The Huguenot-Anglican Refuge in Virginia

ANGLICAN STUDIES

Series Editor
Sheryl A. Kujawa-Holbrook, Claremont School of Theology

This series responds to the growing need for high-quality and innovative research in Anglican Studies made available to the scholarly and ecclesial communities. Anglican Studies as expressed here is an interdisciplinary field, including Anglican history, theology, liturgy, preaching, postcolonial studies, ecclesiology, spirituality, literature, missiology, ethics/moral theology, ministry, pastoral care, ecumenism, and interreligious studies. Studies that engage global Anglicanism, as well as studies related to individual contexts are welcome. The series seeks monographs and edited volumes which explore contemporary issues and forge new directions in interdisciplinary research.

Titles in the series

The Huguenot-Anglican Refuge in Virginia: Empire, Land, and Religion in the Rappahannock Region, by Lonnie H. Lee

The Goldilocks God: Searching for the via media, by Guy Collins

Sacramental Poetics in Richard Hooker and George Herbert: Exploring the Abundance of God, by Brian Douglas

Ministry in the Anglican Tradition from Henry VIII to 1900, by John L. Kater

A Eucharist-shaped Church: Prayer, Theology, and Mission, edited by Daniel J. Handschy, Donna R. Hawk-Reinhard, and Marshall E. Crossnoe

The Huguenot-Anglican Refuge in Virginia

Empire, Land, and Religion in the Rappahannock Region

Lonnie H. Lee

LEXINGTON BOOKS/FORTRESS ACADEMIC
Lanham • Boulder • New York • London

Published by Lexington Books/Fortress Academic
Lexington Books is an imprint of The Rowman & Littlefield Publishing Group, Inc.
4501 Forbes Boulevard, Suite 200, Lanham, Maryland 20706
www.rowman.com

86-90 Paul Street, London EC2A 4NE, United Kingdom

Copyright © 2023 by The Rowman & Littlefield Publishing Group, Inc.

All rights reserved. No part of this book may be reproduced in any form or by any electronic or mechanical means, including information storage and retrieval systems, without written permission from the publisher, except by a reviewer who may quote passages in a review.

British Library Cataloguing in Publication Information Available

Library of Congress Cataloging-in-Publication Data

Names: Lee, Lonnie H., author.
Title: The Huguenot-Anglican refuge in Virginia : empire, land, and religion in the Rappahannock region / Lonnie H. Lee.
Description: Lanham : Lexington Books/Fortress Academic, [2023] | Series: Anglican studies | Includes bibliographical references and index. | Summary: "In The Huguenot-Anglican Refuge in Virginia, Lonnie H. Lee traces the hidden history of a Huguenot emigrant community established in eight counties along the Rappahannock River of Virginia in 1687"—Provided by publisher.
Identifiers: LCCN 2023004319 (print) | LCCN 2023004320 (ebook) | ISBN 9781978714854 (cloth) | ISBN 9781978714861 (epub)
Subjects: LCSH: Huguenots—Virginia—Rappahannock River Region—History. | Anglicans—Virginia—Rappahannock River Region—History. | Rappahannock River Region (Va.)—Church history—17th century. | Rappahannock River Region (Va.)—Church history—18th century.
Classification: LCC BX9458.U5 L44 2023 (print) | LCC BX9458.U5 (ebook) | DDC 284/.5097553—dc23/eng/20230309
LC record available at https://lccn.loc.gov/2023004319
LC ebook record available at https://lccn.loc.gov/2023004320

♾️™ The paper used in this publication meets the minimum requirements of American National Standard for Information Sciences—Permanence of Paper for Printed Library Materials, ANSI/NISO Z39.48-1992.

Contents

List of Maps and Illustrations	vii
Acknowledgments	ix
Introduction: A Distinctive Huguenot Refuge	xi
Chapter One: Cozes, France, 1660	1
Chapter Two: London, 1677	21
Chapter Three: Rappahannock, Virginia, 1687	43
Chapter Four: Powell's Quarter, 1692	67
Chapter Five: Deep Creek, 1694	85
Chapter Six: Whitechapel Parish, 1698	111
Chapter Seven: South Farnham Parish, 1733	133
Conclusion: The Huguenot-Anglican Project in America, 1761	157
Abbreviations	171
Appendix A: Rappahannock Huguenot Refugees, 1677–1710	173
Appendix B: Documenting Rappahannock Huguenot Refugees, 1677–1710	185
Bibliography	191
Index	215
About the Author	227

List of Maps and Illustrations

La Liturgie. Title Page of a French translation of the Anglican *Book of Common Prayer.* Jean Durel's 1662 revision of Pierre de Laune's 1616 translation. Published in 1748 in London by Paul Vaillant.   xiii

Cozes Protestant Baptism Register, 1656–1668. Page includes baptism entry for Charlotte Jolly (1659–1721).   8

Palace of the Bishop of London at Fulham. 1885 print of a 1798 drawing of the inner courtyard. Engraving on wood by an unknown artist.   22

Detail, *A New Map of Virginia, Mary-Land, and the improved parts of Pennsylvania* . . . , John Senex, 1719, showing the area of Huguenot settlement in the Rappahannock region between 1677 and 1710 and the counties that existed in 1687.   45

North Farnham Church, Richmond County, Virginia, c. 1737.   53

Detail, *A New Map of Virginia, Mary-Land, and the improved parts of Pennsylvania* . . . , John Senex, 1719, showing the location of the Bertrand Plantation.   72

Portrait of Charles II issuing the Northern Neck Proprietary Grant in 1649. Painting by an unknown artist.   87

Map of Belle Isle State Park, Lancaster, Virginia, showing the 924-acre Bertrand Plantation as expanded by the 1698 patent.   99

St. Mary's Whitechapel Church, Lancaster, Virginia, showing the older brick of the center section where John Bertrand preached during the 1690s.   120

Detail, *A Map of the Most Inhabited Part of Virginia*, Joshua Fry and Peter Jefferson, 1751, showing *Port Micou*, South Farnham Church, and the Bertrand Plantation.   142

Gravestone of Paul Micou (1659–1736). Vauter's Church, Essex County, Virginia.   162

Acknowledgments

This project could not have been completed without the people and resources of Lancaster County, Virginia. I am grateful for the dedicated volunteers of the Lancaster, Virginia Historical Society and its Mary Ball Washington Museum and Library, Karen Hart, Executive Director. I owe a particular debt of gratitude to the late Carolyn Jett and the late Craig Kilby who extended significant help and encouragement to me during the early phase of this project.

I am thankful for the encouragement of historians and scholars I have consulted for this project. Olga de Saint-Affrique, a La Rochelle-based historian of the French Protestant Church, corresponded with me as I was beginning this project and graciously cited my research in her book on Protestant pastors of Saintonge. Camille Wells, former lecturer in Colonial Architectural History at the College of William and Mary, read early drafts of chapters and offered helpful insights. Pauline Arseneault of the Archives Departmentales Charente-Maritime La Rochelle provided valuable assistance in the task of translating and interpreting seventeenth-century royal notary records of the Archives. Huguenot Historian Robin Gwynn, formerly on the faculty of Massey University in New Zealand, graciously exchanged research information with me. Historian John Grigg of the University of Nebraska Omaha read chapters and gave me invaluable advice and guidance. Historian Owen Stanwood of Boston College read chapters and helped me sharpen my analysis of the documentary evidence as I brought this project to a conclusion. Robert Wuthnow, professor of sociology emeritus and former director of the Center for the Study of Religion at Princeton University, has closely followed my research and writing through every stage of this process—reading numerous drafts and offering insightful comments and helpful advice.

I owe an especially large debt to the people and staff of Westminster Presbyterian Church of Springfield, Illinois. Not only did they support my ministry as their pastor for 17 years, they made possible the renewal leave in Europe that jump-started my research for this project. When I returned from that journey, they listened to my stories and participated in the classes

I taught. I have also been assisted by all those who have participated in the church history classes that I have led, first at Westminster and later at Village Presbyterian Church in Prairie Village, Kansas, and the Lancaster County, Virginia Historical Society.

I am grateful to the very capable Lexington Books/Fortress Academic editors who have guided me through the publication process. Anglican Studies Series editor, Sheryl A. Kujawa-Holbrook, Dean of the Faculty of Claremont School of Theology, and acquiring editors, Gayla Freeman and Neil Elliott, believed in the value of this work and have played an indispensable role in moving it to completion.

I am richly blessed to be part of a family which is exceedingly supportive and places a high value on the written word and the study of history. I am grateful for their unfailing encouragement of my pursuit of this project. My wife, Barbara, has been amazingly tolerant of the long hours I have spent in the solitude of my study probing the mysteries of seventeenth-century records. In addition to being the great love of my life, she is always my most insightful critic and my best fellow traveler.

Introduction

A Distinctive Huguenot Refuge

"It is a form of worship which . . . is ideally suited to inspiring Christian fervor . . . "

—Huguenot theologian Moïse Amyraut endorsing a French translation of the Anglican *Book of Common Prayer,* c.1660

The Huguenot-Anglican Refuge in Virginia required the services of an Anglican minister who could preach in two languages, French and English.[1] The first to perform this bilingual ministry in Virginia was a Huguenot exile named John Bertrand (c. 1651–1701). County court records confirm Bertrand's presence in the North Farnham Parish of Rappahannock County by the end of 1687.[2]

John and his wife, Charlotte Jolly (1659–1721), were members of Protestant leadership families that included ministers, merchants, and nobles from the western French province of Saintonge.[3] They immigrated to Virginia at a time of political and religious peril for England as the Protestant William of Orange was assembling forces for an invasion to challenge the Catholic James II for the throne.[4] Before arriving in Virginia, the Bertrands were part of a massive exodus of Protestants fleeing persecution under Louis XIV in France between 1679 and 1700.[5] They were among the approximately 30,000 Huguenots who poured into London to form the largest community of Huguenot exiles in the world. The size and suddenness of this migration was unprecedented in English history. This momentous event, that Huguenots named *le Refuge*, introduced the word *refugee* into the English language.[6]

Having been educated and ordained as a Protestant minister in France, John Bertrand was re-ordained to the Anglican ministry in England by Bishop of London Henry Compton (1632–1713) in 1677. John lived in London as James

II came to power and Henry Compton scrambled to hold on to his job and keep the nation Protestant. John married Charlotte in London in September of 1686, about the time that England's new Catholic king suspended Bishop Compton from office. Compton then participated in the treasonous plot to invite William of Orange, a Dutch Calvinist and staunch opponent of Louis XIV's expansionist policies, to invade England.

As these dramatic events were unfolding in England, some of the Huguenot refugees there were migrating across the Atlantic to English America.[7] By the early 1680s Huguenots were en route to New York, New England, Virginia, and South Carolina.[8] French Protestant congregations were founded in New York City in 1682, Boston in 1685, and Charleston by 1687. These Huguenot congregations in the new world were heavily influenced by, if not actually under the direction of, the non-conformist French Church of London on Threadneedle Street. The Threadneedle Street Church was accountable to the English government through the Bishop of London, but was not part of the Church of England. The church, about 9,000 members by the late 1680s,[9] conducted its services in French and closely adhered to the Calvinist theology, worship, and governance practices of the Reformed churches in France. The Huguenot congregations in New York City, Boston, and Charleston embraced this style of churchmanship and looked to the Threadneedle Street consistory for assistance in securing their ministers.[10]

By contrast, the Huguenots who began arriving in Virginia in significant numbers during the 1680s were heavily influenced by another London-based French Protestant congregation. The French Church of the Savoy in Westminster, estimated to be slightly more than half the size of the Threadneedle Street Church, had been an Anglican-conformist Huguenot congregation since 1662 and maintained close ties to the English court.[11] The Savoy Church also worshipped in French, but used a French translation of the *Book of Common Prayer*, commonly called *La Liturgie*, produced by its minister, Jean Durel (1625–1683). Durel, who served the Savoy Church from 1662 to 1683, implemented a hybrid style of worship that incorporated both Anglican and Presbyterian practices. As a graduate of the Saumur Academy in France and a student of Moïse Amyraut, the French Reformed theologian who challenged the Scholastic Calvinist theological system that emphasized predestination, Durel made the Savoy Church a less harsh Calvinist alternative to the Threadneedle Street Church.[12]

LA LITURGIE,

OU FORMULAIRE DES PRIERES PUBLIQUES,

Selon l'usage de

L'EGLISE ANGLICANE.

NOUVELLE EDITION,

REVUE ET CORRIGE'E.

A LONDRES,

Chez *PAUL VAILLANT* dans le Strand.

MDCCXLVIII.

La Liturgie. Title Page of a French translation of the Anglican *Book of Common Prayer.* Jean Durel's 1662 revision of Pierre de Laune's 1616 translation. Published in 1748 in London by Paul Vaillant

Courtesy of the author

John Bertrand and the three Huguenot-Anglican ministers who followed him to the Rappahannock region of Virginia were closely aligned with the ecclesiastical and theological emphasis of the Savoy Church.[13] Working under the direction of the Bishop of London, these ministers were accountable to Anglican ecclesiastical authorities rather than to the consistory of the Threadneedle Street Church in London. They were fluent enough in English to secure employment in the Anglican parishes of Virginia where clergy were in short supply. They also played a key role in helping Huguenot refugees quickly integrate into the established Anglican parishes where they settled. The overtly Anglican identity of these French exile ministers, their concurrent work with established Anglican parishes, and the legal requirement that all Huguenot refugees become Anglicans in Virginia set this Refuge apart from all the other Huguenot migrations to English America.

The Huguenot migration that John Bertrand helped lead to Virginia coincided with an imperialist initiative launched by the Bishop of London in 1677.[14] When Henry Compton became Bishop of London in 1675, he assumed direct responsibility for the Anglican churches in the English colonies, where there had never been resident bishops. Compton understood well the fear of his fellow Stuart officials that the English colonies in the new world were susceptible to French cultural hegemony and/or military invasion because they were poorly governed and safe havens for Puritans. To address this concern Compton set out to wrest control of Virginia's Anglican parishes from colonial elites and local governing authorities.[15] Some of these colonial leaders were indeed influenced by Puritanism and they were hiring ministers (some Presbyterian and others untrained) who had never been ordained by an Anglican bishop.[16] Compton put in place a multi-layered strategy for introducing this new imperial policy in Virginia that included the recruitment of Church of England-ordained clergy to carry forward his reforms.

John Bertrand was one of Compton's recruits.[17] Bertrand's mission, and that of his Huguenot-Anglican colleagues James Boisseau, Nicholas Moreau, and Lewis Latané, was to strengthen the Anglican identity of parishes that had long been functionally autonomous and heavily influenced by Puritan (and Presbyterian) doctrine and worship practices. This study offers compelling evidence of the dedication of these ministers to Compton's reform program. That evidence includes their ordinations/licenses by Bishop Compton (Bertrand, Boisseau, and Latané), extant correspondence (Moreau), introduction of the surplice (Bertrand), and deep seated conflict with their vestries (Bertrand, Moreau, and Latané). As these ministers tried to implement Bishop Compton's program, they encountered the fierce resistance of local elites.

A pamphlet published in French at The Hague in July 1687 by a Huguenot exile named Durand de Dauphiné likely influenced some French Protestant exiles to settle in the Rappahannock region of Virginia. After fleeing his estate in southern France, Durand went to London where he decided to immigrate to Carolina. But his ship to America was thrown off course and disabled before he reached his destination. Durand was consequently forced to disembark in Virginia in the fall of 1686. He spent six months in the colony, traveling through its tidewater counties where he was entertained by the governor and other leaders of the colony. By the time he returned to London in the spring of 1687 he had come to the conclusion that Virginia provided a much better opportunity for Huguenot exiles than Carolina or English colonies to the north. Noting that Virginia had not been as well advertised as Carolina, he decided to write a tract to encourage French refugees in Europe to settle in Virginia. He described the rolling hills of Rappahannock and Stafford Counties as ideal terrain for Huguenot settlers to plant vineyards. For both counties, he offered specific information on how Huguenot settlers could obtain land at reasonable prices. Best of all, according to Durand, the availability of servants and enslaved workers in the colony meant the immigrants would not have to work the land themselves.

Perhaps the most important part of Durand's tract was his report that the governor (Francis Howard, Baron of Effingham) had proposed that Huguenot immigrants to Virginia bring a few of their own ministers to preach for them in French. In a conversation with Durand in December 1686, Governor Howard envisioned a dual tract ministry for bilingual Huguenot ministers—serving French immigrants *and* existing Anglican parishes in Virginia. Durand reported the governor's description of the role of these Huguenot ministers in this way: " . . . as for the pastors . . . they would be required to read the book of common prayers when preaching [in English], except when they preached to French people only, they could then do as they were accustomed in France." A servant later informed Durand that Lord Howard had memorialized their conversation in a letter to the Bishop of London.[18]

It is also significant that Durand's tract outlined the details of the fundamental bargain Governor Howard had offered to Huguenots immigrating to Virginia. Huguenot refugees could secure inexpensive land, participate fully in the colony's economy, and enjoy French preaching. In exchange, the French settlers would seek to produce wine for export to Europe and become useful citizens of the empire as members of their Anglican parishes and consumers of England's manufactured goods.

Durand's message was apparently persuasive to Huguenot refugees in Europe who were considering crossing the Atlantic. John Bertrand arrived in Rappahannock County within five months of the publication of Durand's tract to become the first Huguenot minister to perform the dual tract ministry Governor Howard had envisioned the previous year. Dozens more Huguenot refugee households appeared in the Rappahannock region over the next decade and a half. Appendix A-II lists 131 households and thirty-one indentured servants with Huguenot surnames documented for the first time in eight counties of the Rappahannock region between 1686 and 1700. More than 70 percent of these refugees settled in the two counties endorsed by Durand, Rappahannock and Stafford. Records suggest that at least 17 percent of these Huguenot emigrants were from the Protestant Church of Cozes, the Saintonge town where John Bertrand's father had served as pastor from 1650 to 1660. One of them was a physician and merchant named Paul Micou (1659–1736) who would later emerge as a leader of the French exile community in the Rappahannock region. John Bertrand and most of the exiles from Cozes were familiar with the production and distribution of the inexpensive wines of the Charente River Valley of France that were shipped to English and Dutch consumers. The 1686–1700 Huguenot immigrants followed a smaller group of refugees from Louis XIV who began arriving in the colony about 1677.[19]

The county records on which this study is based offer very little information about what motivated Huguenots to migrate to the Rappahannock region rather than other colonies in English America. A core group was clearly motivated by their relationship with a minister they had known in France. But for the other emigrants, the decision to go to the Rappahannock region likely revolved around the one crucial issue that made this Refuge fundamentally different from all the others existing at that time. Whatever else the exiles may have hoped to find in Virginia, they migrated knowing they would be Anglicans once they arrived in the new world. They knew they could not preserve a distinctive French Reformed Church in a colony where the Anglican Church was the only legally recognized communion. Going to Virginia meant giving up the dream of creating a Huguenot Eden in the new world. Those who could not let go of that dream could choose other destinations in the new world—Carolina, New York, or New England—where independent Huguenot congregations were being organized to serve as anchors for their refugee communities. The prospect of living as Anglicans in Virginia may have been particularly appealing to Huguenots who entertained another dream—actively resisting their former king whose proscription of Protestantism had turned their world upside down.

The bottom line for many of these refugees may have been the one outlined by Durand. Huguenots seeking to acquire land (on which others would labor) and enjoy French Protestant preaching in English America could do both in the Refuge that was forming along the Rappahannock River in Virginia. As Durand predicted, a substantial number of the refugees did in fact acquire land. Moreover, through the overlapping ministries of John Bertrand and three other Huguenot-Anglican clergy who followed him to the Rappahannock region (James Boisseau, Nicholas Moreau, and Lewis Latané), the Refuge was served by French ministers from 1687 to 1733. The

1735 arrival of a French emigrant named James Marye, a Catholic priest who converted to Anglicanism, further extended the long succession of French exile ministers in the Refuge across eight decades to 1767.

The Huguenots who began arriving in the 1680s paved the way for a later migration to Virginia, financed by William III, that brought five shiploads of French and other persecuted Protestants to the colony between July 1700 and August 1701.[20] While about 300 of these later exiles helped form a new Huguenot settlement at Manakin Town in the Virginia Piedmont (a short distance west of the present day city of Richmond), county records suggest a significant number of the 1700–1701 refugees joined the settlers who were already established in the upper tidewater counties of the Rappahannock region.[21]

As the Huguenot refugees established themselves in the Rappahannock region, they were quickly drawn into another contested English imperial policy in the colony. Imperial planners in London were keen to use the judicious distribution of land to increase the population of Virginia at a time when the Chesapeake region was experiencing a dramatic decline in immigration.[22] But their strategy was thwarted by the colony's long-standing practice of issuing land patents through the governor with the approval of the wealthy Virginia aristocrats who served on the Council. The members of the Council used their authority over the granting of unassigned land primarily to benefit elite planters like themselves.[23] These wealthy Virginians were amassing huge land holdings (typically 20,000 to 30,000 acres). With newly arriving settlers having to lease land or purchase it at inflated market prices, some were choosing to quickly move on to other colonies.[24]

During the 1690s John Bertrand and other Huguenot emigrants embraced an imperial project that bypassed the governor and Council to distribute unassigned lands north of the Rappahannock River. This alternative method of assigning land in Virginia was created by Charles II when he issued a land grant to reward seven of his supporters in 1649. The grant was for all the land "bounded by and within the heads" of the Potomac and Rappahannock Rivers, several million acres. It gave the Proprietors of Virginia's Northern Neck the right to make grants from these lands to colonial planters and to levy taxes on it. This adaptation of feudalism also gave the Crown a more direct mechanism of control over the assignment and taxation of land in the colony.

When John Bertrand purchased his Lancaster County plantation in 1692, the county's wealthiest citizen, Robert Carter, was leading the opposition to the Proprietary locally and in the House of Burgesses in Jamestown.[25] In this work, Carter made common cause with members of the Council who saw the Northern Neck Proprietary as a threat to their power and future wealth. As John Bertrand worked to expand the size of his plantation he openly allied himself with Proprietary agent William Fitzhugh in opposition to Carter and the Council.[26] The records suggest Fitzhugh deftly used John Bertrand's plantation boundary dispute to outmaneuver Robert Carter and the Council with the timely assistance of commissary James Blair and the political theorist John Locke (a member of the Board of Trade in London). Bertrand's controversial role in this struggle is confirmed by his exchange of angry words with Robert Carter in the Lancaster County Court in September 1699.[27] The sixty-six Huguenot refugee households that acquired land in the Rappahannock region of Virginia after 1693 were beneficiaries of the work Fitzhugh and Bertrand performed on behalf of the Proprietary and the empire planners in London.

Much of the narrative of this study revolves around John Bertrand, and to a lesser degree, Paul Micou and Lewis Latané. As the first Huguenot minister to offer the creative dual-track ministry Governor Howard envisioned in 1686, Bertrand made the Refuge possible. He also played an important role in the controversies over land and religion that pitted empire planners in London against Virginia's native-born aristocracy. In addition, John Bertrand was one of the few members of the Refuge whose activities are reasonably well documented in France, England, and Virginia. Paul Micou, who grew up as a close family friend of the Bertrands in Cozes, became a wealthy physician, merchant, and court justice over the nearly fifty years he lived in Virginia. After John Bertrand's death in 1701, the new Huguenot-Anglican pastor Lewis Latané contributed significantly to the resilience of the Refuge by continuing French language ministry until his death in 1733. Sadly, the loss of county records leaves much of the story of Micou and Latané shrouded in mystery.[28]

An important feature of England's empire in the new world was the cruel exploitation of those who labored on its colonial plantations. Records evaluated for this study expose the ugly face of Virginia's forced labor system. Chapter 3 explores the brutal working conditions of indentured servants and shows how church discipline in the Puritan oriented parishes of Rappahannock County abetted the sexual abuse of servant women (including some Huguenots). Chapters 1, 4, 7, and the Conclusion chronicle the participation of John Bertrand, Paul Micou, Lewis Latané and other Huguenots in Virginia's evolving slave culture and the failure of the French Reformed and Anglican Churches to offer substantive ethical guidance with regard to slavery.

This study follows a largely chronological format. The first chapter presents the Huguenot diaspora through the lens of the Protestant Church of Cozes, France, the congregation that nurtured many of the Rappahannock Huguenot emigrants. The next chapter probes the origin of the Huguenot-Anglican migration to Virginia in the burgeoning Huguenot exile community in London. The ensuing chapters discuss the various migration challenges and controversies of empire, land, and religion that confronted the emigrants in Virginia. The final chapter explores the large 1700–1701 migration to Virginia sponsored by William III and its significance for the Rappahannock Huguenots. The narrative concludes with a consideration of the distinct identity of the Rappahannock Refuge and its contribution to the British American Huguenot diaspora.

The journey of Cyprien and Margaret Prou to seventeenth-century Virginia is in some ways emblematic of the experience of Huguenot refugees along the Rappahannock. Cyprien was a tailor from Poitou who was part of a large wave of Huguenots fleeing the violence of the Dragonnades that began in that province in 1681. On May 31, 1682, he was in London meeting with the consistory of the Threadneedle Street Church to request membership in the congregation. But with no church member vouching for his character or his religious training, the consistory deferred action on Cyprien's request.[29] After attending and perhaps seeking assistance from both the Threadneedle Street and Savoy churches,[30] Cyprien and his wife, Margaret, decided in 1684 to emigrate once again, this time to the new world. Not having the money for their passage, they signed indenture contracts to be transported from London to Virginia.[31] In 1696, they were living in Richmond (formerly Rappahannock) County, and were well enough integrated into its English colonial society for the court justices to appoint Cyprien constable for one of the precincts of the county. In 1699, Prou had at least one indentured servant working for him. By 1704, Cyprian and Margaret had two daughters and had saved enough to purchase 200 acres of Richmond County land through a contract witnessed by Paul Micou.[32] While not all refugees survived the rigors of the ocean passage or the hardships imposed on servants in Virginia, the interests of Cyprien and Margaret Prou were very well aligned with the immigration and land policies designed by English imperialist planners. They were also well connected to the Huguenot refugee network in England and the new world.

The Rappahannock Refuge has remained well hidden for more than 300 years because the usual methods of documenting Huguenot communities in colonial America are not available to researchers of seventeenth-century Virginia. There was no Huguenot Church or Huguenot town in tidewater Virginia through which to identify these refugees. There are very few ship passenger records and no census records to reveal personal or family information for these immigrants. Virginia had no printing presses before the 1730s. Very few personal papers from this period have survived. This Huguenot community (252 households and fifty-three indentured servants) comes to life through the careful examination of extant court records from eight counties of the Rappahannock region. The cross-referencing of these Virginia archival records with French Protestant records from London and western France opens the door to an unexamined feature of the Huguenot migration to America—a distinctive seventeenth-century Huguenot-Anglican Refuge in the upper tidewater area of Virginia.[33]

NOTES

1. Moïse Amyraut, Introduction to *Commentary on the Psalms of David* (dedicated to Charles II in 1662), in Mary K. Geiter and W. A. Speck, "Moïse Amyraut and Charles II," *The Huguenot Society Journal* 30, no. 2 (2014), translated by Janet Davies, 175.
2. Old Rappahannock County, Virginia (ORC) Order Book (OB) 2, 1686–1692, 71–72.
3. Papiers des Baptêmes de l'Eglise Reformee de Cozes . . . Fevrier 1656–Juillet 1668, I-43, 20 (hereafter cited as CZ), Archives Departmentales de la Charente-Maritime, La Rochelle (hereafter ADCMLR).
4. Owen Stanwood, *The Empire Reformed: English America in the Age of the Glorious Revolution* (Philadelphia, 2011), 4–5.
5. Robin Gwynn, *The Huguenots in Later Stuart Britain, Volume II—Settlement, Churches, and the Role of London* (Brighton, UK, 2018), 199.
6. Robin Gwynn, *Huguenot Heritage: The History and Contribution of the Huguenots in Britain*, (Brighton, UK, 2011), 44. For the introduction of the word *refugee* into the English language, see Ibid., 1 and J. F. Bosher, "Huguenot Merchants and the Protestant International in the Seventeenth Century," *The William and Mary Quarterly* (hereafter WMQ), 3rd Series, 52 (January 1995), 1.
7. Roger Howell, Jr., "The Vocation of the Lord: Aspects of the Huguenot Contribution to the English Speaking World," *Anglican and Episcopal History* 61, no. 2 (1987), 133–151.
8. Bertrand Van Ruymbeke, "*Le Refuge*: History and Memory from the 1770s to the Present," in *A Companion to the Huguenots*, ed., Raymond A. Mentzer and Bertrand Van Ruymbeke (Leiden, 2016), 427.
9. Gwynn, *Huguenots in Britain II*, 181.
10. Jon Butler, *The Huguenots in America: A Refugee People in New World Society* (Cambridge, MA, 1983); Bertrand Van Ruymbeke, *From New Babylon to Eden: The Huguenots and Their Migration to Colonial South Carolina* (Columbia, SC, 2006); Paula Wheeler Carlo, *Huguenot Refugees in Colonial New York: Becoming American in the Hudson Valley* (Brighton, 2005).
11. Gwynn, *Huguenots in Britain II*, 108–111.
12. Robin Gwynn, *The Huguenots in Later Stuart Britain: Volume 1—Crisis, Renewal, and the Ministers' Dilemma* (Brighton, 2015), 122, 279–280; Brian G. Armstrong, *Calvinism and the Amyraut Controversy: Protestant Scholasticism and Humanism in Seventeenth-Century France* (Madison, WI, 1969), 71–119.
13. For Huguenot Anglicanism (*un anglicanisme huguenot*) in English America in the late seventeenth and early eighteenth centuries, see Bertrand Van Ruymbeke, "Refuge or Diaspora: Historiographical reflections on the Huguenot dispersion in the

Atlantic World," in *Religious Refugees in Europe, Asia, and North America, 6th–21st century,* ed., Susanne Lachenicht (Hamburg, 2007), 165–166.

14. For the participation of Huguenot refugees (witting or otherwise) in English imperial projects in the new world, see Owen Stanwood, *The Global Refuge: Huguenots in an Age of Empire* (New York, 2020), and "Between Eden and Empire: Huguenot Refugees and the Promise of New Worlds," *American Historical Review* 118, no. 5 (December 2013), 1319–1344.

15. Stanwood, *The Empire Reformed,* 27–30.

16. Kevin Butterfield, "Puritans and Religious Strife in the Early Chesapeake," *The Virginia Magazine of History and Biography* (hereafter VMHB) 109, no. 1 (2001), 36–37.

17. Edward L. Bond, *Damned Souls in a Tobacco Colony: Religion in Seventeenth-Century Virginia* (Macon, GA, 2000), 219–220; Philip S. Haffenden, "The Anglican Church in Restoration Colonial Policy," in *Seventeenth-Century America: Essays in Colonial History,* ed. James Martin Smith (Chapel Hill, NC, 1959), 180–182.

18. Durand de Dauphiné, *A Huguenot Exile in Virginia, or Voyages of a Frenchman exiled for his Religion with a description of Virginia and Maryland,* ed., Gilbert Chinard (New York, 1934), 150–155, 166, and 173–175 (hereafter cited as Durand). Governor Howard's offer of services in French corresponds to the 1686 provisions for the Brent Town settlement in Stafford County which guaranteed freedom of worship to its potential Huguenot settlers, Ibid., 41.

19. Appendix A-I lists forty-five Huguenot households and eleven Huguenot servants arriving in the Rappahannock region between 1677 and 1685. They are documented in Appendix B.

20. David Lambert, *The Protestant International and the Huguenot Migration to Virginia* (New York, 2010).

21. Appendix A-III lists seventy-five households and nine indentured servants with Huguenot surnames appearing in the Rappahannock region for the first time between 1701 and 1710. These immigrants are documented in Appendix B.

22. Lorena S. Walsh, *Motives of Honor, Pleasure, and Profit: Plantation Management in the Colonial Chesapeake, 1607–1763* (Chapel Hill, NC, 2010), 198–200.

23. Manning C. Voorhis, "Crown Versus Council in the Virginia Land Policy," WMQ 3, 3rd series, no. 4 (1946), 500–501; Michael G. Kammen,"Virginia at the Close of the Seventeenth Century, An Appraisal by James Blair and John Locke," VMHB 74, no. 2 (April 1966), 143–144.

24. James Blair and John Locke, "Some of the Chief Grievances of the Present Constitution of Virginia, with an Essay Towards the Remedies Thereof," in Kammen, "Virginia at the Close of the Seventeenth Century," 153–169.

25. For a chronology of the Northern Neck Proprietary, see Douglas Southall Freeman, *Young Washington,* vol. 1, Appendix I-1 (New York, 1948) 447–513.

26. Richard Beale Davis, *William Fitzhugh and His Chesapeake World, 1676–1701: The Fitzhugh Letters and Other Documents* (Chapel Hill, NC, 1963), 42–46.

27. *Lancaster County, Virginia* (LC) OB, *1699–1701,* vol. 4, 78b.

28. Elizabeth Hawes Ryland, "Paul Micou, Chyrurgeon," WMQ 16, no. 2 (April 1936), 241–246.

29. Robin Gwynn, ed., *Minutes of the Consistory of the French Church of London, Threadneedle Street: Calendared with an historical introduction and commentary by Robin Gwynn* (London,1994), 78 (hereafter cited as FCL).

30. William Minet and Susan Minet, eds., *Le Livre Des Tesmoignages de L'Eglise de Threadneedle Street, 1669–1789* (London, 1909), 227 (hereafter all publications of William and Susan Minet cited as Minet).

31. Plantation Indentures, Greater London Record Office, SR02006a, LVA.

32. Ruth and Sam Sparacio, *Richmond County* (RC) OB, *1694–1697* (McLean, VA, 1991), 95 (all Sparacio publications are hereafter cited as SP); SP, RC DB, 1701–1704, 64–67; SP, RC DB, 1705–1708, 110–111.

33. See Appendix A for the listing of 252 households and fifty-three indentured servants with Huguenot surnames arriving in the Rappahannock region between 1677 and 1710. Nine additional households were formed by indentured servants who gained their freedom before 1710. Appendix B provides documentation for these refugees.

Chapter One

Cozes, France, 1660

> When . . . the world is turned upside down . . . the Lord . . . effects this revolution . . . that we may learn that nothing here is of long duration, and may have our whole heart . . . directed to the reign of Christ.
>
> —John Calvin, *Commentary on Isaiah*, 1551

The death of Paul Bertrand in August 1660 forced the Protestant Church of Cozes into a time of transition.[1] Bertrand had served as minister of the church since 1650, leaving a wife, Marie André, and two sons, nine-year-old Jean (c. 1651–1701) and three-year-old Paul (1657–c. 1690). Paul's wife was a member of an influential merchant family in Saintonge. Her brother, Jean André, was a Cozes merchant who served on the consistory of the church where his brother-in-law was pastor.[2] Paul's family had been established in southern Saintonge since at least 1614, when his father became minister of the Protestant Church in Saint-Jean-d'Angle about eighteen miles northwest of Cozes.[3]

With approximately 2,600 members,[4] the Protestant Church of Cozes was one of the major Huguenot congregations in western France.[5] Cozes was located close to the water route between the port cities of La Rochelle and Bordeaux. Situated five miles from the wide mouth of the Gironde River, where it empties into the Atlantic Ocean, Cozes had excellent access to the coastal transportation system of western France and the economic opportunities of the Gironde estuary, the largest in western Europe. Living near Europe's western frontier, seventeenth-century Cozes Huguenots were not limited by their Saintonge or French identity. In a province with seamen who had fished off the banks of Newfoundland and traded with the new world for decades, the people of Cozes had long understood themselves to be part of a larger Atlantic world.

It took about a year for the Cozes congregation to hire its next minister. Parish records indicate that during the interim Protestant ministers from nearby towns—Marennes, Montagne, Saint Seurin d'Uzet, Marnac, Saint Just, Meschiers, Saujon, Saint Fort, Saintes, La Tremblade, Vaux, and Royan—led services and administered baptisms at the Cozes church.[6] A new minister arrived in Cozes in August 1661. Jean Masson was a young man beginning what would prove to be a very successful twenty-two-year pastorate. Jean was a native of Civray in Poitou, where his father was pastor, and a graduate of the Huguenot Academy at Montauban.[7] One of the first tasks of the new minister in Cozes was to resume the education of the older son of his predecessor, the now-ten-year-old Jean Bertrand, for which he was paid by the deceased pastor's widow. Most Huguenot ministers taught their own children, and many, both in France and later in the diaspora, supplemented their income by tutoring boys in their homes.[8]

The people of Cozes lived in the orbit of the port city of La Rochelle. By the early 1600s, that city had emerged as a major seaport with close trading and cultural ties to the Protestant nations of England and the Dutch Republic. As a major hub of European trade, the city became wealthy through its contacts with these nations and the new world to the west. By the end of the sixteenth century, La Rochelle was overwhelmingly Protestant and considered itself to be an independent city state like Geneva. It also functioned as the de facto capital of the Huguenots and the center of French Protestant political and economic influence.[9]

Like La Rochelle, the town of Cozes and the province of Saintonge had been identified with France's church reform movement from its early days. The reform movement began with Renaissance humanist scholars like Jacques Lefèvre d'Etaples, who gained a large following among the French elite in the early decades of the sixteenth century. Lefèvre and some of his followers wanted to examine the theology and organizational structure of the French church in the light of newly discovered biblical texts. As they tried to address the endemic corruption of a church system based on royal patronage, the biblical scholars soon learned that church reform in France could not happen from within.[10] By the middle of the sixteenth century, the reform-minded scholars, inspired by French exiles like William Farel and John Calvin, began organizing Reformed congregations (called temples) along the lines of the churches in Strasbourg (not yet part of France) and Geneva. This was an indigenous French movement that was strongly influenced by Calvin's scripture-centered theology.[11] While the Protestant movement grew rapidly during the 1550s and 1560s, it never exceeded 10 to 15 percent of the population of France. In the 1570s and 1580s, Protestants suffered significant losses from violent religious conflict and periodic persecution. But the Huguenots were able to build durable majorities in some of the Atlantic provinces of southwest France. By the end of the sixteenth century, Protestants heavily outnumbered Catholics in Saintonge. Many

Protestants in the province believed the legend that a young John Calvin had taken refuge there to escape persecution in Paris. Some also believed that Calvin wrote an early draft of his classic theological work, *Institutes of* the *Christian Religion,* in Saintonge.

Late-seventeenth-century Protestants in Cozes were acutely aware of the catastrophe that had devastated La Rochelle in 1628. Henry IV had brought an end to almost four decades of religious warfare in France by converting to Catholicism and then issuing the Edict of Nantes in 1598. The edict granted Protestants the right to worship in existing Protestant churches and authorized them to fortify certain Huguenot majority cities to create safe havens in the event of future persecution by the Catholic majority population. During the 1620s, Louis XIII, son of Henry IV, sought to consolidate his power by removing the military capabilities of Protestant majority cities. When La Rochelle resisted the king, Louis XIII and his chief advisor, Cardinal Richelieu, laid siege to the port city in 1627. By the spring of 1628, the 27,000 to 28,000 inhabitants of La Rochelle had been cut off from the Atlantic world and their European trading partners.[12] When shortages caused the price of grain to skyrocket, most of the city's population faced starvation. Many suffered from poisoning as the result of consuming leather products, pets, and rodents. Civilian casualties were massive, with census data suggesting that as many as 19,800 people died during the final nine months of the siege.[13] Although the Protestant leaders of the city were determined not to surrender, thousands of corpses were piled in the streets because no one had the strength to bury them, making the capitulation of October 28, 1628, unavoidable.

In the eyes of the Protestants of Cozes, the surrender of La Rochelle must have been a human tragedy of biblical proportions. The destruction of the Protestant stronghold and the huge loss of life among its inhabitants left a wound that could not be forgotten. The ensuing disenfranchisement of the Huguenots of La Rochelle had the effect of provoking an exodus from the city and its immediate surroundings—especially among its Protestant merchants. Historian Neil Kamil has observed that, after the siege, Huguenot merchants from La Rochelle began "emigrating to the destination points of their cargoes." Some followed their cargoes to European ports, but others moved west to America.[14] Prohibited by their king from settling in New France, Huguenots who wanted to be part of the new world began looking to the North American colonies of England and the Dutch Republic.

One of the La Rochelle area Huguenots looking west was Antoine Ridouet, Baron de Sance. In 1629, de Sance approached English officials with a proposal to establish a Huguenot settlement in Virginia "to plant vineyards and olive trees, and make silk and salt." Without sufficient influence at court, he was apparently unable to advance his proposal. In 1630, the French nobleman joined forces with English advocates of a settlement scheme to South Carolina. But his efforts to send Huguenots to help establish a colony there fell through as well. As the South Carolina project was coming apart, Baron de Sance reported that potential French settlers from the La Rochelle area were keenly interested in going to Virginia or New England. He claimed to know 100 Huguenots backed by merchants who were ready to settle along the "River St. Jacques" in the southern part of Virginia.[15]

While there is no evidence that Baron de Sance ever organized a migration to the new world, Huguenots from the La Rochelle area were going to Virginia in the 1630s. A land patent filed in 1639 by Nicholas Martiau, a Huguenot from the Ile de Ré near La Rochelle and George Washington's first ancestor in America, lists the names of six emigrants with French or Walloon surnames. One of the emigrants was named John Galliot, whose surname appears frequently in the Cozes records.[16] Other surnames from western France show up in Virginia at about the same time. Thomas Tavernor, Nicholas George, John Nicolas, and Humphrey Clerke formed a partnership and settled in Isle of Wight County sometime before 1638.[17] As Baron de Sance had predicted a few years earlier, these Huguenots established their plantations near the "River St. Jacques," better known to Virginians as the James River. Their decision to settle in Virginia testified to their willingness to conform to the Anglican Church—the only legal option open to them.

The post-siege diaspora from La Rochelle and its suburbs also distributed Huguenot refugees to Protestant-friendly communities in western France.[18] Some Protestant merchant families apparently followed their cargoes into the Cozes region. At a distance of forty-three miles, Cozes was far enough from La Rochelle to be beyond the jurisdiction of its newly installed Catholic government, but close enough for its merchants to maintain business relationships there. Moreover, with its location fifty-three miles north of Bordeaux along the Gironde River, which carried Bordeaux wine to northern Europe, Cozes was well situated to be a center for regional trading activities. It was also a trans-shipment point for Saintonge wine, cognac, salt, and grain through the port channels along the Gironde River that moved local products to a wider European market through La Rochelle. Cozes' proximity to the Charente River Valley—the best wine-growing region in the west of France—made it a good staging area for this trade.[19]

As a Protestant-majority town, Cozes offered a safe haven that Huguenots could no longer find in La Rochelle. While the port city was being forced to live under strict royal and Catholic governance, Cozes was a place where Protestants continued to be in the ascendancy. In Cozes, Huguenots could raise their children in an environment free from the humiliating strictures imposed on them in post-siege La Rochelle. The surnames of pre-1628

La Rochelle leadership families—Allaire, Bernardeau, Chauvin, David, Dourneau, Guerineau, Papin, Prevost, Robin—appear with some regularity in the Cozes baptism register between 1656 and 1668.[20] The transformation of Cozes resulting from the influx of Huguenot merchants from La Rochelle may have encouraged the town's Protestant residents to see themselves as citizens of the Atlantic world.

As Jean Masson was beginning his ministry in Cozes in 1661, Louis XIV, the twenty-three-year-old French king, was taking direct control of his government. In 1643, Louis had assumed the throne as a five-year-old child at the death of his father, Louis XIII. Anne of Austria, mother of the boy king, served as regent, retaining her husband's chief advisor and continuing the policies he established before his death.[21] No one knew what new directions the suddenly empowered king would chart, and no one could predict how his policies would turn the world of his French Protestant subjects upside down. Like most Protestant congregations in France, the Cozes church had enjoyed more than three decades of stability and was ill-prepared for the existential crisis that lay ahead. The church could not have anticipated a crisis that would propel a long-tenured pastor and so many of its younger members into a great exodus from France.

The 1656–1668 Protestant baptismal register offers a rare window into this Huguenot congregation a few decades before Louis XIV banned Protestantism in France. The register reveals a large and vibrant Protestant church that wielded major urban influence. The dominant position of Protestants in Cozes is demonstrated by a comparison of Protestant and Catholic baptisms in the town. During the years of the Protestant baptismal record, an average of 96.6 infants were baptized each year. Of these baptisms, an annual average of seventy-nine were performed in the Protestant church, while only 17.6 per year were celebrated in the Catholic church. These statistics suggest that Cozes had a Protestant community of about 2,610 and a Catholic population of 582—making the town almost 82 percent Huguenot. Taken together, the Cozes Protestant and Catholic baptism records point to a total population approaching 3,200 during the 1650s and 1660s, significantly larger than the town's population a century later. It should be assumed, however, that both congregations drew some worshippers from neighboring settlements.[22]

The Cozes Protestant baptism register shows that French Protestants rejected the Catholic teaching that baptism was necessary for the salvation of infants who died soon after birth. While their Catholic neighbors rushed to baptize infants immediately, Huguenots typically scheduled their baptisms (using the set liturgy of the French Protestant Church) some weeks later. The Cozes record shows that most baptisms in the congregation were celebrated about two weeks after the birth of the child, though some took place as early as a few days or as late as three months following a birth. Baptisms in Cozes were usually held at the church on Sunday morning or Sunday evening, but some are listed in the record for every day of the week.[23]

In Cozes, godparents or sponsors always presented the infant for the sacrament, but the terms *godfather* and *godmother* do not appear in the record. Sponsors were frequently relatives of the parents—sometimes grandparents, but more often aunts or uncles. In many cases, the infants were named for the sponsor. The sponsor was responsible for encouraging the faith development of the child and to provide material support for the child in the event of the death of both parents. In those cases where the sponsor was not a blood relative, there was a close connection between the sponsor and the family of the child—a friendship or patronage relationship.[24] In the Cozes Protestant baptism register, the listing of baptism sponsors offers an important clue to the status and relationships of the family. Paul Micou was a master surgeon in Cozes who had five children with baptisms documented in the register—Paul (1659), Daniel (1661), Marie (1663), Jean (1665), and Elisabeth (1668). Most of the sponsors for these baptisms were easily identifiable relatives, but in 1663, Marie André, widow of the deceased former pastor, Paul Bertrand, was listed for their daughter Marie, and in 1665, pastor Jean Masson was sponsor for their son Jean. These close relationships with two pastoral families suggest that Paul Micou played an important role in the Cozes Protestant Church, perhaps that of an elder.[25]

The baptism register designates the status and/or profession of some of the persons listed. These include eighteen merchants, fifteen members of the local nobility, eleven royal notaries, nine medical doctors/surgeons, four tailors, two shoemakers, two blacksmiths, two gendarmes, two ministers, one hat maker, one gunsmith, one carpenter, one baker, and one teacher. There were obviously more people, both in the church and in the town, who practiced these professions, but they were not fathers of children presented for baptism in the Protestant church during the years covered by the extant record.

The baptismal register points to a large and vibrant economic base, which appears to confirm that Cozes was one of the destinations of La Rochelle's post-siege diaspora. It is noteworthy that the number of merchants and royal notaries in the congregation exceeds the number that a relatively small town in seventeenth-century France could be expected to support. In addition to the eighteen Protestant merchants listed as fathers in the record, another seventeen merchants were named as sponsors at baptisms. There were eleven royal notaries who fathered children and five more who served as sponsors. The notaries worked closely with merchants to record, witness, and legalize business transactions. Trained by clerking with other notaries, most had minimal legal qualifications, although some were lawyers. A town with a large number of merchants would need a robust supply of royal notaries. Some families contained both notaries and merchants.[26]

The Cozes Protestant baptism register suggests that by the 1660s, the Huguenot elite in Saintonge was a mixture of merchants, provincial nobles, clergy, royal notaries, and physicians. The listings also suggest that members of the local nobility did not leave the Protestant fold in significant numbers before 1668, as was the case in other parts of France. The highest-ranking nobleman in the Cozes congregation might have been François de La Rochefoucauld, Chevalier and Seigneur Du Parc d'Archiac. François is believed to have been a member of a junior branch of this distinguished Protestant family in France. Three of François's children were baptized in Cozes during the 1660s: François (1661), Ruben (1664), and Marguerite (1665).[27]

Members of the Jolly de Chadignac family were also prominent nobles in the Cozes Protestant Church. The noble house of this family was located at the Chadignac estate near Saintes, about fifteen miles from Cozes. Before assuming the title of Seigneur de Chadignac, Charles Jolly (d. 1691) lived at the manor house of Vizelle in Grezac, a few miles northwest of Cozes. The baptisms of nine of his eleven children were recorded in the Cozes register, where he was listed as the Sieur d'Esnaux. He acquired the manor of Vizelle from his wife, Judith André (1635–c. 1705), daughter of a wealthy merchant and Protestant elder from the town of Saujon, located about eight miles from Cozes. Charles was the grandson of Jehan Jolly, a Protestant merchant, salt dealer, and royal official who was one of the leading voices advocating for church reform in Saintonge during the 1560s. Jehan Jolly had acquired two estates, Saint-Denis in Saint Seurin d'Uzet and des Salles in Saint-Fort-sur-Gironde, and the channel Port de Maubert on the Gironde River, by 1565. In 1575, Jehan added the estate and noble house of Chadignac. Sometime after 1673, Charles Jolly moved to the family seat near Saintes to become Seigneur de Chadignac, the leader of this Protestant noble family in Saintonge. Two of the sons born to Charles and Judith, who were baptized in Cozes, would follow their father as Seigneur.[28]

Cozes Protestant Baptism Register, 1656–1668. Page includes baptism entry for Charlotte Jolly (1659–1721).
Photo by the author. Courtesy Archives Departmentales de la Charente-Maritime La Rochelle, France.

By 1664, the era of Protestant ascendancy in Cozes was coming to an end. Protestants still made up the overwhelming majority of the population of the town, but they no longer controlled the reins of local government. Louis XIV was three years into his time of direct rule in France and was implementing his policy that every local governing body must be under Catholic control. Local officials pursued the king's interest by turning up the pressure on the Protestant churches of France. On March 1, 1664, the Cozes town council issued an order prohibiting Protestants from singing their beloved psalms in public.[29] The profound significance of this restriction is not obvious to twenty-first-century readers, but one historian has pointed out that for Huguenots the public singing of psalms was an act of "Protestant subversion" that could unite "a Protestant crowd in ecstatic companionship, just as a football chant does today."[30] Louis XIV and his governing officials understood the power of psalms to encourage and energize the Protestant public, and they were determined to put in place a new national policy to ban them outside services of worship in the Protestant temples.

The Protestant Church of Cozes and its new pastor, Jean Masson, faced an even more serious threat in 1664. The 1598 Edict of Nantes limited Protestant worship to the congregations that were in existence at the time the edict was issued. In the early 1660s, Louis XIV began to encourage lawsuits against Protestant congregations to require them to prove they existed prior to 1598. The ones that could not produce adequate documentation of a pre-1598 existence would be closed. Apparently one of these suits was filed against the Cozes congregation, resulting in the investigating commissioner ordering the demolition of the church. In this case, the order was not carried out because of another provision of the Edict of Nantes that created a parallel court system for Protestants. The Protestant commissioner of the court successfully argued for the existence of the Cozes temple before 1598, thereby enabling it to remain open.[31]

The banning of the public singing of psalms was a sign that the Protestants of Cozes had been forced to the periphery of public life. The unenforced order to demolish the temple was an even more ominous indication that the Huguenots of Cozes were entering into a desperate struggle for survival. In the new climate of increasing discriminatory legislation, this town, where Protestants had long been in control, would soon cease to function as a refuge. Like other Huguenots living in western France, they would be faced with horrendous choices about accepting the king's religion or migrating to a Protestant destination in Europe or the new world.

About 1670, the Huguenot diaspora from Cozes was underway as a group of Protestant families set sail for the west. In his *History of the Huguenot Emigration to America*, Charles W. Baird published a census list of Huguenots who relocated to the French islands of the Caribbean at this time. Some of these exiles were from Cozes, including the brothers Jean and Paul Pelletreau; Paul's wife, Ester Gouin; and Paul's sons, Elie and Jean. Other Cozes Huguenots who joined this migration included Jacques Allaire, Jean Bouyer, Pierre Breton, Jean Gaillard, Jean Morin, and Elie Papin. Authorities on the island of Saint Christophe welcomed these merchant-oriented Huguenots and apparently permitted a French Protestant congregation to function there during the 1670s. When the more intense persecution of Protestants by Louis XIV reached the islands in the 1680s, some of these Huguenot settlers (including the Pelletraus and Papins) moved on to New York City.[32]

During the 1670s and early 1680s, Louis XIV continued to impose burdensome restrictions on his Protestant subjects, chipping away at the rights conferred to them in the Edict of Nantes. In 1677, Jean Bertrand, the older son of Paul Bertrand, went to England.[33] Having been educated and ordained in France, Bertrand decided to receive re-ordination as an Anglican by the Bishop of London. Jean migrated several years before the implementation of the worst measures of persecution that decisively turned the increasingly shaky world of the French Protestants upside down. The worst came when the Dragonnades began terrorizing Huguenots in the province of Poitou in 1681. Horrifying tales of the atrocities committed by these French troops against their own people spread quickly into neighboring Saintonge and across France.[34] Quartered in Protestant homes, the Dragoons would confiscate or destroy property and generally abuse the household residents until they signed the renunciations of their Protestant faith known as abjurations. Protestants who resisted abjuring often abandoned their homes to the troops, seeking shelter in the woods or with friends in another town. They would return when the troops moved on, hoping their property had not been totally destroyed.[35] The fear generated by the reports of what the Dragonnades were doing led many Protestants to line up to sign their abjurations when word came that the troops were en route to their town. A few months after the arrival of the Dragonnades in Poitou, Jean Bertrand's younger brother Paul and mother, Marie André, joined him in London.[36] As persecution intensified, the diaspora from Cozes was building momentum.

The destructive consequences of Louis's anti-Protestant crusade played out in an especially painful fashion in Cozes in 1683. Jean Masson was in his twenty-second year of ministry in the town when he was arrested and charged with unlawfully permitting a Catholic convert to worship in the Cozes Protestant temple. Through a campaign of legal pressure and financial inducements, French officials had succeeded in luring less committed members of Huguenot congregations to leave their faith communities, and these new Catholic converts were prohibited by law from returning to a Protestant temple for any reason. If they did, the minister of the congregation, as well as the convert, was in violation of the law. The most damaging consequence of this law was its disruption of the ministries of many Huguenot congregations who saw their pastors placed on trial and sentenced to stiff jail terms.

With Jean Masson in prison waiting to be tried, the Cozes Protestants employed a new pastor, Pierre Forrestier, who had recently been released from a Paris prison. In the spring of 1684, local authorities suspended services in the Cozes church and prohibited Forrestier from practicing his ministry. Forrestier then filed an appeal of this action with a higher court—the Parlement of Bordeaux. These justices reversed the local decision in August 1684, but while Huguenot worship apparently resumed in Cozes by September 1684, the prospects for local Protestants continued to be grim.[37] In December 1684, Jean Masson was finally brought to trial in a regional court in Saintes, where the justices found him guilty and banished him from the kingdom. Masson left France, taking his family with him to the Netherlands.[38]

In the spring of 1685, word reached the Protestants of Cozes that the long-dreaded Dragonnades were finally headed for their province. In his memoirs, Jaques Fontaine, brother-in-law of Pierre Forrestier, offers a vivid portrayal of the anxious mood of the Protestants of Saintonge as they awaited the arrival of Louis XIV's "'missionary' troops." Fontaine lived in Royan, a neighboring town to Cozes. The son and younger brother of pastors who both filled in at Cozes after Paul Bertrand Sr.'s death in 1660, Jaques undoubtedly knew the Bertrand and Jolly families, to which he was loosely connected through the marriage of his brother.[39] Fontaine was only a year younger than Paul Bertrand Jr. Jaques wrote about a dramatic meeting at the Protestant Church of Cozes to develop a coordinated strategy by some of the Saintonge congregations to address the emergency created by the imminent arrival of the Dragonnades. Twelve ministers and a similar number of elders were present for the meeting. Fontaine did not name the ministers who participated in this gathering, but it is clear that some area ministers had, like the Bertrand brothers, already gone into exile. Jean and Paul Bertrand's uncle, the Cozes elder and merchant Jean André, was almost certainly in attendance.

Jaques Fontaine's description of the 1685 gathering of ministers and elders in Cozes is a revealing window into the mind-set of the people who were seeing the 150-year era of Protestant reform in Saintonge crumbling around them as ministers were struggling to manage the unfolding ecclesiastical disaster. Jaques Fontaine was a *proposant,* a candidate preparing for the ministry, when he attended the 1685 meeting in Cozes.[40] He remembered rising during the meeting to call for a Huguenot insurgency to resist the state policy of persecution directed against the Protestants. He boldly criticized the ministers for being too meek in preaching obedience to the king and non-resistance to the Dragonnades. The ministers in Cozes let Fontaine speak, but they were not convinced by the young man's appeal. He later recalled the words by which they put him in his place as an untested *proposant*: "They told me that I did not have the spirit of the Gospel, which was patient and long-suffering, and which gives permission only for flight. . . . They considered me a headstrong youth whose spirit was impure."[41] These ministers were clearly focused on preparing exiles rather than inspiring military insurgents.

Jaques passed through Cozes in the middle of the night following the arrival of the dragoons. He learned there had been very little resistance to them in the town. He later recalled that: "Only about five or six people remained firm so they had all the dragoons. As soon as a person had converted, they took the dragoons away and sent them to those who remained faithful."[42]

A few months after the 1685 imposition of the Dragonnades on Cozes, Louis XIV issued the Edict of Fontainebleau, revoking the Edict of Nantes. He ordered the destruction of the remaining Protestant temples and expelled those Protestant ministers who would not convert to Catholicism. The Protestant Church of Cozes was destroyed without delay, but exiles from Cozes were already en route to England and the Netherlands by that time, and some were contemplating a new life across the Atlantic. The king's new edict in the fall of 1685 sent shock waves across every Protestant community in France. Huguenots understood their world had been cruelly turned upside down by a power they could not hope to resist. To continue practicing their faith, they would have to go underground or make a dangerous, expensive, and illegal journey into exile. Despite the severe punishments Louis threatened to those caught trying to leave France—prison for women and rowing the galleys for men—the French Protestants who fled their country formed one of the largest diasporas of the early modern world.[43]

Historians believe that 150,000 to 200,000 Huguenots left France in response to Louis XIV's persecution of Protestants, with perhaps 500,000 remaining. The refugees poured into the Protestant European countries they could reach. Some took land routes to Switzerland, the German states, and the Dutch Republic. Huguenots with access to the sea sailed to the two countries that hosted the largest populations of refugees: England and the Dutch Republic. This massive exodus would eventually distribute Huguenots across the Atlantic world to divergent locations in Ireland, Scotland, South Africa, Surinam, the West Indies, and the English North American colonies.

Huguenot networks led by ministers and merchants quickly coalesced to offer the refugees financial, social, and spiritual support to help them survive and live their faith in exile.[44] But these migration networks, known to Huguenots as *le Refuge,* were not sufficient to meet the immense challenges that confronted the refugees. Huguenot leaders quickly recognized this massive diaspora required a much larger support system, which could only emerge through alliances with the rulers and churches of Protestant Europe. The exiles quickly became skilled at presenting themselves as valuable citizens—soldiers, ministers, merchants, physicians, vintners, weavers, and artisans—serving the states and colonial empires that supported them.[45]

England might have received the largest number of Huguenot exiles. Of the estimated 50,000 refugees who fled to England between 1680 and 1710,[46] a relatively small number, between 3,000 and 4,000, made their way across the Atlantic to English America. The best-known Huguenot migrations to the new world were to the colonies of Massachusetts, New York, Virginia, and South Carolina.[47] Small numbers of Huguenots were migrating to the new world before their churches were outlawed by Louis XIV. As previously noted, settlers from western France began appearing along the James River in Virginia during the 1630s. French-speaking Walloons from northern France and present-day southern Belgium were prominent citizens of New Amsterdam by 1650. During the 1650s, Waldensian Protestants from eastern France were settling on Staten Island. In 1658, Protestants from northwest France migrated to the Dutch town of Kingston, New York, after having previously settled in the Palatine. Between 1650 and 1680, French-speaking Protestants from the Channel Islands settled in Salem, Massachusetts.[48]

The larger and better-known Huguenot settlements in America were founded after 1680. By 1690, refugees fleeing the persecution of Louis XIV had settled in three of the major English American cities—New York City, Boston, and Charlestown—where they established independent French Protestant congregations. Huguenot exiles had also established rural communities along the Rappahannock River in Virginia (see Chapter 3); Narragansett in Rhode Island; Oxford in Massachusetts; New Rochelle and Staten Island in New York; and Santee, Orange Quarter, Goose Creek, and Wantoot in South Carolina.[49] However, by 1696, the Narragansett and Oxford settlements had failed. In 1700, an additional Huguenot migration to Virginia began arriving in five ships paid for by William III. Some refugees in this large migration joined the previously established Rappahannock Huguenots, and others founded a Huguenot settlement at Manakin Town, a deserted Native American village a short distance west of present-day Richmond (see Chapter 7). All the Huguenots migrating to Virginia worshipped in Anglican parishes, where services were sometimes led by French-speaking ministers.

Most of the Huguenots who migrated to English America were quite willing to make use of enslaved labor if they could afford to do so, especially in the colonies of South Carolina, Virginia, and New York. There is no evidence Huguenots had any ethical qualms about slavery in the English colonies even though some refugees had been in danger of being enslaved themselves on Louis XIV's galleys. Like other seventeenth-century European churches, the French Reformed Church did not teach that slavery was morally wrong. While the National Synod, meeting in 1637, challenged the complicity of Huguenot merchants in the international slave trade, it nonetheless declared that owning enslaved persons was not condemned by the word of God. The moral issue for the Synod was the way the enslaved were treated. The Synod declared that the humane treatment of the enslaved was a moral imperative.[50] While records suggest some Huguenots in South Carolina, Virginia, and New York tried to follow the Synod's directive to treat enslaved persons humanely, there is no reason to believe any of them challenged the English imperial policy of exploiting enslaved labor in its new world colonies.

Records indicate that Huguenots from the Protestant Church of Cozes migrated to six of the North American colonies: Massachusetts, Rhode Island, New York, Maryland, Virginia, and South Carolina. The Cozes Baptism Register includes the names of dozens of Huguenot refugees—perhaps as many as eighty—who found refuge along North America's eastern seaboard.[51] Their geographical distribution made it possible for them to form a clan and kinship network across English America.

The documented merchant activities of Cozes Huguenots in the new world form a common pattern for these exiles. Abraham Tourtellot (born 1666) was the son of the Cozes royal notary Daniel Tourtellot and Ester André, daughter of a prominent Saintonge merchant family. In 1687, he sailed for Boston, where he married Marie Bernon, a Huguenot refugee from La Rochelle. After participating in the failed Narragansett settlement in Rhode Island, Tourtellot helped his merchant father-in-law, Gabriel Bernon, operate ships out of Boston. Some of their trade was smuggling between Boston and French Quebec, but they were also sending their ships to Virginia and the West Indies.[52]

Jean Pelletreau was a wealthy member of a large Cozes Huguenot community of about twenty-five refugees in New York City, where he worked in partnership with his nephews, Elie Pelletreau (born 1665) and Jean Pelletreau (born 1668). As ships' chandlers, they provided necessary supplies to vessels, and their crews docked in New York, which placed them at the center of the city's maritime trading activities. The nephews were sons of a royal notary named Paul Pelletreau and his wife, Ester Gouin, who left Cozes for the island of Saint Christophe about 1670. In France, this family lived in the village of Arces, a few miles down the road from Cozes. The senior Jean Pelletreau served as sponsor at the 1668 baptism in Cozes of his namesake nephew.[53] After arriving in New York City in the early 1680s, Elie Pelletreau married Marie Benoist, the daughter of two other refugees from the Cozes congregation—Jean Benoist and Judith Bourdon.[54]

There was also a significant Cozes presence of about thirteen refugees in the Huguenot settlement in New Rochelle, New York. One of the earliest homes in the settlement was built by Cozes emigrants Louis Guion and his wife, Thomasse Fourestier (born 1657), daughter of Isaac Fourestier and Marie Sequin. The couple's documented Cozes refugee family members in New Rochelle include Thomasse's brother, Jean Fourestier (born 1666); Louis's father, Louis Guion Sr.; two children born in England; and one child born at sea. While this Huguenot settlement was not an economically thriving one, it did construct dock facilities that kept New Rochelle well connected to other Cozes Huguenots in English America.[55] The excellent lines of communication between Cozes Huguenots along the eastern seaboard of English America is illustrated by the presence of Cozes refugee Ambrose Sicard in both New Rochelle and in South Carolina.[56] While the Huguenot emigration to South Carolina was one of the largest in English America, the evidence suggests Sicard was one of a small handful of Cozes exiles who chose to go there.

The documented Cozes refugee community in Maryland was also quite small, but it was led by Paul Bertrand Jr. (1657–c.1690), son of the Huguenot minister who served the Cozes Protestant church from 1650 to 1660. Paul's mother was Marie André of the André merchant family. Through his mother, Paul was a cousin of the New England merchant Abraham Tourtellot. Paul Bertrand migrated to Maryland in 1686 to serve as an Anglican missionary and died there about 1690. Had Paul lived longer in the new world, a larger group of Cozes Huguenots might well have gathered around him.[57]

This study explores in depth the large Huguenot migration to the Rappahannock region of Virginia, where thirty or more Cozes Huguenots settled beginning in 1687.[58] Two leaders of this Huguenot migration were from prominent Cozes families who were closely connected in France. Jean Bertrand, the older son of one Cozes pastor and the student of another, was the organizing pastor of the Rappahannock Huguenots. Paul Micou, a physician like his father, became one of the wealthiest members of the Rappahannock Refuge. Both of these men stayed in Virginia to the end of their lives, and true to the pattern of other Cozes Huguenots in English America, both were also merchants. There is evidence that one of the sons of the banished Cozes pastor, Jean Masson Jr., was part of this Huguenot community along the Rappahannock in 1691. By 1695, Masson was in England, where he was ordained by the Bishop of London and subsequently served as tutor to the sons of the Bishop of Salisbury. Another member of a prominent Cozes Huguenot family who participated in this migration was Charlotte Jolly, daughter of Charles Jolly, Seigneur de Chadignac. She married Jean Bertrand in London and sailed with him to Virginia in 1687, where she also worked as a merchant.[59]

The Virginia trading activities of Jean and Charlotte Jolly Bertrand and Paul Micou put them at the center of a North American Huguenot communication network at a time when common bonds of kinship, friendship, and religious identity were crucial for long-distance traders.[60] The Cozes Huguenot presence up and down the eastern seaboard of English America positioned these exiles for intercolonial trade and kept the French-exile lines of communication open and productive. The relationships of trust that sustained Cozes Huguenots in English America were forged in Saintonge through the Protestant congregation that nurtured them.

This Huguenot diaspora divided many Cozes families as some fled France and others remained behind. The town records of Cozes document the formulaic abjuration statements, to which, in obedience to their king, local citizens placed their signatures in renunciation of their Protestant faith.[61] While the large-scale abjurations began in Cozes in 1685, most of the surviving documented signatures were recorded in 1686. Among those who signed was Jean André, a wealthy merchant and long-serving elder of the Protestant church. André had a very close relationship with the Bertrand and the Masson families. He was the uncle of Jean and Paul Bertrand and the baptism sponsor of the son of Jean Masson. Another example was Charles Jolly, who moved with his wife, Judith André, to Saintes by 1686.[62] With at least two of their sons and one daughter, they abjured as well. One of these sons, Charles Jolly Jr., was a captain in the army of Louis XIV by 1686.[63] But four of the Jolly children, one son and three daughters, had already escaped France to maintain their Protestant identity in England.

The prominent La Rochefoucauld family in Cozes was separated in a similar way. François's son Ruben left France to use his military training to wage war against Louis XIV in the army of the Protestant Dutch leader William of Orange (later William III of England). Ruben's sister Marguerite followed her brother into the Refuge, where she married a French exile military officer. François and his son by the same name abjured and stayed in France. While Paul Micou fled France, his parents, brother, and two sisters converted and remained in Saintonge to the end of their lives. These abjurations were the price Cozes leaders paid for keeping their property and maintaining their titles.[64]

For most Protestants throughout Saintonge, the crucial decision after 1685 was whether to abjure or to emigrate, and Huguenot emigration levels from the region are believed to have been among the highest in France. Many families in the province were, like the Jollys, La Rochefoucaulds, and Micous, permanently torn apart by the process. Some Huguenot families made strategic decisions to separate to save their property and continue their businesses. Family members who emigrated, while sometimes preserving ties to their family businesses based in France, were free to practice their faith openly. Those who remained did what was necessary to convince authorities they were Catholic while practicing their Reformed faith in private.[65] The Protestants who remained in France were sometimes derisively called "New Catholics (*Nouveau Catholiques*)" by authorities who suspected they were continuing Reformed worship in their homes or in the secluded outdoor gatherings of the secret underground church (*églises du désert*). The families that separated believing the king's ban on Protestantism to be temporary, would in time see their hopes disappointed. Those who left, and those who were left behind, were in most cases saying goodbye to family members they would never see again.

From the Netherlands, the exiled Cozes pastor Jean Masson was paying close attention to the unfolding disaster in Saintonge. A few years after Louis XIV ordered the destruction of the remaining Protestant temples in France, Masson decided to leave his family and return to France for a clandestine ministry in the underground church. The sources do not make clear whether he died en route to France or after beginning a secret Protestant ministry there.[66] Like their banished pastor, the Huguenots of Cozes were forced to find new ways to sustain their families and live their faith after their world had been turned upside down.

NOTES

1. John Calvin, *Commentaries on the Old Testament* (Grand Rapids, MI, 1948), cited in William F. Keesecker, ed., *A Calvin Reader: Reflections on Living* (Philadelphia, 1985), 99. The words of Calvin quoted here addressed Isaiah 21:11.

2. Eugene and Emile Haag, *La France Protestante, Deuxieme Edition* (Paris, 1879), Tome Deuxieme, 456. The Cozes Protestant Baptism Register documents Paul Bertrand's ministry in Cozes during the 1650s and his death in 1660, CZ, ADCMLR.

3. Eugene and Emile Haag list Paul Bertrand's father as N. Bertrand, pastor of Saint-Jean-d'Angle from 1614 to 1619, Haag, *La France Protestante*, 456.

4. E. A. Wrigley and R. S. Schofield have concluded that in English churches from 1541 to 1871 30.26 baptisms annually indicates a population of 1,000. On this reckoning the baptisms performed at Cozes between 1656 and 1668 would constitute a community of about 2,600. Gwynn, *Huguenots in Britain II*, 161–62.

5. Van Ruymbeke, *From New Babylon to Eden*, 100.

6. CZ, ADCMLR.

7. CZ, 23, ADCMLR; Elisabeth Forlacroix and Olga de Saint-Affrique, *Les Pasteurs d'Aunis, Saintonge, et Angoumois devant la Revocation: Dictionnaire* (Paris, 2010), 96.

8. Notary Bargignac, 3E 128/49, folio 154–155, ADCMLR.

9. Neal Kamil, *Fortress of the Soul: Violence, Metaphysics, and Material Life in the Huguenots New World, 1517–1751* (Baltimore, MD, 2005), 125–31 and 147–51.

10. Geoffrey Treasure, *The Huguenots* (New Haven, 2013), 56.

11. Armstrong, *Calvinism and the Amyraut Heresy*, 13–22.

12. Ibid., 151; Kevin C. Robbins, *City on the Ocean Sea, La Rochelle, 1530–1650: Urban Society, Religion, and Politics on the French Atlantic Frontier* (Leiden, 1997), 371.

13. Ibid., 352–53; Kamil, *Fortress of the Soul*, 152–53.

14. Ibid., 159–63.

15. W. Noel Sainsbury, ed., *Calendar of State Papers, Colonial Series, vol. 1, America and West Indies, 1574–1660* (London, 1860), 98–121.

16. Nell M. Nugent, *Cavaliers and Pioneers: Abstracts of Virginia Land Patents and Grants, 1623–1666* (Richmond, VA, 1934), vol. 1, xxv, 121.

17. Beverley Fleet, *Virginia Colonial Abstracts* (Baltimore, MD, 1961), 118, 194, and 214 (hereafter cited as Fleet).

18. Robbins, *City on the Ocean Sea*, 400–09.

19. Philip J. Hnatkovich, *The Atlantic Gate: The Anglo-Huguenot Channel Community, 1553–1665* (Penn State University Phd. Dissertation, State College, PA, 2014), 29, 35, 40–44, and 238.

20. Robbins, *City on the Ocean Sea*, 370 (Allaire), 254 and 346 (Bernardeau), 124 (Chauvin), 392 (David), 328 (Dourneau), 346 (Guerineau), 345–46 (Papin) 249 (Prevost), and 327 (Robin); CZ, 4 (Allaire and Prevost), 22 (Chauvin and Bernardeau), 15 (David), 7 (Dourneau and Guerineau), 7 and 15 (Papin), and 25 and 46 (Robin), ADCMLR; Charles W. Baird, *History of the Huguenot Emigration to America* (New York, 1885), vol. 1, 290 and 292 (hereafter cited as Baird); CZ, 34 (Sicard) and 42 (Morin), ADCMLR.

21. Treasure, *The Huguenots*, 301; Van Ruymbeke, *From New Babylon to Eden*, 10–11.

22. CZ, ADCMLR; Controle des Actes de Cozes, Cozes Hotel de Ville.

23. Van Ruymbeke, *From New Babylon to Eden*, 102–03.

24. For the naming and godparenting practices of Protestants in southern France, see Raymond A. Mentzer, *Blood and Belief: Family Survival and Confessional Identity Among the Provincial Huguenot Nobility* (W. Lafayette, IN, 1993), 145–49.

25. CZ, 16, 23, 28, 33, 40, and 52, ADCMLR.

26. Judith Pugh Meyer, *Reformation in La Rochelle: Tradition and Change in Early Modern Europe, 1500–1568* (Geneva, 1996), 38–39.

27. CZ, 22, 32, and 37, ADCMLR.

28. Frédéric Chasseboeuf, *Châteaux, Manoirs, et Logis: La Charente-Maritime* (Prahecq, France, 2008), vol. 2, 137, 517, and 657; Suire Yannis, Region Poitou-Charentes, "Inventaire du patrimoine culturel"; *Bulletin de la Société des Archives historiques de la Saintonge et de l'Aunis* 7 (1880), 455; Charles Dangibeaud, ed., *Minutes de Notaires: Notes de Lecture*, BR 5842, ADCMLR; 1J 115, ADCMLR; Notary Bargignac, 3E 128/49, Folio 23, ADCMLR.

29. Archive Nationale, TT. 246, Bibliothèque de la Société de l'Histoire du Protestantisme Français Paris (hereafter SHPF); Van Ruymbeke, *From New Babylon to Eden*, 103.

30. Diarmaid MacCulloch, *The Reformation: A History* (New York, 2003), 308.

31. Carolyn Chappell Lougee, *Facing the Revocation: Huguenot Families, Faith, and the King's Will* (New York, 2017), 110.

32. Baird, vol. 1, 211, 212, 231, 232, and 286, vol. 2, 39; Butler, *The Huguenots in America*, 42–43, and 157; CZ, 4 (Allaire), 43 (Bouyer), 18 (Breton), 5 (Gaillard), 15 (Morin), 43 (Papin), and 52 (Pelletrau), ADCMLR.

33. Church of England Ordination Records, #9535/3, Guildhall Library, London, #97040; Clergy of the Church of England Database (hereafter CCEd).

34. Gwynn, *Huguenot Heritage*, 26–27.

35. For the experience of Jean Migault, who fled to the woods from his home in Poitou to escape Dragoons in 1681, see Ibid., 8–9.

36. Dangibeaud, *Minutes de Notaires*, BR 5842, ADCMLR; MR/R/R/032/08, London Metropolitan Archives (hereafter LMA).

37. Jaques Fontaine, *Memoirs of the Reverend Jaques Fontaine, 1658–1728* (London, 1992), ed. Dianne Ressinger, 82–83; Archive Nationale TT. 246, SHPF.

38. Elisabeth Forlacroix and Olga de Saint-Affrique, *Les Pasteurs d'Aunis, Saintonge, et Angoumois devant la Revocation: Dictionnaire* (Paris, 2010), 96–97.

39. Jaques Fontaine's brother Pierre was married to Suzanne Brejon, the daughter of a wealthy royal notary and judge in the Saintonge town of Meursac. Suzanne's sister Marguerite was married to Jean André, uncle of Jean Bertrand and his brother Paul. Their sister Marie was married to Jacques Jolly, brother of Charles Jolly. Les Moré, "Descendances et familles allées (XVIe—XIXe siècles)," *Généalogies Protestantes (Angoumois, Aunis, Guyenne, Saintonge)* (2021), 146–47.

40. Fontaine, *Memoirs of the Reverend Jaques Fontaine*, 33, 83–109.

41. Ibid., 111.

42. Fontaine, *Memoirs of the Reverend Jaques Fontaine*, 114–15.

43. Treasure, *The Huguenots*, 356–60.

44. Charles Weiss, *History of the French Protestant refugees from the revocation of the edict of Nantes to the present time*, trans. Frederick Hardman (Edinburgh, 1854), x.

45. Stanwood, *The Global Refuge*, 4–7.

46. Gwynn, *Huguenots in Britain II*, 199.

47. Van Ruymbeke, "Le Refuge: History and Memory from the 1770s to the Present," 427.

48. Butler, *The Huguenots in America*, 43–46.

49. For the Huguenot diaspora to English America, see Van Ruymbeke, *From Babylon to New Eden;* Carlo, *Huguenot Refugees in Colonial New York;* Butler, *The Huguenots in America;* and Lambert, *The Protestant International and the Huguenot Migration to Virginia*.

50. Van Ruymbeke, *From New Babylon to Eden*, 216.

51. Lonnie H. Lee, "The Transatlantic Legacy of the Protestant Church of Cozes," *The Huguenot Society Journal* 32 (2019), 51–54.

52. CZ, 11 and 41, ADCMLR; Bosher, "Huguenot Merchants and the Protestant International," 94–96.

53. CZ, 39 and 52, ADCMLR; Butler, *The Huguenots in America,* 157; Baird, vol. 1, 231–32, vol. 2, 39.

54. CZ, 14, 30, and 38, ADCMLR; Alfred V. Wittmeyer, ed., *Register of the Births, Marriages, and Deaths of the "Eglise Francaise a la Nouvelle York," from 1688 to 1804* (New York, 1886), 37.

55. CZ, 9, 21, and 43, ADCMLR; Baird, vol. II, 39–40; Carlo, *Huguenot Refugees in Colonial New York,* 126; Kenneth Scott and Kenn Stryker-Rodda, eds., *Denizations, Naturalizations, and Oaths of Allegiance in Colonial New York* (Baltimore, MD, 1975), 5.

56. Lee, "The Transatlantic Legacy of the Protestant Church of Cozes," 51–54.

57. CZ, 7, ADCMLR; #97436, CCEd; Le Baron F. De Schickler, *Les Eglises Du Refuge En Angleterre*, tome deuxième (Paris, 1892), 335; Jane Baldwin Cotton, ed., *Maryland Calendar of Wills* (Westminster, MD, 1988), vol. 4, 234.

58. Lee, "The Transatlantic Legacy of the Protestant Church of Cozes," 52–53.

59. F. Edward Wright, *Essex County, Virginia Marriage References and Family Relationships, 1620–1800* (Lewes, DE, 2013), 135; SP, Essex County (EC) WB, 1735–1743, 89–90; Westmoreland County (hereafter WC) OB, 1690–1698, 5.

60. April Lee Hatfield, *Atlantic Virginia: Intercolonial Relations in the Seventeenth Century* (Philadelphia, 2018), 89, 110–15, and 123–27.

61. Controle des Actes de Cozes, Cozes Hotel de Ville, May 3, 1686.

62. Notaire Bargignac, 3E, 128/49, folio 23, February 4, 1692, ADCMLR.

63. "Revue de Saintonge & d'Aunis," *Bulletin de la Société des Archives historiques de la Saintonge et de l'Aunis,* 15, 240.

64. Grace Lawless Lee, *The Huguenot Settlements of Ireland* (Berwyn Heights, MD, 2008), 165–66; Dangibeaud, *Minutes de Notaires*, C224, ADCMLR.

65. Bosher, "Huguenot Merchants and the Protestant International," 93–94.

66. Forlacroix and de Saint-Affrique, *Les Pasteurs*, 96–97.

Chapter Two

London, 1677

Lighten our darkness we beseech thee, O Lord, and by thy great mercy defend us from all perils.

—*Book of Common Prayer,* 1662

On July 4, 1677, a young Huguenot minister was re-ordained to the Anglican ministry by Bishop of London Henry Compton.[1] Jean Bertrand most likely traveled on the bishop's barge the short journey down the River Thames from the city of London to the Bishop's Palace in the village of Fulham. There he disembarked and made the pleasant walk into the palace complex. As Bertrand approached the palace, he would have crossed the ancient moat and passed through a section of the well-landscaped garden. Bishop Compton was an avid horticulturalist and later expanded the garden to include many plant species sent by Anglican clergy in Virginia and other colonies. Among these was the first Virginia magnolia to be planted in England and a Virginia oak that continues to grace the garden today. The ordination service for Jean Bertrand was held in the medieval chapel of the palace, then located on the southeast front of Fulham's Main Hall in space now occupied by a patio and garden area.[2]

Palace of the Bishop of London at Fulham. 1885 print of a 1798 drawing of the inner courtyard. Engraving on wood by an unknown artist.
Courtesy of the author

Jean Bertrand's walk across the palace complex that day was part of a much longer journey on which he had embarked. With the king of France already dismantling Protestantism within his realm, Bertrand had chosen to become part of the Huguenot diaspora that would soon spread across the Atlantic world. Jean Bertrand's journey now brought him from his roots in western France into the center of English religion, culture, and empire to be ordained by one of the pivotal religious and political leaders of late-seventeenth-century England. The spiritual home Bertrand found in the Anglican Church, a new light in his French Protestant darkness, would enable him to straddle his French and English identities and prepare him to serve as an agent of English empire in the new world.[3]

On Jean Bertrand's Anglican ordination day, Henry Compton was still relatively new to his office, having been installed as the spiritual leader of the diocese of London in December 1675. He was the son of an influential noble family that supported Charles I in the English Civil War. He went to France after the execution of Charles I in 1649, where he became fluent in French, and returned to England after the restoration of the monarchy in 1660. During the course of his service as Bishop of London, Compton would ordain about 230 Huguenots to the Anglican ministry.[4] One of Henry

Compton's early accomplishments occurred in 1676, when he secured the permission of Charles II to confirm the princesses and future queens Mary and Anne as Anglicans. Four months after ordaining Jean Bertrand, Compton officiated at the marriage of Princess Mary to the Dutch Protestant leader William of Orange, a couple who would later become England's Mary II and William III.[5]

Huguenot refugees seeking Anglican ordination typically went through two ordination services in England if they had not been previously ordained to the ministry in France. They were ordained first as deacons and then a month or two later ordained again to the priesthood. That Jean Bertrand was ordained as deacon and priest on the same day suggests he had been previously ordained in France and served in ministry there.[6] The course of study for Jean in France would have included four years of philosophy and metaphysics and then three to four years of theology, Hebrew, and Greek. He was almost certainly educated at one or more of the Huguenot academies in France.[7] Approximately twenty-six years of age on his re-ordination date in 1677 (only three years older than the minimum age for an Anglican ordination), Jean could not have been a minister in France for more than a few years.[8]

The transition of Huguenot clergy into the Church of England was not an easy or natural one. The cultural ethos of the two churches was quite different. The egalitarian relationships of Huguenot clergy had to be set aside in favor of the hierarchical structure of the Church of England. Some Huguenot ministers who were presented to Bishop Henry Compton in 1686 were bewildered by the instruction that they were to put a knee to the ground to greet him.[9] The requirement that Huguenot clergy must be re-ordained to practice ministry in the Church of England was established as part of Charles II's *Act of Uniformity* in 1662.[10] Though it was controversial among French Protestants, about 60 percent of the almost 600 Huguenot ministers who were exiled in England eventually accepted re-ordination as Anglicans.[11]

Jean Bertrand's arrival in England by 1677 places him in exile about two years before the time frame historians typically use to calculate the twenty-one-year exodus of 150,000 to 200,000 Huguenot refugees.[12] By the mid-1670s, the life of Huguenots "under the cross" in France was becoming increasingly difficult. Authorities had already destroyed a significant number of Protestant temples. Huguenots could no longer expect to receive justice in a French court of law. Many of the cemeteries where Protestants had always buried their dead were no longer open to them.[13] The Protestant academies that trained ministers and other leaders were being squeezed out of existence. The future of the Protestant Church in France was becoming ever more tenuous.[14]

The early date of Jean Bertrand's arrival in England also put him at the forefront of a large-scale exodus of family and friends from the congregation in Cozes, France, where Jean was raised and where his father had served as pastor. The flow of French immigrants into England increased dramatically as the persecution of Huguenots intensified during the 1680s. Like Jean Bertrand, many of the Cozes Huguenot exiles had more than one reason for leaving France. To be sure, they wanted to openly embrace their Protestant identity. But they also wanted to participate fully in the Atlantic world from which Louis XIV was cutting them off. The merchants and seamen of Saintonge were leaving France in droves, knowing this was the only way for them to remain fully connected to the transatlantic economy that had been part of their communities for centuries.[15] For many of the exiles from Cozes, England did not prove to be their final destination. It was, instead, the first stop on a journey that would take them to Ireland, to Scotland, or to English America. With his arrival in England just before this large Huguenot migration gained traction, Jean was in position to prepare the way for the relatives and friends who chose to follow him there.

One of the ways Jean assisted newly arriving Cozes emigrants was the pastoral leadership he provided to them as a minister. There is reason to believe that Jean Bertrand arrived in England fully prepared to become an Anglican clergyman.[16] The evidence suggests that Jean and his brother Paul found in the Church of England a firm anchor to secure their Protestant identity in the face of the catastrophic destruction of their Huguenot world in France. For them, ordination into the Church of England was not something to be endured as a matter of professional or financial necessity as it was for some Huguenot ministers. The French training and theological orientation of the Bertrand brothers prepared them to embrace the Anglican Church without relinquishing their Huguenot identity. Records show that Jean Bertrand's brother Paul was educated at the Saumur Academy and was deeply influenced by its more moderate version of Calvinist theology.[17] While there is no record showing which Huguenot academy awarded Jean's master's degree, there is much evidence to confirm Jean shared this theological identity with his brother. As J. F. Bosher has pointed out, the world of seventeenth-century Huguenots was one of "families and religious clans, not an age of individualism in . . . custom or thought."[18]

The Saumur theology was at the center of a bitter controversy that shook the French Protestant Church by the middle of the seventeenth century.[19] It was championed by Moïse Amyraut (1596–1664), who began teaching at the Saumur Academy in 1626.[20] Amyraut, who was also pastor of the Protestant Church of Saumur, challenged the formulation of Calvinist orthodoxy adopted by the Synod of Dordt in 1619, especially its doctrine that Christ died only for the elect. In his *Brief Traitte de la Predestination*, published in 1634,[21] Amyraut argued that his teaching was faithful to John Calvin's emphasis on justification by faith. The defenders of the theological formulations of the Synod of Dordt, however, found Amyraut's theology heretical. The critics of Amyraldean theology, especially Scholastic Calvinists like Pierre du Moulin, were particularly alarmed by the fact that graduates of the prestigious Saumur Academy were almost always devoted to Amyraut's teaching. As this controversy continued to grow in intensity, some Huguenots feared it was becoming a theological civil war that would lead the French Protestant Church into schism.[22]

Moïse Amyraut's continuing appeal to Huguenots like the Bertrands was also driven by his multi-faceted career as a theologian, a parish pastor, and a political leader of national prominence. He enjoyed a long and amiable relationship with Cardinal Richelieu, who gave the Huguenot theologian an entree into French politics at the highest level. Amyraut also had a close relationship with Richelieu's successor, Cardinal Mazarin. Amyraut nurtured ongoing dialogue with leading Catholic theologians with whom he maintained close friendships. Cosmopolitan Huguenots, especially those who lived in or near Paris, welcomed Amyraut's close cooperation with Catholic leaders, but his theological opponents viewed these relationships with great suspicion.[23]

Amyraut's impassioned advocacy of the divine right of kings led him to condemn the radical Puritans in England who executed Charles I in 1649. This opened the way for Amyraut to develop a close relationship with members of the inner circle of Charles II (the English king-in-waiting) during his exile in Paris during the 1650s. When Charles II came to power in England in 1660, Amyraut publicly endorsed the anticipated religious settlement of the new king that would soon disestablish all of the Puritans in England, including the more moderate Presbyterian Puritans whose views on theology and polity were closely aligned with his.[24]

Amyraut dedicated his 1662 *Commentary on the Psalms of David* to Charles II. In his introduction to the book, he praised Charles II as a Protestant prince who would oppose the abuses of Catholicism. Having carefully studied a French translation of the Anglican *Book of Common Prayer*, he declared it to be "ideally suited for inspiring Christian fervor" and "devoid of poisonous content." He went on to offer a "Presbyterian" rationale for bishops in England and called on the English Calvinists, who were expected to resist the new church settlement, to obey their king and accept it:

> If there are any people in your kingdom who are still somewhat hostile to the Episcopacy, they should take care, with all the thoughtful and religious fervor they can, not to stir up trouble in the Church because of it, and not to cause any offense to Your Majesty in state affairs. . . . Experience of former times has certainly taught us that those who wanted not just to restrict the power of bishops in England but actually to abolish it sent the unwary headlong into anarchy, and there is nothing more damaging in the whole of society than that kind of plague.[25]

Amyraut's suspicion of the tendency of English Calvinists toward anarchy and regicide was internalized by the Bertrand brothers. This conviction gave the Bertrands an important point of agreement with Henry Compton and his Stuart monarchical vision of empire. The Stuart officials who were working to bring more thorough imperial control over English colonies in the new world were motivated by fear of Louis XIV's France and by fear of Puritan dissenters. They believed the colonies were at greater risk of being overrun by the French because of the Crown's lax governance at the local level that in turn enabled Puritan dissenters to flourish. For Henry Compton, unchecked local governance that tolerated Puritan dissenters in the colonies constituted a threat to the Protestant empire he was hoping to build in the new world. That Jean and Paul Bertrand had internalized these concerns made them ideal emissaries of Stuart imperial policy when they sailed for America bearing clergy licenses from Stuart church officials.[26]

Amyraut's teaching heavily influenced the development of the first Huguenot congregation in England that conformed to the Anglican Church. The French Church of the Savoy was established as the English civil war was breaking out in 1642. When its future was in question at the time of the restoration of the monarchy in 1660, Charles II offered to pay the minister and to let the church use the Savoy Chapel if it would conform to the Church of England. This meant the Savoy church would come under the direct supervision of the Bishop of London as a truly Huguenot-Anglican congregation. This model was in direct contrast to the non-conformist French Church of London on Threadneedle Street and the other previously existing exile congregations in England. These congregations had been organized a century earlier under a royal charter that gave them the privilege of being independent from English church authorities and governing themselves as they had in France. The reorganization of the Savoy church marked the beginning of a new policy on refugee churches in England, as the government required all congregations organized between 1661 and 1687 to follow its conformist model.

The pastor who implemented the Huguenot-Anglican Savoy model was John Durel (1625–1683), a student of Moïse Amyraut. In 1662, Durel joined his teacher in making the argument that the Anglican settlement of Charles II should be unconditionally affirmed by Reformed Protestants on the Continent.[27] Durel designed a compromise system for the Savoy church based on the one he experienced while serving on the Channel Island of Jersey. It was a Huguenot-Anglican model that met the basic Anglican requirements while retaining familiar Presbyterian practices valued by his Huguenot parishioners. The Savoy church followed the Huguenot pattern of singing psalms, but it also used the liturgy of the Anglican *Book of Common Prayer* (translated into French by Pierre de Laune in 1616 and revised by Durel in 1662). The pastors of the non-conformist Threadneedle Street church preached without notes and wore their hats into the pulpit as they had in France. While the clergy of the Savoy church preached bare-headed in deference to Anglican practice, they probably delivered sermons in Huguenot fashion rather than reading from manuscripts and/or notes as Anglicans typically did.[28] But to avoid offending their Huguenot parishioners, the Savoy ministers never wore the Anglican surplice and never made the sign of the cross when leading worship. The Savoy church had a Huguenot-style governing consistory, but it was subject to the direction of the Bishop of London. While all the Huguenot churches organized in England between 1661 and 1687 are believed to have followed the Savoy model, most Huguenots in the pews accepted it with genuine reluctance.[29]

The Huguenot-Anglican model of church organization and practice Durel implemented at the Savoy also provided a spiritual center for Amyraldean Huguenots arriving in London. Durel was still in London when Jean Bertrand emigrated in 1677, but by then he was dividing his time between the Savoy and the string of other ecclesiastical appointments he had received from Charles II. A certificate issued by one of the ministers of the French Church of the Savoy in November 1681 confirms that Jean and Paul Bertrand were active participants in the congregation at that time. The presence of the Bertrands at the Savoy church encouraged the Protestants from Cozes exiled in London to gravitate to this conformist Huguenot congregation.[30]

The Amyraldean and Huguenot-Anglican identity of the Bertrands was on display in the first pastorate of Paul Bertrand. Paul was twenty-four years old and apparently a *proposant,* candidate for ministry, when he was ordained by Bishop Compton in January 1682 and assigned to a newly organized Huguenot refugee church in the English coastal town of Rye.[31] The membership of this church consisted largely of Huguenot master-fishermen and their families. Leaders of the French Church of London on Threadneedle Street worked with Henry Compton to organize this church. Like all the refugee congregations formed during the reign of Charles II, the Rye church was required to conform to the Church of England following the Savoy model.[32]

Problems between Paul Bertrand and the Rye congregation surfaced within the first year of his ministry. With the help of Bishop Compton, some reconciliation was achieved by March of 1683.[33] But Paul's ministry at Rye continued to be controversial as members were making bitter complaints to Compton about their minister. The usual unhappiness arising from the differences between Huguenot expectations and Anglican requirements was made more difficult by the fact that the Rye parishioners were communicating with their merchant friends at the Threadneedle Street Church, a congregation that operated by a different set of ecclesiastical rules. According to Paul Bertrand, these merchants were giving unhelpful advice about how to resolve the crisis. Worse yet, in sympathy with their friends at Rye, some of these Threadneedle

Street members were apparently circulating rumors in London that Paul Bertrand was neglecting his duties. If this were not enough, English Puritan nonconformists in Rye were trying to influence the Huguenots there to reject the Church of England altogether. Needless to say, the Rye congregation was a very difficult challenge for a minister as young and inexperienced as Paul Bertrand.[34]

In the end, Paul Bertrand's ministry at Rye failed. In a letter Paul wrote to Anglican authorities to defend himself, he complained that his parishioners were unwilling to embrace the Church of England because they considered it "too un-Calvinist."[35] In turn, the Rye Huguenots challenged Paul Bertrand's legitimacy as a minister. The differences between the congregation and its minister apparently had to do with deeply held theological views. The evidence suggests Paul Bertrand and his parishioners at Rye were on opposite sides of the Huguenot theological "civil war" over the nature of French Calvinism.[36] The young minister's identification with the theology of Saumur appears to have been the one pastoral deficiency neither Bertrand nor Bishop Compton could overcome. By July 1685, Paul Bertrand was no longer serving the Rye congregation. Records show he was by then seeking financial assistance from the Bishop of London, the Archbishop of Canterbury, and the French Church of London on Threadneedle Street.[37] The following year, the master-fishermen at Rye sent Bishop Compton a letter thanking him for finally sending them a "real minister of Christ," and Paul Bertrand was beginning his work as an Anglican missionary in the English American colony of Maryland.[38]

Jean Bertrand's embrace of the Anglican Church would have expanded his employment opportunities after he arrived in England, where he could have served as a minister, a chaplain, or a tutor. The available records reveal very little about Jean's ministry activities in his adopted country. The loss of the register of the French Church of the Savoy for this period adds to the difficulty of documenting the Bertrand family in England. A 1681 record offers the only solid clue to Jean's professional activities in England. A census conducted by officers of the French Church of the Savoy to certify that refugees were committed Protestants and not Catholic agents in disguise, lists "Jean Bertrand, minister" in the household of Louis Casimir de La Rochefoucaud, Esq., Sieur de Fontrouet on Castle Street near the Black Bull's Head.[39] While the record does not specify Jean's role in this large household of fifteen persons, it is likely he was serving as domestic chaplain and tutor for this French noble family. Louis Casimir was connected by marriage to the Du Parc d'Archiac branch of the La Rochefoucaulds, a prominent Protestant noble family in Saintonge and Aunis.[40] Jean Bertrand's relationship with this family likely began in Cozes, where Francois de La Rochefoucauld, Seigneur

Duparc d'Archiac et Salut, was one of the highest-ranking nobles in the Protestant Church Jean's father served as pastor.

Serving as a tutor was the most likely employment option for Jean Bertrand in London. Since most Huguenot clergy could not find employment serving churches in England, many worked as tutors. Well-educated Frenchmen were in demand as tutors for the children of English aristocrats and well-to-do French families in London.[41] Jean was very well qualified for such a position. His university master's degree went beyond the basic qualification of a bachelor's degree that most English noble families required in a tutor.[42] Since an important part of the tutor's responsibility in seventeenth-century England was the religious education of students, Jean's Anglican ordination would have enhanced his marketability for this role. His well-documented competence as a tutor in Virginia suggests Jean developed this skill during his decade-long residence in England.[43]

In the fall of 1684, Jean Bertrand apparently applied for a part-time position with the non-conformist Threadneedle Street Church.[44] The consistory minutes for November 16, 1684, describe the opening for the position of "lecteur." The person in this role led the singing of psalms, offered prayers, and read scripture during the portion of the service that preceded the sermon. Because this was a part-time role, Bertrand could have combined this work with serving as a household chaplain and tutor in London. According to the consistory minutes, there were five candidates for the position. Each was to lead worship for a month "to see who reads best," and be paid twenty-five shillings for doing this work. The record does not reveal which month was assigned to Jean Bertrand, but he was one of four candidates who subsequently participated in the audition. Jean did not, however, secure this paid position. In the consistory minutes for April 1, 1685, the name of the successful candidate for the lecteur position is listed as Moïse Avisseau.[45]

Avisseau and one of the other candidates were identified in the record as members of the Threadneedle Street Church and a third candidate as a member of the Savoy congregation. Bertrand was apparently the only minister under consideration. With the large surplus of exiled clergy in London, it is understandable that ministers would be willing to take on a part-time role ordinarily filled by laymen.[46] With reports of Paul Bertrand's problems at Rye circulating at Threadneedle Street, the consistory was well aware of the Bertrand family identification with the theology of Saumur and their strong Huguenot-Anglican convictions. This would not have helped Jean's candidacy.

That Jean Bertrand made himself available for the position is revealing in several ways. His candidacy to serve as lecteur indicates that, like most Huguenot clergy in London, he did not have a full-time pastoral position in late 1684. Huguenot-Anglican congregations such as the Savoy church are known to have hired ministers as lecteurs, expanding their duties to include presiding at some baptisms, and Bertrand might have served in that role with one of them.[47] Jean's candidacy to be the Threadneedle Street lecteur also makes clear that his Anglican ordination had not taken him out of the Huguenot refugee network. This apparent attempt to straddle his French and English identities suggests he saw himself as both a Huguenot and an Anglican. Serving for a month in this high-profile role at the Threadneedle Street Church gave him significant exposure in the largest French congregation in the city of London.

A year and a half after his tryout for the lecteur position, Jean Bertrand married a woman he knew in Cozes. On September 23, 1686, he married Charlotte Jolly (1659–1721) at St. Paul's Covent Garden Church in London. Charlotte was the daughter of Charles Jolly, Sieur d'Esneaux and Seigneur de Chadignac, a leading nobleman in Cozes, and Judith André, the daughter of a prominent Saintonge merchant.[48] The Jolly family had a close relationship with the Bertrand family in Cozes. Charles Jolly and Paul Bertrand Sr. were both married to women who were members of the André family of Saintonge merchants. Charlotte's mother was probably a cousin of Jean's mother (or stepmother), Marie André. Jean's father baptized Charlotte at the Cozes Church on February 22, 1660, about six months before his death.[49] This marriage in London brought together Huguenot noble, merchant, and clergy families that had played important leadership roles during the last half century of Protestantism's legal existence in western France.

The couple's marriage record estimates Charlotte's age to be about twenty-five.[50] The entry for her baptism in the Cozes Baptism Register shows that she was, in fact, three months short of her twenty-seventh birthday at the time of her marriage to Jean. The marriage record also underestimates Jean's age by about two years, describing him as a man of thirty-three rather than his more likely age of thirty-five. While Charlotte was old enough to be a widow, the instability of the times suggests otherwise. It is unlikely that her family could have made marriage arrangements on a normal schedule when their Huguenot world was turning upside down. The postponement of Charlotte's marriage may also point to her role as caretaker of two of her younger sisters who emigrated with her. Charlotte arrived in England about 1685 with her brother Henry (age thirty) and her sisters Marie (age twenty-two) and Elizabeth (age twenty). Her parents and at least three of her siblings remained in France and were unable to attend her wedding.[51]

The London addresses listed on their marriage record show that Jean and Charlotte had lived near one another. While there is no evidence to confirm that Jean was still a member of the household of Louis Casimir de La Rochefoucaud in 1686, the marriage record shows he was living in the parish of St. Paul's Covent Garden. Charlotte lived at Exeter Court, Strand, a neighborhood wedged between Covent Garden and the Savoy palace. Both resided in very close proximity to the French Church of the Savoy and about a mile and a half from the French Church on Threadneedle Street. This was an area well populated with French merchants and artisans.[52]

The year before Jean Bertrand's marriage to Charlotte Jolly, Paul Bertrand strengthened his Amyraldean network through his marriage to Marie Gribelin at the French Church of the Savoy.[53] Marie was from a Huguenot family that had emigrated from the French town of Blois on the Loire River, where their pastors were well-known supporters of Amyraut.[54] The Gribelins were highly skilled in making and decorating watches and watch cases. Marie's grandfather was watchmaker to Louis XIII, and her brother, Simon, became one of the most gifted London-based engravers of watches and prints of his generation.[55] This marriage shows that the Bertrands were mixing with the skilled Huguenot émigré artists and craftsmen who were able to produce luxury goods that had previously been in short supply in England. French engravers and goldsmiths like the Gribelins, who were clustering in this part of London, were in the right place at the right time to develop very successful businesses. In 1691, Simon Gribelin married Anne Mettayer, daughter of another Amyraldean Huguenot minister. The Gribelin family, true to its Amyraldean roots, was also firmly established in the French Church of the Savoy, where many family baptisms are recorded.[56]

During his last few years in London, Jean Bertrand made the decision to follow his brother across the Atlantic. This is confirmed by Huguenot records in London that suggest the newly married couple was preparing to emigrate to the new world. Charlotte was one of the 215 Huguenots in London who received assistance between 1685 and 1688 for the stated purpose of settling in English America. Her grant of fifteen pounds sterling is the level of support reserved for "persons of quality." Refugees of lesser rank received substantially less. The average grant for Huguenots wishing to settle in America was eight pounds sterling. The cost of passage from London to America for these refugees is estimated to have been five or six pounds sterling per person.[57] With his license to serve as a clergyman in Virginia, Jean Bertrand would have received the Royal Bounty grant of twenty pounds awarded by the Crown to Anglican clergy for their passage to America. But the fact that he received a small grant from the same Huguenot relief fund as Charlotte also suggests the couple began their marriage with modest financial resources.[58]

Since 1680, Bishop of London Henry Compton had been recruiting clergy to implement his program of Anglican reform in England's new world colonies. In 1685, Compton strengthened his recruitment program by securing approval of a generous royal bounty grant to transport ministers to the colonies.[59] This program was part of the Stuart imperial policy to strengthen the Crown's governance of English American colonies at the local level to make them less vulnerable to French hegemony or invasion.[60] For Compton, this imperial program was ultimately about building a Protestant bulwark to counter the spread of militant Catholicism in the new world.

Henry Compton's vision of Protestant empire in the new world would prove especially compelling to Huguenot exiles who wanted to strike a blow against the French king who had turned their world upside down. The Bertrand brothers appear to be among the first of at least fourteen Huguenot-Anglican clergy Compton would send to the new world between 1682 and 1713. The others were Laurentius Van den Bosch,[61] James Boisseau,[62] Nicholas Moreau,[63] Daniel Bondet, James Gignilliat, Francis Le Jau, John La Pierre, Lewis Latané,[64] Stephen Fouace,[65] Benjamin de Joux,[66] Jean Cairon,[67] and Claude Philippe de Richebourg.[68] Six ministers with French surnames were licensed or received travel grants for English America during Compton's tenure, but they do not appear in colonial records. The decisions of these ministers to become part of England's new world empire confirms their expectation that Huguenots would not be going back to France. They had given up the dream of creating an ideal French Protestant community in exile that would be ready to return to the old country if and when the politics of the French court were reversed.[69]

It is possible that Jean Bertrand was initially preparing to join the Huguenot migration to Carolina. Charlotte Jolly's Royal Bounty grant, issued between June 4, 1686, and August 28, 1687, noted that she was planning to immigrate to Carolina.[70] Henry Compton was interested in Huguenot migration to Carolina, and he might have seen Bertrand as a good fit for the task of bringing newly arriving English and French settlers together under the Anglican umbrella in a new colony with no established church and no permanent Anglican clergy.[71] This may have been the mission of the Huguenot-Anglican minister Laurentius Van den Bosch, who went to Carolina with Huguenot refugees in 1682. If so, the failure of his ministry there by 1685 and the subsequent arrival of non-conforming Huguenot ministers Florent-Philippe Trouillart and Elie Prioleau would have made such a Huguenot-Anglican mission in Carolina problematic.[72]

In the end, Bishop Compton approved Virginia as the location for Jean Bertrand's imperialist mission to the new world. At about the same time, Durand de Dauphiné published his French language pamphlet that aimed to dissuade Huguenots from immigrating to Carolina in favor of Virginia. The publication of Durand's tract at The Hague in July 1687 put Virginia on the map of Huguenots considering immigrating to the new world. After traveling through Virginia in the fall and winter of 1686–1687, Durand returned to London in the spring. He then wrote about his journey, giving specific reasons for settling in Virginia rather than Carolina.[73] He described the rolling hills of Rappahannock and Stafford Counties as ideal locations for

Huguenot settlers who wanted to plant vineyards. In Virginia, Durand met with some of the highest-ranking leaders of the colony, including the governor, Francis Howard, Baron of Effingham[74]; Ralph Wormeley, a wealthy Middlesex County landowner and member of the Council of Virginia; other unnamed members of the Council; and William Fitzhugh, a wealthy Stafford County lawyer and landowner. Durand reported that all of them were strongly encouraging Huguenot immigration to Virginia, perhaps in response to the precipitous downturn in immigration to the Chesapeake. Before leaving Virginia in March 1687, Durand received word that Governor Howard had written Bishop Compton about their conversation in which the governor proposed using bilingual French ministers to serve both the emigrants and existing Anglican parishes. If such a letter was received by Compton or his representatives in the spring of 1687, it could well have influenced John Bertrand's migration planning.[75]

In his tract, Durand outlined specific opportunities for Huguenots to acquire land in the Rappahannock region. Ralph Wormeley wanted to sell or lease 10,000 acres at Portobago in Rappahannock County near present-day Port Royal. Nicholas Hayward, a London merchant and part owner of the 30,000-acre Brent Town Development in Stafford County for which William Fitzhugh was the lawyer, offered favorable terms for 100-acre tracts to Huguenots.[76] While surviving records offer no information about Huguenot land purchases from Ralph Wormeley, at least one Huguenot emigrant, Paul Micou, acquired land in the Portobego area. Records also suggest that at least fifteen Huguenot households settled at or near Brent Town.[77] Understanding that it was unlikely that Huguenot emigrants would include many experienced farmers, Durand emphasized refugees going to Virginia would not need to know anything about agriculture or perform any work on their land. He assured his readers that in Virginia's plantation economy, they could easily employ knowledgable overseers and acquire servants. Durand's emphasis on using the land for tobacco *and* wine production demonstrates his awareness of the interest of English imperial planners in using Huguenots to produce wine that could be exported to Europe.

Perhaps the most significant contribution of Durand's tract was his attempt to overcome religious impediments to Huguenot migration to Virginia, a colony where only the Anglican Church could legally exist. Durand's narrative stated more than once that the main barrier preventing him from settling in Virginia was his inability to live in a place where the gospel was not being preached in French. But he also assured his readers that this deficiency could be overcome by a Huguenot migration that included one or more French ministers. Durand reported the offer of Governor Howard that French ministers could lead services in French for Huguenot settlers—an offer Bishop Compton would certainly have endorsed.[78]

However reassuring Durand's message might have been, one potential religious impediment remained for Huguenots immigrating to Virginia. These refugees would have to make their peace with the Presbyterian/Anglican hybrid worship of the French Church of the Savoy. Those who could not let go of the Reformed worship style they knew in France could migrate to Carolina, New York, or New England, where independent Huguenot congregations were being organized under the sponsorship of London's Threadneedle Street Church. While Durand's tract offers no indication that he was attuned to the contrasting worship styles of London's two large Huguenot congregations, his reported interactions with Huguenot ministers were limited to Isaac Dubourdieu of the Savoy Church and Charles Piozet, the only Threadneedle Street pastor who was a dedicated supporter of the Church of England.[79]

Durand returned to London from Virginia on May 7, 1687, two months before his tract was published at The Hague. If Durand communicated with Compton[80] or with Huguenot ministers Dubourdieu or Piozet after arriving in London, Bertrand and his fellow emigrants might have known about the tract before it was circulated to a wider European readership. If indeed Durand's report influenced the selection of the Rappahannock region as the destination of the exiles, the planning timeline was exceedingly tight. Nonetheless, records show that by the end of 1687, Jean Bertrand and a group of Huguenot refugees migrated to the same Rappahannock County Durand promoted in his pamphlet, probably leaving England in August or September 1687.[81] The publication of Durand's tract in Europe and the subsequent arrival of Bertrand's Huguenot preaching in Virginia, by coincidence or design, were two key ingredients in the gradual development of a large Huguenot-Anglican Refuge in the Rappahannock region.

Through his relationships with refugees from Cozes and exiles worshipping at the French Church of the Savoy, Jean Bertrand was in position to help organize a Huguenot migration to the new world. There are no surviving ship passenger records to identify the first wave of Huguenot exiles traveling with Jean Bertrand to Virginia. With the loss of the Savoy church records, it is not possible to connect exiles directly to Jean Bertrand during their time in London. Some of the several dozen Cozes Huguenots who joined Jean Bertrand in Virginia during his early years in the colony were probably part of a London organizing group for this migration. These might have included Paul Micou; his relatives Edward Danellin and James Roy[82]; Jean Bertrand's close friends or relatives James and Marie Foushee; and their relatives John Foushee, John and Elisabeth Morrice, Elias and Bridgett Morrice, and Michal and Katherine Connele.[83] It may be that some of the emigrants knew Cozes Huguenots like George Lascaille and Claude Vallet, who had been in the Rappahannock region since the early 1680s.[84] Additional

Virginia-bound Huguenots who received assistance through the Royal Bounty in England between June 1686 and August 1687—Marquis Calmes, John de la Chaumette, Abraham Depree, Benjamin and Mary Renoe, and Lewis and Anne Renoe—might also have made contact with Jean Bertrand and his Cozes friends in London.

Jean Bertrand and the new world migrants who went with him sailed to Virginia at a time of great change for the Huguenot community in England. In 1687 and 1688, French Protestant refugees were pouring into London and would soon swell London's Huguenot population to 30,000 thousand people.[85] The Huguenot congregations in London were hard-pressed to meet the needs of the new arrivals. The Threadneedle Street Church was overwhelmed by the 2,800 new members it received during these two years. The church opened a new building at a second location to accommodate its exploding growth in worship attendance.[86] The French Church of the Savoy also struggled to accommodate rapid growth during this period as it launched a building expansion and acquired two additional church buildings at other locations.[87]

The status of the Huguenot churches was also a flash point in the political crisis that had England in its grip as the Bertrand group sailed for America. Early in 1686 England's new Catholic king, James II, instructed Bishop of London Henry Compton to end the remaining Presbyterian practices of the French Church of the Savoy. This new model of pure Anglican conformity also had an Amyraldean connection. It was launched with the founding of the Jewin Street Church in May 1686 under the leadership of a Saumur-educated minister Pierre Allix, former pastor of the celebrated Charenton church near Paris.

Compton understood that James II's order to end the "half-way house" ministry of the Savoy church would greatly reduce its ability to attract a reasonable share of the refugees who were pouring into London. Such a development could severely damage the Huguenot-Anglican new world projects being led by ministers like the Bertrand brothers. James II also declared his intention to found a Jesuit school in the Savoy neighborhood to counter the Protestant influence of the French church there. Recognizing this to be the first volley of a campaign to expand the footprint of Catholicism in London, Compton did not comply with the order of the king. In a letter directed to the Archbishop of Canterbury on May 12, 1686, he wrote, "It would be an insolent demand of me to require more of the French Church in the Savoy than the late king himself did in the constitution of them . . . where neither surplice or sign of the cross were ever used or required: and where they have long taken care of their Churches by way of Consistory."[88]

Henry Compton's problems with his new king became even more severe when he chose not to implement James II's order that anti-Catholic preaching be banned from the pulpits of the diocese of London. Three months later, James created a commission to oversee church affairs, which quickly summoned Compton to appear before them. In September 1686, the commissioners suspended him from office for disobedience to the king. Three other bishops (Crewe, Sprat, and White) were appointed to administer the diocese of London in Compton's absence, but they failed to close down the growing half-way house ministry of the French Church of the Savoy.[89] As Jean Bertrand boarded a ship for Virginia in 1687, no one could predict what these turbulent events would mean to the English nation and its fragile Protestant empire across the Atlantic.

After his suspension, Henry Compton withdrew to his beloved Fulham Palace. But he did not remain idle. When James II issued a Declaration of Indulgence in the spring of 1688 to open the way for Catholics to assume leading roles in the government and the military, Compton helped to coordinate the resistance of seven other bishops who refused to have the document read in their churches. James had them arrested, sent to the Tower, and placed on trial in June 1688. When the trial judges found them "not guilty" on June 30, the verdict was celebrated in the streets, and the king's position was weakened. A few months later, Paul Bertrand's Huguenot brother-in-law, Simon Gribelin, produced an engraving called "The Seven Bishops" to celebrate the verdict and the courage of these religious leaders. It is archived in the British Museum today.

As these events unfolded, Henry Compton had even more dangerous business to pursue. He was one of seven conspirators who issued an invitation to William of Orange to invade England to replace his father-in-law, James II, on the throne.[90] One year after Jean Bertrand arrived in Virginia, William of Orange and his army landed in England with the financial support of Huguenot merchants. Of William's invasion force of 21,000 soldiers, almost 20 percent were Huguenots.[91] Huguenot senior officers also formed an important part of William III's inner circle of trusted military aids.[92] James II chose not to engage William's army, leaving the country instead. Just two months before fleeing to the safety of France, James ironically granted citizenship to a Huguenot-Anglican minister in Virginia named Jean Bertrand.[93]

The French Protestant military contingent in William's invasion force included at least two soldiers from Saintonge who were cousins of Charlotte Jolly. Francois and Henri d'Aulnis were the sons of Charlotte's aunt and baptism sponsor, Judith Jolly, widow of Francois d'Aulnis. Judith fled to the Netherlands in 1685, where her teenaged sons enlisted in the army of William of Orange in 1686 to fight against Louis XIV. They joined their older half-brother Pierre, a veteran of the French army who had switched sides. Before invading England, the brothers could have seen action against their cousin Charles Jolly, Charlotte's brother, who was made a captain in the army of Louis XIV in 1686. After arriving in England with William's army, Pierre d'Aulnis was commissioned as a captain and led Huguenot troops in the Battle of the Boyne in July 1690, which secured the English crown for William III and Mary II.[94]

For Jean Bertrand, London was the first stop in his Atlantic Refuge.[95] He migrated to the city looking to regain his footing as his world was turning upside down. He arrived in London connected to a network of relationships from western France and the Amyraldean wing of the French Reformed Church. In London, Bertrand underwent a profound personal transformation as he layered new relationships and networks onto his Huguenot identity. After ten years in England, he embarked for the new world as a Huguenot-Anglican clergyman firmly connected to the international networks of the French Church of the Savoy and the Bishop of London.[96]

Bertrand was also transformed by the mission at the center of his journey to the new world. Like his wife's cousins who were putting their French military training at the service of the Protestant William of Orange, Bertrand was placing his French theological training and professional skills at the service of the bishop who was helping make William the king of England. As the refugee soldiers would put their lives on the line against the militant Catholic empire of Louis XIV at the Battle of the Boyne in Ireland, Bertrand would labor in Virginia to bolster England's defense against Louis's grand ambitions in the new world. After going to England as *Jean* Bertrand, he would cross the Atlantic as *John* Bertrand, agent of English empire.

Serving Bishop Compton's imperialist program in the new world would make it possible for Bertrand to help create a refugee network that would largely define the rest of his life, the Huguenot-Anglican Refuge in Virginia.

NOTES

1. Third Collect from the Order for Evening Prayer, Church of England, *Book of Common Prayer from the Original Manuscript attached to The Act of Uniformity of 1662* (Cambridge, UK, 1760); John Bertrand Ordination #9535/3, Guildhall Library, London; John Bertrand Ordination #97040, CCEd.

2. Sibylla Jane Flower, *A Walk Round Fulham Palace and Its Garden* (London, 2002); Sandra Morris, "Legacy of a Bishop: The Trees and Shrubs of Fulham Palace Gardens Introduced 1675–1713," *Garden History* 19, no. 1 (Spring, 1991), 47–59.

3. Bertrand Van Ruymbeke, "Minority Survival: The Huguenot Paradigm in France and the Diaspora," in *Memory and Identity: The Huguenots in France and the Atlantic Diaspora,* eds., Bertrand Van Ruymbeke and Randy Sparks (Columbia, SC, 2008), 11–12; David J. B. Trim, "The Huguenots and the Experience of Exile (Sixteenth to Twentieth Centuries): History, Memory, and Transnationalism," in *The Huguenots:*

History and Memory in Transnational Context, ed., David J. B. Trim (Leiden, 2011), 4–10.

4. Gwynn, *Huguenots in Britain I*, 151; Edward Carpenter, *The Protestant Bishop: Being the Life of Henry Compton, 1632–1713, Bishop of London* (London, 1956), 323–24.

5. Ibid., 8–14, 29, and 33–36.

6. Gwynn, *Huguenots in Britain I*, 150.

7. Karin Maag, "Pulpit and Pen: Pastors and Professors as Shapers of the Huguenot Tradition," in *A Companion to the Huguenots,* eds., Raymond A. Mentzer and Bertrand Van Ruymbeke (Leiden, 2016), 154.

8. James B. Bell, *Empire, Religion and Revolution in Early Virginia, 1607–1786* (Basingstoke, UK, 2013), 100. My estimate of Jean Bertrand's age is based on his role as baptism sponsor on September 8, 1665, CZ, 39, ADCMLR. Sponsors were required to be at least fourteen years old, Van Ruymbeke, *From New Babylon to Eden,* 102. This would indicate that Jean was born no later than September 1651. Since his London marriage record estimates his year of birth as 1653, it is reasonable to conclude that Jean was not much over the minimum age of fourteen when he served as baptism sponsor in Cozes. G. J. Armytage, ed., *Allegations for Marriage Licenses Issued by the Vicar-General of the Archbishop of Canterbury, July 1679 to June 1687* (London, 1890), 245.

9. Elisabeth Labrousse, "Great Britain as Envisaged by the Huguenots of the Seventeenth Century," in *Huguenots in Britain and their French Background, 1550–1800,* ed., Irene Scouloudi (Basingstoke, UK, 1987), 149–50.

10. Gwynn, *Huguenot Heritage,* 124–25.

11. Gwynn, *Huguenots in Britain I*, 157–58.

12. Bertrand Van Ruymbeke defines the post-Revocation exodus of Huguenots as the approximately 200,000 who left France between 1679 and 1700; Van Ruymbeke, *From New Babylon to Eden,* 57.

13. The Musee du Protestantisme in La Rochelle, France, displays a printed 1630 decision by the intendant of the province forbidding Huguenots to bury their dead in cemeteries attached to Protestant churches that were awarded to Catholics in 1628.

14. Elisabeth Labrousse, *Bayle* (Oxford, UK, 1983), 7–10.

15. David van der Linden, "The Economy of Exile: Huguenot Migration from Dieppe to Rotterdam, 1685–1700," in *The Huguenots: France, Exile, and Diaspora,* eds., Jane McKee and Randolph Vigne (Brighton, UK, 2013), 99–112.

16. Bernard Cottret, "Frenchmen by Birth, Huguenots by the Grace of God," in *Memory and Identity,* eds., Van Ruymbeke and Sparks, 311.

17. #9535/3, Guildhall Library, London; #97436, CCEd; # 97040, CCEd. A fragmentary record suggests Jean Bertrand might have attended the Montauban Academy in 1672 (after its 1659 forced removal to the village of Puylaurens). Another record documents a Jean Bertrand in Bordeaux a few months later on June 14, 1672; *Un Album Bernois de 1672,* 514–15, SHPF.

18. Bosher, "Huguenot Merchants," 100.

19. F. P. Van Stam, *The Controversy Over the Theology of Saumur, 1635–1650: Disrupting Debates Among the Huguenots in Complicated Circumstances* (Amsterdam, 1988).

20. Armstrong (1969), 263–69.

21. Moïse Amyraut, *Brief Traitte de la Predestination et de ses Principales Dependances* (Saumur, 1634).

22. Armstrong, *Calvinism and the Amyraut Controversy*, 73, 88–96, 114–15.

23. Ibid., 6–7.

24. Geiter and Speck, "Moïse Amyraut and Charles II," 160–65.

25. Ibid., 170 and 175.

26. Stanwood, *The Empire Reformed*, 27–29.

27. John Durel, *A View of the Government and Public Worship of God in the Reformed Churches Beyond the Seas: Wherein is Shewed Their Conformity and Agreement with the Church of England, as it is Established by the Act of Uniformity* (London, 1662).

28. Robin Gwynn has argued it is unlikely Savoy preachers read their sermons because the practice would have been "a divisive issue" for Huguenot worshippers, Gwynn, *Huguenots in Britain I*, 120–21.

29. Gwynn, *Huguenot Heritage*, 122–27; Gwynn, *Huguenots in Britain I*, 118–26, 279–80. For John Durel's relationship with Moïse Amyraut, see Geiter and Speck, "Moïse Amyraut and Charles II," 163.

30. MR/R/R/032/08, LMA.

31. *Proceedings of the Huguenot Society of London* 7 (1901–1904), 148–49.

32. Gwynn, ed., FCL, 68–69.

33. *Proceedings of the Huguenot Society of London* 7 (1901–1904), 148–49.

34. Bernard Cottret, *The Huguenots in England: Immigration and Settlement, c. 1550–1700*, trans. Peregrine and Adriana Stevenson (Cambridge, UK, 1992), 162–63, 170, 180–81; Robin Gwynn, "Strains of Worship: The Huguenots and Non-Conformity," in *The Huguenots: History and Memory in Transnational Context*, ed., David J. B. Trim, 128–32.

35. Paul Bertrand Letter in the papers of Henry Compton, Bishop of London, April 13, 1684, Rawlinson Papers, Ms C 984, Bodleian Library, Oxford University.

36. While not identifying the theology of Saumur as the source, Bernard Cottret observed that this episode suggests "a crisis probably existed in Calvinist society *before* the Revocation of the Edict of Nantes." Cottret, *The Huguenots in England: Immigration and Settlement, c. 1550–1700*, 163.

37. Gwynn, ed., FCL, 148; *Bulletin Historique et Litteraire*, Tome XXXIV, Troisieme Series, Quatrieme Anee, 479, SHPF; *Proceedings of the Huguenot Society of London* 7 (1901–1904), 149.

38. Carpenter, *The Protestant Bishop*, 333; F. De Schickler, *Les Eglises Du Refuge En Angleterre* (Paris, 1892), Tome Deuxieme, 335; Nelson Waite Rightmyer, "List of Anglican Clergy Receiving a Bounty for Overseas Service, 1680–1687," *Historical Magazine of the Protestant Episcopal Church* 17 (June 1948), 177–78.

39. The fifteen residents listed in this household were Louis Casimir de la Rochefoucaud, Diane de la Rochefoucaud, Magdelaine de la Rochefoucaud, Lidie de la

Rochefoucaud, Mary Bertrand (Jean's mother or stepmother), Jean Bertrand/minister, Paul Bertrand, Jean Fiefbeard, Jean Robert, Pierre Lambert, Susanne Testafolle, Marie Testafolle, Ann Testafolle, Marguerite Chien, and Marie Vias. For the certificate issued by Pastor Lortie and Elder Lewis de la Faye on November 29, 1681, see MR/R/R/032/08, LMA.

40. According to two sources, Louis de la Rochefoucauld, Sieur de Fontrouet, married Isabeau de la Rochefoucauld, granddaughter of Pierre de la Rochefoucauld (Seigneur du Parc Archiac) and daughter of Charles de la Rochefoucauld (de la Renaudie), in 1639. Pere Anselme, *Histoire Genealogique et Chronologique de la Maison Royale de France* (Paris, 1712), vol. 4, 426, and Haag, *La France Protestante*, vol. 6, 358. Louis Casimir's appearance as a sponsor at a Huguenot baptism in Canterbury in March 1683 confirms he was still living in England at that time. Charles Edmund Lart, *Huguenot Pedigrees* (Baltimore, 2009), vol. 1, 74. For a detailed treatment of the Du Parc Archiac branch of the La Rochefoucauld family during the final decades of the seventeenth century, see Lougee, *Facing the Revocation*.

41. Gwynn, *Huguenot Heritage*, 133.

42. Michael Green, "A Huguenot Education for the Early Modern Nobility," *The Huguenot Society Journal* 30, no. 1 (2013), 91.

43. Davis, *William Fitzhugh and His Chesapeake World*, 270, 271, and 371.

44. Records from the Royal Bounty and the Threadneedle Street Consistory point to two Jean Bertrands in London in 1687; RBP, Ms 1 (Bertrand), HL. Jean Bertrand, son of Nicholas Bertrand of Dieppe, first appears in the records when he joined the Threadneedle Street Church in April 1687. He could not have been the candidate for the lecteur position in 1684; Gwynn, ed., FCL, 190.

45. Ibid., 136, 139–45.

46. Ibid., 359.

47. Gwynn, *Huguenots in Britain I*, 147.

48. CZ, ADCMLR; Dangibeaud, Minutes de Notaires, BR 5842, ADCMLR; NS, 284, SHPF; Chasseboeuf, *Châteaux, Manoirs, et Logis: La Charente-Maritime*, vol. 1, 144.

49. CZ, 20, ADCMLR.

50. The summary of the marriage record reads, "Jean Bertrand of St. Paul, Covent Garden, Midd., Clerk, Bachr, abt 33, and Mrs Charlotte Jolly, of Exeter Court, Strand, co. Midd., Spr, abt 25, at own disp.; at St Paul afsd"; Armytage, ed., *Allegations for Marriage Licenses*, 245.

51. RBP, Ms 1, fol. 88 (Joly), HL; CZ, 20, 28, and 38, ADCMLR; NS 284, SHPF. For the experience of older daughters in Huguenot refugee families postponing marriage to care for younger siblings, see Lougee, *Facing the Revocation*, 322.

52. Baird, vol. 2, 219.

53. Paul Bertrand married Mary Gribelin on October 20, 1685, FM 1/10, Lambeth Palace Library, London.

54. Gwynn, *Huguenots in Britain I*, 414; Armstrong, *Calvinism and the Amyraut Controversy*, 84, 87, 90–92, 94, 96, and 99.

55. Treasure, *The Huguenots*, 388.

56. Gwynn, *Huguenots in Britain I*, 360–61; Vanessa Brett, *Bertrand's Toyshop in Bath: Luxury Retailing, 1685–1765* (Wetherby, UK, 2014), 15–36.

57. RBP, Ms 1, fol. 88 (Joly), HL; Van Ruymbeke, *From New Babylon to Eden*, 66–70.

58. Jean Bertrand's Huguenot grant from the Royal Bounty in 1686 was for a little over three pounds sterling; RBP, Ms 1 (Bertrand), HL. For the Royal Bounty grants to Anglican clergy for passage to America, see Haffenden, "The Anglican Church in Restoration Colonial Policy," 181.

59. Ibid., 181.

60. Stanwood, *The Empire Reformed*, 27–30; Bond (2000), 215–20.

61. Van Ruymbeke, *From New Babylon to Eden*, 116–18.

62. Frederick Louis Weis, *Colonial Clergy of Virginia, North Carolina, and South Carolina* (Boston: 1955), 6.

63. SP, EC RB, 1699–1702, 33, 83, 87, and 117.

64. John Clement, "Clergymen Licensed Overseas by the Bishop of London, 1696–1710 and 1715–1716," *Historical Magazine of the Protestant Episcopal Church* 16 (December 1947), 329, 331, 334, and 335.

65. Rightmyer, "List of Anglican Clergy Receiving a Bounty for Overseas Service," 176–78.

66. Gwynn, *Huguenots in Britain I*, 316.

67. R. H. Rife, ed., "The Vestry Book of King William Parish, Virginia, 1707–1750," VMHB 11, no. 3 (January 1904), 303.

68. Ibid., 303 and Van Ruymbeke, *From New Babylon to Eden*, 135–37.

69. Stanwood, "Between Eden and Empire," 1319–20.

70. RBP, Ms 1, folio 88, HL.

71. Stanwood, *The Global Refuge*, 86.

72. Van Ruymbeke, *From New Babylon to Eden*, 116–18.

73. For Durand's five specific reasons for preferring Virginia to Carolina, see Durand, 172–73. For Durand's counter-promotional purpose regarding Carolina, see Van Ruymbeke, *From New Babylon to Eden*, 42–44.

74. Francis Howard, Baron of Effingham, was governor of Virginia from 1684 to 1689. John W. Raimo, *Biographical Dictionary of American Colonial and Revolutionary Governors, 1607–1789* (Westport, CT, 1980), 480.

75. Durand, 166.

76. Ibid., 154–55, 179–80. Brent Town was patented by the Northern Neck Proprietary on February 10, 1687, with Nicholas Hayward, George Brent, Robert Bristow, and Richard Foote as co-owners. For the creation of Brent Town and Durand's visit to the site during his travels through Virginia, see Davis, *William Fitzhugh and His Chesapeake World*, 41 and 191.

77. Huguenots who appear to have settled in the Brent Town area between 1687 and 1704 include Lewis Renoe, Benjamin Renoe, John de la Chaumette, Marquis Calmes, Abraham Delander, Samuel Duchinenia, Isaac Duchimenia, John Gayot, Michel Mauzy, John Marr, Clement Chevalle, Rynhart de la Fayolle, Peter Lehew, Louis Tacquet, and James Gallahough.

78. Durand, 144.

79. Gwynn, *Huguenots in Britain I*, 268–69, and 375–76; Durand, 85–88.
80. Ibid., 176.
81. ORC OB 2, 1686–1692, 71–72.
82. Edward Danellin's surname was a shortened form of the surname of Paul Micou's mother—Denillanialle, CZ, 16, ADCMLR. Paul Micou's aunt, Judith Micou, was married to Elie Roy in France. Dangibeaud, *Minutes de Notaire*, BR 5842, ADCMLR. Two of Micou's grandchildren married Roys in Virginia. Raleigh Travers Green, *Genealogical and Historical Notes on Culpeper County, Virginia* (Culpeper, VA, 1900), 75–76. Mungo Roy was named in Paul Micou's will. SP (1989), EC *Will Abstracts, 1735–1743*, 11–12.
83. James Foushee's mother was Marie Morice. CZ, 38, ADCMLR. Jean Connil was the baptism sponsor of James's sister Marthe in Cozes in 1667. CZ, 45, ADCMLR.
84. For George Lascaille and Claude Vallet, see Appendix A-I.
85. Robin Gwynn, *The Huguenots of London* (Brighton, UK, 1998), 4.
86. Robin Gwynn points to the end of James II's policy of persecuting dissenters in 1686 as opening the way for large-scale immigration of French Protestants into England in 1687, Gwynn, ed., FCL, 1, 2, 8–9.
87. Gwynn, *Huguenots in Britain II*, 108–09.
88. Gwynn, *Huguenots in Britain I*, 132–36; Carpenter, *The Protestant Bishop*, 86.
89. Ibid., 97, 100–01; Warren M. Billings, ed., *Papers of Francis Howard, Baron Howard of Effingham, 1643–1695* (Richmond, VA, 1989), 274.
90. Carpenter, *The Protestant Bishop*, 121.
91. Bosher, *Huguenot Merchants*, 98; Matthew Glozier, *The Huguenot Soldiers of William of Orange and the "Glorious Revolution of 1688: The Lions of Judah* (Brighton, UK, 2002), 66; David J. B. Trim, "The Huguenots and the European Wars of Religion," in *The Huguenots: History and Memory in Transnational Context*, ed., David J. B. Trim, 183–84.
92. Gwynn, *Huguenot Heritage*, 102.
93. David C. A. Agnew, *Protestant Exiles from France in the Reign of Louis XIV: or, The Huguenot Refugees and Their Descendants in Great Britain and Ireland* (London, 1874), 51.
94. T. P. Le Fanu and W. H. Manchee, ed., *Dublin and Portarlington Veterans, King William III's Army* (Frome, UK, 1946), 32; "Revue de Saintonge & d'Aunis," *Bulletin de la Société des Archives historiques de la Saintonge et de l'Aunis* 15, 240; file for the Daulnis Famille, G 34/D2, SHPF.
95. Van Ruymbeke, "Minority Survival: The Huguenot Paradigm in France and the Diaspora," 1–13.
96. Carolyn Lougee Chappell, "Family Bonds Across the Refuge," in *Memory and Identity*, eds., Van Ruymbeke and Sparks, 183.

Chapter Three

Rappahannock, Virginia, 1687

> When I saw the beauty and fertility of the Rappahannock province . . . I realized that this country was unknown and as it had no proprietors, no one had taken the trouble to print accounts of it, such as those of Carolina and Pennsylvania.
>
> —Durand de Dauphiné, *A Huguenot Exile in Virginia*, 1687

When John Bertrand arrived in English America in 1687, he settled in the region publicized by Durand de Dauphiné, Virginia's upper tidewater county of Rappahannock (soon to be renamed Richmond County and more recently designated "Old Rappahannock" to differentiate it from another Virginia county of the same name created in 1833).[1] There he was surrounded by other Huguenot emigrants whose world had been turned upside down by Louis XIV. Most of the Huguenots who found their way to the Rappahannock region were from western French provinces that had a long history of maritime interactions with the new world.[2] Many were leaving the southern part of the province of Saintonge, where they lived along the Gironde estuary, the largest in western Europe. In the new world they settled near the Chesapeake Bay, the largest estuary in English America. These refugees brought with them their knowledge of trade, seamanship, and the Saintonge wine production and distribution economy—skills that were highly valued by empire planners in London. The willingness of these Huguenots to integrate themselves into the struggling and Puritan-influenced Anglican parishes of Virginia made them even more useful to England's empire projectors.

There is no evidence the Huguenots who migrated to the Rappahannock region in the 1680s and 1690s arrived in the new world in a way that attracted wide attention or that they traveled in large groups on chartered ships, as was the case with the 1700–1701 Huguenot migration sponsored by William III. The surviving county court records suggest this was a migration *process* that began about 1677 and spanned more than three decades. This study has documented 252 households and fifty-three indentured servants with Huguenot surnames who arrived in the Rappahannock region between 1677 and 1710.³ Some exiles were apparently able to pay their passage to Virginia. Some were assisted by the Royal Bounty and possibly the French Church of the Savoy. Some who traveled in 1700–1701 arrived on ships paid for by William III. Others traveled to the new world by obligating themselves to indentured servant contracts, which typically ran four to five years.⁴

These migrants were a diverse group of merchants, seamen, physicians, ministers, artisans, skilled laborers, and unskilled workers apparently unified by their hope that Virginia would welcome French Protestants, make affordable land available to them in the Rappahannock region, and permit them to worship in French (as Durand de Dauphiné had claimed in his 1687 tract). Durand's description of the opportunities that would be afforded to Huguenots in the Rappahannock region is confirmed by the fact that the Refuge continued to grow well into the next century as it assimilated refugees from later waves of immigration. Durand's positive view of Huguenot prospects in Virginia is also confirmed by records showing about a third of the Huguenot emigrant households acquired land.

The most cohesive group of refugees were likely those from the western French town of Cozes. Of the 131 households documented between 1686 and 1700, about 17 percent can be tied to Cozes through documented name matches and family relationships. Given the near impossibility of identifying Cozes women in Virginia county records or men born in Cozes after 1668, it is likely the percentage of households with connections to the town was even higher. Refugee surnames provide another indicator of Cozes participation in this migration with 43 percent of these 131 households headed by persons with surnames found in the Protestant Baptism Register of the town. The Cozes Protestant network extended well beyond the town as many of its Protestant citizens had kinship relationships in other communities across the southern half of Saintonge. Most of the refugees with identifiable Cozes connections settled in the three counties closest to the Bertrands (see Appendix B). Many of these exiles had grown up with John Bertrand or with his wife, Charlotte, who was eight years younger than her husband. Most knew the Bertrand and Jolly families in Cozes, and some, like Paul Micou and Charlotte Jolly Bertrand, had been baptized by John's father.

This long-standing attachment to a minister whom Huguenot refugees knew in France fits a pattern that powered the proliferation of new Huguenot congregations in London during the last decade and a half of the seventeenth century. At the Revocation of the Edict of Nantes in the fall of 1685, there were only three Huguenot congregations in London. By 1700, the flood of refugees caused the number of French churches in and around the city to swell to twenty-six. With the support of people they had known in France, refugee ministers who could not secure positions in the established congregations of

London were forming new ones. As a minister who was apparently unable to secure a church position in London, John Bertrand was a rare (and possibly unique) example of this dynamic playing out in a transatlantic context.[5]

The Huguenots who formed this Huguenot-Anglican Refuge adhered to the tobacco coast settlement pattern. Like other immigrants to Virginia, they settled on plantations rather than in towns—though larger plantations functioned much like small villages. Most of these Huguenot refugees were scattered along a forty-mile segment of the Rappahannock River, occupying portions of eight counties centered roughly on the present-day town of Tappahannock, Virginia (see the 1719 John Senex map on this page).[6] Most tried to live as close to the river as they could, though two clusters of refugees, one at Brent Town in Stafford County and another along the Mattapony River in New Kent County,[7] were more distant from the Rappahannock River. The river provided the refugees with a dependable communication system and the ability to maintain a loosely structured exile community. Records documenting many of these Huguenot immigrants in two or more counties suggest they traveled, formed marriages, engaged in business, and migrated freely throughout the Rappahannock region. The coastal waterways of upper tidewater Virginia, which connected the exiles to the estuary marine life of the Chesapeake Bay, also linked them to the intercolonial and transatlantic shipping routes.

Detail, *A New Map of Virginia, Mary-Land, and the improved parts of Pennsylvania,* **John Senex, 1719, showing the area of Huguenot settlement in the Rappahannock region between 1677 and 1710 and the counties that existed in 1687.**
Courtesy Library of Congress, Geography and Map Division

When John Bertrand arrived in the Chesapeake,[8] he was reunited with his brother Paul. Paul Bertrand and his wife, Marie Gribelin, had immigrated to Calvert County, Maryland, in 1686. The Church of England had commissioned Paul to serve as a missionary to Maryland, a colony with a strong Catholic identity and a solid Puritan presence but very few Anglican congregations during the late seventeenth century.[9] Paul's presence in the Chesapeake region gave John a trusted partner in Bishop Compton's Anglican reform program.

Very little is known about Huguenots migrating with Paul Bertrand, but records suggest there were at least a half-dozen households who did. Paul settled along the Patuxent River on 100 acres he purchased or leased from the Cox–Hay tract. To visit his brother, John would have traveled by sloop to the Chesapeake Bay, proceeded north past the Potomac River, and followed the Patuxent River to Paul's small waterfront plantation. Records suggest Paul Bertrand was struggling with poor health soon after arriving in the new world. In March 1687, as John and Charlotte were making final preparations for their voyage to English America, Paul wrote a will, leaving his land and personal effects to his wife.

England was embroiled in political and religious crises as John Bertrand arrived in America. In November 1688, as the Bertrands were completing their first year of residence in Virginia, the Dutch Calvinist William of Orange landed in England with an army strengthened by battle-tested Huguenot soldiers. Like everyone in English America, the Bertrands were anxiously waiting for news from England about the struggle for the throne. There can be little doubt that the Huguenot-Anglican settlers in Virginia were hoping that William, long a favorite of Huguenots in Europe, would prevail.

When news arrived that Bishop Compton had officiated at the coronation of William and Mary in the spring of 1689, the Rappahannock-area Huguenots almost certainly celebrated. But this good news did not end the anxiety that had gripped English America. Rumors spread from New England to the Chesapeake that the French were supporting the cause of James II by inciting North American Indians to launch murderous raids against Protestant settlers throughout the colonies. A conspiracy theory took hold that implicated colonial officials appointed by James II and Catholic settlers in a vast plot to massacre Protestants. Huguenots who settled in Stafford County, Virginia, experienced this conspiracy scare through the so-called tumult instigated by Anglican minister John Waugh. George Brent, a Catholic partner in the Brent Town development where some Huguenots lived and leased land, was pursued by an angry Protestant mob. He fled for safety to the home of his law partner, William Fitzhugh, who served as a Stafford court justice.[10]

Fears of a Catholic/Native American conspiracy were especially potent in Maryland, where many leaders of the colony were Catholic.[11] In a letter to Bishop Compton, written in French in September 1689, Paul Bertrand described the terror of had overwhelmed the settlers in his neighborhood a few months earlier. In response to reports of Seneca warriors massing at the head of the Patuxent River, Paul evacuated his family to the house of a neighbor five miles away. There he joined with other panic-stricken settlers who were bringing their valuables and arranging a common defense against an eminent attack from a Seneca war party. But they soon learned they were victims of a false alarm. Scouting parties quickly confirmed there were no native warriors pouring in from the north. Paul's long letter to Compton gave the names of radical Protestant militia leaders who were promoting the conspiracy and using this manufactured crisis to unseat the legal proprietary government of Maryland. Paul wrote at the request of jailed Calvert County officials who hoped the Bishop of London would bring their plight to the attention of the English court.[12]

Paul Bertrand's involvement in this civil unrest could not have had a very positive influence on his tenuous health. The date of his death is not known, but it most likely took place during 1690. His will was filed in 1691 at the request of Michel Morin, a Huguenot refugee with a Cozes surname.[13] The published abstract of the will confirms that Paul was a Huguenot-Anglican who sought to straddle his French and English identities. In his will, Paul described himself as a "minister of the gospel," the same title that was applied to his father in the Huguenot Baptism Register at Cozes.[14] Paul's widow remained in America long enough to give birth to Paul Bertrand III and then sailed with her son for England, never to return.[15] The death of John's younger brother, still in his early thirties, so soon after their arrival in English America gave the Virginia Bertrands an extremely painful introduction to the high mortality rate that stalked the settlers of the Chesapeake region. During their tumultuous early years in Virginia, John and Charlotte were having children, too. In 1688, Charlotte gave birth to a son named William and in 1690 a daughter named Mary Ann.

Paul Micou's arrival in Virginia was documented in Rappahannock County twenty-one months after John Bertrand first appeared in county records. At the court session of November 5, 1690, Micou was granted payment from the estate of Richard Clifton for medical treatment he provided to the deceased.[16] This is the first of many records showing Micou using the county courts to collect payment for his work as a physician. The abundance of these records led Beverley Fleet, a compiler of colonial Virginia record abstracts and a descendant of Micou, to quip that his ancestor was "pretty good at collecting debts, particularly from the widows and orphans of his patients."[17] While there is much about Micou's early years in Virginia that is not known, records suggest he arrived about the same time as John Bertrand and initially lived near him on the north side of the Rappahannock in North Farnham Parish. He was still residing north of the river in May 1697—but now farther upriver in Sittenbourne Parish—when he purchased 100 acres on the other side of the river in Essex County.[18] By 1702, Micou had moved across the Rappahannock, but he continued to treat patients on both sides of the river.[19]

The most intriguing mystery of Paul Micou's early years in Virginia is whether he arrived in the colony with a Huguenot wife. The earliest documented reference to Paul Micou's Virginia wife comes in the will of his mother-in-law, Margaret Cammock, a member of a wealthy and well-established English colonial family, drafted in the spring of 1709.[20] Given the high mortality rate in tidewater Virginia during this period, the frequent occurrence of serial marriages, and the approach of his fiftieth birthday, the possibility that Paul was in his second marriage by 1709 must be taken seriously. A family tradition cited in 1880 held that Micou arrived in the colony with a wife. An undocumented source in 1900 reported that Micou's first wife was a member of the Huguenot Roy family.[21] The close relationships between the Micou and Roy families in France and Virginia gives a measure of credence to this legend. The theory of a Huguenot first wife is also supported by the 1740 will of Paul's widow, Margaret, in which she did not list one of her husband's sons, James, who was documented as living two years later.[22]

The available evidence indicates the Huguenots who migrated with John Bertrand and Paul Micou were unusually successful in integrating into English colonial society in the Rappahannock region. One reason for this was the presence of French and Walloon families who had been established in this part of Virginia for two or more generations. Some of these families initially settled along the James and York Rivers in the 1630s and 1640s (see Chapter 1) and moved to the Rappahannock region when Europeans poured into that area after 1650. Geographical clustering and marriages among French-surnamed settlers suggest this may have been a sizable community. Like the second- and third-generation Huguenots who served on the consistories of the French churches in London during the 1680s, these French Protestants were in position to assist the newcomers to Virginia who had fled the persecution of Louis XIV. Some of them were major landowners in the Rappahannock region and leaders in their Anglican parishes.

Another reason for the successful integration of the Huguenots who arrived with John Bertrand is that some of them came with education, skills, and Atlantic networks urgently needed in the still-developing Rappahannock region. While the occupations of most Huguenots arriving between 1677 and 1710 are not known, records show eight merchants, five physicians, four ministers, three teachers, three ministerial candidates, one ship captain, one pharmacist, four carpenters, one tailor, one shoemaker, and one weaver of tapestries. After integrating into colonial society, one exile served as court justice, four as constables, one as tobacco receiver, one as tax collector, one as millwright, one as overseer, one as builder of tobacco houses, one as tavern keeper, and two as coopers (see Appendix A).

While it is not possible to determine the number of Rappahannock Refuge emigrants who entered marriages with English settlers, the high Chesapeake mortality rates and resulting serial marriages combined with the quick integration of Huguenots into Anglican parishes suggests exogamous marriages were taking place earlier and more often in Virginia than in other English American colonies. This observation is supported by the exogamous marriages of high-profile immigrants such as Paul Micou, Samuel Demonvill, James Foushee, and Lewis Latané. The refugees who read Durand de Dauphiné's tract understood that exogamous marriage was an avenue for Huguenots to advance their prospects in the colony. Durand described in detail the marriage celebration of a French immigrant who had served his term as an indentured servant, worked as an overseer, and then married into a well-established English slaveholding family. Later, Durand further affirmed exogamous marriage by characterizing his opportunity to marry an English widow with a 1,000-acre plantation as a Providential blessing.[23]

That Paul Micou used his exogamous marriage to Margaret Cammock to enter the governing elite of the colony is confirmed by the governor's appointment of him in 1710 to serve as one of the Essex court justices who governed the county.[24] While the date of Micou's marriage is not known, the surviving records suggest he was rising to a position of prominence during the second half of the decade of the 1690s. In this capacity, Micou probably paved the way for some of his relatives to immigrate to the Rappahannock region, and he could well have influenced the hiring of Huguenot-Anglican ministers Nicholas Moreau and Lewis Latané to serve in Essex County.[25]

One refugee who probably did not have skills that were in demand in the Rappahannock region, but had elevated status within the Huguenot community, was the Marquis de Calmes. Calmes, who apparently traveled to Virginia under the auspices of Nicholas Hayward to participate in the Brent Town settlement, appears in records with John Bertrand and Paul Micou during the 1690s. He patented land in Stafford County by 1706.[26] At the other end of the Huguenot social hierarchy were fifty-three refugees documented as indentured servants between 1677 and 1710—another role for which there was high demand in the colony by the 1680s (see Appendix A).

Perhaps thinking of his friend's advantageous wedding, Durand de Dauphiné offered an overly positive view of indentured service in Virginia. While he correctly reported that servant contracts for adults were never more than five years in duration, his description of former servants being in high demand as well-compensated overseers (like his friend) seems optimistic. Moreover, Durand was apparently unaware of the crushing living and working conditions that were all too often imposed on servants and the exceedingly high mortality rate they suffered in Virginia.[27] While about 20 percent of the Huguenot servants documented in this study survived their indenture contracts to build families and acquire property in Virginia, most disappeared from the records. The court proceedings offer significant insight into the hardships they faced. Of the fifty-three Huguenot refugees who arrived in the colony as servants, twenty-three appeared before the justices in a county court and two more filed cases with the general court of the colony. Eight women and one man were convicted of moral and criminal offenses. Four men and two women were punished for running away. Another five men and two women had to sue their employers to gain their freedom and/or their freedom benefits of clothing and corn. One man sued his master for mistreatment. Two complained to colonial officials that fellow Huguenots had maneuvered them into becoming servants by trickery or by withholding information.

John Bertrand's first effort to implement Bishop Compton's church reform program was through his pastoral service to the North Farnham Parish. In this role he was obliged to move beyond his Huguenot identity to be the spiritual leader for a parish of the established Anglican church of Virginia. In this capacity, Bertrand worked with people from every level of Virginia society—from the gentry who served on his vestry to the servants and enslaved persons who labored on the Rappahannock plantations. To do this work, John had to accommodate himself to the unique cultural and ecclesiastical norms of seventeenth-century Virginia. With no resident bishop in Virginia, Bertrand was accountable to the colony's governor, Francis Howard, Baron of Effingham, and later to the commissary James Blair.[28] He was obligated to present to the governor his certificate of ordination and the license for ministry issued by the Bishop of London or his representative.[29]

Virginia's version of Anglican polity gave the parish vestry the responsibility to hire its minister and recommend him to the governor, who would then induct him. Induction would give the minister permanent tenure, provided there were no proved charges of moral laxity or dereliction of duty. In England, the bishop would perform the induction of a minister after the recommendation of the patron of the parish. The colony had adapted the Church of England system to place the governor and the vestry in these roles. But the vestries did much more than hire clergy. With no bishop in the colony and Anglican-ordained ministers in short supply, colonial Virginia vestries assumed the primary responsibility for the theological identity and governance of the parishes.[30] The vestries set the worship style of the parish and sought clergy who would be willing to implement their vision. Governor Howard was struggling with limited success to curb the power of the vestries over their parishes and to make sure the churches were using the 1662 *Book of Common Prayer.* He undoubtedly welcomed the arrival of a clergyman who was properly ordained and ready to aggressively pursue Bishop Compton's reform program. He could not have overlooked the fact that Bertrand was the first bilingual French minister to perform the dual-tract ministry he had envisioned in a conversation with Durand the previous year.[31]

Anglican clergy were almost never given the titles of rector, priest, or reverend in seventeenth-century Virginia. They were commonly referred to as ministers and are therefore identified by that title in this study.[32] The county records often identified a member of the clergy as "Clerk" of the parish or "Clerk" associated with a particular county. This title was also used in the English records of the time, as evidenced by John Bertrand's 1686 marriage record in London listing him as "John Bertrand, Clerk." The Church of England's listing of clergy receiving funds for their passage to America between 1680 and 1688 did not use the title of priest. All the ministers were referred to as "Clerks."[33] The title of "Clerk" for a clergyman as seen in seventeenth-century Virginia records challenges present-day readers to pay attention to the context of the reference because county courts and parish vestries also had clerks to record official proceedings and carry out other administrative duties. The complexity confronting the reader of seventeenth-century records is made even more daunting by the evolution in the use of the term "clerk" in the next century. By the middle of the eighteenth century, the clerk of an Anglican parish in Virginia was a lay reader who would assist the minister in leading worship.[34]

John Bertrand and his clergy colleagues in Virginia were essentially civil servants. The parish churches were part of the governmental system of the colony and were supported by tax revenues. The ministers received salaries generated by tax income and were accountable to parish vestries and colonial officials. Governmental officials periodically instructed ministers to post announcements on the doors of the churches. Sometimes the governor issued proclamations that the ministers were required to read from the pulpit during the course of a service of worship. There were times when the Virginia Assembly called for a day of celebration, thanksgiving, fasting, or penance, and the ministers were required to organize these public observances and preach special sermons in the parish churches.[35]

The intertwining of church and state in the Rappahannock River basin is illustrated by an incident reported in the Lancaster court records in 1671. The court justices were given reserved seats in places of honor for Sunday morning services.[36] But on Sunday, November 1, 1671, a member of the St.

Mary's Whitechapel Parish refused to abide by this priority-seating system. According to the record, Richard Price "did after a rude irreligious and uncivil manner intrude himself into ye seat purposely designed and made for use by His Majesties' justices of the peace for this county." After engaging in a shoving match with one of the justices, Mr. Price was charged with misconduct. He was packed off to James City to be placed on trial before the governor and Council of State. Once there, Price decided to throw himself on the mercy of the colony's highest court. The Lancaster court record notes with satisfaction that Price asked forgiveness for "his turbulent and contentious carriage against this court."[37] Enforcing the priority-seating arrangements in parish churches was not beneath the dignity of the governor.

It is not possible to offer a detailed history of John Bertrand's ministry in Virginia. All the early parish records and many of the seventeenth-century records kept in the colonial offices in Jamestown and Williamsburg have been lost.[38] Information about Bertrand's ministry must be pieced together from the land, estate, and court records of the counties where he lived or had business activities. It is not possible to determine precise starting and ending dates of Bertrand's ministry to particular parishes in the colony. Some of the county records naming John Bertrand are ambiguous in nature so that one cannot be certain if they refer to his ministry activities or his business dealings. Some of the conclusions that can be drawn about Bertrand's ministry come into focus by analyzing his records alongside documents describing other ministers serving in the same area at about the same time.

Surviving records confirm that John Bertrand began his ministry in Virginia in the North Farnham Parish in Rappahannock County by the end of 1687. Upon their arrival in Virginia, the Bertrands were living at a home owned by Richard King.[39] With this home located adjacent to the North Farnham Church, it was a convenient residence for the parish minister. Records indicate this earliest North Farnham church building was built about 1661 and included some brick construction. It was near the heads of Richardson and Farnham Creeks, several miles above the present-day North Farnham Church. Originally called Farnham Parish and incorporating territory on both sides of the Rappahannock, the parish became North Farnham in 1684, when the area across the river was made South Farnham Parish. During John Bertrand's ministry to this parish, the church was still commonly called Farnham Church.[40]

North Farnham Church, Richmond County, Virginia, c. 1737.
Photo by the author. Courtesy North Farnham Episcopal Church, Farnham, Virginia

When John Bertrand began his ministry in Virginia, vestries rarely recommended their ministers for induction. Instead, they retained them on a year-to-year basis. This arrangement put the vestries in position to dismiss ministers without cause by not renewing the employment agreement.[41] John Bertrand most likely began his ministry with a one-year contract, subject to annual renewal by the vestry. The compensation package would have included a home with about 100 acres of land and some livestock provided by the parish. Salaries were paid in tobacco. The annual salary for ministers in the colony was 13,333 pounds of tobacco, an amount established by the Virginia Assembly in 1662, though it is possible that Bertrand, like a colleague in a neighboring parish, was paid at a higher rate.[42] In 1696, nine years after Bertrand's arrival in the colony, the salary for ministers was upgraded by 20 percent to 16,000 pounds of tobacco per year. Bertrand would have received additional compensation for special services provided to his parishioners. The

1696 action on salaries by the Virginia Assembly also established set fees for these services. Ministers were to receive forty shillings or 400 pounds of tobacco for a funeral sermon, twenty shillings or 200 pounds of tobacco for officiating at a marriage service, and five shillings or fifty pounds of tobacco for reading the marriage banns (the advanced announcements of marriages required by law in the colony).[43]

John Bertrand's imperialist mission soon placed him in conflict with leaders of his North Farnham Parish. As a Huguenot-Anglican minister, Bertrand was the first clergyman at North Farnham to make regular use of the *Book of Common Prayer* and to advocate the policies Henry Compton was seeking to impose on the parishes of the colony. From their inception, North Farnham and the other Rappahannock County parishes (dating from 1651, when they were part of Lancaster County) were able to organize worship in the way they saw fit. The parish vestry expected their ministers to follow its ecclesiastical vision and was willing to terminate those who did not.

The long history of autonomy in seventeenth-century Virginia parishes created a level of theological diversity in the colony that was no longer present in England. Puritan-oriented parish leaders had far more staying power in Virginia's Anglican Church than Puritan leaders enjoyed in England. One historian has noted that prior to 1650, there were as many Puritans in Virginia as there were in New England.[44]

It is important to note, however, that Virginia Puritans reflected a variety of views that were not tolerated in early New England. Massachusetts was settled by Separatist Puritans at Plymouth in 1620 and Congregationalist Puritans at Boston in 1630. Both these groups were committed to immediately ridding the church of what they considered to be "Catholic" governance and worship practices. While Virginia had these strains of radical Puritanism in its parishes, it also had settlers with Puritan views not typically found in New England. Presbyterian Puritans and Anglican Puritans, who were more moderate and less alienated from the Church of England, played an important role in the colonial Virginia churches. While they affirmed Calvinist theology and wanted many of the same changes the Separatists and Congregationalists advocated, they were more willing to work within the Anglican Church for gradual change. The variety of Puritan parties in Virginia sometimes led to conflict between them within Puritan-oriented parishes.[45]

Many of Virginia's more moderate Puritans considered themselves to be dedicated Anglicans, though Calvinist Anglicans to be sure.[46] The governor and the Council of State consistently made pronouncements that favored the anti-Puritan policies of the Stuart kings, but they rarely had the tools to enforce them. For most of Virginia's first century, it was the vestries, local court justices, and longer-tenured ministers who negotiated how particular parishes would align themselves in relation to England's competing theological parties.[47]

In Rappahannock County and later in Lancaster County, John Bertrand had to contend with the well-established Puritan identity of the parishes. Many of the early settlers of the two counties were from Puritan families relocating from the counties south of the James River.[48] In addition, the Rappahannock region parishes had a long history of being served by ministers with Puritan views. The earliest identifiable predecessor of John Bertrand in what would become North Farnham Parish was a Presbyterian Puritan named Charles Grimes, who is documented in the area between 1653 and 1661.[49] Grimes's successor in Rappahannock County was Francis Doughty, a Puritan minister who migrated to New England in 1642 and moved on to Virginia in 1662 to serve North Farnham and the neighboring Sittenbourne Parish.[50] When two members of the vestry filed charges against him in 1669, Doughty left for Maryland.[51] Doughty was replaced in North Farnham Parish by another non-conformist Puritan, Charles Dacres, who was accused by a colleague of lacking credentials to be a minister, fraudulently claiming to be a Doctor of Divinity, and wearing a scarlet hood into the pulpit.[52] Dacres's death in 1687 created the opening for Bertrand to serve the parish.[53]

John Bertrand's Huguenot-Anglican identity made his relationship with the Puritan-oriented population of his first Virginia parish a complex one. As a French Protestant, he was grounded in a Calvinist tradition that Puritans valued. That Bertrand remained a Calvinist to the end of his life is made clear by the theological language of his 1701 will, in which he used the term *elect* to describe those who receive the gift of salvation.[54] But French ministers, who never called themselves Calvinists, took John Calvin's theology for granted and never felt the need to wear it on their sleeves the way many Puritans did. As a Huguenot minister, Bertrand would have been trained to preach without notes and in a more emotional style than was typical for Anglican ministers trained after the restoration of the Stuart kings in 1660. While John Bertrand's Puritan-oriented parishioners likely appreciated his core theological views and the preaching style in which he was trained, they would have been suspicious of their pastor's Anglican identity. Bertrand's identification with London's French Church of the Savoy exposed him to the same caustic criticism that theological purists directed against its pattern of worship. The Savoy church's use of a French translation of the *Book of Common Prayer* combined with Calvinist preaching led some to say it had an Anglican face and a Presbyterian heart. While most Rappahannock Puritans could embrace John Bertrand's Presbyterian heart, many would have been repulsed by his Anglican face.[55]

John Bertrand had reasons of his own to be wary of his Puritan parishioners in Virginia. He likely grew up with a very negative view of the English

Puritans whose rebellion against their king put Huguenots on the defensive in France. In addition, John had seen firsthand how English Puritan nonconformists tried to discourage Huguenot refugees in England from associating with the Church of England, thereby damaging his brother's ministry at Rye. John Bertrand's French Protestant background and experiences in England probably made him as suspicious of Virginia's Puritans as they were of him.

The issue that made John Bertrand's relationship with the Puritans of Rappahannock County most difficult was his identification with the imperialist reforms of Henry Compton. These reforms were designed to reduce the power of the local officials who governed the parishes through the vestries. In parishes like North Farnham, Anglican reform also meant undoing thirty-six years of Puritan-influenced worship and preaching. After arriving in Virginia, John Bertrand would have quickly recognized how difficult his mission was going to be. With no bishop in Virginia and local church governance firmly in the hands of vestrymen, Bertrand's only tool was the power of persuasion.

On the other hand, events on the world stage gave positive momentum to Bertrand's ministry with the Puritans of Rappahannock County. With the success of the Glorious Revolution, England's posture toward the Catholic powers of Europe dramatically changed. William of Orange had established himself as an opponent of French expansionism on the continent of Europe before his invasion of England. As the king of England, William continued his military opposition to the French king by committing England to the Nine Years' War against France. During these years, anti-Catholicism moved to center stage as a driving force of English patriotism. As the conspiracy theory–induced panic of 1688–1689 had shown, many in English America already believed European Catholics and their Native American allies in the new world constituted their most threatening enemy.[56]

As dramatic victims of militant Catholicism on the continent, Huguenots became an important symbol for England's patriotic struggle against Louis XIV for Anglicans and Puritan non-conformists alike. New England Congregationalist Puritan leaders Increase and Cotton Mather were preaching and writing about the sufferings of the Huguenots and lifting them up as examples of courage and faith. John Bertrand's ministry in a Puritan-oriented county of Virginia served as a powerful reminder of the rationale for William's long war with France and an invitation to non-conformists to identify more fully with English imperial policies.[57]

Moreover, Virginia records show that Bishop Compton's Anglican reform program was not directed against Puritan standards of church discipline. All citizens of the colony were required to attend worship on Sundays and holidays or to pay a shilling fine when they were absent. Parishioners were obligated to have their children baptized, observe sabbath regulations, and refrain from swearing, fornication, and adultery. Pastors were obligated to counsel with members who failed to fulfill these responsibilities and to take legal action against those who did not reform their behavior.[58]

The leading advocate for Bishop Compton's reform program in Virginia was James Blair, whom Compton appointed in 1689 to represent him as commissary of the colony's Anglican Church. That moral discipline was an urgent priority for this leader of the church in Virginia can be seen in the agenda of the meeting of colonial clergy called by the commissary and held in Jamestown on July 23, 1690. Blair issued a proclamation at the conclusion of the meeting that included the following words:

> Now know ye . . . with the advice of the clergy of this colony at their general meeting certify to all persons concerned I intend to revive and put in execution the ecclesiastical laws against all cursers, swearers and blasphemers, all whoremongers, fornicators and adulterers, all drunkards, ranters and profaners of the Lord's day and contemners of the Sacraments, and against all other scandalous persons, whether of the clergy or laity within this dominion and colony of Virginia.[59]

While Blair was never accused of being a Puritan, no Puritan could have issued a more pointed call for moral purity. Reaching back to his roots in the dual Presbyterian/Episcopal system of the Restoration Church of Scotland, the commissary announced the division of the colony into four presbytery-like districts to better administer discipline.[60]

The one aspect of church discipline that is most visible in the records of the Rappahannock County court was the punishment handed out to those found guilty of fornication. Women who had children out of wedlock were brought before the justices and charged with fornication. The standard punishment for this offense was a fine of 500 pounds of tobacco to be paid to the parish where the woman resided. If the father of the child was identified, he would be assessed the same fine. The fines given to the women were usually paid by a family member or by the masters of indentured servant women in exchange for having time added to the indenture contract. When fines could not be paid, the offender (usually a woman) would be sentenced to twenty-one lashes on the bare back.

The birth of children out of wedlock was a common event in Rappahannock County and throughout the Chesapeake region during the years when John Bertrand was a minister there. Between March 5, 1690, and March 3, 1692, county records show twenty-eight women and seven men charged with fornication.[61] Of the women charged, twenty-two were indentured servants who had six months or more added to their time of service because of their offense. Three of the women were sentenced to be publicly whipped. Of the thirty-five fornication cases coming before the justices within this two-year period, thirteen of the offenders were from John Bertrand's North Farnham Parish.[62] The potential income to the parish of 6,500 pounds of tobacco from this "sin tax" was substantial—providing a new meaning to the biblical expression "wages of sin." While the stated purpose of the fines was to reimburse the parish for costs it might incur to support the children produced by extramarital liaisons, the vestries were likely using this significant income stream for general parish expenses as well. The North Farnham vestry had a strong financial interest in making sure every unwed mother appeared in court.

Masters of indentured servant women also had a clear incentive to bring unwed mothers before the bar of justice. Women serving as indentured servants were not allowed to marry. With women greatly outnumbered by men both in the colony and in the workplace, young female servants were inevitably sexual targets. Since masters clearly benefited from the fornication convictions that extended the term of service of their servants, some would have recognized it was to their advantage to tolerate a degree of sexual permissiveness among their servants. Moreover, some of the masters were sexual predators.[63] There is evidence to suggest that some masters impregnated their female servants with a view toward extending their indentures.[64]

County records document sixteen women with Huguenot surnames who became indentured servants when they arrived in the Rappahannock region between 1677 and 1710. These women were clearly not immune from the sexual abuse that so many female servants suffered. In 1689, Sarah Lafeavour was prosecuted in Rappahannock County for having a child out of wedlock and was sentenced to a longer term of service. She was sentenced again for her next child in 1693. Margaret Connil (Lancaster, 1695), Mary Pew (Richmond, 1700), Margaret Gerrard (Lancaster, 1701), Elizabeth Maurice (Richmond, 1706), and Mary Carnee (Richmond, 1710) were given similar sentences. In 1699, Ellinor Deinne, a servant of John Bertrand, was one of a group of servants convicted of stealing a hog belonging to Bertrand's foreman. When given a choice between having time added to her contract or receiving lashes on her bare back, she chose the whip. Ellinor Deinne's decision raises questions about the kind of abuse she might have been suffering.[65]

One can only guess what the Huguenot-Anglican exiles thought of this system for regulating sexual morality. There can be no doubt they had no previous experience with anything remotely similar to it. The governing consistories of the Protestant churches in France and the Huguenot refugee churches in England could never call on civil authorities to enforce their moral codes. Their influence was limited to moral persuasion and social pressure.[66] John Bertrand's mission to Virginia required him to assist his parish in its work as a disciplinary arm of governing authorities in a Puritan-oriented county.

An important part of John Bertrand's dual-track ministry was his role as spiritual leader of the Huguenot-Anglican refugees. The size and significance of this community is confirmed by the arrival in Virginia of additional Huguenot-Anglican ministers. Bertrand was the first of seven documented French émigré ministers serving in Virginia during his lifetime, four of them in the Rappahannock region. Stephen Fouace immigrated to Virginia in 1688 and served Anglican parishes in York County, outside the bounds of the Rappahannock Refuge, until he returned to England in 1703.[67] James Boisseau was a Huguenot from Saintonge, ordained and licensed by Bishop Compton, who served St. John's Parish near the Mattapony River in New Kent County on the southwest edge of the Rappahannock Refuge (eighteen miles from present-day Tappahannock, Virginia). He served the parish from 1690 until at least 1693. Due to the loss of records, nothing more is known of Boisseau's ministry except that he remained in Virginia until about 1705.[68] Nicholas Moreau went to St. Peter's Parish in New Kent County in 1696 and moved to Essex County, where he served from 1698 to 1702 at South Farnham Parish and was a practicing physician. One of the few Virginia ministers of this period for whom correspondence has survived (see Chapter 6), he might have been related to the prominent Moreau family in Cozes that included a Huguenot elder and a physician.[69] Three Huguenot ministers ordained by Henry Compton traveled to Virginia on the ships financed by William III in 1700 and 1701. Benjamin de Joux and Claude Philippe de Richebourg served the new Huguenot community founded at Manakin in the Virginia Piedmont, and Lewis Latané went to Essex County along the Rappahannock.[70]

Most of these Huguenot ministers were engaged in bilingual ministry. The four serving in the Rappahannock region (Bertrand, Boisseau, Moreau, and Latané) had dual-track ministries, preaching both in English and in French. As the first Huguenot-Anglican minister to arrive in the colony, John Bertrand likely had a role in helping his French colleagues make the transition to the unique ministry context they encountered in Virginia.

A major focus of the ministry of the French exile ministers was assisting their fellow refugees integrate into the Anglican parishes where they lived. For many of these Huguenots, their Virginia parish was their first experience of the Anglican Church or worship in the English language. Their worship life in England, where most had lived only a few years, was most likely limited to one or more of the refugee congregations that worshipped in French. One of the strategies Bertrand and his Huguenot-Anglican colleagues likely used was to offer Anglican services in French following the model of the French Church of the Savoy in London, consistent with the vision of Governor Howard as reported by Durand de Dauphiné.[71] French language worship could have been scheduled at North Farnham or other churches along the Rappahannock River at an alternate time on Sundays. These services would also have served as a "half-way house" for training Huguenot refugees to participate more fully in their Anglican parish churches. This "half-way house" format was also implemented in Huguenot-Anglican congregations that would later be formed in South Carolina, the Manakin Town settlement in the Virginia Piedmont, and New Rochelle, New York. All of them were modeled on the worship practices of the Anglican conformist French Church of the Savoy in London.[72]

There is intriguing, though fragmentary, evidence that Huguenot ministerial candidates might have led services in French for Huguenot-Anglican refugees in the Rappahannock region. Jean Masson (1666–1747) was the son of the minister who succeeded John Bertrand's father at the Protestant Church of Cozes in France. The appearance of his name in a 1691 Westmoreland County, Virginia, court record points to the possibility that he was in the Rappahannock region with other young adults from Cozes during the interval between his 1689 approval as a ministerial candidate in the Netherlands and his 1695 Anglican ordination in England. If his English skills were good enough, Masson could have served Cople Parish for a few years. If not, he might have been specifically assigned to lead French-language services for Huguenot exiles.[73] A similar ministry could have been performed by Jean Marion, who was documented in Stafford County in 1702, and Jaques Joyeux, whose name appears in Essex County in 1710 (see Appendices A and B). Their names match Huguenots identified by the Royal Bounty in London as *proposants*—French Protestant ministerial candidates. These Huguenot-Anglican ministerial candidates were, in fact, much better educated and far more qualified than the largely untrained nonconformist ministers frequently employed by Anglican vestries in the Rappahannock region before 1710.

While the effective integration of Huguenot-Anglican refugees into the parishes of the Rappahannock region could be helpful to John Bertrand's mission, it could not guarantee its success. Virginia records point to a major backlash against John Bertrand's work to implement Bishop Compton's Anglican reforms. Bertrand's ministry in North Farnham Parish came to an end about the time Rappahannock County passed out of existence at the close of 1692.[74] On June 1, 1692, the court justices of the newly created Richmond County called a "free election" of North Farnham Parish for July 22 to choose a new vestry.[75] This was an unusual process in a colony where Anglican vestry vacancies were usually filled through appointment by the remaining vestrymen and/or court justices. It is not clear whether the scheduled election was an open one or just a way to "rubber-stamp" the candidates chosen by local officials.

While the surviving county records do not reveal the identities of the new vestrymen, the June 1 action of the Richmond justices suggests the new vestry might have included more Puritan dissenters. Three of the justices were empowered to swear in the newly elected vestrymen using the "oaths enjoined by Act of Parliament" after its passing of the 1689 Act of Toleration. This simple oath of allegiance to William and Mary replaced the previous oaths of supremacy and allegiance that emphasized the English monarch's status as head of the church. The new oath was used in New England after 1689 to enable Puritan dissenters to be sworn in as officials of the Crown.[76] Its use with the North Farnham vestry in 1692 suggests a new opening for Puritan dissenters to be members of the governing body of the parish.

In April 1693, three influential members of the parish—William Tayloe, John Loyd, and John Tavernor—appeared before the Council in James City to file a complaint against the action taken by the Richmond court justices to reorganize the North Farnham vestry. John Tavernor was a Huguenot whose family had been in Virginia since the late 1630s and was a well-established lawyer in Rappahannock County when John Bertrand arrived in the colony.[77] The previous year, Tavernor had witnessed the deed for John Bertrand's purchase of a plantation from another member of this parish delegation, John Loyd.[78] When they addressed the Council, Tavernor, Loyd, and Tayloe alleged that "the court of that County had turned out the vestry of the said parish, and appointed a new vestry." The Council summoned the Richmond County justices to submit a "full and particular account of their actions to the next meeting of the Council." In July 1693, the Council received the report of the Richmond justices and summoned Tayloe, Loyd, and Tavernor to appear at their October 23 meeting. The Council record has no further entry to reveal what happened next.[79]

The surviving records suggest the newly created vestry at North Farnham had decided not to renew the annual contract of John Bertrand as minister of the parish. The complaint filed by three of Bertrand's supporters in the parish was most likely their attempt to overturn his dismissal. The new opening for Puritans to be sworn into office and the just-completed division of the county probably shifted the balance of power for the parishes north of the river. Control of the vestry apparently moved away from the Anglican Puritan justices and vestrymen who held sway when John Bertrand was hired five years earlier. With the newly constituted vestry under the control of more radical Puritans, John Bertrand's Huguenot-Anglican ministry was no longer viable in the parish. By January 1693, the nonconformist Puritan minister John Davis was serving North Farnham and filing court actions on behalf of the parish. Davis had previously been the minister of two other Rappahannock parishes, Sittenbourne (1684–1686) and St. Mary's (1688).[80]

The dissolution of John Bertrand's pastoral relationship with North Farnham at the close of 1692 is confirmed by the court action he filed against the church wardens of the parish in October 1693. The suit was dismissed when the minister did not appear, but it suggests Bertrand was having difficulty collecting back salary from his former parish.[81] John Bertrand's dismissal after five years at North Farnham was a serious setback to his Huguenot-Anglican mission to the Rappahannock region. The backlash against Bishop Compton's imperialist reforms proved to be exceedingly strong. This would not be the only imperialist project in which John Bertrand would be harshly rebuffed. The next chapter opens the narrative of Bertrand's purchase of a Rappahannock River plantation—a development that placed him at the center of another imperialist initiative elite Virginians bitterly resisted.

NOTES

1. Durand, 155.
2. Philip P. Boucher, "Revisioning the French Atlantic," in *The Atlantic World and Virginia, 1550–1624*, ed., Peter C. Mancall (Chapel Hill, NC, 2007), 274–306.
3. Nine of the fifty-three indentured servants eventually gained their freedom and helped create nine additional households, bringing the documented household total to 261. For documentation of these refugees, see Appendices A and B.
4. For the length of servant contracts in the seventeenth-century Chesapeake region, see James Horn, *Adapting to a New World: English Society in the Seventeenth-Century Chesapeake* (Chapel Hill, NC, 1994), 66.
5. Gwynn, *Huguenots in Britain I*, 183–85. Bertrand Van Ruymbeke, in his detailed study of the Huguenot migration to South Carolina, found no evidence to support a tradition that some refugees arrived in that colony with a minister they knew in France. Van Ruymbeke, *From New Babylon to Eden*, 118–19.
6. The Rappahannock region Huguenot refugees were scattered over portions of Rappahannock (later Richmond and Essex), Lancaster, Westmoreland, Northumberland, Middlesex, Stafford, New Kent (later King William and King and Queen) Counties. Six of these counties shared Rappahannock waterfront. The exceptions were Northumberland, which was adjacent to Lancaster and Richmond, and New Kent, which was adjacent to Essex. Seven of these counties were part of Virginia's upper tidewater, while Stafford straddled the tidewater and the piedmont.
7. The Mattapony River–area Huguenots in New Kent County became part of the newly organized King and Queen County in 1691. With the creation of King William County on the west side of the river in 1702, the Huguenot households were divided between King William and King and Queen.
8. ORC OB 2, 1686–1692, 71–72.
9. De Schickler, *Les Eglises Du Refuge En Angleterre*, Tome Deuxieme, 335; Rightmyer, "List of Anglican Clergy Receiving a Bounty for Overseas Service," 177–78.
10. Davis, *William Fitzhugh and His Chesapeake World*, 37–38.
11. Stanwood, *The Empire Reformed*, 86–112.

12. Monsieur Bertrand to the Bishop of London, September 12, 1689, in W. H. Browne, ed., *Archives of Maryland* (Baltimore, 1883), vol. 1, 114–18.

13. Records for the Royal Bounty list Michel Morin receiving assistance in 1686 to migrate to Virginia. RBP, Ms 1 (Morin), HL.

14. Jane Baldwin Cotton and R. B. Henry, eds., *Maryland Calendar of Wills* (Baltimore, 1928), vol. 4, 234.

15. Brett, *Bertrand's Toyshop in Bath*, 27–36.

16. SP, ORC OB, 1689–1692, 42.

17. Fleet, vol. 1, 295.

18. SP, EC DWB, 1695–1697, 69–70.

19. John Bailey Calvert Nicklin, "An Annotated Copy of the Rent Roll of 1704," WMQ 21, no. 4 (October 1941), 402.

20. Ryland, "Paul Micou, Chyrurgeon," 244–45.

21. Philip Slaughter, *Memoir of Col. Joshua Fry, Sometime Professor in William and Mary College* (Richmond, 1880), 16–17; Green, *Genealogical and Historical Notes*, 75–76.

22. SP, EC WB 6, 1735–1743, 100–01, 135–36.

23. Durand, 137–39, and 150.

24. ORC OB 2, 262; Wright, *Essex County Marriage References*, 135; Ryland, "Paul Micou, Chyrurgeon," 241–46; Paul Micou, "Paul Micou, Huguenot Physician and His Descendants," VMHB 46, no. 4 (October 1938), 362–70.

25. Refugees to the Rappahannock region who might have been related to Paul Micou include James Roy (1692), Edward Danellin (1695), Thomas Roy (1697), John Roy (1700), William Roy (1704), Francis Lafon (1710), and Nicholas Lafon (1710).

26. RBP, Ms 2/5, HL; SP, LC OB, 1691–1695, 87; SP, *SC DWB*, 1699–1709, 68; Northern Neck Grants (hereafter cited as NNG) No. 3, 1703–1710, 147, LVA.

27. Horn, *Adapting to a New World*, 155.

28. Billings, *Papers of Francis Howard*, 260–61.

29. Carpenter, *The Protestant Bishop*, 95–100; H. L. McIlwaine, ed., *Executive Journals of the Council of Colonial Virginia* (Richmond, 1925), vol. 1, 323.

30. Bond, *Damned Souls*, 204–06.

31. Warren Billings, *Virginia's Viceroy: Their Majesties' Governor General: Francis Howard, Baron of Effingham* (Fairfax, VA, 1991), 78–81.

32. In a 1690 letter, William Fitzhugh describes John Bertrand as a "minister." Davis, *William Fitzhugh and His Chesapeake World*, 270–72. See also Parke Rouse Jr., *James Blair of Virginia* (Chapel Hill, NC, 1971), 58.

33. Rightmyer, "List of Anglican Clergy Receiving a Bounty for Overseas Service," 177.

34. John K. Nelson, *A Blessed Company: Parishes, Parsons, and Parishioners in Anglican Virginia, 1690–1776* (Chapel Hill, NC, 2001), 354, note 2.

35. McIlwaine, *Executive Journals*, 245, 290, 291, 292, 293, 378, and 386.

36. For worship seating in colonial Virginia churches by social rank, see Brent Tarter, "Reflections on the Church of England in Colonial Virginia," VMHB 112, no. 4 (2004), 352.

37. SP, *LC OB, 1670–1674*, 41 and 59.

38. McIlwaine, *Executive Journals*, 393.

39. Richard King's November 1689 deed for the sale of his 300-acre plantation and house near the head of Farnham Creek identified Mr. John Bertrand as a recent tenant, ORC DWB, No. 8, 80.

40. George Carrington Mason, "The Colonial Churches of Essex and Richmond Counties," VMHB 53, no. 1 (Jan., 1945), 16–19.

41. William H. Seiler, "The Anglican Parish Vestry in Colonial Virginia," *The Journal of Southern History* 22, no. 3 (August 1956), 320–21.

42. Bell, *Empire, Religion, and Revolution*, 124–25. For the salary of Deuel Pead at Christ Church in Middlesex County, see C. G. Chamberlayne, *The Vestry Book of Christ Church Parish, Middlesex County, Virginia, 1663–1767* (Richmond, 1947), 41.

43. William Wilson Manross, ed., *The Fulham Papers in the Lambeth Palace Library, American Colonial Section*, Calendar and Indexes (Oxford, UK, 1965), 159; Robert Beverley, *The History and Present State of Virginia by Robert Beverley: A New Edition with an Introduction by Susan Scott Parish* (Chapel Hill, NC, 2013), 209–10.

44. Brent Tarter, "Evidence of Religion in Seventeenth-Century Virginia," in *From Jamestown to Jefferson: The Evolution of Religious Freedom in Virginia*, eds. Paul Rasor and Richard E. Bond (Charlottesville, VA, 2011), 28–31.

45. Michael Raymond Bradley, *The Puritans of Virginia: Their Influence on the Religious Life of the Old Dominion, 1607–1659* (Vanderbilt University Dissertation, Nashville, 1971).

46. George MacLaren Brydon, "The Huguenots of Manakin Town and Their Times: An Address Delivered before the Annual Meeting of the Huguenot Society of Manakin Town on April 14, 1934," VMHB 42, no. 4 (October 1934), 325–35.

47. Bell, *Empire, Religion, and Revolution*, 81.

48. Horn, *Adapting to a New World*, 182–85; John Bennett Boddie, *Seventeenth Century Isle of Wight County, Virginia* (Baltimore, 1973), 54, 56, and 515; Carolyn Jett, *History of Lancaster County: Where the River Meets the Bay* (Lancaster, VA, 2003), 40–43; Tarter, "Evidence of Religion in Seventeenth Century Virginia," 30; Butterfield, "Puritans and Religious Strife in the Early Chesapeake," 5–37.

49. Thomas Hoskins Warner, *History of Old Rappahannock County, Virginia, 1656–1692* (Tappahannock, VA, 1965), 131 and 133; SP, LC DWB, 1654–1661, 130; J. A. Venn and John Venn, eds. *Alumni Cantabrigienses: a biographical list of all known students, graduates, and holders of office at the University of Cambridge* (Cambridge, UK, 1922–1954), vol. 1, 268; #26310, CCEd. Other early ministers in Rappahannock County include Mr. Clemovant (1652), who died in 1652, Warner, *History of ORC*, 132–33, 142–43, and William White (1655–1658), Warner, *History of ORC*, 132–33, LC OB, 1656–1666, 14 and 56. William G. Stanard, "Christ Church, Lancaster County, Virginia," in *Colonial Churches: A Series of Sketches of Churches in the Original Colony of Virginia*, edited by W. M. Clarke (Richmond, VA, 1907), 96, #90466, CCEd.

50. ORC DWB, no. 1, 1665–1677, 38–39.

51. ORC DB, 1656–1664, Part II, 191–92; #86798, CCEd; ORC DB, 1668–1672, 21, and 61–67; Stanard, "Abstracts of Rappahannock County Wills," VMHB 5, no. 3 (January 1898): 283, 290; Warner, *History of ORC*, 140.

52. SP, ORC DWB, 1672–1676, Part I, 60, 75–77; SP, ORC OB, 1685–1687, 81; ORC WB, 1656–1692, 113–14; SP, NC OB, 1677–1679, 60 and 101; Various Authors, *Colonial Records of Virginia* (Baltimore, 1964), 318–23; George MacLaren Brydon, *Virginia's Mother Church and the Political Conditions Under Which It Grew* (Richmond, 1947), vol. 1, Appendix VII, 513; SP, LC OB, 1674–1678, 49; SP, ORC DWB, 1677–1682, Part II, 72; SP, RC OB, 1697–1699, 115–16.

53. SP, ORC OB, 1685–1687, 81.

54. LC WB, 1690–1709, no. 8, 105.

55. Gwynn, *Huguenot Heritage*, 122–27.

56. Stanwood, *The Empire Reformed*; Thomas S. Kidd, *The Protestant Interest: New England after Puritanism* (New Haven, CT, 2013).

57. Paula Wheeler Carlo, "Huguenot Identity and Protestant Unity in Colonial Massachusetts: the Reverend Andre Le Mercier and the 'Sociable Spirit,'" *Historical Journal of Massachusetts* 40, nos. 1 and 2 (Summer 2012), 122–47.

58. Warner, *History of ORC*, 128–29.

59. Parke Rouse, *James Blair of Virginia*, 39–40.

60. P. G. Scott, "James Blair and the Scottish Church: A New Source," WMQ 33, no. 2 (April, 1976), 300–08.

61. Betty Wood, "Servant Women and Sex in the Seventeenth-Century Chesapeake," in *Women in Early America*, ed., Thomas A. Foster (New York, 2015), 103.

62. SP, ORC OB, *1689–1692*.

63. Warren M. Billings, "The Law of Servants and Slaves in Seventeenth-Century Virginia," VMHB 99, no. 1 (January 1991), 50. For the unsuccessful attempt of three female servants to bring charges of rape against their master in Accomack County in 1669, see Irmina Wawrzyczek, "The Women of Accomack County versus Henry Smith: Gender, Legal Recourse, and the Social Order in Seventeenth-Century Virginia," VMHB 105, no. 1 (Winter 1997), 5–26.

64. David Hackett Fischer, *Albion's Seed: Four British Folkways in America* (New York, 1989), 303.

65. Wright, *Essex County Marriage References*, 58; SP, ORC OB, 1687–1689, 94; SP, RC OB, 1692–1694, 59; SP, LC OB, 1691–1695, 90; SP, LC OB, 1699–1701, 12–15, 87; SP, RC OB, 1699–1701, 38; SP, RC OB, 1705–1706, 18.

66. Labrousse, *Bayle*, 3–4.

67. Mary D. Micou, "The Colonial Churches of York County, Virginia," in *Colonial Churches: A series of Sketches of Churches in the Original Colony of Virginia*, ed., W. M. Clarke (Richmond, VA, 1907), 242, and Gwynn, *Huguenots in Britain I*, 293.

68. Weis, *Colonial Clergy*, 6; #97686, #85066, CCEd; McIlwaine, *Executive Journals*, vol. 1, 280; Gwynn, *Huguenots in Britain I*, 227–28.

69. C. G. Chamberlayne, ed., *The Vestry Book and Register of St. Peter's Parish, New Kent and James City Counties, Virginia, 1684–1786* (Richmond, 1937), 49, and 53–54; SP, EC RB, 1699–1702, 33, 83, 87, and 117; SP, RC OB, 1697–1699, 86 and 110; John Frederick Dorman, WC OB, 1698–1705, Part Two, 1700–1701

(Washington, DC. Printed by the author, 1978), 48, 74, and 83 (all John Frederick Dorman publications are hereafter cited as Dorman); RBP, Ms 4/1, Ms 4/2, Ms 9/4, Ms 9/7, Ms 11.

70. R. A. Brock, ed., *Documents, chiefly unpublished, relating to the Huguenot emigration to Virginia and the settlement of Manakin-Town* (Baltimore, 1962), 29–34 (hereafter cited as Brock); # 98676 (de Richebourg), #98702 (de Joux), CCEd.

71. Durand, 144.

72. For the Huguenot-Anglican practices of the conformist church in New Rochelle, see Carlo, *Huguenot Refugees in New York*, 78–102. For the use of the term *half-way house* by historians to describe the ministry of the conformist New Rochelle church and the French Church of the Savoy in London, see Ibid., 94, and Gwynn, *Huguenots in Britain I*, 122. For the Anglican annexation of Huguenot congregations in South Carolina, see Van Ruymbeke, *From New Babylon to Eden*, 131–60.

73. WC OB, 1690–1698, 5a; RBP, Ms 1, HL; # 164848, CCEd; Marcia Watson, *Hugo*, e-letter of the Huguenot Society of Australia Inc, no. 15 (February 2017); Forlacroix and de Saint-Affrique, *Les Pasteurs d'Aunis, Saintonge, et Angoumois devant la Revocation*, 96–97; CZ, 46, ADCMLR.

74. John Bertrand returned to the North Farnham Parish about 1696 (see Chapter 6). Bertrand was probably the minister of North Farnham for approximately ten years, from late 1687 to late 1692 and from about 1696 until his death in 1701.

75. RC OB, 1692–1694, no. 1, 20.

76. For the use of this oath in Boston in 1692, see *A true copy of the oaths that are appointed by act of Parliament in the first year of their present Majesties' reign . . .* Boston, 1692, rbpe, 033 0250b, Library of Congress, Washington, DC.

77. John Tavernor's family was in partnership with the Nicholas, George, and Clerke families in Isle of Wight County by 1638. In the 1650s, members of this clan began moving to Lancaster and Rappahannock Counties. Fleet, vol. 1, 118, 124, 145, 155, 194, and 214; Nugent, *Cavaliers and Pioneers*, vol. 2, 217 and 295; SP, ORC WB, 1682–1687, 17–18.

78. LC DWB, vol. 7, 1687–1700, 56–57.

79. McIlwaine, *Executive Journals*, 285 and 288.

80. SP, ORC OB, 1687–1689, 9 and 22; SP, RC OB, 1692–1694, 41, 49, 53, and 57; Bell, *Empire, Religion, and Revolution*, 66, 92, and 216.

81. RC OB, 1692–1694, no. 1, 98.

Chapter Four

Powell's Quarter, 1692

> But accidentally meeting with a French Minister, a sober, learned, and discreet Gentleman, whom I persuaded to board and tutor [my son] . . . in whose family there is nothing but French spoken.
>
> —William Fitzhugh to Nicholas Hayward, July 10, 1690

The most successful feature of Stuart imperialist policy in Virginia was the regulation of trade through the Navigation Acts, which had first been put in place by Commonwealth officials.[1] While Charles II displayed little interest in the religious life of the colonies, he was determined that Virginians ship their tobacco on English ships to ensure the lucrative tax revenues would go to the Crown. This meant Virginia planters could no longer benefit from the competition offered by Dutch traders in negotiating for the best price for their tobacco. After 1662, English authorities aggressively blocked foreign traders from participating in the English colonial market, ensuring that Virginia agricultural products would be directed to the sole benefit of the merchants and government of the mother country at the expense of Virginia's tobacco growers.[2] While Virginia elites fought hard to have this Stuart imperialist policy reversed, their efforts met with no success.

When John Bertrand sailed for Virginia in 1687, these regulations had been in place for a quarter of a century. As a member of a Huguenot trading family, John probably saw this imperial policy through the eyes of the English merchants who benefited from it. The nature of his business ambitions is revealed by his 1692 acquisition of a plantation on a navigable section of the Rappahannock River that could serve as a port of call for transatlantic ships. By the end of the decade, Paul Micou had followed Bertrand's example by acquiring his own Rappahannock River plantation that could accommodate transatlantic ships to support merchant activities.

Through their families in western France, John Bertrand and his wife, Charlotte Jolly, understood how regional and international markets operated.[3]

Their decision to immigrate to America was likely driven in part by the mercantilist orientation of their families and their network of trading relationships on both sides of the Atlantic.[4] Like their families in western France, John and Charlotte pursued their merchant ambitions by working in partnership. Women from seventeenth-century merchant families in Saintonge, in contrast to English merchant wives of this period, worked alongside their husbands and inherited these businesses when their husbands died. A 1690 French legal record offers a snapshot of the role of women in business affairs within Charlotte's family. This document was a contract to sell vine cuttings from the Jolly Chadignac estate near the town of Saintes to a Saintonge merchant. It was signed by Judith André, Charlotte's mother.[5]

Virginia's intercolonial trade sent tobacco, grain, lumber, livestock, and meat to New York, New England, and the West Indies in exchange for enslaved workers, Dutch cloth, sugar, rum, and molasses. Virginia's transatlantic trade sent tobacco and agricultural products to the European markets through England in exchange for European manufactured goods.[6] The role of Virginia in the intercolonial and transatlantic trade of the latter seventeenth century can be seen in the operations of the prominent New York City merchant Jacob Leisler. A member of a Dutch emigrant trading family with Huguenot roots, Leisler established regular trade routes between New York City, the Chesapeake Bay, the West Indies, and ports in England and the Netherlands. Leisler's intercolonial trading connected the various English American colonies to one another, and his transatlantic trading connected all these colonies to Europe. He had agents or factors in each of these locations. The role of these agents was to distribute the goods he sent or to procure the goods he needed for customers at various locations on both sides of the Atlantic. With Thomas Hawkins of Rappahannock County as his Virginia agent, Leisler's ships sailed to and from the colony by way of the Chesapeake Bay and the Rappahannock River.[7]

As described in Chapter 1, the Protestant Church of Cozes gave John Bertrand and Paul Micou a network of relationships in Huguenot settlements up and down the eastern seaboard of North America.[8] Most importantly, Bertrand and Micou were connected to at least three prominent merchant families in America. Members of two of the leading Huguenot merchant families in New York City were from Cozes: the Pelletreaus and the Papins.[9] John Bertrand was connected to Gabriel Bernon, a leading New England merchant, through his cousin, Abraham Tourtellot, who married Bernon's daughter and worked for him.[10] John's connection to this important New England entrepreneur and native of La Rochelle was strengthened by the marriage of Diane de La Rochefoucauld to one of Bernon's agents in Massachusetts about 1690. This young noblewoman was recorded living in the same household with John Bertrand in London in the fall of 1681, when the minister was serving as chaplain and tutor for the La Rochefoucauld family.[11]

John Bertrand and Paul Micou also knew Cozes Huguenots who were established in the West Indies by the early 1670s. The island of Barbados dominated the economy of the English colonial world in the second half of the seventeenth century and was Virginia's most important colonial trading partner when Bertrand and Micou immigrated to English America. Some Cozes Huguenots in the Caribbean, like the Pelletreaus and Papins, had moved from there to New York City about 1686. John Bertrand and Paul Micou clearly had the network of relationships to engage extensively in intercolonial trade.[12]

With family trading connections in France and his long residence in England, John Bertrand almost certainly knew Huguenot merchants based in London, Bristol, and other English ports. The Bertrand and Jolly families in Saintonge were producing wine to be exported (probably as brandy or cognac) to England and the Netherlands.[13] After John and Charlotte emigrated, their family members remaining in France abjured their Protestant faith and continued their wine production and trading activities well into the eighteenth century. The members of the Micou family who remained in France (Paul's parents and at least two of his siblings) followed the same path to retain their property and business operations in Saintonge.[14] It may be that these families who remained in France hoped to use their emigrant relatives as Virginia-based factors for trading with the new world.[15]

In Virginia, the business model for John Bertrand and Paul Micou called for developing a Rappahannock River landing from which to receive goods shipped from Europe and to load tobacco onto the same ships. A plantation with such a facility could also become a trans-shipment location where planters could store the tobacco they were ready to send to England. The landings these refugee merchants envisioned would fully utilize the Chesapeake water transportation system to put them in position to serve as agents or factors for merchants in New York, Boston, London, Amsterdam, or La Rochelle. Both Bertrand and Micou aggressively pursued this business model by acquiring waterfront plantations on the Rappahannock River.

Operating plantations in Virginia and participating actively in intercolonial trading activities placed John Bertrand and Paul Micou at the center of the colony's slave culture. The slave trade and the profits it generated was one of the most destructive features of England's imperialist ambitions. The slave trade also helped to create the Atlantic world Bertrand and Micou knew as a space defined by relationships between Europe, Africa, and the Americas. The slave trade was a large and highly profitable transatlantic business by the time Dutch traders delivered the first enslaved Africans to planters in Virginia in 1619.[16] As the English began to make use of slave labor, they followed the established norms of their Atlantic context. They closely observed the slave system the Spanish developed in their Caribbean colonies. The slave culture of Virginia developed gradually. Until the last quarter of the seventeenth century, Virginia addressed its labor needs primarily through the importation of indentured servants.[17]

Through their Saintonge merchant families and friends, the Huguenot emigrants to Virginia understood that the slave trade was a major international business and that Protestant merchants from La Rochelle and Bordeaux participated in it. By the time they embarked for Virginia, they also knew that enslaved Africans were going to the colony in significant numbers. The earliest record of John Bertrand's participation in Virginia's slave system is found in Rappahannock County. In July 1690, Bertrand made a court appearance to present two enslaved boys. The first was judged to be eight years old. The second was considered by the court to be six years old. Each was declared to be "levey free until he shall arrive to the age limited by Act of Assembly."[18] Four years later, Paul Micou made a similar visit to the same court (now Richmond County) to present an enslaved girl named Moll, who was judged to be ten years old. These Huguenot emigrants were complying with an act passed by Virginia's House of Burgesses in 1680 requiring that all enslaved children be brought before county court justices to have their ages legally confirmed and recorded so that taxes could be levied on their labor when the children reached the age established for that purpose by Virginia law.[19]

With a small number of elite planters owning most of Virginia's enslaved labor during the last two decades of the seventeenth century,[20] it is not surprising that records indicate most of John Bertrand's laborers were indentured servants.[21] Nonetheless, enslaved African Virginians formed an important part of Bertrand's workforce. John's 1701 will names three of the estimated five or six enslaved workers at his plantation.[22] For Paul Micou's first twenty years in Virginia, very few records have survived to document his family relationships, his business activities, or his use of enslaved workers. With his marriage to Margaret Thatcher/Cammock (probably at the end of the 1690s), he became part of a wealthy English slave-holding family.

One can only guess whether the Huguenot-Anglican refugees had any ethical qualms about participating in the colony's evolving slave system. They clearly did not receive much help in sorting out the ethics of slavery from the Reformed Church of France or the Church of England. Like other seventeenth-century European churches, neither taught that slavery was morally wrong.[23] William Fleetwood, the Anglican Bishop of St. Asaph, addressed the theological implications of slavery in a book published in

1705. Interpreting the apostle Paul's instruction in 1 Corinthians that servants must obey their masters in all things, he drew a sharp distinction between servants in covenantal relationships with their rulers and those who were "captives and downright slaves." While the first kind of servant might disobey an unjust ruler like James II, as people like Fleetwood had done in the Glorious Revolution of 1689, the "captives and slaves" must always obey their masters to make their chains as easy as possible by their submission. By this distinction, Fleetwood provided a quasi-theological rationale for the enslaved people on English American plantations to render absolute submission to their masters.

In a sermon he preached in 1711, Fleetwood went on to insist on the full humanity of enslaved Africans and to recommend their inclusion in the church. He admitted that a good theological case could be made for setting the enslaved free. But in the end, he concluded that freeing enslaved laborers was not a good idea. To do so would inflict damage on the "trade" by which the English lived, leaving them helpless before their competitors and their enemies in the international arena. For Bishop Fleetwood, slavery could not be ended because it was integral to England's imperialistic ambitions. He advised his listeners and readers that where slavery was concerned, theological considerations must give way to national and economic necessity. Bishop Fleetwood's conclusion was one that profit-driven Virginia planters and merchants could readily understand.[24]

In 1692, John Bertrand found a plantation with the potential to support his ambitious mercantilist goals. It was located in Lancaster County near its boundary with Rappahannock (Richmond) County. The plantation was on the north shore of the Rappahannock River near the point where Deep Creek flowed into the river. True to its name, Deep Creek was, in fact, deep enough for John Bertrand to create a protected landing for transatlantic ships if he could control enough of its shoreline. This plantation, eventually named *Belle Isle*,[25] was purchased by the Commonwealth of Virginia in transactions completed in 1992 and 2015. Virginia subsequently created Belle Isle State Park, consisting of virtually all of the plantation the Bertrands had purchased 300 years earlier, including seven miles of shoreline. Archeological studies were conducted in Belle Isle State Park in 1992, 1995, 2004, 2006, and 2020. An earlier archeological study was performed in 1974, when the site was privately owned. These studies have provided an important window into the rich history of this Rappahannock River plantation.[26]

Detail, *A New Map of Virginia, Mary-Land, and the improved parts of Pennsylvania,* John Senex, 1719, showing the location of the Bertrand Plantation.
Courtesy Library of Congress, Geography and Map Division

When the Bertrands purchased their plantation, it had been under European management for more than forty years. However, it had a much longer history as a Native American settlement. When the English adventurer, Captain John Smith, explored the Rappahannock River in 1608, he mapped a series of Moraughtacund villages (loosely bound to the Powhatan Algonquins) on the north bank of the river. The resulting 1612 map shows a "Kings house" and other native buildings at the site that would become the Bertrand plantation. There were about 300 Indians living in this area at the time, and they tended to live close to the river as it was their main source of food.[27] From 1634, Virginia's colonial government officially set aside the land between the Rappahannock and Potomac Rivers, later called the Northern Neck, for Native Americans, but pressure quickly grew from English settlers who wanted to move into the area.[28] When the authorities officially opened the Northern Neck to Virginia planters in 1648, thousands of settlers poured into the region within a few years.[29]

John Bertrand's plantation was located on a small neck of land protruding into the Rappahannock River bounded on the east by Deep Creek and on the west by Mulberry (sometimes called Mud) Creek. When the plantation was first patented October 14, 1650, it was known as *Powell's Quarter* for Thomas Powell (d. 1670), who received a 500-acre grant.[30] Powell moved to Lancaster from Isle of Wight County, where he owned land on the south side of the James River.[31] His brother, Howell, joined him in the Rappahannock River basin by 1654.[32] Thomas gradually became a one of the most prominent planters in Lancaster County,[33] acquiring additional land on the Corrotamon River.[34] He became a Lancaster court justice in 1659.[35] After the death of his first wife, Powell filed a jointure for a marriage with a younger woman named Jane Catesby, who might have been an indentured servant.[36] The terms were very generous, as he promised her 200 pounds sterling plus one-third of his Rappahannock River plantation to enter into this marriage.[37]

When Powell died in 1670, the provisions of his will set in motion a chain of events that generated long-term questions about the administration of *Powell's Quarter*.[38] He left his estate to Rawleigh Powell, his four-year-old son by Jane Catesby Powell. He named his older son by his first wife, the twenty-eight-year-old Thomas Powell Jr., who had earlier received generous gifts from his father, the co-executor and overseer of the estate and co-guardian of Rawleigh in partnership with a nephew named John Gibson.[39] Since the will makes no mention of Thomas Powell's adult daughter, Ann, whose mother had been accused of adultery, Powell might have doubted she was his daughter.[40] A year later, Thomas Powell Jr. also died, and the court named Nathaniel Browne, a *Powell's Quarter* neighbor, as co-executor.[41] Then Jane Catesby Powell appeared before the court with her new husband, John Kyrby.[42] She petitioned the justices for two-thirds of *Powell's Quarter*, one-third from the jointure and one-third from her lifetime interest as a widow. She and her husband also petitioned the court to give them guardianship of young Rawleigh, the remaining share of *Powell's Quarter* and the executorship of the other assets of the estate. The court granted her the two-thirds share of *Powell's Quarter*, but left the other assets and custody of Rawleigh in the hands of the court-appointed overseers.[43]

What the court declined to turn over to John and Jane Kyrby, the overseers subsequently provided. John Gibson and Nathaniel Browne withdrew from their positions as court-appointed guardians and overseers, in which they had served only one year. The court then appointed John Kyrby to be the guardian of Rawleigh Powell and overseer of the estate, putting him and his wife in full control of *Powell's Quarter* and all the Powell assets.[44] There is no way to know if John Gibson and Nathaniel Browne received any compensation from the Kyrbys for stepping aside to let them take full control of Thomas Powell's estate, but the relationship between the Kyrbys and their longtime neighbor Nathaniel Browne would prove to be a vexing issue for John Bertrand when he purchased *Powell's Quarter* twenty years later.

Rawleigh Powell was single and about twenty-one years of age at the time of his death in the spring of 1687. Having come into his inheritance at the age of eighteen, he was apparently sharing the management of the plantation with his stepfather, John Kyrby.[45] Jane Catesby Kyrby was deceased, leaving John Kyrby control of her one-third life share of *Powell's Quarter*. Rawleigh was living at the lower or east end of the plantation near Deep Creek, where archaeological studies have found evidence of an early eighteenth-century building.[46] His will assigned 300 acres of this section of *Powell's Quarter* to his sister, Ann Powell Dacres,[47] wife of North Farnham minister Charles Dacres.[48] John Kyrby was living in the original home of Thomas Powell Sr. at the upper or western end of the property where evidence of seventeenth-century European settlement has been unearthed.[49] Rawleigh's will gave Kyrby 200 acres of this portion of the plantation. Receiving this land as a bequest gave him the legal authority to sell his interest in the plantation, an action he could not have taken with his wife's life interest.[50]

When John Bertrand purchased the plantation, he oriented it to the Deep Creek side to exploit its potential for trading operations. Consequently, he chose to live in or near Rawleigh Powell's house in the eastern section of the plantation rather than the western site favored by Thomas Powell and John Kyrby.[51] The location John Bertrand selected also gave his home the kind of panoramic view of the Rappahannock River and the wide mouth of Deep Creek that was favored by aristocratic Virginians of the seventeenth century.[52] Locating the plantation house near the water also emphasized its connection to the superb water transportation system of the Chesapeake region that opened onto Virginia's Atlantic world.

Powell's Quarter did not remain divided for long. After the death of her husband, Ann Dacres re-married and by the fall of 1690 had sold her 300 acres to William Loyd. She knew Loyd as one of the most prominent members of the North Farnham Parish, where her deceased husband had served as minister. In December 1690, William Loyd filed a patent on this land.[53] In February 1692, John Kyrby, then living in Rappahannock County, also gave up his portion of the plantation, which he had patented in 1691. A few months after William Loyd's death, Kyrby sold the remaining 200 acres to William's son John for 20,000 pounds of tobacco.[54] With this transaction, John Loyd completed the pair of acquisitions that had been delayed by his father's death in late 1691.[55] With these transactions the family had put back in place the original 500-acre tract of Thomas Powell.

The surviving records indicate that John Bertrand was serving two parishes in the spring of 1692: North Farnham in Rappahannock County and St. Mary's Whitechapel in Lancaster County. Bertrand appears in records of both counties from 1690 to 1693.[56] Since these two parishes had a history of sharing ministers with adjacent parishes, it is not surprising that John Bertrand was dividing his time between the two during the early 1690s. Neither parish had a glebe house for a minister at this time. When Whitechapel shared a minister with the neighboring Christ Church Parish, the clergyman lived in the glebe house located near that church. In 1692, Andrew Jackson was serving as minister of Christ Church and was in possession of its glebe.[57]

Powell's Quarter was centrally located to the two parishes John Bertrand was serving when he purchased the plantation in 1692. It was five miles by land or water from Whitechapel Church and eleven miles by water from the North Farnham Church. John Loyd could have rented the *Powell's Quarter* homes of John Kyrby or Rawleigh Powell to the Bertrands before selling the plantation to them. The possibility that the Bertrands moved to the plantation early is supported by the language of the 1692 deed for the plantation identifying John Bertrand already residing in Lancaster County.

The Loyds certainly knew that John Bertrand had arrived from England with money to purchase a plantation. Bertrand made a down payment on a Rappahannock County plantation soon after arriving in Virginia. The failure of the seller, Henry Lucas, to close on the sale in early 1688 was adjudicated in the Rappahannock County court during William's time as a justice.[58] As merchants themselves, the Loyds would have valued John Bertrand's Huguenot Atlantic trading network and could have been pursuing joint mercantile ventures with him.

John Bertrand's merchant ambitions and ministry responsibilities were not the only factors that influenced his choice of a plantation. By the end of 1689, John was boarding and educating the sons of a wealthy Virginia lawyer and planter. On July 10, 1690, William Fitzhugh wrote to Nicholas Hayward in London that he had been planning to send his oldest son, William, to school in London because there were no adequate schools in Virginia. He went on to explain he changed his mind after a chance meeting with John Bertrand. He wrote, "But accidentally meeting with a French Minister, a sober, learned, and discreet Gentleman, whom I persuaded to board and tutor him, which he had undertaken, in whose family there is nothing but French spoken which by continual Converse, will make him perfect in that tongue, and he takes great pains to teach him Latin, both which go on hitherto very well together."[59]

Fitzhugh then placed an order for the books that were needed for his son's course of study: three Latin grammars, three French common prayer books (*La Liturgie*), and a French and Latin dictionary. He then added that the French minister/tutor had asked for a "chaise roulant," a small buggy for ground transportation. He placed that order in these words, "Therefore Sir, I desire you will purchase me one of them and send it in the first Conveniency. I would have one as strong, plain, and light as I could, for as he says he approves of the lightest sort for this Country."[60] Fitzhugh was compensating Bertrand in part by delivering a surrey without "the fringe on top." War with

France and problems with pirates apparently delayed delivery of the "chaise roulant," but Fitzhugh was also making payments to Bertrand in pound sterling. These payments provided a substantial boost to Bertrand's annual income, and payment in sterling protected him from the wild fluctuations in the price of tobacco that played havoc with his clergy salary, which was paid in tobacco. Letters from Fitzhugh to Nicholas Hayward in London on July 14, 1692; July 23, 1692; July 31, 1693; and December 19, 1693, authorize Hayward to make fourteen pound sterling payments to "Mr. Bertrand."[61]

Fitzhugh's decision to place his son with John Bertrand was no doubt influenced by the fact that French language and French culture were of major importance for European aristocrats by the middle of the seventeenth century. Fitzhugh would have known that Huguenot ministers were in high demand as tutors in England. John Locke, who had made an extensive tour of France, was a leading advocate of hiring Huguenot tutors.[62]

The records suggest Bertrand was augmenting his income by tutoring the Fitzhugh sons and perhaps a small number of other "live-in" students.[63] Combining ministry with teaching had long been a common practice among Huguenot ministers.[64] Bertrand's teaching relationship with the Fitzhugh family would continue until 1698 and include William's second son, Henry. Writing to George Mason on July 21, 1698, Fitzhugh reported that he was sending Henry to London to continue his education, which had been supervised by "A most ingenious French Gentleman, a Minister who had the government and tutorage of him, and indeed did it singularly well, but the unhealthfulness of his Seat and the sickliness of the child, occasioned his remove from thence."[65] Fitzhugh correspondence and family records suggest Henry lived with his French tutor from 1689 to 1697 (from age three to age eleven). The adult Henry Fitzhugh was recognized as a distinguished scholar who served the colony in significant governance roles.[66]

William Fitzhugh had emigrated from England as a young man in 1672. He was from a Bedford, England, family that had been successful in business and civil service. His father was a well-to-do woolen draper who had fallen on hard times but nonetheless found a way to provide his son with a good education. William had used his legal education and an advantageous Virginia marriage to become a wealthy lawyer and planter in the new world. The account of Durand de Dauphiné calls attention to the wealth and status Fitzhugh attained in Virginia by describing the hospitality he provided to travelers. When Durand arrived at Fitzhugh's home on the Potomac in December 1686, he was part of a group of twenty travelers. Fitzhugh had enough beds for all the guests, with most sleeping two to a bed. Durand was impressed by the high style in which Fitzhugh entertained them: "He treated us royally, there was good wine and all kinds of beverages, so there was a great deal of carousing. He had sent for three fiddlers, a jester, a tight-rope dancer, an acrobat who tumbled around, and they gave us all the entertainment we could wish for."[67] Fitzhugh's hospitality did not end when the travelers departed from his home. He sent them wine and bowls of punch to enjoy at the shore as they prepared to cross over to Maryland. He also loaned them his sloop so they could make the crossing in comfort.[68]

William Fitzhugh's close relationship with the Northern Neck Proprietary put him in position to be very helpful to John Bertrand as he looked to acquire a plantation. Fitzhugh was the lawyer for the Proprietary when the 30,000-acre Brent Town tract for Huguenot immigrants was patented in 1687. He was known to be sympathetic toward the Proprietary at a time when most Virginia elites living within its boundaries wanted to challenge its authority. This led to Fitzhugh and his law partner, George Brent, being named as agents of the Proprietary. While they received their formal instructions from the Lords Proprietors on November 3, 1693, Fitzhugh claimed to have been a lawful agent of the Proprietary as early as January 6, 1692, a few months before John Bertrand purchased his plantation.[69]

On May 11, 1692, John Loyd sold the 500-acre *Powell's Quarter* plantation to John Bertrand for 200 pounds in current English money. Payment in pound sterling was unusual in Virginia during this era, when most land transactions were done in tobacco.[70] The fact that John Loyd sold this property only three months after acquiring the final portion of it suggests he and his father purchased it with John Bertrand in mind. The desirable location of the plantation made it a prime property that would have attracted interest from some of Lancaster's leading merchants. The extensive shoreline of the plantation relatively near the mouth of the Rappahannock River and the potential for Deep Creek to provide a protected landing for transatlantic ships would almost certainly have drawn the attention of Lancaster's merchant families. The circumstances of the sale suggest John Loyd did not take the time to test the market with members of the Lancaster gentry.

The evidence also suggests the Loyds did not "flip" this property to John Bertrand for a large profit. Based on the 1688 conversion rate of tobacco to pound sterling, the cost of the 200 acres purchased from John Kyrby was just over eighty pounds sterling. If a similar price per acre was paid by the Loyds for Ann Dacres's 300 acres, their cost for acquiring *Powell's Quarter* was approximately the same as the sales price to John Bertrand. These transactions apparently resulted in a modest profit or loss for the Loyds. The language of the deed and later litigation between Loyd and Bertrand indicate John Bertrand paid something less than sixty-six pounds sterling as a down payment at the time the sale was closed. Bertrand still owed 134 pounds sterling several years later and remained in debt to John Loyd for more than a decade. By setting the sales price and future mortgage payments in pound sterling rather than tobacco, Loyd protected himself from the wild fluctuations in the price of tobacco that were common during these years, leaving John Bertrand heavily exposed to this significant risk.[71]

The deed drawn up by John Loyd was unusually long for a land document of this period. It gave the standard boundaries of *Powell's Quarter* and described the descent of the property from Thomas Powell to his son Rawleigh Powell, who passed it on to his sister and stepfather, from whom the Loyds purchased it. The deed stated that John Loyd owned the full 500 acres through his inheritance from his father, William Loyd. The reference in the deed to the property being "discharged . . . from all former gifts, grants, and joyntures" suggests Loyd knew that one-third of the plantation had gone to Jane Kyrby as a jointure for her marriage to Thomas Powell. There can be little doubt that Loyd's father was familiar with some of the details of the Thomas Powell/Jane Catesby marriage and the subsequent Powell estate proceedings. Loyd's deed was predicated on the understanding that the will of Rawleigh Powell had "discharged" the Catesby jointure and any residual life share accruing to Kyrby so that the plantation was legally in his possession.

The deed also states that the sale of the property to John Bertrand was in accordance with the provisions of William Loyd's will. While no record of the will survives, the language of the deed implies that William Loyd set out to acquire the property to make it available to John Bertrand, perhaps with the knowledge that Bertrand could not pay the full price up front. The deed offers no explanation for the instructions William Loyd issued to his son in his will. Did he offer *Powell's Quarter* to John Bertrand on favorable terms to seal a business relationship between them or to tie the minister to the North Farnham Parish? William Loyd's motive for acquiring the plantation for John Bertrand remains a matter of conjecture.

One of the witnesses to the deed was Robert Carter, the wealthiest citizen of Lancaster County, whose niece was married to John Loyd. The other witnesses were Edwin Conway of Lancaster County and John Tavernor of Rappahannock County and North Farnham Parish.[72] The witnessing signature of John Tavernor makes clear the continuing interest of leaders of North Farnham in John Bertrand. Tavernor might also have been interested in Bertrand because he was a member of a Huguenot family that had been in Virginia since the late 1630s. The involvement of Tavernor and Loyd in John Bertrand's acquisition of *Powell's Quarter* and their support of him the next year, when the North Farnham vestry, which had hired Bertrand, was dissolved, points to a significant level of investment by both of them in the welfare of this Huguenot-Anglican minister.

The name of Robert Carter on this deed is ironic because when controversy erupted the year after Bertrand's purchase of *Powell's Quarter*, it went to the court where Carter was a leading justice. When John Bertrand purchased the plantation, he knew it came with surplus land that had never been patented. The marsh land Thomas Powell had chosen not to patent in 1650 had, through the changing course of the river, gradually developed into more solid ground by the time Bertrand acquired the plantation, and 444 acres of this now-valuable land was situated along Deep Creek between the plantations of John Bertrand and Nathaniel Browne. As the new owner of one of the plantations framing this land, John Bertrand expected to control a significant portion of it. Because the Deep Creek shoreline contained in the 500-acre Thomas Powell tract was not sufficient to support a protected landing and tobacco trans-shipment business, John Bertrand was keen to acquire a healthy slice of the surplus land. With William Fitzhugh's appointment to be one of the agents of the Northern Neck Proprietary about the time John Bertrand purchased *Powell's Quarter*, he had every reason to believe he had the "inside track" to acquire a major portion of the plantation's now-valuable contiguous property.[73]

There was, however, a serious obstacle standing in John Bertrand's way. Lancaster records suggest that Bertrand's neighbor Nathaniel Browne was already making regular use of the surplus land. Browne's construction of a house relatively near *Powell's Quarter* indicates that he was actively managing most of the unassigned land long before John Bertrand became his neighbor.[74] The question that cannot be answered from the records is whether the Kyrbys gave Browne a deed or lease permitting him to do what he wanted with the surplus land in exchange for his decision in 1671 to give up his court-appointed position as overseer of the Powell estate and guardian of Rawleigh Powell.

Nathaniel Browne was Thomas Powell's neighbor on Deep Creek by 1656. Court records show that when Browne and fellow emigrant George Vezey arrived in the colony about 1650, they were servants of Thomas Cooper, a neighbor of Powell on Deep Creek. When Cooper died in January 1657, the servants convinced the court that their master intended to bequeath his estate to them but died before drawing up his will.[75] Together they patented Cooper's 200 hundred acres on Deep Creek and purchased 250 contiguous acres from David Fox, a Lancaster merchant and court justice.[76] Vezey signed his Deep Creek holdings over to Browne in 1665, the year before his death. In 1668, Browne took out a patent in his name for 480 acres on Deep Creek he had previously owned with Vezey. While Nathaniel Browne's plantation was clearly a successful one, he was not in the upper echelon of Lancaster County planters.[77]

Any understanding that John Kyrby and Nathaniel Browne had for the division of the surplus land would have been confirmed through a procedure established by the Virginia Assembly in 1662 and implemented by local parish leaders. This law called for the church wardens of each parish to head off property disputes by walking property lines with landowners once every four years. Boundary markers were to be refreshed, and new owners were to be appraised of the landmarks that demarcated the lines. If landowners disagreed about the boundaries, the church wardens reviewed the documents and if necessary appointed two disinterested residents to make the determination.[78] The parish records that could document the results of this processioning during the twenty years Kyrby and Browne shared this unassigned land have been lost. However, extant parish records that begin in 1739 indicate that processioning in Whitechapel Parish was performed on a regular basis every four years. If processioning was also performed in the parish during the last quarter of the seventeenth century, parish officials would have recorded the boundaries to which these two men agreed.[79]

The understanding that apparently existed between Nathaniel Browne and John Kyrby (and possibly Rawleigh Powell and Ann Dacres) allowing Browne to control most of the surplus land was not one John Bertrand was willing to accept. In July 1693, Bertrand filed a lawsuit that was the opening act of a documented land controversy that would drag on for more than five years. The next chapter will show that this legal dispute was part of a hard-fought struggle over another imperialist policy Virginia elites aggressively resisted.

NOTES

1. Davis, *William Fitzhugh and His Chesapeake World*, 270–71; Jack P. Greene, "From John Smith to Adam Smith: Virginia and the Founding Conventions of English Long-Distance Settler Colonization," in *Virginia 1619: Slavery and Freedom in the Making of English America*, ed. Paul Musselwhite, Peter C. Mancall, and James Horn (Chapel Hill, NC, 2019), 305–07.

2. Bond, *Damed Souls*, 177–179; April Lee Hatfield, "Dutch and New Netherland Merchants in the Seventeenth-Century English Chesapeake," in *The Atlantic Economy During the Seventeenth and Eighteenth Centuries: Organization, Operation, Practice, and Personnel*, ed., Peter A. Coclanis (Columbia, SC, 2005), 207.

3. For the internationalist orientation of Huguenot merchants from western France, see R. C. Nash, "Huguenot Merchants and the Development of South Carolina's Slave-Plantation and Atlantic Trading Economy, 1680–1775," in *Memory and Identity: The Huguenots in France and the Atlantic Diaspora*, eds., Van Ruymbeke and Sparks, 194–203.

4. CZ, 5 and 25, ADCMLR.

5. Notaire Tourneur, 3E, 26/1086, folio 244–245, ADCMLR.

6. Hatfield, *Atlantic Virginia*, 97–103, and 145–48.

7. Hermann Wellenreuther, "The Meaning of Early Modern North Atlantic History: Jacob Leisler, Commerce, Piety, Kinship, and Politics," in *Jacob Leisler's Atlantic*

World in the Later Seventeenth Century: Essays on Religion, Militia, Trade, and Networks, ed., Hermann Wellenreuther (Munster, 2009), 166–67.

8. For documentation of the Cozes Huguenot network in English America, see Lee, "The Transatlantic Legacy of the Protestant Church of Cozes," 36–54.

9. CZ, 7 and 52, ADCMLR; Butler, *Huguenots in America,* 157.

10. Bosher, *Huguenot Merchants,* 94–96; Baird, vol. 2, 141 (note 2); CZ, 41, ADCMLR.

11. MR/R/R/032/08, LMA. After receiving a grant from the Royal Bounty to immigrate to Boston, Diane (Dina) married Isaac Bertrand du Tuffeau in Massachusetts about 1690. Tuffeau helped organize Gabriel Bernon's ill-fated Huguenot settlement at Oxford, RBP, Ms 2, fol. 7 (Rochefoucault), HL; Baird (1885), vol. 2, 259.

12. Hatfield, *Atlantic Virginia,* 39–59, and 145–50.

13. For the wine-producing activities of Charlotte Bertrand's mother, Judith André, and John Bertrand's uncle, Jean André, see Notaire Bargignac, 3E 128/49, folio 23, ADCMLR, and Notaire Tourneur, 3E 26/1086, folio 244–45, ADCMLR. For the common practice of distilling Saintonge wines into brandy and cognac for export, see Lougee, *Facing the Revocation,* 28 and 168, and Karen MacNeil, *The Wine Bible* (New York, 2001), 157–59.

14. Dangibeaud, *Minutes de Notaires,* BR 5842, ADCMLR.

15. For the Huguenot merchant practice of connecting Protestant family members in exile with the "Catholic" home office in France, see Susanne Lachenicht, "Diaspora Networks and Immigration Policies," in *A Companion to the Huguenots,* eds., Raymond A. Mentzer and Bertrand Van Ruymbeke (Leiden, 2016), 261.

16. J. H. Elliott, "The Iberian Atlantic and Virginia," in *The Atlantic World and Virginia, 1550–1624,* ed., Mancall, 554–57.

17. Hatfield, *Atlantic Virginia,* 137–38.

18. ORC OB, 1686–1692, no. 2, 297.

19. "Colonial Tithables," Research Notes No. 17, 2, LVA.

20. John C. Coombs, "A New Chronology for the Rise of Slavery in Early Virginia," WMQ 68, no. 3 (July 2011), 352–54.

21. SP, LC OB, *1695–1699,* 103; SP LC OB, 1699–1701, 12–15, 23, 35, 65, 68, 77, and 81.

22. LC WB, 1690–1709, 10. Three enslaved women were named in John Bertrand's will: Sue, Katy, and Doly. Two enslaved runaways named Jack and Tom were returned to John Bertrand by Lancaster County officials in 1700.

23. Van Ruymbeke, *From New Babylon to Eden,* 216.

24. Jon Butler, *Awash in a Sea of Faith: Christianizing the American People* (Cambridge, MA, 1992), 135–42.

25. The earliest documented use of the name *Belle Isle* is in the 1778 obituary of John and Charlotte Bertrand's great-grandson Thomas Bertrand Griffin, *The Virginia Gazette,* Dixon and Hunter, May 8, 1778, 7, Colonial Williamsburg Digital Library.

26. William and Mary Center for Archeological Research, William H. Moore, David W. Lewes, and Joe B. Jones, *Archeological Evaluation of Sites 44LA147 and 44LA175, Belle Isle State Park, Lancaster County, Virginia* (Williamsburg, VA, 2006), 3–16 (hereafter cited as WMCAR-2006).

82 Chapter Four

27. Ibid., 3, 4, and 17. For a description of the Powhatan Algonquins, see Hatfield, *Atlantic Virginia*, 8–13.

28. Jett, *Lancaster County, Virginia*, 17–19, 32–35, and 39.

29. Robert A. Wheeler, *Lancaster County, Virginia, 1650–1750: The Evolution of a Southern Tidewater Community* (Brown University Phd. Dissertation, 1972), 14–16. Wheeler estimates that as many as 15,000 settlers might have moved into the Northern Neck within a few years.

30. Land Office Patents No. 2, 1643–1651, 288 (hereafter cited as LOP), LVA.

31. Nugent, *Cavaliers and Pioneers*, vol. 1, 76. More detailed information about Thomas Powell is offered in Lee, *A Brief History of Belle Isle Plantation*, 7–13.

32. William Lindsay Hopkins, *Isle of Wight County, Virginia Deeds, 1647–1710, Court Orders, 1693–1695, and Guardian Accounts, 1740–1767* (Athens, GA, 1993), 4; SP, LC DWB, 1654–1661, 6.

33. SP, LC OB, 1656–1661, 39 and 96; SP LC OB, 1662–1666, 12, 31, 62, and 92.

34. Thomas Powell patented 700 acres on the west side of the Corrotoman in June 1658. LOP no. 4, 1655–1664, 223, LVA. He probably controlled more acres in that area in partnership with his brother Howell. Records show that the brothers aggressively speculated with this land, finally selling a large tract in June 1659, SP (1991), LC DWB, 1654–1661, 12–13, 67–68, and 110, Fleet, vol. 1, 131 and 219, and Nugent, *Cavaliers and Pioneers*, vol. 1, 360.

35. SP, LC OB, 1656–1661, 50. Neither this Thomas Powell nor his son Thomas Powell Jr. should be confused with the Thomas Powell who married Mary Place, daughter of Francis Place, on September 30, 1666, in Rappahannock County. Robert K. Headley, *Married Well and Often: Marriages of the Northern Neck of Virginia, 1649–1800* (Baltimore, 2003), 287.

36. SP, LC OB, 1662–1666, 19.

37. SP, LC DWB, 1661–1702, 42–43.

38. LC OB, I, 141. Thomas Powell's will was never recorded and is archived among the loose papers at LVA. Craig M. Kilby located the will and abstracted it.

39. SP, LC DWB, 1661–1702, 62.

40. Horn, *Adapting to a New World*, 365.

41. SP, LC OB, 1666–1669, 101.

42. More detailed information about John Kyrby is provided in Lee, *A Brief History of Belle Isle Plantation*, 18–23.

43. SP, LC OB, 1670–1674, 21 and 26.

44. Ibid., 27.

45. SP, LC OB, 1682–1687, 50 and 52.

46. WMCAR-2006.

47. SP, ORC DWB, 1672–1676, Part I, 60; SP, ORC OB, 1685–1687, 81. Ann Dacres next married William Tomlyn and died before September 2, 1691. SP, ORC OB, 1689–1692, 19 and 71.

48. Raleigh Powell's will divides the plantation at "the bridges." The bridges are also mentioned in a lease agreement between William Bertrand and Charles Ewell in 1719. Taken together, these references suggest the bridges were located near the head of Thomas Creek on a part of the plantation that extends northwest into the low-lying

land and marshes running to Mulberry Creek. LC DWB, no. 11, 136–37. A 1670 map by Augustine Hermann confirms the description of *Powell's Quarter* in Rawleigh Powell's will.

49. James River Institute for Archeology, Inc., *Phase I Archeological Survey of Belle Isle, Lancaster County, Virginia* (Jamestown, VA, 1992), 54–55.

50. LC WB, vol. 5, 1674–1689, 109; SP, LC OB, 1682–1687, 106.

51. The decision of John and Charlotte to live on the eastern side of the plantation is confirmed by the power of attorney issued to Charlotte Bertrand in England in 1706. This legal document lists her living in Lancaster County "upon Deep Creek in Virginia," SP, LC DB, 1706–1710, 13.

52. Rhys Isaac, *The Transformation of Virginia, 1740–1790* (Chapel Hill, NC, 1982), 32, 33, and 35.

53. NNG no. 1, 1690–1692, 16–18, LVA.

54. LC DB, vol. 7, 1687–1700, 54; Brock Collection, BR Box 227-3, folio 119, Huntington Library, San Marino, California. Kyrby died in Richmond County in 1698. SP, RC OB, 1697–1699, 38.

55. William Loyd, who was a court justice in Rappahannock County, does not appear in court records after October 1691. He married the wealthy widow of Moore Fauntleroy in 1666. Wright, *Essex County, Virginia Marriage References*, 71.

56. SP, LC WB, 1690–1709, 12–13; SP, ORC OB, 1686–1692, no. 2, 297 and 316.

57. Robert Teagle, "Mean Tobacco and a Well-Beloved Minister: Andrew Jackson of Christ Church Parish, 1686–1710," *Northern Neck of Virginia Historical Magazine* 52 (December 2002), 6238.

58. ORC OB, 1686–1692, no. 2, 68, 71, 72.

59. Davis, *William Fitzhugh and His Chesapeake World*, 270–71.

60. Fitzhugh acknowledged receipt of the French books in a letter to Hayward dated July 14, 1692. Ibid., 270–71, 290, 291, and 306.

61. Ibid., 306, 313, 318, and 320.

62. Green, "A Huguenot Education for the Early Modern Nobility," 73–91.

63. Richard Beale Davis, *Intellectual life in the Colonial South, 1585–1763* (Knoxville, TN, 1978), 302.

64. For Huguenot ministers in London combining ministry and teaching, see Anthony Chamier, "A Refugee Minister Comes to London: Daniel Chamier, 1661–1698," *The Huguenot Society Journal* 30, no. 1 (2013), 52–72.

65. Davis, *William Fitzhugh and His Chesapeake World*, 361.

66. Stuart E. Brown Jr., *Annals of Clarke County, Virginia* (Berryville, VA, 1983), 226–36; George Harrison Sanford King, *The Register of Overwharton Parish, Stafford County, Virginia, 1723–1758*, and *Sundry Historical and Genealogical Notes, Fredericksburg, Virginia* (Fredericksburg, VA, 1961), 224–25.

67. Durand, 158.

68. Ibid., 159.

69. Davis, *William Fitzhugh and His Chesapeake World*, 42, note 80. Fitzhugh's partner, George Brent, had an official role with the Northern Neck Proprietary from 1683, when he was appointed to serve as receiver general for the counties of Stafford and Rappahannock. SP, ORC DWB, 1682–1686, 24.

70. LC DWB, Book 7, 1687–1700, 56–57.

71. For the wild fluctuations in the price of tobacco between 1688 and 1705, see Emily Jones Salmon and John Salmon, "Tobacco in Colonial Virginia," *Encyclopedia Virginia*, Virginia Foundation for the Humanities.

72. John Loyd married Robert Carter's niece, Elizabeth, daughter of the deceased John Carter, in 1690. Elizabeth died of the measles in November 1693. Headley, *Married Well and Often,* 229. Edwin Conway had a close relationship with John Tavernor. These two were co-administrators of the estate of Thomas Georg, a member of a French Protestant family who died in 1683. SP, ORC WB, 1682–1687, 17–18.

73. John Bertrand's 1698 patent from the Northern Neck Proprietary references 424 acres of surplus land on Deep Creek adjacent to the original 500-acre Thomas Powell patent. NNG No. 2, 1694–1700, 293–95, LVA.

74. Lancaster court records reveal that Nathaniel Browne was renting a house on the surplus land to Thomas Norser. SP, LC OB, 1691–1695, 64–65.

75. Browne and Vezey were two of the ten persons on the transportation head-right list by which Thomas Powell patented his Rappahannock River plantation in 1650. Nugent, *Cavaliers and Pioneers,* vol. 1, 209. For the George Vezey/Nathaniel Browne partnership, see Ibid., 345, 346, 438, and 514, and SP, LC OB, 1656–1661, 55 and 61. For their role as servants of Thomas Cooper and their inheritance of his estate, see SP, LC DWB, 1652–1657, 132, and SP LC DWB, 1654–1661, 63.

76. For Nathaniel Browne and George Vezey's patent of Thomas Cooper's Deep Creek land, see LOP No. 5, 1661–1666, vols. 1 and 2, Part 1, 369 and 537, LVA. For their purchase of more Deep Creek land from David Fox, see LOP No. 4, 1655–1664, 137, LVA.

77. For George Vezey's gift of his share of the Deep Creek land to Nathaniel Browne and documentation of their 1657 deed for property bordering the land of Thomas Powell, see SP, LC DWB, 1661–1702, 66. For Nathaniel Browne's April 20, 1668, patent for 480 acres on Deep Creek, see LOP and Grants No. 6, 1666–1679, Parts 1 and 2, 138, LVA. For tithable listings for Nathaniel Browne, see SP, LC OB, 1666–1669, SP, LC OB, 1674–1678, SP, LC OB, 1678–1681, SP, LC OB, 1682–1687, and SP, LC OB, 1687–1691.

78. For the processioning of boundary lines in colonial Virginia, see Tarter, "Evidence of Religion in Seventeenth-Century Virginia," 32, and William H. Seiler, "Land Processioning in Colonial Virginia," WMQ 6, 3rd series (1949), 426–30.

79. For the processioning activities regularly carried out by the Parish of St. Mary's Whitechapel for 1739 and following years, see Margaret H. Tupper, ed., *Christ Church Parish, Lancaster County, Vestry Book, 1739–1786* (Irvington, VA,1990), 8, 22, 29, 36, and 41.

Chapter Five

Deep Creek, 1694

> It might be . . . fit to transport some of . . . the poor French Protestants who might all live comfortably there, and have land at an easie rate.
>
> —James Blair and John Locke, *The Present Constitution of Virginia*, The Board of Trade, London, September 2, 1697

The controversy ignited by John Bertrand's legal claim to the surplus land along Deep Creek was contested under the shadow of a much larger struggle between Virginia elites and empire planners in London over the distribution of unassigned land in the colony.[1] English imperial policy emphasized the granting of available land in small parcels to encourage immigration to the colony. But the aristocratic Virginians serving on the Council, who controlled the process of granting land, regularly subverted the policy by using this resource to benefit large planters like themselves. During the 1690s, the aggressive activities of the Virginia agents of the Northern Neck Proprietary became a flashpoint in this struggle over the distribution of land. The Proprietary was an imperialist project that loomed as a truly ominous threat to Virginia elites as well as most Northern Neck landholders. The lawsuit John Bertrand filed in Lancaster County Court in July 1693 offers a revealing window onto this larger land-distribution controversy.

By 1690 patent holders in Lancaster County had been locked in a twenty-year struggle to secure the titles to their long-standing land grants and to clarify their obligations to pay taxes on these grants. The county was part of the Northern Neck Proprietary, which encompassed at least one million acres of land and by some estimates as much as five million acres bounded by the Potomac and Rappahannock Rivers. This huge land grant was contrived in 1649 by King Charles II to reward seven of his supporters while he was in exile in France following his father's execution. This gift of Virginia land, which had opened for European settlement the previous year, held no value to the Proprietors until Charles II returned to England to assume the throne in 1660.

Colonial proprietary ventures were a common feature of the Atlantic world in the sixteenth, seventeenth, and early eighteenth centuries. Spain, France, the Netherlands, and England made use of this device to spread their Atlantic empires. The English used proprietorships to encourage the settlement of Virginia, Maryland, Pennsylvania, South Carolina, and the West Indies. Charters were issued to corporations or individuals giving them power to recruit settlers, defend frontier boundaries, carry out governmental functions, and own land as a way of developing colonies. This method of extending imperial influence across the Atlantic was an adaptation of the medieval system of feudalism. Authority was delegated to loyal subjects who ruled on behalf of the sovereign and in return received certain benefits for rendering faithful service. Proprietors sometimes worked in concert with local colonial interests and were sometimes very much at odds with them.[2]

The language of Charles II's grant to the "Lords Proprietors" of the Northern Neck makes no reference to recruiting or organizing settlers and speaks in the most vague terms of governance responsibilities. The grant spells out the rights and privileges of the Proprietors to operate as barons over their domain. They are empowered to build castles and fortresses as needed; collect rents from tenants; hold mineral rights (reserving gold and silver for the king); establish towns, churches, schools; and appoint clergy and teachers. This grant looks less like a charter for colonization than a scheme by which a king rewards feudal vassals and creates a mechanism for assigning and taxing land.[3] Between 1649 and the return of Charles II to England to claim his throne in 1660, settlers from other parts of Virginia (and some from England) poured into the Northern Neck. They patented land, established counties, and built churches by the authority of the governor and the Council, all the while oblivious to the Lords Proprietors the king had delegated to rule over them. With Virginia's governor and the Council busy making Northern Neck land grants, usually to benefit the colony's wealthiest planters, they were already on a collision course with the king's chosen barons of the Northern Neck.[4]

Portrait of Charles II Issuing the Northern Neck Proprietary Grant in 1649. Painting by an unknown artist.
Courtesy Westmoreland County Museum, Westmoreland, Virginia

By 1670, the Proprietors began to pay attention to their Northern Neck domain. It soon became clear that while they had no interest in living in Virginia, they were keen to manage the land. They launched an effort to register the grants in place prior to 1669 and to issue new grants for lands not yet assigned. Colonial landowners in Virginia were subject to a form of taxation on their land called "quit rents." These were to be paid to the Crown to support the cost of administering the colony. This tax, however, was only sporadically collected at the direction of the governor and the Council. When landowners in the Northern Neck learned in 1670 that they were suddenly required to pay this tax to the Proprietary and not to colonial officials, their resistance to paying it became much stronger. Recognizing how threatening the Northern Neck Proprietary was to his governing authority, Governor William Berkeley worked to delay its implementation while he developed a plan to buy out the Proprietors, a plan that collapsed when Bacon's Rebellion emerged as an even greater threat in 1676.[5] In response to the controversy surrounding the taxes claimed by the Proprietary, its Virginia-based agents were, until about 1690, rather half-hearted in their attempts to collect them.[6]

By 1681, Thomas Lord Culpepper succeeded in buying out most of the other shareholders in the Proprietary.[7] His efforts to cash in on his valuable asset during his brief residence in Virginia as governor (1682–1683) met with little success.[8] While Lord Culpepper left Virginia frustrated by this turn of events, his blatant attempt to enrich himself at the colony's expense drew the ire of the next governor, Francis Howard, Baron of Effingham. Lord Howard campaigned against the Northern Neck Proprietary in letters to Charles II and the Lords of Trade, the special committee of the King's Privy Council responsible for the colonies. In these letters, Howard warned of the danger of unrest among colonists who were irate over the prospect of paying taxes to Culpepper. Writing in 1685, he urged his superiors to recognize "how improper and inconvenient it will be that there should be a proprietor in the midst of his Majesties' Dominion and render that part in some measure distinct from the Government, only his Majesty hath the worst part of it, the Trouble, the Proprietor the advantage."[9]

Neither Charles II nor the monarchs who followed him were convinced by Lord's Howard's warning about the destructive nature of the Proprietary. In 1688, King James II issued a new grant that was renewed the following year by William III.[10] Both wanted to strengthen the Crown's control over colonial affairs. With a huge swath of Northern Neck real estate yet to be assigned, they chose to keep in place the proprietary mechanism for distributing and taxing land in that part of Virginia.

At Thomas Lord Culpepper's death in 1689, his five-sixth share of this vast area went to his daughter Catherine Culpepper and her husband, Thomas, fifth Lord Fairfax of Cameron after their marriage in 1690. The remaining one-sixth was soon in the hands of Catherine's mother, Margaret Lady Culpepper. At their direction the agents for the Proprietary became much more aggressive in their efforts to collect "quit rents" in Lancaster and the other counties of the Northern Neck. By this time, the process of coming to terms with the Proprietary over the tax had become even more threatening for Northern Neck landholders because doing so required negotiating the payment of back taxes from the previous twenty years.[11]

The new level of assertiveness by which the agents of the Proprietary sought to collect "quit rent" taxes after 1690 is documented in the journals of the Council of Virginia. On June 5, 1690, the Council made a formal request to the Lords of Trade in London for the Crown to purchase the rights of the Proprietors. At the meeting of the Council on October 23, 1690, the board was informed that Proprietary agent Phillip Ludwell "pretendeth to be attorney or agent of the heirs of the late Lord Culpepper . . . and those acting under him may give great disturbance to the Inhabitants of the said Neck, and by that meanes hazard the Peace of this their Majesties' Dominion." This pre-eminent governing body and highest court of the colony (now working with Lieutenant Governor Francis Nicholson) was clearly threatened by the Proprietary's newly aggressive effort to usurp their authority to make land grants, manage escheated properties, and collect taxes. They issued an order to the Stafford County Court that it should no longer register deeds issued by the Proprietary as it had done the previous summer.[12] The Council also made another urgent appeal to the Lords of Trade in London to intervene on their behalf, "to implore his most Sacred Majesty to take the matter into his Gracious Consideration and to take Such Measures for the reliefe of the Inhabitants from their Great Oppression that they Justly feare may happen to them, as his Majesty in his Princely Clemency and Wisdom shall think fitt."[13]

The Council desperately wanted the king to buy out the Lords Proprietors to bring their disruptive activities in the colony to an end. There can be little doubt that the growing desperation of the wealthy members of the Council was less about protecting the "peace of the colony" than protecting the immense power they hoped to exercise in parceling out the huge swath of unassigned land in the Northern Neck. They soon recognized they could strengthen their campaign by making common cause with small and middling planters in the Northern Neck who had reasons of their own to resist paying "quit rents" to the Proprietors.[14]

One of the ways in which the Proprietary agents were giving "great disturbance" was through the filing of lawsuits. The authority of the Proprietary to tax landowners was closely related to its power to issue land grants. The first legal test for these grants was getting them registered in the county courts as the Stafford justices began doing in July 1690.[15] When legal disputes arose concerning these grants, lawsuits could be appealed to the governor and Council, who constituted the General Court of the colony. The full implementation of the authority of the Proprietary to issue land grants and levy taxes required legal recognition in the General Court and in all the the county courts of the Northern Neck. By 1690, the agents of the Proprietary were initiating test cases designed to establish the necessary legal basis for their activities.

Fitzhugh vs. Dade was a suit filed by John Bertrand's friend and client, William Fitzhugh, in June 1690. After receiving a deed from the Northern Neck Proprietary on escheated land, Fitzhugh tried to use it to evict Francis Dade, who held a lease from a deceased former owner. When Dade refused to leave, Fitzhugh filed a trespassing suit against him. Fitzhugh won his case in the Stafford County Court where he was an influential justice. The court ruled that the Northern Neck Proprietary deed issued to Fitzhugh was valid and then ordered that Francis Dade be evicted for trespassing.[16] However, when Francis Dade appealed the case to the governor and Council, the result was different. The record does not show the reasons the Council might have cited for overturning the case, but their ruling suggests they were unwilling to recognize the validity of a Proprietary deed. While Fitzhugh was not yet serving as the official agent of the Northern Neck Proprietary, he was already filing cases intended to force the Council to accept the authority of the Proprietary to manage escheated land and issue patents.[17]

In June 1692, the Council reacted with alarm to the litigation that was being initiated by agents of the Northern Neck Proprietary. In response to reports that these lawsuits were clogging the county courts, the Council complained that colonial subjects were suffering the burden of lawsuits they could not afford. The minutes of June 24, 1692, declared, "Complaints are made thereof by poore people who alleadge they are not able to stand Law-Suites," which disrupt the "peace and quiet of the Inhabitants of this Colony."[18] Claiming to be the advocates of the poor, the Council bemoaned the lawsuits generated by the Proprietary and its threat to their power.

When John Bertrand acquired *Powell's Quarter* in 1692, Lancaster County landholders were caught up in the "great disturbance," and most were resisting the payment of taxes to the Proprietors.[19] They were led in this struggle by Robert "King" Carter. It is not surprising that Carter was allied with the Council in this campaign. As the largest landholder in the county, he supported the efforts of the aristocratic members of the Council to subvert the policy of the Crown to encourage immigration to the colony through the wide distribution of unassigned lands in relatively small tracts.[20] In 1688, Carter had been very active in opposing the renewal of the Northern Neck Proprietary. He clearly wanted the governor and the Council to continue favoring people like him in the patenting of Northern Neck lands and the decisions they were making about the assessment of taxes on these lands. He used the attempt by the Proprietors to levy "quit rent" taxes on an annual schedule rather than the occasional basis of the Council as a populist "talking point" to unite the interests of elites like himself with small and middling planters.[21]

The deed for John Bertrand's purchase of *Powell's Quarter* from John Loyd included a surprising endorsement of the Northern Neck Proprietary. The deed noted that John Bertrand was to pay the stipulated "quit rent" on the property to the "Lords Proprietors." Most deeds at this time made no reference to "quit rents," and precious few specified this tax would be paid to the Proprietary. The deed further stated that the "Lords Proprietors" had the authority to issue deeds and grants on this property. The provisions of this land sale make clear that John Bertrand was affirming the legitimacy of the Northern Neck Proprietary in a way most of his neighbors were not willing to do in 1692. Bertrand's unusually positive view of the Northern Neck Proprietary was likely grounded in his close personal relationship with William Fitzhugh. The language of the deed also suggests Bertrand viewed English America through a Stuart imperialist lens that placed a high value on the Crown's control of colonial affairs.

John Bertrand's 1692 purchase of *Powell's Quarter* apparently coincided with an important transition in the use of the 444 acres of contiguous surplus land along Deep Creek. The marsh land that Thomas Powell apparently considered not worth patenting in 1650 gradually became a good resource as its vegetation was an excellent source of food for cattle. Virginia planters never penned up their livestock and sometimes let them graze and feed in marshes. The next stage in the evolution of this particular marsh land was the transition of part of it into a field for planting tobacco. As the river changed course creating new marshes, some of the older marsh land gradually dried out and at a certain point could be cultivated for crops. Some of the unassigned land on Deep Creek had by 1692 become a valuable agricultural asset for whomever controlled it.

The surplus land along Deep Creek was valuable to John Bertrand for another reason. Deep Creek offered a protected inlet along the Rappahannock River, deep enough for transatlantic ships to anchor for loading tobacco and unloading manufactured goods from the British Isles. As the surplus land along Deep Creek became less marshy, it could be developed as a trans-shipment point where planters could deliver their tobacco and store it for later shipment to England. This staging area would require a significant amount of land along the creek with road access for a tobacco warehouse and loading dock or wharf. The designation of Deep Creek as an official tobacco landing by the early 1720s[22] and the the appointment of John Bertrand's son, William, as county tobacco receiver in 1722[23] confirms this Bertrand business plan for their plantation.

By 1693, Nathaniel Browne had determined that some of the surplus land along Deep Creek was ready to be planted in tobacco. He found a tenant to live in the house he had previously built a short distance from the *Powell's*

Quarter boundary line. The tenant, Thomas Norser, was given the assignment of converting some of this former marsh land into a tobacco field.[24] The first step in developing a new tobacco field was to construct a fence to protect the field from the cattle and hogs grazing in the nearby woods and marsh.[25] When Norser brought in a large supply of fence posts and tobacco hogsheads, John Bertrand knew his neighbor was preparing to plant tobacco on the surplus land.

Bertrand decided to take action before the fences could be constructed and the fields planted. On July 12, 1693, he filed a trespassing suit against the tenant.[26] The legal basis of Bertrand's trespassing suit is not elucidated in the records. His deed from his purchase of *Powell's Quarter* would not have given him the ownership of this unassigned land that would be necessary to file such a suit. It seems likely that Bertrand had received some form of deed from the Northern Neck Proprietary granting him control of a major portion of the surplus land. If so, it is reasonable to imagine that William Fitzhugh was orchestrating this legal action on behalf of the Proprietary. To ensure that Browne and his tenant could not create the tobacco field while the court deliberated, Bertrand took possession of the fence posts and hogsheads. The justices referred the case to the court's next session so that Nathaniel Browne could be present to respond to Bertrand's allegation against his tenant.

Unexpected developments delayed the legal process John Bertrand had set in motion. Nathaniel Browne never appeared in court to answer Bertrand's suit. Less than two months after the minister filed the lawsuit, Browne was dead. On September 13, 1693, Nathaniel's widow, Ann Browne, filed his will for probate. John Bertrand's lawsuit could not go forward until the ownership of the Browne estate had been resolved.[27] Then on October 11, 1693, Thomas Norser notified the Lancaster County Court that he was leaving the county. He would not be creating the new tobacco field for the Brownes after all, and he would, therefore, no longer be a party to the lawsuit. When the court met on December 14, four Lancaster residents reported that Norser had left the county and had not settled his debts with them before leaving. He owed more than 3,000 pounds of tobacco, of which 1,000 was back rent for the Browne house in which he was living. The court authorized the creditors to seize any marked cattle belonging to Norser that happened to be grazing in the area. He, too, had been making use of the unassigned land for running cattle.[28]

Another twist in the court case unfolded during the December 14 court session. Stephen Tomlyn appeared on behalf of his wife, Ann, the widow and executrix of Nathaniel Browne.[29] Tomlyn, who had been a planter in Lancaster County for more than twenty years and a close associate of Nathaniel Browne, asked to be admitted as the defendant. Tomlyn had participated with Browne and George Vezey in the purchase of land in the northern part of Lancaster County in 1664.[30] Stephen Tomlyn's role as a witness to Rawleigh Powell's 1687 will suggests he was living in the Deep Creek area by that time.

Tomlyn presented to the court the title for the land his wife, Ann Browne Tomlyn, had inherited through Nathaniel Browne. Tomlyn claimed this document gave him ownership of Nathaniel Browne's plantation on Deep Creek and control of the land referenced in Bertrand's trespassing charge. After registering his ownership of the Browne property, Stephen Tomlyn requested that the court delay taking any action until a later date. The justices admitted Tomlyn as defendant and granted his request for a delay.[31] With this action by the court, *Bertrand vs. Norser and Browne* became *Bertrand vs. Tomlyn*.

When the Lancaster County Court next took up this lawsuit on February 14, 1694, the minister's relationship with the Northern Neck Proprietary was the elephant in the room. As the justices examined Bertrand's deed for *Powell's Quarter*, the language affirming the authority of the Proprietary would have leaped from the page. If Bertrand had another deed issued by the Proprietary for the surplus land, the atmosphere in the courtroom would have been even more highly charged. At this court session, Stephan Tomlyn made his case for his possession of the unassigned land he claimed his wife had inherited from Nathaniel Browne.[32]

In response to Tomlyn's argument, the justices determined that a new survey should be made of the original 500-acre patent made to Thomas Powell in 1650. The record makes no reference to any additional deed issued by the Northern Neck Proprietary. The justices appointed George Heale, a member of their court, to perform the survey. They also directed the county sheriff to appoint a jury to attend the survey. At the next meeting of the court on March 14, 1694, the survey results were reported. With the approval of the jury, the survey determined that Bertrand's plantation consisted of 573 acres—the 500-acre original Powell tract plus seventy-three acres of the surplus land. This result would, in effect, allocate the rest of the unassigned land to the Tomlyns—empowering them to exploit 371 acres any way they wished. The justices then approved the new survey that clearly favored the Tomlyns.[33]

John Bertrand recognized that this verdict was a devastating blow to his hope to control a significant portion of the surplus land. The land assigned to him by the survey was not enough to sustain his trespassing suit to block the creation of the tobacco field by his neighbor. This in turn almost certainly prevented Bertrand from developing the landing and tobacco transit point he had envisioned at Deep Creek. John immediately filed an appeal to the governor and the Council. At the same time, Stephen Tomlyn filed a complaint against Bertrand for taking possession of items left on the disputed property: a crosscut saw, a set of wedges, boards for constructing tobacco hogsheads, and fence rails.[34]

This follow-up case was taken up by the Lancaster Court on November 14, 1694. The court record of that day's proceedings confirms the basic outline of *Bertrand vs. Tomlyn*. The Tomlyns were at that moment in occupation of the disputed land on Deep Creek that Ann Tomlyn claimed she had inherited from Nathaniel Browne. John Bertrand was represented in court by Thomas Loyd, brother of the man who sold him *Powell's Quarter*. Loyd admitted Bertrand was in possession of the items named in the suit, but argued that the current litigation should not go forward until the General Court in Jamestown settled the "controversy" over the ownership of the disputed land. The justices immediately ruled in favor of the Tomlyns by fining John Bertrand 10,000 pounds of tobacco to compensate Tomlyn for the damage he had suffered.[35] It seems unlikely that Bertrand could afford to pay such a large fine (equal to 20 percent of his purchase price for *Powell's Quarter*). Once again, Bertrand appealed this verdict and fine to the governor and the Council.[36]

The missing link in this narrative is the evidence John Bertrand submitted and the arguments he made to support his trespassing allegation. Since the court rejected these, the court clerk chose not to record them. This raises many questions that cannot be answered. Did Bertrand submit a deed for the surplus land issued by the Northern Neck Proprietary that the Lancaster court refused to register? While court records offer no evidence that Lancaster was registering any Northern Neck patents during this period, Richmond County was registering them in 1692 and Westmoreland followed suit by 1694.[37] Did Bertrand challenge the validity of Tomlyn's deed, given that the 480-acre deed Nathaniel Browne filed in 1668 could not have included the surplus land?[38] Did he move that the case be referred to the agents of the Proprietary? Did he challenge the authority of the county justices to adjudicate the case?

There can be little doubt that Nathaniel Browne had taken possession of much of this surplus land some years before Bertrand became his neighbor. He had, after all, built a house on the property near the *Powell's Quarter* boundary. It is possible John Kyrby had issued a deed giving Browne a legal claim on the unassigned land (to compensate Browne for relinquishing his court-appointed role as executor of Thomas Powell's estate so that full control would pass to Kyrby?). Browne's long-term use of the land enabled the Tomlyns to argue that the Kyrbys had always recognized Browne's claim on the surplus land. The parish records for the "processioning" of the boundaries between the Kyrby and Browne properties could well have supported such a claim.

The Lancaster County justices' attempt at a narrow ruling based on a survey of Bertrand's property was intended to avoid crossing the line of making a de-facto award of surplus land to the litigants. They understood they had no legal authority to grant land that had not been previously patented. That authority resided with one of the two entities contending for it—the governor and Council of Virginia or the Northern Neck Proprietary. One can easily imagine Bertrand's appeal challenging the Lancaster verdict on just this point. By framing the case as a simple boundary dispute, the justices presented it as the kind of case they had authority to adjudicate.

The most prominent of the justices who ruled against John Bertrand in the Lancaster court cases was Robert Carter.[39] Carter's well-documented anger toward the Proprietary might have been inflamed by the refusal of one of its agents to grant him a tract of escheated land for which no heirs could be confirmed in Lancaster County in 1693.[40] The blunt rejection of his proposal drove home to Carter that the Proprietary was not favoring the elite colonial planters as consistently as the Council had. While Lord Howard and the Council were awarding escheated land in the Northern Neck as late as 1687, within a few years Proprietary agents were aggressively challenging the Council's authority to use this resource to benefit the colony's wealthiest citizens.[41]

After losing his case before the Lancaster justices in 1694, John Bertrand would have understood the ultimate disposition of the issue was in the hands of William Fitzhugh. If Fitzhugh could ensure the authority of the Northern Neck Proprietary was confirmed in London and James City, he would be in position to issue Bertrand a deed for the valuable land that the Lancaster justices could not overrule. But Bertrand could not take much comfort from knowing this. He must also have known that as he was losing his lawsuit and being assessed a huge fine in Lancaster County Court in the fall of 1694, the Proprietary was in crisis. On May 10, 1695, Robert Carter, a member of Virginia's House of Burgesses, issued on the floor of that body a vicious attack against the Proprietary for the "mischief" it was creating for Northern Neck planters. He railed against William Fitzhugh and George Brent for abusing their power as Proprietary agents. He accused them of engaging in "strange and exorbitant practices." Carter specifically challenged the authority of the Proprietary to tax landowners and to issue letters of escheat.[42] As chairman of the Burgesses' Committee on Propositions and Grievances, Carter drafted a resolution to eliminate the authority of the Proprietary. While the resolution passed in the House of Burgesses, it was not taken up by the Council.[43]

William Fitzhugh was angry about the personal nature of Carter's attack and the half-truths and exaggerations at the center of his charges. Fitzhugh was alarmed that Robert Carter's inflammatory rhetoric had apparently succeeded in uniting the governor, the Council, and small Northern Neck planters in opposition to the Proprietary. Fitzhugh acknowledged the crisis in letters to his good friend Roger Jones.[44] In a letter to Jones dated May 11, 1697, the Stafford lawyer emphasized the importance of the Proprietor, Lord Fairfax, making sure their case was effectively presented to the Lords of Trade in London. Fitzhugh described the challenge he faced as a game of cards in which the opponent has the better hand:

You ... will see what a hard game we have to play, the contrary party that is our Opposers, having the best cards and the Trumps to boot, especially the Honor. Yet would my Lord Fairfax there, take his turn in Shuffling and Dealing the Cards and his Lordship with the rest see that we were not cheated in our game, I question not but we should gain the Sett, tho' the game is so far plaid, but if we be not as we have now and always urged, supported from thence not only our Master's money will be lost, but we shall hardly be able to keep our just and legal standing.[45]

As John Bertrand was struggling to appeal the 1694 verdict against him and the exorbitant fine imposed on him by the Lancaster justices, William Fitzhugh was doing everything he could to overcome the early advantage of the Council and Robert Carter in the "hard game." As his 1697 letter to Roger Jones makes clear, Fitzhugh believed the game would be won or lost in London where a newly organized Board of Trade had replaced the ineffective Lords of Trade in the summer of 1696.[46] Fitzhugh was looking to Lord Fairfax to convince the Board of Trade that the Crown would reap greater rewards from the Northern Neck by utilizing the mechanism of proprietorship—an efficient and dependable instrument of empire. Because the unassigned lands of the Northern Neck were such a valuable asset of empire, their distribution and taxation should not be delegated to colonial governors who would always be constrained by the self-dealing of the aristocratic Virginians who made up the Council. Fitzhugh hoped Fairfax could convince the Board of Trade that the Proprietary would more effectively serve the Crown's policy of distributing land in a way that would reverse the colony's dramatic decline in immigration.[47] In an era when England sought to consolidate and streamline the administration of its colonial empire, the Proprietors of the Northern Neck, as Fitzhugh understood, were holding potent cards.[48]

The surviving records do not reveal whether the governor and Council ever ruled on John Bertrand's appeals. By this time, Council members were apparently realizing that their ability to curtail the growing power of the Proprietary over the citizens of the Northern Neck was severely limited. The Council minutes show that well before 1694, the Council had given up making direct appeals to the king to buy back the Northern Neck Proprietary and put its agents out of business.[49] Instead, it was making life difficult for the agents by complaining about them and challenging their activities on procedural grounds.[50]

As William Fitzhugh looked to Lord Fairfax in May 1697 to bring the "hard game" to a successful conclusion, he could not have known that the final hand in London would would be played over the next four months. This hand would not be directed by the strategy of Lord Fairfax, but by a far more skillful player, the political theorist John Locke. When the Board of Trade was formed in the summer of 1696, Locke was appointed to be one of its eight members. While Locke's health did not permit him to attend all the meetings during his four years as a member, he played a vital role in helping the board investigate important issues in the colonies and develop rational policies to better serve the goals of England's empire.

Some of the first reports submitted to the Board of Trade in the summer of 1696 contained allegations that members of the Council of Virginia were abusing their power in two important ways. Council members were violating the Crown's land distribution policy by taking up huge tracks for themselves and their friends so that very little land remained for the purpose of inducing settlers to populate the colony. According to these allegations, the Councilors were also holding themselves above the law to avoid paying their debts to English merchants.[51] In the summer of 1697, John Locke encouraged the Board to carefully examine these allegations by interviewing knowledgable Virginians who happened to be in London at the time. James Blair, the commissary of the Bishop of London in Virginia, was in London to raise money for the fledgling William and Mary College and to seek the removal of Governor Edmund Andros. During the week of August 23, 1697, Blair testified before the board about conditions in Virginia. His testimony alleged that the governor had failed to implement England's imperialist goals for the colony. According to Blair, the governor's failure was caused in part by the excessive power and privileges of the Council. He confirmed the members of the Council were self-dealing in the issuance of land grants as they accumulated personal holdings of 20,000 to 30,000 acres, were not accountable to the legal system of the colony, and were not subject to Virginia's tax levies.

Recognizing the value of Blair's testimony, Locke conducted a longer personal interview with the commissary and helped him put his observations in writing. Locke apparently edited Blair's written testimony into a position paper for presentation to the Board of Trade the following month.[52] In October 1697, Blair's case against the Council became part of a larger report for the Board of Trade: *The Present State of Virginia and the College*.[53] The position paper produced by Blair and Locke and the larger report that followed severely damaged the credibility of the Council with the Board of Trade and undoubtedly undermined the case it had been making against the Northern Neck Proprietary.[54] Governor Andros was subsequently dismissed. When the next governor, Francis Nicholson, arrived in Jamestown in December 1698, his instructions (drafted by the Board of Trade) significantly reduced the powers of the Council.[55]

An apparent turning point in Fitzhugh's "hard game" was the negotiated settlement with Richard Lee II, a member of the Council and one of the most influential men in the Northern Neck. In July 1695, Lee was refusing to deal with the Proprietary as evidenced by the petition filed by Fitzhugh and Brent to the Council complaining that they could not obtain common process against Colonel Lee. The petition challenged the Council to declare whether it considered its members "above the law" in their dealings with the king's Proprietors. The Council, possibly suspecting a legal trap, responded that the problem was the negligence of the sheriff in serving papers, not Lee's resistance to due process.[56] Richard Lee eventually had a change of heart that was described by contemporary Robert Beverley in 1705: "At last Colonel Richard Lee, one of the Council, an Inhabitant of the Northern Neck, privately made a Composition with the Proprietors themselves for his own Land. This broke the Ice, and several were induced to follow so great an Example; so that by Degrees, they were generally brought to pay their Quit-Rents into the Hands of the Proprietors Agents."[57] Beverley did not give a date for Richard Lee's change of heart. However, Lee's decision to make an arrangement with the Proprietors suggests the Council had finally come to understand that its campaign against the Northern Neck Proprietary had failed.

In the fall of 1698, the Deep Creek controversy came to an end. On October 17, the Northern Neck Proprietary issued a new patent for John Bertrand's plantation.[58] This time neither the Lancaster County Court nor the Council, sitting as the General Court in Jamestown, was able to ignore or countermand it. The final result of the "hard game" pitting William Fitzhugh against the Council and Robert Carter, apparently decided in London in the fall of 1697, was likely reported in Virginia in the spring of 1698. John Bertrand's 1698 Northern Neck patent confirms the struggle over the Proprietary, still very much in doubt in May 1697, was decisively resolved by the summer of 1698. By that time, the Board of Trade's October 20, 1697, report on Virginia (exposing the Council's excessive privileges and self-dealing) had reached the colony.

The new patent issued to John Bertrand was clearly written to refute the 1694 opinion of the justices of the Lancaster County Court. The patent was a "deed of escheat" for 500 acres of land obtained from the Proprietary office. It identified the land as a neck lying on the north side of the Rappahannock River "commonly called *Powell's Quarter.*" The deed explained that Thomas Powell had received a patent for the land on October 14, 1650, and passed the land on to his son, "who died without heir or otherwise disposing of the said land." The deed stipulated that a grant of escheat was then given to John Bertrand who had paid for the land to be "resurveyed and re-measured by virtue of a warrant directed to one of our surveyors whereupon and by the survey finds and reports that by the winding of the Rappahannock River in the said County of Lancaster . . . there is contained four hundred and twenty-four acres within the ancient bounds of the original patent of five hundred acres. . . . "[59] The patent went on to say the rules of their office "give preference of all surplus lands within any grant contained to the possessor" if he surveys it and pays all fees.

To make sure there would be no misunderstanding, the deed stated in explicit terms that John Bertrand was granted both the 500-acre original Powell tract *and* 424 surplus acres as substantiated "by a just survey." The new survey superseded the Lancaster County survey by county surveyor George Heale making 371 acres of surplus land available to the Tomlyns. The Proprietary survey reduced the Tomlyn's share to only twenty surplus acres.[60] Then followed the detailed coordinates extending Bertrand's land to the head of Deep Creek. The descriptions contained in the 1694 and 1698 surveys confirm that the surplus land controversy was over the middle to upper reaches of Deep Creek's western shoreline.

The location of the disputed land along Deep Creek is further indicated by the extension of the boundary of John Bertrand's land beyond the house owned by the Tomlyns. The property line is described as reaching the head of Deep Creek near a "marked poplar (standing above Mr. Tomlyn's house)." The naming of the neighbor who had prevailed against John Bertrand in the Lancaster County Court emphasized the decisive manner in which the justices' verdict had been overturned. It also indicated that the house Nathaniel Browne had built on the surplus land to strengthen his claim on it was transferred to the ownership of John Bertrand. This home, just within the the northeast boundary line of the enlarged plantation, was in the general location of the 1767 *Belle Isle* plantation house.[61] The deed concluded by noting that the "quit rent" John Bertrand will owe for these 924 acres is "nineteen shillings yearly."

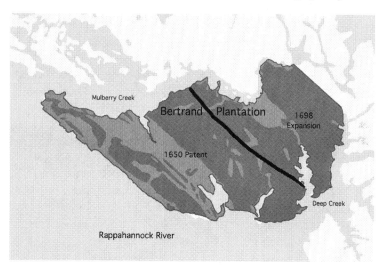

Map of Belle Isle State Park, Lancaster, Virginia, showing the 924-acre Bertrand Plantation as expanded by the 1698 patent.
Created by the author

The 1698 deed makes clear that the agents of the Northern Neck Proprietary had resolved the Deep Creek controversy in John Bertrand's favor. But more than that, the patent asserted in very explicit terms the authority of the

Proprietary to make land grants, to settle disputes over land boundaries, and to levy taxes on the land within its jurisdiction. Over the next twelve months, John Bertrand doubled his workforce, confirming that by the middle of 1698 Northern Neck Proprietary patents could no longer be ignored by Lancaster officials or by the Council in Jamestown.[62]

The chronology of the Deep Creek controversy raises the question of whether John Bertrand's 1698 patent restated elements of an earlier Proprietary deed he submitted in 1693 to the Lancaster Court justices, who then decided not to admit it into evidence. Such a deed would certainly have provided a legal basis for Bertrand's trespassing suit and would have made *Bertrand vs. Tomlyn* essentially a rerun of *Fitzhugh vs Dade*. This interpretation of the Deep Creek controversy casts William Fitzhugh as its legal architect. In this scenario, *Bertrand vs. Tomlyn* provided Fitzhugh with another opportunity to do what *Fitzhugh vs. Dade* failed to achieve—elicit from the Council its formal recognition of the impeccable legal standing of deeds issued by the Proprietary.

William Fitzhugh's work as agent of the unpopular Northern Neck Proprietary made him a controversial figure among the leaders of the colony. He was never fully accepted as a member of Virginia's colonial elite despite his wealth and his service in the House of Burgesses. In some ways the arc of Fitzhugh's life was similar to that of John Bertrand. Both were emigrants who pursued their careers in the colony at a time when the majority of Virginians were native born.[63] Both saw the new world through the lens of the imperialist policies of Charles II. Under the influence of these policies, they willingly embraced their roles as vassals or servants of Charles's appointed Barons of the Northern Neck. Neither was the product of the Virginia cultural mind-set that governors like Francis Howard, Edmund Andros, and Francis Nicholson found so troubling in the aristocrats with whom they dealt in the colony.[64]

In the immediate aftermath of the "hard game," John Bertrand would face the wrath of Robert Carter and other members of the Lancaster aristocracy. When the Northern Neck Proprietary issued to John Bertrand the 1698 patent that was, in turn, duly recognized by colonial authorities, Carter's anger toward the Proprietary and Bertrand must have been intense. It was not in Carter's temperament to graciously accept losing to William Fitzhugh or seeing the Stafford lawyer reward John Bertrand for his loyalty.[65]

An incident in Lancaster County Court on September 14, 1699, illustrates the bad blood between Carter and Bertrand. Less than a year after receiving his new patent, John Bertrand was in court to address a problem he was having with some of his indentured servants. He accused two servants of killing some of his livestock for personal use without his permission. Hogs typically ran loose on seventeenth-century Virginia plantations, and wild animals that were not branded by their owners could legally be captured by servants or anyone else. The legal issue in cases like this was whether servants had killed marked or unmarked hogs.[66] The first servant pleaded guilty to the charge and was sentenced to having two years added to his term of service. The second servant, Owen Lord, pleaded not guilty. A jury was brought in, and the court found in favor of Lord.[67]

John Bertrand then tried to appeal the case, and his appeal was ruled out of order. Recognizing the justices were not favorably inclined toward his master, Owen Lord petitioned the court to end his term of service immediately. A jury was then impaneled to consider setting Lord free before he had served his full term. As Bertrand made his argument against setting the servant free early, he apparently directed angry words toward Justice Robert Carter. The exchange between the two men in open court degenerated into verbal fisticuffs. The court record reads: "John Bertrand offered many unhandsome words against . . . Colo. Robert Carter, Esqr." The record goes on to quote Bertrand telling Carter "that he vented too much spleen against him." The justices then found John Bertrand in contempt of court and fined him five pounds sterling.[68] Lancaster citizens in attendance at that day's court proceedings were apparently very well entertained.[69] After fining John Bertrand for contempt and requiring him to post bond to assure he would not repeat his "indecent behavior," the court deferred its decision on Owen Lord's petition until the next month.[70]

It may be that John Bertrand saw his treatment by the Lancaster justices as retaliation for his role in the "hard game." The following month he petitioned the governor and Council to overturn the September 14, 1699, action the Lancaster justices took against him and to refund the five-pound-sterling fine assessed against him. The decision of the Council to grant Bertrand's appeal and refund the fine represented an important legal vindication for the minister. One can well imagine Robert Carter's reaction to that.[71] The explosive exchange between these two in the Lancaster Court shows the degree to which the differences between John Bertrand and Robert Carter operated on a visceral level. The emotional intensity of this incident confirms that the resolution of the Deep Creek controversy was a watershed moment for both men. After four years of delay, Bertrand could move forward with the development of his landing for transatlantic ships. But with the Board of Trade moving to reduce the the authority of the Council to distribute land patents to their friends, Carter's ambitious plans for expanding his holdings and his wealth would have to be placed on hold.

John Bertrand's exchange with Robert Carter in the Lancaster court violated one of the most important precepts of Virginia colonial society. This was a culture built on deference to those who occupied the highest social positions. As a parish minister, John Bertrand was a civil servant in a position considerably below that of a wealthy court justice like Robert Carter. But his public altercation with Carter suggests Bertrand did not feel constrained by his assigned place on the social pyramid of the colony.

Like elite Huguenot émigrés in Europe, Bertrand might have seen himself and his fellow refugees as distinct from and superior to his host community and its leaders.[72] Moreover, as an agent of English empire, John Bertrand was driven by a loyalty that took precedence over the deference system that existed within the colony. His primary loyalty to his host nation was not to the court justices or the governor of Virginia, but to Bishop Compton and the Lords Proprietors of the Northern Neck. Bertrand saw Virginia through the lens of the imperialist projects that were at the heart of his Huguenot-Anglican mission. Still, it is noteworthy that Bertrand was willing to repudiate in public and challenge before the Council the most influential official in Lancaster County and a man who was on his way to becoming the most powerful leader in Virginia and perhaps the wealthiest citizen in British America.

John Bertrand's work with William Fitzhugh in the "hard game" helped pave the way for other Huguenot refugees to acquire land in Virginia. About one-third of the Rappahannock Refuge Huguenot emigrant households identified in this study appear to have acquired land in the colony (forty-six refugees north of the Rappahannock River, thirty-two living south of the river, and four with land on both sides of the river).[73] The relative ease with which some of the Huguenot refugees secured land in the Rappahannock region is illustrated by the experience of Andrew Barbee, who arrived in Lancaster County in 1684. After completing his four-year contract as an indentured servant, he moved to Stafford County, where he purchased 300 acres in 1691.[74] William Fitzhugh understood the difficulties Huguenot families experienced in Stafford and sometimes used his position as Northern Neck agent to help them. When, in 1690, the widow of Huguenot Nicholas Burnard was left destitute by her deceased husband's debts, Fitzhugh came to her aid. In 1695 the proprietary awarded escheated land in Stafford County to this impoverished widow.[75]

A complicating factor for Huguenots looking to acquire land in Virginia was their status as aliens in an English colony. When an alien accumulated real property, it reverted to the Crown at his or her death. Some of the Rappahannock Refuge Huguenots addressed this concern before leaving England by applying for letters of patent from the king making them subjects of the Crown. Lewis and Benjamin Renoe (and their wives) received word that their letter of patent applications had been approved soon after their 1688 arrival in Stafford County. Others sought citizenship in Virginia by utilizing the naturalization statutes passed by the Virginia General Assembly in 1680 (Leonard Dozier) and 1705 (James Foushee).[76] Theodore de Rosseaux was included in the blanket naturalization given to the Manakin Huguenots in 1705 before he moved from there to Richmond County.[77] The records suggest some of the Rappahannock Refuge Huguenots were never naturalized but found ways to work around this impediment to acquiring land and passing it on to their children. Lewis Tacquet was a silent partner in Lewis Renoe's 1711 grant from the Northern Neck Proprietary. After Tacquet's death his son received his father's share of the patent as a gift from the Renoe family, and he subsequently registered it.[78] In 1704, Cyprian Prou signed a contract for a lifetime lease on 200 acres as the landowner signed a commitment to make a gift of that land to Prou's daughters when Cyprian and his wife were both deceased. Paul Micou's role as a witness to both agreements suggests he was helping a fellow Huguenot through this complex legal process. That Huguenot John Orion filed identical contracts in 1708, with Prou serving as a witness, suggests such boilerplate documents were circulating within the Rappahannock Refuge to help aliens acquire land.[79]

While some Huguenot immigrants were, like John Bertrand, in a position to purchase land when they arrived in Virginia,[80] records suggest most of the landholding Huguenot refugees began leasing tracts of land and later became landowners. This pattern is illustrated by a group of exiles in Stafford County. By 1690, Lewis Renoe and James Gallahough were in Stafford County, where they were leasing small plots of land at Brent Town, the development for Huguenots advertised by Durand de Dauphiné in his 1687 pamphlet.[81] By 1700, Huguenot John Marr was one of their neighbors.[82] Records suggest that by the early 1700s, they were joined by five more Huguenots: Clement Chevalle, Rynhart de la Fayolle, Samuel Duchemin, Peter Lehew, and Louis Tacquet, who were apparently leasing land at Brent Town, too.[83] By the end of the decade, most of these Huguenot neighbors were busy securing their own land grants. About 1708, Samuel Duchemin had secured land in Richmond County. In 1710, he received a grant of 440 acres in Westmoreland County, where Isaac Duchemin had purchased land in 1698. That same year, John Marr secured a grant of 588 acres in Richmond County.[84] In 1711, Rynhart de la Fayolle received a grant of 123 acres in Stafford. Also in 1711, Lewis Renoe and Clement Chevalle secured a joint grant of 968 acres across Cedar Run from the Brent Town tract in Stafford,[85] with Renoe dividing his share with Louis Tacquet.[86] In 1724, Peter Lehew received a Stafford County grant of 972 acres.[87] There is no evidence of land acquisition by James Gallahough, who was apparently deceased by 1710. However, by 1748, his son Darby had become a landowner in the part of Stafford that became Prince William County while retaining the lease on his father's acreage at Brent Town.[88]

The members of the Rappahannock Refuge who made these mostly smaller land acquisitions fit the profile of the kind of settlers English imperial planners wanted to attract to the colony with the offer of land at a time when immigration to the Chesapeake region had dramatically declined.[89] The written report James Blair and John Locke prepared for the Board of Trade in 1697 called for reining in the abuses of the Council in order to make land available at "an easy rate" to "poor French Protestants" who could become productive new citizens of the empire.[90] While these Huguenot patent holders were beneficiaries of the difficult battle Fitzhugh and Bertrand waged in the "hard game" (with the help of Blair and Locke), they also benefited from being settlers whose interests overlapped with the priorities of the planners of England's new world empire.[91]

Court records confirm John Bertrand and his wife, Charlotte, were generating business as merchants by the end of the seventeenth century. With his 1698 deed giving him 924 acres and complete control of the entire western shoreline of Deep Creek from its mouth to its head, John Bertrand had more than enough land for a protected deep-water landing for transatlantic ships, tobacco storage facilities, and a Bertrand store, all of which were documented by the 1720s.[92] With its major expansion along Deep Creek, the plantation gradually took on a new name. *Powell's Quarter* was becoming *Deep Creek* as John Bertrand placed his personal stamp on Thomas Powell's Rappahannock River plantation.[93]

While there are no records showing the Bertrands used their family expertise in wine production to develop vineyards in Virginia, it would be surprising if they did not at least make an attempt. If they brought vine cuttings from family vineyards in Saintonge, they, like other French emigrants, probably discovered that the delicate European grape varieties were especially vulnerable to Virginia's unpredictable climate, destructive pests, and bacterial and fungus infections.[94] If the Bertrands hoped to import Saintonge wine from their families in France, world events would have made such a plan difficult. England's Nine Years' War with France made legal trade between these nations impossible from late 1688 until the latter part of 1697. The Bertrands had a brief window for legally importing family wine from 1698 until 1701, before the War of Spanish Succession renewed hostilities between England and France.[95] Records showing the grandson of John and Charlotte's closest friends, Cozes Huguenots James and Marie Foushee,[96] marketing wine to prominent Virginians, including President Monroe, suggest these families were either producing it or more likely importing it from France into the late eighteenth century.[97]

While there is very little documentation for Paul Micou's work as a merchant, Richmond County court proceedings demonstrate that in the fall of 1707, Micou was serving as a factor for a Bristol merchant named Edward Foye. The power of attorney Foye filed for this purpose identifies Paul Micou not as a physician, but as a merchant.[98] The work of Paul Micou and John Bertrand as merchants likely strengthened their ties to Cozes Huguenots in other English American colonies with whom they were trading. Their merchant activities put them at the center of a North American Huguenot communication network along the eastern seaboard of North America.[99]

While supporting the struggling Northern Neck Proprietary proved to be a winning strategy for the Bertrand family and other Huguenots who had acquired land in Virginia, John Bertrand would pay a heavy price in the form of the deep-seated resentment of the Lancaster aristocracy. The decidedly negative portrayal of Bertrand in the *Lancaster County Order Book,* after his 1698 patent was issued, reveals the contempt in which the Lancaster justices held him. As the next chapter shows, these damaged relationships with elite Virginians would also pose a significant threat to John Bertrand's other imperialist project in Lancaster County—the implementation of Bishop Compton's Anglican reforms.

NOTES

1. Blair and Locke, "Some of the Chief Grievances of the Present Constitution of Virginia," 158.

2. For an overview of proprietary ventures of European powers seeking early modern Atlantic empires, see Louis H. Roper and Bertrand Van Ruymbeke, eds., *Constructing Early Modern Empires: Proprietary Ventures in the Atlantic World, 1500–1750* (Leiden, 2007), 1–18.

3. The full text of the 1649 Northern Neck Proprietary charter is published in Freeman, *Young Washington,* vol. 1, 513–19.

4. For the effectiveness of the elite planters who served on the Council in using their land grant powers to benefit people like themselves, see Voorhis, "Crown versus Council in the Virginia Land Policy," 500–01.

5. Brent Tarter, "Bacon's Rebellion, the Grievances of the People, and the Political Culture of Seventeenth-Century Virginia," VMHB 119, no. 1 (2011), 11 and 15.

6. For the chronology of the Northern Neck Proprietary, see Freeman, *Young Washington,* vol. 1, 447–513.

7. Ibid., 471–72.

8. Thomas Lord Culpepper was appointed governor at William Berkeley's death in 1677, but did not travel to Virginia until May of 1680. After a short stay in colony, he returned to England. His second residence in Virginia began in December 1682 and ended in May 1683; Raimo, *Biographical Dictionary of American Colonial and Revolutionary Governors,* 479.

9. Billings, *Virginia's Viceroy,* 52–53.

10. Freeman, *Young Washington,* vol. 1, 481.

11. Ibid., 481–86.

12. SP, SC DWB, 1689–1693, 21–23, 44–45.

13. McIlwaine, *Executive Journals,* vol. 1, 119, and 131–132.

14. For Virginia's ruling elite seeking to protect their interests by courting small planters in the 1690s, see Susan Scott Parish, "Introduction," in *The History and Present State of Virginia by Robert Beverley,* xviii.

15. SP, SC DWB, 1689–1693, 21–22.

16. SP, SC OB, 1664–1668 and 1689–1690, 114.

17. Davis, *William Fitzhugh and His Chesapeake World*, 36–37, 280–84.

18. McIlwaine, *Executive Journals*, vol. 1, 252.

19. Freeman, *Young Washington*, vol. 1, 488.

20. Voorhis, "Crown versus Council in the Virginia Land Policy," 499–514.

21. For Robert Carter's evolution from chief opponent of the Proprietary to become its agent, see Katharine L. Brown, *Robert "King" Carter: Builder of Christ Church* (Irvington, VA, 2010).

22. William Walter Hening, ed., *Statutes at Large: Being a Collection of All the Laws of Virginia* (Richmond, VA, 1821), vol. 6, 173.

23. LC OB, 7, 1721–1729, 65.

24. The surname of Thomas Norser appears with a variety of spellings in Lancaster County records—Norser, Nonrser, and Nornser. In Richmond County records in 1694, he appears as Nurser. This narrative uses the Norser spelling.

25. Warner, *History of ORC*, 106.

26. LC OB, 1686–1696, 257.

27. SP, LC OB, 1691–1695, 57. For the will of Nathaniel Browne, see SP, LC WB, 1690–1709, 32–33.

28. LC OB, 1686–1696, 273, 274, and 283.

29. Ibid., 270.

30. Nugent, *Cavaliers and Pioneers*, vol. 1, 514; SP, LC WB, 1690–1709, 33.

31. LC OB, 1686–1696, 270. Ann Browne Tomlyn should not be confused with Ann Dacres Tomlyn, the sister of Rawleigh Powell and previous owner of 300 acres of *Powell's Quarter*.

32. LC OB, 1686–1696, 280.

33. Ibid., 282.

34. Ibid., 286.

35. Ibid., 290.

36. Ibid., 297.

37. SP, RC DB, 1692–1695, 26–27; NNG No. 2, 1694–1700, 76–77, LVA.

38. LOP and Grants No. 6, 1666–1679, Parts 1 and 2, 138, LVA. Nathaniel Browne's deed was for the same tract that George Vezey patented in 1657. SP, LC DWB, 1661–1702, 66.

39. LC OB, 1686–1696, 257, 279, 281, 289, and 296.

40. Clifford Dowdey, *The Virginia Dynasties: The Emergence of King Carter and the Golden Age* (New York, 1969), 161.

41. SP, OR DWB, 1686–1688, 93.

42. Davis, *William Fitzhugh and His Chesapeake World*, 43.

43. Dowdey, *The Virginia Dynasties*, 161–62.

44. Davis, *William Fitzhugh and His Chesapeake World*, 325–26.

45. Ibid., 352.

46. Kammen,"Virginia at the Close of the Seventeenth Century," 142. For a detailed analysis of the transition from the Lords of Trade and Plantations to the Board of Trade in 1696, see Winfred T. Root, "Lords of Trade and Plantations, 1675–1696," *American Historical Review* 23, no. 1 (October 1917), 20–41.

47. For the dramatic decline in immigration to the Chesapeake after 1680, see Walsh, *Motives of Honor, Pleasure, and Profit*, 198–200.

48. For the strong movement toward imperial consolidation during this period, see Stanwood, *The Global Refuge*, 142.

49. The requests from the Council for the Crown to buy out the Proprietary were authorized on June 4, 1689, and June 5, 1690. McIlwaine, *Executive Journals*, vol. 1, 523 and 119.

50. Ibid., 252.

51. Kammen, "Virginia at the Close of the Seventeenth Century," 143–44.

52. Blair and John Locke, "Some of the Chief Grievances of the Present Constitution of Virginia," 153–69.

53. Henry Hartwell, James Blair, and Edward Chilton, *The Present State of Virginia, and the College,* ed. Hunter Dickinson Farish (Williamsburg, VA, 1940).

54. Voorhis, "Crown versus Council in the Virginia Land Policy," 503; Kammen, "Virginia at the Close of the Seventeenth Century," 146–49.

55. Robert A. Bain, "The Composition and Publication of *The Present State of Virginia and the College*," *Early American Literature* 6, no. 1, Special Southern Issue (Spring 1971), 31–54.

56. McIlwaine, *Executive Journals*, vol. 1, 333–34.

57. Beverley, *The History and Present State of Virginia*, 71.

58. NNG No. 2, 1694–1700, 293–95, LVA.

59. Ibid., 294.

60. In 1699 Tomlin filed a trespassing suit against his neighbor, John Matthews. The survey of his land showed that his original patent of 480 acres had grown to 500 acres. SP, LC OB, 1699–1701, 58–60.

61. The Belle Isle plantation house was built by John Bertrand's great-grandson Thomas Bertrand Griffin. A dendrochronological study authored by Camille Wells, Edward R. Cook, and William J. Callahan determined the cutting date for the wood in the oldest section of the house to be 1767, per correspondence from Camille Wells to the author, March 20, 2014.

62. Lancaster County, Virginia Tithable Records, 19, Mary Ball Washington Library, Lancaster, Virginia.

63. Hatfield, *Atlantic Virginia*, 228.

64. Billings, *Virginia's Viceroy*, 64–76; Parke Rouse, *James Blair of Virginia* (Chapel Hill, NC, 1971), 70–116 and 152–74.

65. For Robert Carter's determination to get his own way, see Carolyn Jett, "The Strange Case of Col. Robert 'King' Carter versus Capt. Richard Haynie," *The Bulletin of the Northumberland County Historical Society*, 39 (2002), 15–20.

66. Warner, *History of ORC*, 106.

67. LC OB, 7, 1696–1702, vol. 4, 78a–78b.

68. Ibid., 78b.

69. For the public nature of court proceedings in seventeenth-century Virginia, see Carl R. Lounsbury, *The Courthouses of Early Virginia: An Architectural History* (Charlottesville, VA, 2005).

70. SP, LC OB, *1699–1701,* 23–24.

71. McIlwaine, *Executive Journals*, vol. 2, 13–14.

72. Susanne Lachenicht, "Huguenot Immigrants and the Formation of National Identities, 1546–1787," *Historical Journal* 50, no. 2 (June 2007), 320–23.

73. See Appendix A for Huguenots owning land.

74. SP, LC OB 1687–1691, 50; SP, SC OB, 1692–1693, 30.

75. SP, SC OB, 1664–1668, 1689–1690, 92–93; SP, SC DWB, 1699–1709, 33.

76. SP, SC DWB, 1686–1689, 79–80; Research Notes Number 9, "Virginia Naturalizations, 1657–1776," LVA. Leonard Dozier is not listed in Appendix A of this study because he arrived in Virginia before 1677.

77. "Virginia Huguenot Naturalization, 1705," Library of the Huguenot Society of the Founders of Manakin, Richmond.

78. NNG No. 5, 1713–1719, 65, LVA; NNG F, 1742–1754, 274, LVA.

79. SP, RC DB, 1701–1704, 64–67; SP, RC DB, 1705–1708, 110–11.

80. SP, ORC OB, 1687–1689, 12, 14, and 15.

81. SP, SC DWB, 1686–1689, 79–80; SP, SC OB, 13.

82. SP, SC DWB, 1699–1709, 17, 25, and 47.

83. Fairfax Harrison, *Landmarks of Old Prince William: A Study of Origins in Northern Virginia* (Richmond, VA, 1924), 189–90. Samuel Duchimenia and his brother, Isaac, were apparently transported to Stafford County about 1690 by one of the owners of Brent Town, RBP, Ms 2/6 (Hayward), HL.

84. Crozier, *Virginia County Records*, New Series, vol. 1, Westmoreland County; Dorman, WC DW No. 2, 1691–1699, 38; NNG No. 4, 1710–1712, 94, LVA.

85. NNG No. 4, 1710–1712, 43 and 53, LVA.

86. NNG No. 5, 1713–1719, 65, LVA; NNG F, 1742–1754, 274, LVA.

87. NNG A, 1722–1726, 128, LVA.

88. Prince William County Land Causes, 1789–1793, 67–68; SP, PWC OB, 1754–1755, 5. By 1735, Darby Gallahue owned 150 acres in the part of Essex that became Caroline County. This tract was inherited by his wife, Charlotte Ewell (a granddaughter of John and Charlotte Bertrand), LC OB 12, 334; Caroline County Court Order Book, 1740, 42.

89. Walsh, *Motives of Honor, Pleasure, and Profit*, 198–200.

90. Kammen, "Virginia at the Close of the Seventeenth Century," 155 and 158.

91. Stanwood, *The Global Refuge*, 82–87.

92. LC WB, 1690–1709, 110–11; LC OB, 5, 1702–1713, 18, 44, 45, 51, 102, and 113; LC DB, 9, 1701–1706, 25 and 45; SP, LC DB, 1701–1706, 45–46; SP, LC OB, 1695–1699, 55; LC WDB, 13, 1736–1743, 21–22.

93. The use of the name *Deep Creek* for the Bertrand plantation is cited in the tripartite deed for the property issued by William Bertrand in 1760, LC WB, 16, 105–06.

94. Andrew A. Painter, *Virginia Wine: Four Centuries of Change* (Fairfax, VA, 2018), 2.

95. That trade between England and France resumed during the interim between the Nine Years' War and the War of Spanish Succession is confirmed by Jaques Fontaine, who reported receiving shipments of French wine and salt in Ireland in 1698 and sending fish to La Rochelle. Fontaine, *Memoirs of the Reverend Jaques Fontaine*, 153–54, and 157.

96. In his will, Bertrand named James Foushee as the custodian of his children and administrator of his estate in the event of Charlotte's death. The Foushees' daughter, Susannah, married John and Charlotte's son, William, in 1713. More information about the Foushee family is provided in Lee, *A Brief History of Belle Isle Plantation*.

97. For William Foushee marketing wine to prominent Virginians, see George Hay to James Monroe, November 22, 1824, Mss 2H3218a1, Virginia Historical Society Library, Richmond. William Foushee became mayor of the city of Richmond in 1782.

98. Ryland, "Paul Micou, Chyrurgeon," 243.

99. Hatfield, *Atlantic Virginia*, 89, 110–15, and 123–27.

Chapter Six

Whitechapel Parish, 1698

Though the whole country of Virginia hath great respect for my Lord Bishop of London, they do resent . . . his Lordship has sent here Mr. Blair a Scotchman, to be commissary.

—Nicholas Moreau, Virginia, April 12, 1697

As the crisis over the distribution of unassigned land in Virginia drew to an end in 1698, John Bertrand and the refugees who supported his ministry were caught up in another crisis—this time over religion.[1] It was a propitious time for help to arrive in the form of a bilingual Huguenot-Anglican minister named Nicholas Moreau, who moved from New Kent County at the far edge of the Refuge to Essex County on the Rappahannock River in 1698. Moreau, who was also a physician, was attracted to Essex in part because its larger Huguenot population gave him a much better opportunity to practice both of his professions. In a 1697 letter to the Archbishop of Canterbury, Huguenot-Anglican minister Stephen Fouace reported from Virginia that he had helped Moreau find a good parish where he could also practice medicine.[2]

Like Paul Micou and other Huguenot physicians, Moreau practiced in at least three counties—Essex, Richmond, and Westmoreland—on both sides of the river. Before moving to Essex, he wrote a letter to the Bishop of Lichfield in England expressing a positive view of Native American medicine and a very negative view of the condition of Virginia's Anglican Church. He was horrified by the unqualified ministers parish vestries were hiring, describing them as "so basely educated and so little acquainted with the excellency of their charge and duty that their lives and conversation are fitter to make Heathens than Christians."[3]

Bishop of London Henry Compton was well aware of the sad condition of the Anglican Church in Virginia. He believed the underlying problem was the way colonial elites dominated the parish vestries, hiring and firing ministers according to their whims. His program to reform the colonial church sought to wrest the parishes from the control of these local aristocrats. After hearing bitter complaints from ministers about their treatment at the hands of the vestries, Compton reported to English authorities that these vestries had too much power over their ministers.[4] Compton was alarmed by the same complaints Robert Beverley wrote about in 1705, that ministers lived in a constant state of fear because vestries could dismiss them at any time without cause.[5] Abuse of power by vestries was magnified by the lifetime tenure of vestrymen who often influenced the selection of new members when vacancies occurred.[6] Grievances registered by Virginia citizens in the aftermath of Bacon's Rebellion in 1676 highlighted the lack of accountability of the vestries in managing the parishes and setting the tax rates to support them.[7] Accusing the vestries of maintaining a "pretended authority" to run the church, Bishop Compton was determined to dramatically reduce their power.

When Henry Compton was ready to implement a reform program to free the colonial parishes from the control of the vestries, he took it to the Lords of Trade. This committee, of which Compton was a member, was the guiding instrument for shaping and implementing England's imperialist policy toward the colonies. Compton could be confident of a favorable hearing from the Lords of Trade because this body was seeking to strengthen the Crown's governance of colonies at the local level to make them less vulnerable to French hegemony or invasion.[8] They would quickly grasp the threat posed by the power of the vestries in Virginia, which were free to set the direction of their churches and were in some cases heavily influenced by Puritan theology and worship practices. By the end of 1677, Henry Compton secured the approval of the Lords of Trade for his Anglican reform program.[9]

John Bertrand's Huguenot-Anglican ministry in Lancaster County reveals the dynamic interplay among the three components of Henry Compton's strategy for implementing this reform. Compton designed a reform process that would begin with the governors. He made sure the specific instructions delivered to Virginia's governors emphasized their responsibility to ensure that vestries hired ministers who were Anglican-ordained and duly licensed by the Bishop of London. The next step was to make certain the colony had a more adequate supply of Anglican ministers who willingly practiced obedience to their bishop and the king. At Compton's urging, the Crown directed that ministers be empowered to meet regularly with their vestries.[10] By the early 1680s, Compton's aggressive clergy recruitment program was sending an unprecedented number of ministers with Anglican ordinations to Virginia. The final agent of Compton's strategy for Virginia was put in place in 1689 with his appointment of James Blair to serve as commissary—the personal representative of the Bishop of London in Virginia. The commissary was to superintend the ministry of the clergy and give them greater authority in their parishes. Compton was looking to the combined contributions of these imperialist agents—governor, commissary, and parish ministers commissioned by him—to break the stranglehold the vestries held on the parishes.[11]

All these components were falling in place when John Bertrand extended his dual-track ministry into Lancaster County in the fall of 1690. But Bertrand soon learned the mission Bishop Compton had assigned him would be extremely difficult to carry out. As his Huguenot-Anglican ecclesiology collided with the churchmanship that had been dominant in Lancaster County over four decades, the support of the governor and the commissary proved ineffective, as their energies were sapped by the growing conflict between them. Moreover, Bertrand's mission was further undermined by his pastoral colleague in Lancaster, a Scots-Irish Presbyterian named Andrew Jackson, who was very much in tune with the county's well-established theological identity and a very good friend of Robert Carter.

From its inception in 1652, Lancaster County, like the rest of the Rappahannock region, was a magnet for settlers and ministers with Puritan leanings.[12] The county's Puritan roots are clearly revealed in what may be the earliest reference to worship in local records. On August 6, 1652, the court justices made specific preparations for what they described as "the next meeting when there shall be a sermon."[13] Like other Puritans, these Lancaster leaders believed worship should always be sermon-centered.

Seventeenth-century Puritans in Virginia were part of a large movement within the Church of England in which there was general agreement on a set of broad goals. Puritans were united in seeking to reform the Church of England to make it more Calvinist in its theology and worship practices. They agreed in their opposition to particular features of Anglican worship they considered too Roman Catholic. All Puritans wanted their clergy to wear black academic gowns in worship rather than the white or cream-colored surplice favored in the Anglican Church of the Stuart kings. Puritans of every stripe were also adamantly opposed to kneeling for Communion and the use of the sign of the cross by clergy in baptism.

However, Puritans did not agree about how far reform should go or the best strategies for achieving it. Separatist and Congregationalist Puritans wanted a thorough program of reform to be implemented immediately, while Presbyterian and Anglican Puritans were more comfortable working within the structure of the Church of England and the Anglican Church in Virginia for more gradual change. Both of these more moderate Puritan groups affirmed the connectional polity of the Anglican Church, with the Anglican Puritans endorsing governance by bishops and Presbyterian Puritans working to replace bishops with governing bodies called presbyteries.[14]

Early Lancaster records suggest the county's ecclesiastical identity was shaped by a partnership between the Presbyterian and Anglican Puritans with the Presbyterians holding the stronger hand. This identity was forged by leaders such as Henry Fleete and William Underwood, who represented Lancaster in the House of Burgesses in 1652.[15] It was maintained through the vestries that hired the clergy and set local church policy with little or no interference from the colonial governor or the Bishop of London.

Lancaster County was formed during the Commonwealth period, quickly attracting clergy who shared its residents' moderate Puritan views. These ministers were John Rosier (1649–1652),[16] Alexander Cooke (1652–c. 1654),[17] Charles Grimes (1653–c. 1660),[18] and Samuel Cole (1657–1659).[19] Rosier, Cooke, and Grimes were graduates of Puritan-leaning colleges at Cambridge. Only Grimes is documented as having an Anglican ordination, while Cole appears on a 1645 list of Presbyterian Puritan ministers in England. The ministers who served Lancaster County during the early years of settlement set the direction for its moderate Puritan churchmanship and Presbyterian worship.

In 1645, the English Parliament abolished the Anglican *Book of Common Prayer* and replaced it with the *Directory for the Public Worship of God*, commonly known as the *Directory for Worship*.[20] The *Directory for Worship* was produced by the Westminster Assembly to be a centerpiece of what Parliament hoped would be a Presbyterian Church of England and Scotland ultimately supported by the monarchy. While that Parliamentary dream died when Colonel Thomas Pride and his regiment of musketeers forcibly removed the Presbyterian majority from their seats in 1648, the *Directory for Worship* was widely used in England and its colonies from 1645 to 1660.[21]

The *Directory for Worship* was not a Calvinist version of the *Book of Common Prayer*. It was instead a guidebook for ministers leading worship. It defined the elements of worship, including the sacraments, and provided an outline for how worship should be structured. The *Directory for Worship* called for worship to be centered on the sermon rather than on formal liturgies. The theologians who produced it believed the *Book of Common Prayer*'s heavy emphasis on standardized liturgies had devalued the importance of the sermon in worship.[22]

The Puritan-oriented ministers who arrived in Lancaster County in the 1650s would have followed the example of their colleagues in England by making use of the Parliament-approved *Directory for Worship*. Virginia law during the Commonwealth period did not constrain them from organizing worship in this way. The 1651 articles of the colony's surrender to the Commonwealth gave Virginia vestries the authority to decide whether or not to use the *Book of Common Prayer*. While this agreement has often been cited to support the continuing use of the prayer book in the colony during the Commonwealth era, the articles also affirmed the freedom of the vestries to structure worship according to the *Directory for Worship* then favored by Parliament. During the first decade of Lancaster County's existence, its leaders were legally empowered to work with their ministers to shape the theological identity and worship practices of its parishes along Presbyterian Puritan lines.[23]

During most of the decade of the 1660s, Lancaster vestries north of the Rappahannock were unable to secure the regular services of ministers in their parishes.[24] Tumultuous political events in England caused the flow of new ministers into the colony to slow to a trickle. By one estimate, there were only twelve clergymen for the 26,000 people who lived in the colony in 1661.[25] Lancaster officials looked to ministers in the neighboring parishes, mostly Puritans, to lead services as they were able. David Lindsay (a Scottish Presbyterian at Wicomico),[26] Francis Doughty (a radical Puritan at North Farnham and Sittenbourne),[27] and Richard Morris (a moderate Puritan at Christ Church south of the Rappahannock)[28] were almost certainly guided by the *Directory for Worship*. Presbyterian Puritan worship that was sermon-centered, and largely unconnected to the *Book of Common Prayer*, apparently continued for a second decade in Lancaster County.

In 1669, Lancaster officials recruited Benjamin Doggett (1636–1682) to serve both of its parishes. Lancaster leaders hired Doggett knowing that he would continue the county's Presbyterian Puritan theological identity and worship practices. Doggett had studied at St. John's College Cambridge from 1655 to 1662, where the master was Anthony Tuckney (1599–1670), a leading Presbyterian Puritan theologian. Tuckney, who was a member of the Westminster Assembly of Divines that produced the *Westminster Confession of Faith* and the *Directory for Worship,* would have made certain Benjamin Doggett was thoroughly trained in both. The Westminster Assembly also produced a *Form of Church Government* to guide the church into an era without bishops. Doggett was certainly well versed in that document as well.[29]

The timing of Doggett's graduation in March 1662 from a Presbyterian-oriented college at Cambridge put him in a very precarious position from which to launch an ordained ministry in the Church of England.[30] The monarchy had been restored in 1660, but the status of Presbyterian Puritans would not be sorted out until May 1662. Understanding that waiting for the Cavalier Parliament to act would further damage his chances of being ordained, Doggett moved quickly to find a bishop to ordain him before Parliament could put the new church settlement in place. He succeeded in making such an arrangement with a newly restored Scottish bishop. Thomas Sysderf (1581–1663) returned from exile with Charles II to become Bishop of Orkney in 1661 at the age of eighty. Sysderf ordained Benjamin Doggett on March 30, 1662.[31]

On May 19, 1662, Parliament passed the *Act of Uniformity,* establishing a well-defined Anglican orthodoxy and requiring all ministers to take an oath before their congregations endorsing the new settlement and a revised *Book of Common Prayer.* The Parliament established an early deadline for swearing the oath, St. Bartholomew's Day on August 24, knowing the new prayer book could not be published by that date. Puritans complained that they could not endorse a prayer book revision they could not yet read. When the deadline arrived, 3,000

Puritan clergy had not yet sworn the oath. They were summarily ejected from their Church of England pulpits and teaching positions. The century-old Puritan party with all its diverse elements (Independents, Presbyterians, radicals, and moderates) suddenly had no place in the Church of England and no legal existence within the realm.[32] Doggett's master at Cambridge was one of those who lost his position. However, the acute shortage of clergy created by the expulsion of more than 20 percent of the ministers of the Church of England meant that most new graduates, even those with questionable Presbyterian educational backgrounds, could find employment.[33]

Five months after his March 30, 1662, ordination, Benjamin Doggett was serving Stoke-by-Clare as minister and schoolmaster, probably securing the position from another minister who had held the rights to it. As required by law, he publicly swore the oath.[34] Many of the Puritan-trained ministers who, like Benjamin Doggett, complied with the *Act of Uniformity* to keep their church positions were treated with contempt by orthodox Anglicans and Puritans alike.[35] There can be little doubt Doggett found ministry in this highly polarized environment to be very difficult. By 1669, the opportunity to serve a parish in a county of Virginia in which his Presbyterian Puritan training would be an asset rather than a millstone around his neck could well have been very attractive to Doggett.[36]

In Lancaster County, where the *Directory for Worship* had shaped religious identity and worship from the beginning, Benjamin Doggett was free to preach and teach the Calvinist theology and Presbyterian churchmanship he learned at Cambridge. That Doggett was an excellent fit for the theological culture of Lancaster County is confirmed by his nomination by the two vestries to be inducted into a tenured position.[37] This was a rare occurrence in seventeenth-century Virginia, where vestries much preferred keeping their ministers on twelve-month contracts from which they could be dismissed without cause. By the time of his death in 1682, Doggett had created the template for a successful and long-tenured Presbyterian Puritan minister in the county.

When Lancaster officials began the search for Doggett's successor in 1682, they were confronted with an ecclesiastical landscape still in transition following the 1662 expulsion of moderate Puritans. Two decades had passed since the last Puritan minister had been formally trained and ordained in the Church of England. Two Rappahannock region parishes, Sittenbourne and Washington, were able to work around the anti-Puritan Anglican regulations during the 1670s by hiring the Cambridge-educated brothers Amory Butler (1649–1678) and William Butler (1647–1681). They were not ordained in the Church of England and most likely received theological and ecclesiastical training from their ejected Presbyterian Puritan minister father and his non-conformist colleagues. Both of the Butlers had successful ministries in Virginia.[38] Another Rappahannock region parish, Christ Church in Middlesex, hired the Oxford-educated John Shepard (1646–1683), who had a successful ministry in Virginia without being ordained by a bishop.[39]

Lancaster leaders knew these ministers and might have considered this model in their search for a Presbyterian successor to Benjamin Doggett. They would also have understood that ministers with Anglican ordinations and credentials were a decided minority among the clergy in their part of Virginia. Of the seven ministers serving Lancaster's neighboring parishes in the Rappahannock region in 1680, only one is known to have been ordained by an Anglican bishop. Lancaster officials would also have recognized that Anglican-ordained ministers were in the minority in the colony as a whole. Of the thirty-four ministers on the 1680 Virginia clergy list, evidence of Anglican ordination exists for only nine. But records showing as many as twenty-six of these ministers had higher-education credentials suggests a significant number fit the pattern of the Butlers and John Shepard.[40]

Lancaster vestrymen might well have been surprised by how suddenly both the supply and demographics of ministers in Virginia were changing. With England finally recovering from the acute shortage of clergy created by the expulsion of Puritan ministers in 1662, Henry Compton was successfully recruiting Anglican-credentialed ministers for Virginia. By June 1680, the supply of clergy had improved significantly, with only two of the forty-eight parishes served exclusively by readers.[41] During the next three and a half years, Virginia received fifteen additional ministers to complement the thirty-four who were in place in 1680. This was the largest wave of new clergy to enter the colony in its seventy-eight-year history. In a dramatic turnaround, Virginia was making major progress toward having as many ministers as parishes. More importantly for Compton, he was closing in on his goal of replacing the nonconformist ministers who filled so many of Virginia's pulpits with Church of England–ordained clergy. This significant influx of new ministers into the colony, just as the Lancaster vestries were beginning their search in 1682, suggests they did not have to wait until 1686 to hire Benjamin Doggett's replacement.[42]

With neighboring parishes hiring two of Bishop Compton's Anglican-ordained recruits (Deuel Pead at Christ Church in Middlesex County in 1683 and Abraham Kenyon at Washington Parish in Westmoreland County in 1684), the theological profile of the clergy of the Rappahannock region was already changing. There can be little doubt that Lancaster officials were under pressure to make a similar hire in 1683 and 1684. Nonetheless, they chose not to employ a minister from the growing pool of ordained Anglicans Henry Compton was sending to the colony. Instead, they conducted their own transatlantic search in the hope of finding a minister who would fit the Presbyterian Puritan identity of the county. For this purpose, they were prepared to make use of the excellent business contacts maintained by wealthy merchant planters, such as the Carters and the Balls, with the British Isles.

By the late 1670s, some Puritan-oriented Virginia parishes were looking to Scottish-educated Presbyterians to help fill the void created by the removal of Presbyterian Puritan clergy from the Church of England. Two Anglican parishes in Lower Norfolk County, south of the James River, employed a series of Presbyterian-ordained ministers. The Scots-Irish Presbyterian James Porter had served Lynnhaven Parish from 1678 to 1683.[43] At his death, another Scots-Irish minister, Francis Makemie (c. 1658–1708), provided pastoral services to Lynnhaven and neighboring Elizabeth River Parish.[44] Makemie was educated at the University of Glasgow in Scotland and ordained by the Presbytery of Laggan in Ireland. In 1685, Makemie moved on to Accomac County, where he married the daughter of a wealthy merchant, engaged in trade, registered as a dissenter, and helped organize the first presbytery in the new world at Philadelphia.[45] Makemie's replacement at Lynnhaven Parish was another Scottish-trained Presbyterian, Josias Mackie, who was a graduate of Edinburgh.[46] Since these South-side parishes had so recently been able to employ ordained Presbyterian ministers to lead their Anglican congregations, Lancaster officials had reason to believe they could do the same.[47]

In 1686, the search of the Lancaster vestries finally led them to Andrew Jackson,[48] a Scots-Irish minister who, like Josias Mackie, was a graduate of Edinburgh.[49] By then events had further paved the way for Jackson's approval by the governor. Bishop Compton's impressive clergy recruitment campaign had come to a screeching halt in the summer of 1685. Compton had fallen out of favor with the new king, James II, and was suspended from his office in September 1686.[50] Governor Howard recognized the colony was once again suffering a serious shortage of clergy that was getting worse and begged London for help in 1686.[51] Diseases spawned by the harsh winter of 1686–1687 took the lives of some of Virginia's clergy. At the same time, other ministers were leaving their positions to avoid contracting one of these illnesses. In the second half of the decade, only five new ministers arrived in Virginia, of whom two were Huguenot-Anglicans. But they were not enough to cover the mounting losses by death and attrition.[52]

The suddenly desperate situation of 1686 made Governor Howard's decision to approve Andrew Jackson's employment in Lancaster County less difficult. While the governor's instructions from London specified that ministers in the colony were required to have Anglican ordinations and licenses,[53] seventeenth-century colonial officials remained reluctant to veto the decisions of vestries that displayed a strong preference to recruit and maintain nonconforming ministers.[54] Recognizing the Lancaster County parishes of Christ Church and St. Mary's Whitechapel were determined to employ a minister with Presbyterian credentials and having no realistic alternative, Governor Howard gave formal approval for the hiring of Andrew Jackson.[55]

In the spring of 1686, the governor summoned the clergy of the colony to James City to meet with him. He reported afterward that some of these ministers were not episcopally ordained, thereby confirming what the records suggest. Even more disturbing to him were nonconformist clergy whom he described as being ministers "only by their own direction of themselves to the ministry."[56] In some parishes, vestries chose not to hire ministers to save the money they would be required to spend on a clergyman's salary. They could employ a part-time reader for much less. The likelihood that some of these readers were gradually elevated to serve as ministers would explain the presence of "clergy" who did not have any kind of educational or ecclesiastical credentials.[57] Governor Howard assured officials in England he was addressing this problem by forbidding ministers who were not episcopally ordained to read absolution in public worship or to celebrate Holy Communion.[58]

By the spring of 1690, events in England had changed the course of the church in Virginia once again. In response to William of Orange's invasion, James II fled England, clearing the way for William and Mary to take the throne in 1689. Henry Compton, now back in place as Bishop of London, renewed his Anglican reform campaign in Virginia by adding one more component. In 1689, Compton appointed James Blair, a Scottish minister who had served in Virginia since 1685, as the commissary representing the bishop in Virginia. One of Blair's most important responsibilities was to help the governor rein in the power of the vestries.

By this time, Governor Howard had left Virginia and had passed governance responsibilities to Lieutenant Governor Francis Nicholson, a military man and determined advocate for the Church of England. In June 1690, Nicholson called for stricter enforcement of existing ecclesiastical laws. Reports coming to him from county court justices confirmed that in many places ministers were not conforming to the doctrine and rules of the Anglican church and were not using the prayer book. In response, the Council issued the following order on May 15, 1691: "Order that for the future noe Vestry presume to entertain any Minister in their parish who doth not in all things Comply with the Canons of the Church of England, nor suffer any Such Minister to Preach in their Church."[59] This was precisely the kind of action for which Compton had been pressing. At this time, Andrew Jackson and Josias Mackie were the only two Presbyterian-ordained ministers serving Anglican parishes in the colony. Nicholson's order put vestry leaders in Lancaster and Lower Norfolk on notice that the positions of their ministers could well be in jeopardy. When Francis Nicholson dismissed Josias Mackie from his parish in the spring of 1692, Lancaster leaders would have understood how perilous Andrew Jackson's situation had become.[60]

The 1689 Act of Toleration, passed in the aftermath of the Glorious Revolution that brought William and Mary to the throne, gave nonconformist

Protestants the right to form their own churches. It provided Mackie another avenue for ministry in Virginia after his dismissal from his Anglican parish.[61] He registered as a nonconformist and led services for Presbyterians in the South-side counties.[62] Lancaster officials, however, were determined to keep Andrew Jackson in his Anglican pulpit and they had an answer for Francis Nicholson and Bishop Compton that Mackie's vestry could not provide. By the fall of 1690, Andrew Jackson had handed over the Whitechapel Parish to John Bertrand, while retaining his position at Christ Church. With Bertrand's Huguenot-Anglican mission in place at Whitechapel, Lancaster officials could argue the following spring that they were moving toward full compliance with the May 15, 1691, directive of the Council.

St. Mary's Whitechapel Church, Lancaster, Virginia, showing the older brick of the center section where John Bertrand preached during the 1690s.
Photo by the author. Courtesy St. Mary's Whitechapel Episcopal Church, Lancaster, Virginia

This apparent compromise could well have given Andrew Jackson sufficient "cover" to hold his job until the crisis passed. But colonial records also show Jackson weathered every crisis that threatened his ministry in the county. He served in Lancaster for twenty-four years, until his death 1710. Jackson would be remembered as a very competent and well-loved minister. As William Meade, who had access to the lost vestry book of Christ Church Parish, wrote in 1857, Andrew Jackson "had been serving the parish faithfully . . . was much esteemed and beloved . . . and the people were very unwilling to part with him."[63]

John Bertrand's ministry in Lancaster County is documented by a will drafted in November 1690. In it, George Spencer authorized a payment to John Bertrand to preach his funeral sermon at St. Mary's Whitechapel.

Spencer was a wealthy member of the parish who was bequeathing funds to the parish to care for the poor and to purchase items needed to enhance the worship life of the church. He gave money to buy a communion plate and a surplice for the church.[64] The bequest of a surplice suggests the nature of the transition John Bertrand was initiating in Lancaster County. Since the early 1650s, Lancaster ministers had almost certainly officiated in the black Geneva pulpit gowns worn by all Presbyterian Puritan clergy. By introducing the surplice in worship at Whitechapel, John Bertrand was calling into question one of the defining symbols of the county's long-standing ecclesiastical identity. In the eighteenth century, a compromise between Puritan worship attire and Stuart-era Church of England clerical garb became common in Virginia's Anglican churches. The minister typically wore the white or cream-colored surplice when reading liturgy and administering sacraments. He then removed the surplice and put on a black academic gown before climbing into the pulpit to preach the sermon. The usual eighteenth-century practice was for the parish to provide the surplice and the minister to procure his own preaching gown.[65] Could John Bertrand have been one of the first clergymen to implement this compromise in Virginia?

The surplice also symbolized the English imperialist reform process Bertrand was charged to put in place in Lancaster. This is the type of innovation ministers recruited by Henry Compton were implementing across the colony. John Clayton arrived in Virginia in 1684 to serve the church in James City, the colony's capital. He introduced the surplice and the *Book of Common Prayer*, neither of which had been in use when he arrived. Deuel Pead, who was well known for his high-church Anglican identity, arrived at Christ Church Middlesex County in 1683. In April 1686, he preached a sermon in Jamestown to celebrate the first anniversary of the coronation of James II, in which he called on Virginians to make daily use of the prayer book.[66] By 1688, Pead was also serving South Farnham Parish.[67] His presence in South Farnham meant there could well have been two surplice-wearing Anglican ministers in Puritan-oriented Rappahannock County. This is a development that would have warmed the heart of Francis Nicholson, who was the colony's lieutenant governor at the time. Both Pead and Clayton, however, found the challenge of introducing Virginia parishes to Bishop Compton's Anglican reforms to be a decidedly daunting task. Both returned to England for successful careers as clergymen in the mother country. Clayton left Virginia in 1686, and Pead followed in 1690.[68]

The changes implemented by Bishop Compton's imperialist project in Virginia through the early 1690s did not continue. By the middle of the decade, Virginia ministers were clearly disappointed by the performance of the commissary. When Bishop Compton appointed Scottish clergyman James Blair to represent him as commissary in Virginia in 1689, the ministers had good reason to expect Blair to help restore a sense of balance between the authority of the vestries and that of the clergy. But to their great disappointment, the ministers found Blair supporting the influential lay leaders who were expanding the power of the vestries in Virginia far beyond anything that existed in the Church of England. It might be that Blair's background in the Anglican Restoration Church of Scotland, with its emphasis on the governing authority of elders at the local level, predisposed him to see strong vestries in a more positive light than Compton.[69]

Blair's marriage into one of the elite families of Virginia most likely influenced his perspective. His new status clearly increased his political clout in Virginia and might also have given him a more sympathetic ear to the desire of leading families to maintain control of their parish churches.[70] Not surprisingly, Blair had a much better relationship with these wealthy planters than he did with his fellow clergy.[71] In his 1697 letter to the Bishop of Lichfield, the Huguenot-Anglican Nicholas Moreau expressed his bitter disappointment with Blair's failure to rein in the vestries. Having given up on the commissary as an effective instrument for checking the power of the vestries, Moreau called for the appointment of a bishop in Virginia to institute "a severe observation of the Canons of the Church."[72]

Henry Compton's Anglican reform project in Virginia was also sabotaged by conflict between its two most important agents—the commissary and the governor. By the end of 1696, James Blair was locked in a desperate power struggle with Governor Edmund Andros, leaving Virginia ministers on their own to continue Compton's reform process with vestries that were no longer constrained by colonial authorities. The bad blood between Blair and Andros led to a complete breakdown of trust between them as the commissary launched a campaign to have Andros removed from office. In the spring of 1697, Blair sailed for England to lobby for the governor's dismissal. Bishop Compton agreed to support his commissary's recommendation to fire the governor. Perhaps Blair was able to convince him that malpractice by Virginia's governor was a greater threat to his imperialist program than the machinations of the vestries. With Blair's departure from England delayed until late in the summer of 1698, the campaign to reduce the power of the vestries in Virginia was on hold for two years or more.[73]

By the time Blair arrived home in the fall of 1698, John Bertrand was no longer serving in Lancaster County. A record, preserved in the *Lancaster County Deed Book*, offers compelling evidence that Andrew Jackson replaced John Bertrand as Whitechapel minister by the fall of 1698. This deed, from Jackson to Mary Pullen on October 12, 1698, identifies him as serving both Christ Church and Whitechapel.[74] While the records give no indication of the circumstances of the dissolution of Bertrand's pastoral relationship with

Whitechapel, the sequence of events points to the vestry refusing to renew his annual contract or forcing his resignation.

Bertrand was vulnerable to being terminated in this way for several reasons. A minister leading worship in a surplice and making regular use of the 1662 prayer book challenged the Presbyterian Puritan identity of the county. According to one Virginia minister, resistance to the surplice by Anglicans in Virginia continued to be strong as late as 1724.[75] Any attempt by Bertrand to implement Bishop Compton's policy of weakening the authority of the vestry would have certainly threatened county leaders. While the clergy shortage in Virginia could be a deterrent to releasing a minister, Lancaster County had the well-regarded Presbyterian Andrew Jackson in place at Christ Church. Once Lancaster officials were satisfied Jackson's position was secure, a return to the earlier arrangement of having him serve both parishes would have been appealing to those who wished to reassert the county's long-standing Calvinist identity and resist Bishop Compton's imperialist reforms.

The strong affinity of Lancaster leaders for Andrew Jackson's ministry was spelled out in a 1704 letter from the Christ Church vestry to the governor. Once again, colonial officials were contemplating a new church policy that would reduce the power vestries wielded over their ministers and place Jackson's employment in jeopardy.[76] In its letter, the vestry expressed strong opposition to the proposed policy and deep appreciation for Jackson's eighteen-year ministry to that point. In describing his ministry as a "singular blessing," they affirmed in particular Jackson's character, conversation, and *doctrine*.[77] Jackson's *doctrine* was grounded in the very precise Calvinist formulations of the *Westminster Confession of Faith,* in which he had been trained at Edinburgh. John Bertrand's more nuanced Huguenot-Anglican Calvinism would have struck his Whitechapel parishioners as a very different *doctrine* from the one espoused by Andrew Jackson and Benjamin Doggett before him.

John Bertrand was placed at a severe disadvantage by Jackson's identification with the *Directory for Worship* from the Westminster Standards.[78] As a French Protestant, Bertrand had not been trained in the *Directory for Worship.* Having grown up with the liturgies of the French Reformed Church, some of which were written by John Calvin, he would not have understood the appeal of the liturgy-free *Directory for Worship* in the Rappahannock region.[79] In a parish that was well versed in the *Directory*'s sermon-centered worship, Bertrand's commitment to the prayer book could only weaken the support for his ministry in the county.

Perhaps the most compelling reason to doubt that Bertrand's ministry could have survived at Whitechapel through the end of 1698 was his frayed relationship with Robert Carter and other county leaders resulting from Bertrand's role in the bitter controversy over Virginia's land policies. The ruling from the Board of Trade in London reducing the power of the Council to grant land likely arrived in the colony by the spring of 1698. With the dramatic convergence of the imperialist controversies over land and religion, both challenging the power of colonial elites, Bertrand's ministry in Lancaster became untenable. Moreover, Robert Carter's well-documented appreciation for Andrew Jackson[80] made it easy for him to advocate returning the Whitechapel Parish to the pastoral leadership of the Scots-Irish minister.

John Bertrand was not the only agent of Henry Compton's imperialist project to suffer failure in Virginia during this turbulent period. In Puritan-oriented counties like Lancaster, the resistance to Compton's efforts to reduce the power of vestries was fierce.[81] Bertrand's experience at North Farnham and Whitechapel parishes fits the larger pattern, which can be identified in most of the parishes of the Rappahannock region where Anglican reform clearly generated a recognizable backlash. Compton's Anglican-ordained recruits were employed in six Rappahannock region parishes during the 1680s and early 1690s: Cople[82] and Washington[83] in Westmoreland, Sittenbourne[84] in Essex/Richmond, North Farnham in Richmond, Whitechapel in Lancaster,[85] and Christ Church[86] in Middlesex. Of these six parishes, five replaced Compton's recruits with ministers who did not have Anglican credentials. Like most of the ministers Henry Compton sent to the Rappahannock region during the 1680s and early 1690s, John Bertrand's Huguenot-Anglican mission to Lancaster County appears to have met with little success. Both Lancaster parishes remained devoted to their Scots-Irish Presbyterian minister.[87]

Henry Compton's Anglican recruits quickly learned the vestry-dominated Virginia church was notoriously hard on ministers, especially those who believed they were entitled to the security afforded to their colleagues serving in England. That John Bertrand stayed in Virginia to the end of his life when other well-educated and competent clergy licensed by Bishop Compton chose to return to England testifies to his strong sense of calling to his dual-track ministry in Virginia. Bertrand's willingness to remain in Virginia was undoubtedly strengthened by his role as spiritual leader of the French Protestant refugee community, which included family and friends from his hometown in western France. He bore special responsibility for helping these settlers integrate into Virginia society and its Anglican Church. While this work added a layer of complexity to Bertrand's ministry in Virginia, it also tied him to the colony in a way his English-born clergy colleagues were not. John Bertrand was firmly bound to a community whose members understood they could never go home again.

Nicholas Moreau returned to England in 1702 to rejoin his wife, who was not willing to immigrate to the new world. While the court records offer no information about Moreau's dual-tract ministry in Essex County, he described his previous parish in New Kent as "the very worst parish in Virginia and most troublesome."[88] One can imagine that after his move to South Farnham, he faced many of the same challenges John Bertrand did. With Paul Micou emerging as an influential leader in Essex County by the end of the seventeenth century, Moreau enjoyed a powerful Huguenot ally whom Bertrand had never had in Lancaster.

As John Bertrand's Lancaster County ministry was collapsing, he was once again serving the North Farnham Parish in Richmond County, where he had started when he first arrived in the colony in 1687. North Farnham ended its relationship with nonconformist John Davis in 1695. When their next pastor was disabled after a few months on the job, the parish vestry rehired John Bertrand, perhaps reluctantly, in 1696.[89] North Farnham had a much larger Huguenot refugee population than the Lancaster parishes and had leaders like second-generation Huguenots John Tavernor and his Georg/Nicolas/Clerke relatives. It is likely that Bertrand continued serving North Farnham until his death in 1701. As the seventeenth century drew to an end and John Bertrand's time on earth grew short, his Huguenot-Anglican mission to Virginia was very much alive.[90]

NOTES

1. Mr. Nicholas Moreau to William Lloyd, the Right Honorable the Lord Bishop of Lichfield and Coventry, His Majesty's High Almoner, 12 April 1697, in William Stevens Perry, ed. *Historical Collections Relating to the American Colonial Church*, vol. 1 (Hartford, CT, 1870), 29–32.

2. Manross, *Fulham Papers in Lambeth Palace Library*, 159.

3. Mr. Nicholas Moreau to William Lloyd, in Perry, ed., *Historical Collections*, 29–32.

4. Seiler, "The Anglican Parish Vestry in Colonial Virginia," 1, 320, and 321; Bond, *Damned Souls*, 215.

5. Beverley, *The History and Present State of Virginia*, 211.

6. Warner, *History of ORC*, 125–26.

7. Tarter, "Bacon's Rebellion, the Grievances of the People," 21, 34–35.

8. Stanwood, *The Empire Reformed*, 27–30.

9. Carpenter, *The Protestant Bishop*, 256.

10. Ibid., 257.

11. Ibid., 262.

12. For the early history of the churches in Lancaster County, see George Carrington Mason, "The Colonial Churches of Northumberland and Lancaster Counties, Virginia (Concluded)," VMHB 54, no. 3 (July 1946) 233–43.

13. LC DB, 1652–1657, 2.

14. John T. McNeill, *The History and Character of Calvinism* (Oxford, UK, 1954), 322–30.

15. Bradley, *The Puritans of Virginia*, 68–69; Jett, *Lancaster County, Virginia*, 31; Hening, *Statutes at Large*, vol. 1, 374. For Fleete's relationship with pioneer Puritan minister John Rosier, see LC DWB, 2, 119. Rosier's son married Underwood's daughter.

16. Warner, *History of ORC*, 124, 125, and 131; Venn, *Alumni Catabrigiences*, vol. 3, 488; Mason, "The Colonial Churches of Westmoreland and King George Counties, Virginia, Part I," VMHB 56, no. 2 (April 1948), 172.

17. LC DWB, 1652–1657, 41–42, 129–30; Venn, *Alumni Catabrigiences*, vol. 1, 382; Mason, "The Colonial Churches of Northumberland and Lancaster Counties, Virginia (Concluded)," 234.

18. Warner, *History of ORC*, 131 and 133; SP, LC DWB, 1654–1661, 130; Venn, *Alumni Catabrigiences*, vol. 1, 268; #26310, CCEd.

19. William A. Shaw, *A History of the English Church During the Civil Wars and Under the Commonwealth* (London, 1900), vol. 2, 370; LC OB, 1656–1666, 1 and 91; Mason, "The Colonial Churches of Northumberland and Lancaster Counties, Virginia (Concluded)," 235.

20. C. H. Firth and R. S. Raitt, eds., *Acts and Ordinances of the Interregnum, 1642–1660* (London, 1911), Table of Acts 1645, XXX–XIiii, 4 January 1647.

21. Diane Purkiss, *The English Civil War: Papists, Gentlewomen, Soldiers, and Witchfinders in the Birth of Modern Britain* (New York, 2006), 234; John Gwynfor Jones, "The Growth of Puritanism, c. 1559–1662," in *The Great Ejectment of 1662: Its Antecedents, Aftermath, and Ecumenical Significance*, ed., Alan P. F. Sell (Eugene, OR, 2012), 44–48.

22. John H. Leith, *Introduction to the Reformed Tradition* (Atlanta, 1977), 180–82.

23. Hening, *Statutes at Large*, 364; George MacLaren Brydon, *Religious Life of Virginia in the Seventeenth Century: Faith of Our Fathers* (Williamsburg, VA, 1957), 37.

24. LC OB, 1656–1666, 153.

25. Brydon, *Religious Life of Virginia in the Seventeenth Century*, 37; Bond, *Damned Souls*, 181.

26. David Lindsay served Wicomico Parish from 1655 to 1667. Though he was apparently from a family that supported James I's appointment of bishops for the Church of Scotland, his training at St. Andrews University was grounded in the *Directory for Worship*, LC OB, 1655–1666, 59 (1658) and 290 (1664); Warren, "Gossip and Slander in Northumberland County in the Last Half of the Seventeenth Century," 41–52; NC WB, 1666–1678, 11; Fleet, vol. 1, 566; WMQ 16 (1907), 136; Mason, "The Colonial Churches of Northumberland and Lancaster Counties, Virginia (Concluded)," 235.

27. Francis Doughty served North Farnham and Sittenbourne Parishes from 1662 to 1669. ORC DB, 1656–1664, Part II, 191–92; #86798, CCEd; ORC DWB, no 1, 1665–1677, 38–39; ORC DB, 1668–1672, 21, and 61–67; Stanard, "Abstracts of Rappahannock County Wills," 290; Bell, *Empire, Religion, and Revolution*, 90.

28. Richard Morris served Christ Church south of the Rappahannock from 1663 to 1666. Joseph Foster, ed., *Alumni Oxonienses, the members of the University of Oxford, 1500–1714* . . . (Oxford, 1891), 1026–49; Chamberlayne, ed., *The Vestry*

Book of Christ Church Parish, Middlesex County, Virginia, 1663–1767, 2, 6, and 9; Bond, *Damned Souls*, 205; Bell, *Empire, Religion, and Revolution*, 180.

29. Robert Forsyth Scott, *St. John's College Cambridge* (London, 1907), Chap. V. When pressured to hire radical Puritans, Tuckney refused, saying, "They may deceive me in their godliness, they cannot in their scholarship."

30. Syndics of Cambridge University Library, UA, Subscriptions 2, 92.

31. Benjamin Doggett ordination record, #101399, CCEd. The listing notes that the wrong date, March 30, 1651, was entered into the record. There was no Bishop of Orkney in 1651, and Thomas Sydserf's tenure in that position was 1661–1663. Given the dates of Doggett's graduation and license to serve in ministry, it is likely he was ordained on March 30, 1662. Thomas Sydserf also ordained Jean Durel in Paris in 1660. Durel immigrated to London by 1662 to lead the French Church of the Savoy.

32. MacCulloch, *The Reformation: A History*, 530.

33. John Raithby, ed., *Statutes of the Realm* (London, 1810–1829), vol. 5, 1628–1680, 364–70; David J. Appleby, "From Ejectment to Toleration in England, 1662–1689," in Sell, *The Great Ejectment of 1662*, 80.

34. Syndics of Cambridge University Library, UA, Subscriptions 2, 92; #101399, #135799, and #135800, #23842, CCEd.

35. Appleby, "From Ejectment to Toleration in England, 1662–1689," 74–75.

36. Jett, *Lancaster County, Virginia*, 58.

37. *General Court Will Book, no. 2*, 37, in "Notes from the Council and General Court Records, 1641–1672," VMHB 8, no. 3 (January 1901), 244.

38. For Amory Butler, see Venn, *Alumni Catabrigiences,* vol. 1, 271 and 274; ORC DB, 1672–1676, Part I, 29–30. For Amory's brother, William, see Dorman, WC DWB, 1665–1677, Part 3, 41; Dorman WC OB, 1675/6–1688/9, Part 2, 1679–1682, 63.

39. Foster, *Alumni Oxoniences, 1500–1714*, 1322–50; National Society of Colonial Dames of America (Virginia), ed., *Christ Church Middlesex County Parish Register* (Richmond, VA, 1897), 8.

40. Other area ministers known to Lancaster officials who fit the pattern of having educational qualifications without Anglican credentials include Richard Morris at Christ Church south of the Rappahannock (1663–1666), John Farnefold at Fairfield Parish in Northumberland County (1670–1702), Samuel Dudley at Sittenbourne (1678–1682), and John Davis of Sittenbourne, St. Mary's, and North Farnham (1684–1695). Charles Dacres of North Farnham and Wicomico Parishes (1672–1687) is the only neighboring minister for whom neither educational nor ordination records have yet been found. The only documented Anglican-ordained minister in the Northern Neck in 1680, other than Benjamin Doggett, was John Scrimgeour (identified as Scrimmington on the 1680 Virginia clergy list) at Cople Parish in Westmoreland County, serving from c. 1680 to 1691.

41. For a list of the thirty-four clergy serving Virginia parishes in 1680, see "A List of the Parishes in Virginia in 1680," in Various Authors, *Colonial Records of Virginia*, 318–23. Two of these ministers, John Wood and Paul Williams, are known to have been ordained and/or licensed by Bishop of London Henry Compton just before sailing for Virginia, where they arrived by early 1680. #97244 and #78001, CCEd.

42. The 1680 Virginia clergy list cited previously can be cross-referenced with lists published by Nelson Rightmyer and James B. Bell to identify most of the ministers arriving in Virginia between June of 1680 and 1685. Rightmyer, "List of Anglican Clergy Receiving a Bounty for Overseas Service," 176–77, and Bell, *Empire, Religion, and Revolution*, 189–91. See also Dell Upton, *Holy Things and Profane: Anglican Parish Churches in Colonial Virginia* (New Haven, CT, 1997), 175–92. The fifteen ministers arriving in the colony as the Lancaster search was underway were James Blair, John Carr, John Clayton, John Davis, Superior Davis, Thomas Finney, Abraham Kenyon, Josias Mackie, Francis Makemie, William Mullett, William Paris, Deuel Pead, Thomas Perkins, James Sclater, and Isaac Vary. Of these, seven ministers (Blair, Clayton, Finney, Kenyon, Mullett, Pead, and Sclater) had documented Anglican ordinations.

43. Brydon, *Virginia's Mother Church*, vol. 1, 252, 255, and 479.

44. For a genealogical exploration of records treating Francis Makemie, see Richard S. Uhrbrock, "Francis Makemie (c. 1658–1708)," *Colonial Genealogist* 8, no. 3 (1976), 115–25, no. 4 (1977), 189–95. The close relationship of the family of Charles Ewell, husband of John Bertrand's daughter, Mary Ann, with Francis Makemie is documented in Lee, *A Brief History of Belle Isle Plantation*, 58.

45. McIlwaine, *Executive Journals*, 427; *Accomac County OB, 1697–1705*, 74; James H. Smylie, *A Brief History of the Presbyterians* (Louisville, KY, 1996), 39–43; I. Marshall Page, *The Life Story of Rev. Francis Makemie* (Grand Rapids, MI, 1938).

46. Bell, *Empire, Religion, and Revolution*, 193.

47. Teagle, "Mean Tobacco and a Well-Beloved Minister," 6230.

48. In their recruitment of Andrew Jackson, Lancaster officials might have had help from Josias Mackie and Francis Makemie. Makemie likely had a role in recruiting Josias Mackie for Elizabeth River Parish. Page, *The Life Story of Rev. Francis Makemie*, 65–72. See also Brydon, *Virginia's Mother Church*, 252–53.

49. The sudden increase in the supply of ministers in Virginia just as Lancaster began its search raises questions about the reported statement of Lancaster's Christ Church vestry in 1704 that no other minister wanted this position after Benjamin Doggett's death. Brydon, *Virginia's Mother Church*, vol. 1, Appendix VIII, 531–32; Seiler, "The Parish Vestry in Colonial Virginia," 322–24.

50. Carpenter, *The Protestant Bishop*, 97, 100, and 101; Billings, *Papers of Francis Howard*, 274.

51. Ibid., 282.

52. Bond, *Damned Souls*, 221–22. The ministers arriving in Virginia during the second half of the 1680s were John Bertrand (1687), Cope D'Oyley (1687), Stephen Fouace (1688), John Gordon (1688), and Samuel Eburne (1688), as noted by Bell, *Empire, Religion, and Revolution*, 189–90, and Rightmyer, "List of Anglican Clergy Receiving a Bounty for Overseas Service," 176–77.

53. Bell, *Empire, Religion, and Revolution*, 117.

54. James B. Bell sees the reluctance of colonial officials to intervene in local parish affairs as a key reason for the hiring of Presbyterians Josias Mackie and Andrew Jackson. Ibid., 105–06.

55. Teagle, "Mean Tobacco and a Well-Beloved Minister," 6233.

56. For Governor Howard's conference with Virginia clergy, see Billings, *Papers of Francis Howard*, 458–59. While the conference is described in an undated letter to Bishop Nathaniel Crew, the content of the letter points to the spring of 1686.

57. Leaving parishes vacant and employing readers as a cost-saving alternative were among the abuses Bishop of London Henry Compton reported to the Lords of Trade and Plantations in July 1677. Bell, *Empire, Religion, and Revolution*, 111.

58. Billings, *Papers of Francis Howard*, 458–59.

59. McIlwaine, *Executive Journals*, 176.

60. For the dismissal of Mackie by August 1692, see the October 4, 1699, record abstract from Princess Anne County published in WMQ 2, 1st series, 179–80. The record is a report from the county justices to the Council on the dissenting Presbyterian congregations Mackie was leading after registering as a dissenting minister on August 15, 1692. This incident is also described in Brydon, *Virginia's Mother Church*, 254–56.

61. For the importance of the Glorious Revolution to nonconformists in England and America, see Kidd, *The Protestant Interest*, 1–28.

62. Josias Mackie's dismissal may also indicate that some of the more radical Puritan residents of his Lower Norfolk County parish were not pleased to be served by a Presbyterian minister. Bond, *Damned Souls*, 155–57.

63. Meade, *Old Churches, Ministers, and Families of Virginia*, vol. 2, 123.

64. LC WB 8, 1690–1709, 11–12.

65. Nelson, *A Blessed Company*, 361, note #70.

66. Richard Beale Davis, ed., "A Sermon Preached at James City in Virginia the 23rd of April 1686 Before the Loyal Society of Citizens Born in and about London and Inhabiting Virginia by Deuel Pead," WMQ 17 (1960), 371–94.

67. The research of Thomas Hoskins Warner uncovered an April 13, 1688, land record and a November 7, 1689, marriage record listing "Dewell Prad" in South Farnham Parish in Rappahannock County. Warner, *History of ORC*, 142.

68. Bond, *Damned Souls*, 216–22; SP, *Middlesex County* OB, 1690–1694, 21; Chamberlayne, *The Vestry Book of Christ Church Parish, Middlesex County*, 69–70.

69. For James Blair's participation in the Restoration Church of Scotland, with its combination of episcopal rule at the national church level and Presbyterian practice at the local level, see P. G. Scott, "James Blair and the Scottish Church: A New Source," 300–08.

70. Bernard Bailyn, "Politics and Social Structure in Virginia," in *Seventeenth-Century America: Essays in Colonial History*, ed. James Morton Smith (Chapel Hill, NC, 1959), 113.

71. For a striking example of the frustration of Virginia ministers with James Blair, see "Account of the Proceedings of the Clergy of Virginia at the Church at Williamsburg, 1705," in *Historical Collections*, ed. Perry, vol. 1, 144–53.

72. Nicholas Moreau to William Lloyd, Bishop of Lichfield and Coventry, April 12, 1697, in *Historical Collections*, ed. Perry, vol. 1, 29–32.

73. Rouse, *James Blair of Virginia*, 96–116. For Blair's successful indictment of Andros before Bishop of London Henry Compton and Archbishop of Canterbury Tenison at Lambeth Palace in London on December 27, 1697, see Manross, ed., *The*

Fulham Papers in the Lambeth Palace Library, American Colonial Section, Calendar and Indexes, 160–61.

74. LC DB, 1687–1700, 162.

75. Hugh Jones, *The Present State of Virginia* (London, 1724), 69–70.

76. "Sir Edward Northey's Opinion Concerning Induction of Ministers in Virginia, July 29, 1703," in *Historical Collections*, ed. Perry, vol. 1, 127–28.

77. Brydon, *Virginia's Mother Church*, vol. 1, Appendix VIII, 517–32.

78. Bell, *Empire, Religion, and Revolution*, 90.

79. For the Huguenot use of set prayers by John Calvin and his mentor, Martin Bucer, see E. B. Holifield, "Worship," in *Encyclopedia of the Reformed Faith* (Louisville, KY, 1992), ed. Donald McKim, 410–12.

80. When Robert Carter became the agent of the Northern Neck Proprietary, his office awarded 2,146 acres in Richmond County to Andrew Jackson in 1704. Teagle, "Mean Tobacco and a Well-Beloved Minister," 6236–42.

81. Stanwood, *The Empire Reformed,* 85–112; Kidd, *The Protestant Interest*, 17.

82. Anglican-ordained John Scrimgoeur served Cople Parish in Westmoreland County from c. 1680 to 1691 and was replaced by John Bolton, for whom no ordination record exists. #102340, CCEd; Venn, *Alumni Catabrigienses,* Part I, vol. 4, 44; WC OB, 1690–1698, 122 and 144a; WC DWB, 1698, February 3; Bertha Lawrence Newton Davison, "First Fifty Years in the Life of Cople Parish," *Northern Neck of Virginia Historical Magazine* 40, no. 1 (December 1990), 4592–600.

83. Anglican-ordained Abraham Kenyon served Washington Parish in Westmoreland from 1684 to 1686 and was replaced by Harvard-trained Puritan William Thompson. Dorman, WC OB, 1675/6–1688/9, Part Six, 1687–1688/9, 11; #82132, CCEd; Lothrop Withington, "Virginia Gleanings in England (Continued)," VMHB 13, no. 2 (October 1905), 193–95; Bell, *Empire, Religion, and Revolution*, 87, 91, and 92.

84. Anglican-ordained Abraham Kenyon served Sittenbourne Parish from 1686 to 1690 and was replaced by Thomas Vicars, for whom no ordination record exists. Warner, *History of ORC*, 136; SP, EC DWB, 1692–1693, 23, 59, 70, and 87; Nugent, *Cavaliers and Pioneers*, vol. 2, 363.

85. John Bertrand was replaced by Puritan nonconformist John Davis at North Farnham in 1693 and Presbyterian Andrew Jackson at Whitechapel about 1698.

86. Deuel Pead, Anglican-ordained clergyman who served Christ Church in Middlesex from 1683 to 1690, had a properly credentialed Anglican successor in Samuel Gray. Chamberlayne, *The Vestry Book of Christ Church Parish, Middlesex County, Virginia, 1663–1767*, 41 and 69–70; Warner, *History of ORC*, 142; #6554, #92506 and #82019, CCEd; Bond, *Damned Souls*, 216–22; Kilby, *Christ Church Parish Register, Middlesex County Virginia, 1651–1821,* 254; Bell, *Empire, Religion, and Revolution*, 178; Davison, "First Fifty Years in the Life of Cople Parish," 4605–15.

87. Andrew Jackson's years of service at St. Mary's Whitechapel were from 1686 to 1690 and from c. 1698 to 1710.

88. Nicholas Moreau to William Lloyd, Bishop of Lichfield and Coventry, April 12, 1697, in *Historical Collections*, ed. Perry, vol. 1, 29–32.

89. The last appearance of John Davis in the records of Richmond County was August 9, 1695. RC OB, 1694–1697, 79. Davis had been replaced at North Farnham

by John/Alexander Burnett, who was serving the parish by February 1695. By June 1695, Burnett was ill and disabled. He died in the fall of 1699. SP, RC OB, 1694–1697, 22 and 40; RC OB, 1697–1699, 64 and 123.

90. John Bertrand's renewed activity in Richmond County is documented from April 1697. Ibid., 91. His preaching of a funeral sermon at North Farnham in July 1698 confirms Bertrand's renewed ministry there. Fleet, vol. 1, 306–07; *TLC Genealogy, Richmond County Virginia Miscellaneous Records, 1699–1724*, 62.

Chapter Seven

South Farnham Parish, 1733

> About ten of the clock, we mounted our horses, Mr. Beverley with us, and we went about seven miles to his parish church, where we had a good sermon from a French man named Mr. De Lattiny, who is minister of this parish.
>
> —John Fontaine, November 17, 1715

By the end of the seventeenth century, the Huguenot-Anglican Refuge in the Rappahannock region of Virginia was firmly planted.[1] However, John Bertrand did not live to see the fulfillment of his ecclesiastical mission or the full impact of the Refuge he helped to launch. He died, apparently at his Lancaster County plantation, during the summer of 1701.[2] Yet Durand's Virginia Huguenot dream and Bishop Compton's imperialist program continued to move forward after John Bertrand's death, as the Huguenot-Anglican Refuge grew in numbers and influence during the first four decades of the eighteenth century. Some of the émigrés and their children were assuming leadership roles in their counties and parishes as they acquired land and built wealth.

As a new century dawned, other forces were lending strength to the work of Henry Compton's French exile ministers in America. The Society for the Propagation of the Gospel in Foreign Parts (SPG) was founded in 1701 to provide new focus and energy to the Anglican Church in the new world.[3] The SPG sent missionaries to overseas parishes, along with money, books, and Bibles. The society was particularly effective in reaching out to Huguenot congregations in America that were willing to entertain conformity to the Church of England.[4] Financial support from the society played an important role in encouraging independent Huguenot congregations in the colonies of South Carolina and New York to become Anglican during the first decade of the eighteenth century. With the establishment of the Anglican Church in South Carolina in 1706, four rural Huguenot congregations and annexes chose to be absorbed into the newly created parishes of Saint Denis,

Saint James Santee, Saint James Goosecreek, and Saint John's Berkeley. In 1709, the Huguenot congregation in New Rochelle voted to become an Anglican parish. Evidence suggests these new Anglican parishes embraced the Calvinist theology and hybrid Huguenot-Anglican worship practices of London's French Church of the Savoy.[5]

By the end of the seventeenth century, the English imperialist enterprise was becoming more successful in America. In the context of a long-running war with France, English colonial residents in America were more willing to accept centralized authority imposed by the Crown as the necessary price of security against raids by Native Americans allied with the French. English officials learned how to play on these fears to create momentum for the empire. As Owen Stanwood has written: "By the eighteenth century . . . Anglo-Americans embraced their identity as subjects of a powerful English monarch."[6] The Huguenots of the Rappahannock region were becoming part of a larger mosaic of English Americans who found their personal interests closely aligned with the English imperial enterprise.

One important imperialist project for Huguenots in America came to fruition during the last year of John Bertrand's life. In 1700, a large wave of Huguenot refugees began to pour into Virginia on five ships financed by William III.[7] The first two ships to arrive were the *Mary and Ann* in July 1700 and the *Peter and Anthony* in September 1700. Surviving passenger lists for these ships document 384 French and other European refugees.[8] Most of these emigrants are believed to have formed a new Huguenot settlement at Manakin Town in the Virginia Piedmont near the present-day city of Richmond. The profile of the Manakin settlers was quite different from the Rappahannock Huguenots. They were less merchant-oriented and much less likely to be from the Atlantic provinces of western France. Benjamin de Joux, the first pastor at Manakin Town, was from the Vaudois region of Dauphiné in southeast France.[9]

Many of the French settlers who were transported on the first two ships were less than satisfied with the location of the Manakin Town settlement. Manakin was situated on the frontier of European settlement in 1700 and was considered to be vulnerable to attack by Native Americans. Unlike the Rappahannock region in Virginia's upper tidewater counties, Manakin was isolated from the water transportation system of the colony that connected Virginians to the Atlantic world. While the refugees who went to Manakin Town formed a homogeneous French community where they would not need to be bilingual, they never had the range of economic opportunities afforded the Huguenots who settled earlier along the Rappahannock. Moreover, the isolated location of Manakin Town forced them to become farmers, a vocation most knew nothing about before arriving in Virginia. For many, this was a slow and difficult transition that left the settlement dependent on charitable assistance from Virginia and England during its early years of existence. The capacity of the Manakin refugees to financially support their newly established Anglican parish, named King William, was severely compromised by their difficult economic circumstances.[10] The Huguenot-Anglican ministers who served this French-speaking parish were not required to be fluent in English because they were not engaged in the dual-track ministry that characterized the Rappahannock Refuge.

When the first ship, the *Mary and Ann,* arrived in Virginia in June 1700, it was met by representatives of a Huguenot named Bertrand Servant, a native of Saintonge who lived near the mouth of the James River. Servant was naturalized in 1698 and became a court justice for Elizabeth City County. He provided the weary passengers fruit, cider, milk, and salt. When Servant, or his men, observed the ship captain abusing the refugees, he offered a written statement to document the abuse. Durand de Dauphiné had also met Bertrand Servant in 1686. His account noted his overnight stay at the home of "Monsieur Servant."[11]

At least two immigrants arriving on the second ship, the *Peter and Anthony,* continued their journey into the Rappahannock Refuge. Theodore de Rousseau and Isaac Trocq settled in Richmond County, where they formed close relationships with members of the 1680s migration. Rousseau became the godfather of Elizabeth Foushee (likely a daughter of James and Marie) and bequeathed his land to her when he died in 1712. By 1717, Isaac Trocq was married to Mary Cammock, a close relative of Paul Micou's wife, Margaret.[12]

When the third refugee ship (name unknown) landed in Virginia on October 20, 1700, the passengers were dispersed to other areas of the colony with the approval of Governor Nicholson and the Council. The Rappahannock region, where county records show Huguenot-surnamed indentured servants beginning their service during this period, was likely one of the destinations for the settlers arriving on this ship. The fourth ship was the *Nassau,* arriving in Virginia on March 9, 1701. Although its passengers included Swiss, Genevese, German, and Flemish Protestant refugees, most were French. While the earlier ships delivered their passengers to ports along the James River closer to Manakin Town, the *Nassau* went up the York River to landings more convenient to refugees en route to the Rappahannock region by way of the Mattapony River. Fifty of these passengers made their way to the Manakin Town settlement, while 141 went to other Virginia locations.[13] It is reasonable to assume that most of the larger group went to the Rappahannock region, where some of them—Daniell Braban, Jean Chaperon, Estienne Cheneau, Pierre des Maizeaux, James Merchand, Antoine Laborie, Lewis Latané, and John Roy—were later documented.[14]

Huguenot exiles living along the Rappahannock were paying particular attention to the arrival of the *Nassau* because one of the passengers was the Huguenot-Anglican minister Lewis Latané. Nicholas Moreau, John

Bertrand's Huguenot-Anglican colleague at South Farnham Parish in Essex County beginning in 1698, was planning to return to England because he had been unable to convince his wife to cross the Atlantic.[15] The arrival of Latané, another French-speaking minister, gave Moreau a convenient opening to make his departure. Latané's Huguenot-Anglican credentials were impeccable. His father was Henri Latané, a Huguenot minister in the southwestern French province of Guyenne who died in prison after being incarcerated by local authorities.[16] Having immigrated to England as a child or youth, Latané was educated there and ordained to the Anglican ministry by Bishop Compton. The Royal Bounty supported Latané with a 1692 grant for his education and a 1699 grant for his immigration to America.[17]

According to Latané's papers, he began serving as minister of the South Farnham Parish on April 5, 1701.[18] The beginning of his ministry in Essex County less than a month after the *Nassau* landed in Virginia suggests the position was offered to him before he left England. As minister of South Farnham Parish, Lewis Latané continued the dual-track ministry envisioned by Governor Howard and first implemented by John Bertrand. As a French-speaking minister in Essex County, he was well placed to receive the mantle of spiritual leadership for the Rappahannock Refuge upon John Bertrand's death in the summer of 1701.[19]

The fifth and final ship financed by William III was the *William and Elizabeth*, arriving on August 9, 1701. No passenger list has survived for this ship. While nothing is known of the identity or final destination of these passengers, there is evidence they were in Stafford County in the fall of 1701. They also appear to have been in contact with William Fitzhugh, who had recently returned from a trip to England.[20] A letter from the Stafford County militia commander, George Mason II, to Governor Nicholson was likely written in response to an inquiry from the governor about French refugees in the county. Mason wrote, "Sir, We have no news in these parts, only that ye french refugees is, most of them, gone to Maryland, and have left an ill distemper behind them, ye bloody flux, which has affected some of our neighbors. Ye french refugees' great friend, Col. Fitzhugh, died tuesday, ye 21st at night, Nov'r 6th 1701."[21]

Was William Fitzhugh trying to settle these emigrants on his Ravensworth property in Stafford County, which he had been advertising as a potential Huguenot settlement for some years? The emigrants described by Mason appear not to have been well settled since most of them had so quickly moved on to another Chesapeake location, fleeing the local residents who blamed them for the deadly epidemic that apparently arrived with them. George Mason's letter reporting William Fitzhugh's death confirms the lawyer's alliance with Virginia's Huguenot exiles, some of whom had already received Northern Neck patents through his office. William Fitzhugh's widow began filing legal papers on his estate on November 16, 1701,[22] about two months after Charlotte Bertrand filed the will of her husband, one of Fitzhugh's Huguenot friends.

The 1700–1701 wave of Huguenot emigration brought an infusion of new refugees to the Rappahannock region, where seventy-six arriving households and eleven servants are documented between 1701 and 1710 in Appendix A-III.[23] More than half of these households settled in the community that formed around the Bertrands and Paul Micou in and near the former Rappahannock County. About one-third of the 1700–1701 Huguenot refugees were making their way to the other county promoted by Durand de Dauphiné, Stafford. A group of thirteen refugees who identified themselves as French "strangers" and petitioned the Stafford County justices in March 1702 to exempt them from taxation because of their poverty were likely passengers on the *Nassau*.[24] Some Huguenots from the 1680s wave of the migration were relocating to Stafford, where unclaimed land was more plentiful. Some refugees from the early and later immigration waves found available land by moving across the Essex County line to the Mattapony River, close to the York River landing place of the *Nassau*, along the border that would soon be established to separate the newly created King William County from King and Queen County in 1702.[25]

The 1700–1701 infusion of new immigrants points to the gradual formation of what might have been the largest Huguenot community in English America, with perhaps as many as 261 households recorded by 1710.[26] The Rappahannock Huguenot population looks quite large in comparison to the other centers of North American Huguenot migration at the beginning of the eighteenth century. The research of Jon Butler shows eighty-six Huguenot households, including 155 adults, in New York City; ninety-eight Huguenot adults in New Rochelle; sixty-four adults in New Paltz; 100 adults on Staten Island; and fewer than sixty adults in Boston.[27] Bertrand Van Ruymbeke has studied the Huguenot Churches in South Carolina, where he found 195 members in the Charlestown congregation, eighty members in its rural Orange Quarter annex, thirty-one members in its Goose Creek annex, 111 members in the rural Santee congregation, and forty-five members in the rural Wantoot community.[28] While the Rappahannock Huguenot community appears significantly larger than the others listed here, it was also scattered over eight or nine counties along the Rappahannock River. Evidence suggests that well over half of the Rappahannock Huguenots lived in or near a parish with a long-tenured French minister. Another 15 percent lived in or near parishes where French pastors apparently had short-term ministries.[29] The others followed the pattern of the Charlestown Huguenot Church annexes, traveling by river to the places where French-language services were offered and receiving occasional visits from their French pastors.[30]

The significant expansion of the Rappahannock Refuge to as many as 261 households formed the centerpiece of a major Huguenot presence in the colony of Virginia at the turn of the eighteenth century. Another seventy-six households, about 300 refugees, of the 1700–1701 immigration were establishing their homes at Manakin Town.[31] At the same time, several hundred additional undocumented refugees from William III's ships scattered to unknown locations in Virginia and beyond. The addition of the 1700–1701 refugees may have made Virginia the host of the largest French exile population in English America, exceeding the estimated Huguenot populations in the colonies of New York (800) and South Carolina (500).[32]

In a 1702 journey through the colony, a French-speaking Swiss merchant named Francis Louis Michel managed to visit both the Piedmont and upper tidewater sections of Virginia's Huguenot Refuge. His journal described newly arrived refugees at Manakin Town and Rappahannock Huguenots in both Essex and King William Counties. Michel and another contemporary observer reported that the Manakin exiles had found a way to make a tolerably good claret from local grapes. These reports offered a thin measure of hope to the English empire planners who dreamed Virginia might become a major producer of wine for export to Europe.[33]

The strong emphasis Durand de Dauphiné placed on acquiring land in Virginia became a defining characteristic of Huguenots in Virginia. Records evaluated for this study show about one third of the documented Rappahannock Huguenots, eighty-two households, acquiring land.[34] In early eighteenth-century Virginia, land was not just a resource for agricultural pursuits. In the colony's plantation culture, land was also an indicator of wealth and status. While most Huguenot land holdings were a few hundred acres or less, some refugees, like Bertrand and Micou, acquired much larger tracts. Many of the refugees had apparently been persuaded by Durand's assertion that they would not have to labor on the land they acquired in Virginia.[35] There is no reason to believe more than a few of them had any agricultural experience in Europe.

No doubt aware of the significant land holdings secured by Rappahannock Huguenots, Manakin Huguenots pressed the governor to issue personal land grants in the area where they were living. Allocation of these individual grants, 133 acres per household to original refugees, was finally concluded in 1710, after the refugees were granted citizenship. These land grants were not large, but did exceed the fifty acres theoretically allocated to all new Virginia immigrants.[36] While officials warned that selling the Manakin land to any buyer who was not an original French settler was strictly forbidden, this rule was not enforced over time. Four Huguenot refugees who were residing in Stafford County in 1702 decided by 1705 to move to the Manakin settlement, where local business was typically conducted in the French language. They secured tracts in the Piedmont through the land allocated to the refugees there: John Calvet (100 acres), Isaac Lafite (133 acres), Abraham Micheau (850 acres), and Charles Perrault (133 acres).[37] The significantly larger

Manakin holdings of Micheau suggests he purchased land from other refugees. The success of so many Huguenot refugees in securing land confirms the effectiveness of the 1697 decisions of the Board of Trade in London to make smaller patents more available in the colony.

Paul Micou may have amassed the largest land holdings of any of the Huguenot immigrants in Virginia. He was living in Richmond County on the north side of the river when he made what appears to be his initial land purchase of 150 acres on the south side of the river in Essex County in 1697.[38] In 1702, then living in Essex, he began gradually purchasing 374.5 acres in Richmond. He later made numerous land acquisitions in Essex, including purchases of 406 acres in 1708, 250 acres in 1712, seventy-five acres in 1714, 696 acres in 1723, and a 650-acre patent filed in 1727. Some of his land acquisitions are difficult to trace because the carving out of new counties from Essex (Spotsylvania in 1721 and Caroline in 1728) and Richmond (King George in 1720) apparently shifted the jurisdiction of some of his holdings. Over time, he expanded his *Port Micou* plantation in Essex to about 1,600 acres. Some of the documentary references to Paul Micou's land do not provide specific acreages, but his holdings in Essex, Richmond, Spotsylvania, Caroline, and King George Counties likely gave him more than 3,000 acres.[39]

Lewis Latané also acquired major land holdings in the colony during his thirty-two-year ministerial career in Virginia. He purchased 200 acres in Essex in 1717 and received 663 acres in Essex as a dowery for his wife, Mary Deane, in 1718. In 1722, Lewis received a Land Office patent for his share of 24,000 acres in Spotsylvania County, a land speculation partnership with nine other grantees.[40]

John Bertrand's work to establish the authority of the imperialist Northern Neck Proprietary helped to dramatically increase the size of his plantation, a development that eventually paid large dividends to his family. Ironically, the largest beneficiary of the work of Bertrand and Fitzhugh on behalf of the Lords Proprietors was Robert Carter, whose attempts to undermine the Proprietary in the Lancaster County Court in 1694 and in the Virginia House of Burgesses in 1695 had utterly failed. In 1702, Lord Fairfax needed a new Virginia agent to administer the Proprietary, and he settled on "King" Carter as his man.[41] Carter's stewardship of the Proprietary from 1702 to 1710 and again from 1719 to 1732 generated significant profits for the Proprietors, while propelling his rise to become one of the wealthiest men in English America. It is estimated that Carter secured almost 200,000 acres for himself and members of his family during his years as agent of the Proprietary, giving him control of well over 300,000 acres at the time of his death.[42] While Carter's relationship with the Northern Neck Proprietary after 1702 multiplied his large fortune, his aggressive program to open the unassigned western lands of the Northern Neck in Stafford County helped at least twenty-three

Huguenot refugees who acquired land north of the Rappahannock River after 1702.[43] These later developments in Carter's career could not be foreseen at the time he was so bitterly contesting and decisively losing the "hard game" against William Fitzhugh.

At John Bertrand's death in 1701, his wife, Charlotte, assumed full responsibility for managing the Bertrand plantation and trading operations, following the Saintonge cultural tradition in which women typically worked alongside their merchant husbands and inherited these businesses when their husbands died.[44] Charlotte was faced with numerous challenges in the wake of John's death. Though confronted by major social and cultural impediments to administering an English colonial plantation as a woman, Lancaster County Court records confirm that Charlotte was managing it by July 1701.[45] This was a difficult task in the best of circumstances, but the challenges Charlotte faced following John's death were especially daunting. While their 924-acre plantation was a valuable asset, its mortgage had not been retired at the time of John's death, and much remained to be done to create the trading businesses John and Charlotte envisioned for the plantation. Charlotte had to make the plantation self-sustaining without John's income from parish ministry and tutoring.

In 1703, Charlotte was in Lancaster County Court contesting eight separate lawsuits. The most threatening litigation she faced was an attempt by John Loyd to collect the balance of the 1692 mortgage on the plantation. The mortgage terms to which John and Charlotte had agreed were exceedingly difficult to fulfill. In 1690s Virginia, most land was purchased with tobacco. John's salary as a minister was paid in tobacco. But the Bertrands were obligated to pay their mortgage in pound sterling. A few years after they signed the purchase agreement, the price of tobacco plummeted, substantially reducing their ability to pay off this obligation. While John and Charlotte had succeeded in reducing the mortgage by about 50 percent over the previous six years, Charlotte still owed sixty-six pounds sterling to John Loyd in 1703.[46] On September 6, Loyd's lawyer was in court, pressing the case on behalf of his client, who had by then moved to England. But Charlotte was also initiating litigation against people who owed her money and having some success in Lancaster Court.[47]

Other Lancaster lawsuits show Charlotte was engaged in transatlantic business. In September 1704, Charlotte took legal action against Bristol merchant William Lawson for his refusal to honor letters of credit he had issued to a customer of Charlotte's. After reviewing the case, the Lancaster justices ordered Lawson's representative to make good on the letters of credit. In this and other cases like it, the Lancaster County Court was functioning as an arbiter of transatlantic business.[48] Court records show Charlotte was doing business with other merchants from Bristol and Liverpool between 1701 and 1705.[49] Since the court records mainly document litigation, Charlotte's trading activities with more trusted clients are not listed there.

The prospects for the Bertrand trading business were enhanced by the marriage of John and Charlotte's daughter Mary Ann to Charles Ewell (c. 1682–1722) about 1710. Ewell was the son of an emigrant from Kent who settled on Virginia's Eastern Shore about 1665. Charles moved to the Bertrand plantation and used his skills as a builder to enlarge the plantation house and improve the infrastructure for the Bertrand landing and tobacco storage business. Charlotte continued to appear in court for the family trading operations until 1713, when her twenty-five-year-old son, William, began to assume these duties. This was the year William married Susannah Foushee (1695–c. 1745), daughter of Rappahannock Huguenots James and Marie Foushee. Charlotte's capable management of the Bertrand plantation and trading interests for twelve or more years forged a successful business partnership among her son, daughter, and son-in-law, propelling them into the Lancaster, Virginia, aristocracy.

Charlotte's children continued the family trading partnership after her death in 1721. After Charles Ewell's death in 1722, Mary Ann's next husband, a transatlantic ship captain named William Ballandine (d. 1736), joined the partnership. By the time of Mary Ann's third marriage in 1742 to the wealthy merchant and court justice James Ball (1678–1754), cousin of George Washington's mother, Mary Ball Washington, her sons Charles Ewell and Solomon Ewell were married to two of James's daughters. As Mary Ann was forging a merchant dynasty with the Ball family, her brother William formed a planter dynasty through the 1734 marriage of his daughter Mary Ann (c. 1717–1770) to Leroy Griffin (1711–1750), son of a wealthy Richmond County court justice. By 1744, Leroy owned more than 3,000 acres.[50]

With Paul Micou's move to Essex County in the late 1690s, he married into a prominent English family, continued to practice medicine, served as a factor for English merchants, and acquired a stake in a water mill. At the same time he was gradually accumulating significant land holdings and enslaved workers.[51] He established a landing for trading purposes at *Port Micou*, his large plantation on the Rappahannock River. Micou had eight children, at least seven of whom appear to have been by his exogamous marriage to Margaret Thatcher Cammock. He had four sons: John, James, Henry, and Paul. His four daughters were Elizabeth (husband, James Scott), Mary (husbands, Leonard Hill and Joshua Fry), Margaret (husband, Moore Fauntleroy), and Judith (husband, Lundsford Lomax).[52]

In 1710, the governor and Council appointed Micou to serve as a court justice for Essex County.[53] In this influential position in the county, Micou helped to manage local government operations and ruled on litigation between local citizens. Micou's son Paul Jr. also served as an Essex court justice while another son, John, was a justice in Caroline County.[54] By 1724, John and Paul Micou Jr. were partners with English merchants from Bristol in a King George County iron works. John Bertrand's grandson Charles Ewell also entered an iron works partnership in the same county by 1737.[55] And like the son of John and Charlotte Bertrand, Paul Micou's sons served on parish vestries.[56] A son-in-law of Paul Micou, a former mathematics teacher at William and Mary named Joshua Fry, second husband of Mary Micou, also served as a court justice in Essex before moving to the frontier county of Abermarle. Joshua later gained recognition through the publication of the "Fry–Jefferson Map" he produced with Peter Jefferson, father of Thomas Jefferson, and through his disastrous command of Virginia forces in the French and Indian War in 1754. The "Fry–Jefferson Map" clearly displays the location of *Port Micou*, shown as Port Micow, and the Bertrand plantation house, labeled "Ball" for Mary Ann Bertrand's third husband, James Ball. While the map does not identify the South Farnham Parish Church, it clearly shows Hoskins Creek, on which the church was located.[57]

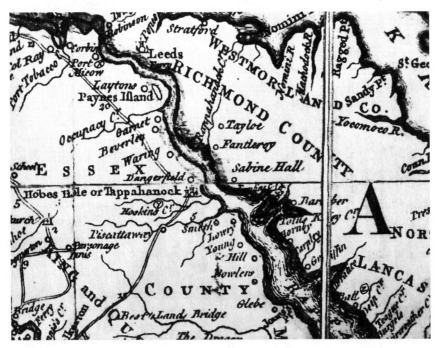

Detail, *A Map of the Most Inhabited Part of Virginia*, Joshua Fry and Peter Jefferson, 1751, showing *Port Micou* (X), South Farnham Church (Y), and the Bertrand Plantation (Z).
Courtesy Library of Congress, Geography and Map Division

By the second decade of the eighteenth century, Rappahannock Huguenots who could afford to do so were deeply enmeshed in Virginia's growing slave culture. For Huguenots like the Bertrands and Micous, enslaved workers might also have provided a liquid asset that could be readily transferred within and between families in a cash-poor society. In June 1718, Paul Micou gave five enslaved persons to his daughter, Margaret Fauntleroy, apparently as a dowery for her recent marriage.[58] Records suggest Charlotte Bertrand made a similar transfer of enslaved workers to her daughter, Mary Ann, at her 1710 marriage to Charles Ewell.[59]

The significant growth of African slavery in Virginia during the eighteenth century can be seen in the records of the Bertrand family in Lancaster County. John Bertrand's late-seventeenth-century labor force was mostly indentured servants but included five or six enslaved workers. The 1722 inventory of John Bertrand's son-in-law Charles Ewell lists twenty-five enslaved persons and only one indentured servant. The 1761 inventory of William Bertrand shows he had twenty-eight enslaved workers and no indentured servants at the time of his death. The 1778 inventory of William's grandson, Thomas Bertrand Griffin, who inherited the Bertrand plantation, lists thirty-nine enslaved persons and three servants.[60] Cross-referencing the Bertrand family inventory lists from 1722 to 1778 reveals the longevity of the plantation's enslaved African Virginian labor force. The repetition of names over that fifty-six-year period suggests many of the enslaved laborers remained on the plantation through a succession of patent holders and thereby retained essential knowledge of the plantation and its landing as they contributed valuable skills. Their long tenure lent a high degree of stability to the Bertrand agricultural and business operations.

The wills of other Huguenot refugees document their participation in Virginia's slave culture. James Foushee's 1729 will lists twelve enslaved persons while Lewis Latané's 1732 will names twenty-one enslaved African Virginians.[61] Apparently the wealthiest member of the Huguenot-Anglican migration to Virginia by 1710, Paul Micou was probably the largest slaveholder among the refugees. His 1736 will, conveying sixty-three enslaved persons to various members of his family, confirms his major stake in the colony's slave system.[62] While the evidence suggests John Bertrand and his son-in-law Charles Ewell presented the children of their enslaved workers for baptism, this was not a common practice in Virginia. Most Virginia slaveholders were reluctant to permit their enslaved workers to participate in the life of the church, fearing it would make African Virginians proud and less obedient. They also suspected that church membership for the enslaved would inevitably lead to their emancipation.[63]

Huguenot-Anglicans were leaders in a largely ineffectual effort to extend church membership, education, and somewhat more humane conditions for enslaved persons in English America. A Huguenot from Saintonge named Elie Neau had been enslaved on a French galley after being caught by a French warship on a business trip between New York and London in 1693. When Neau returned to New York in 1699, after more than six years as a slave and prisoner of Louis XIV, he decided he no longer wanted to be a merchant. Having undergone a spiritual transformation during his incarceration in France, he came to appreciate the desperate condition of the enslaved in New York City and decided to launch a ministry to assist them.[64] With the financial support of the SPG, Neau offered catechism classes to prepare enslaved workers for membership in the Anglican church. By 1707, more than 100 were enrolled. In the face of unrelenting resistance to this ministry by New York's slaveholding elites, Neau faithfully continued this work until his death in 1722.[65]

One of Henry Compton's Huguenot-Anglican clergy recruits was Francis Le Jau, who arrived in South Carolina in 1706. Serving the Huguenot-Anglican Goosecreek Parish, he was successful in securing the consent of a considerable number of planters for their enslaved workers to be baptized. Apparently the plantation owners were reassured by Le Jau's requirement that the enslaved persons make public statements before their baptisms asserting they were not seeking freedom from their masters, only the salvation of their souls.[66] Whatever the Rappahannock Huguenots might have thought about England's evolving slave system in the new world, there is no evidence any of them challenged it on moral grounds. Had they done so, they would have betrayed the English imperialist system they went to the new world to serve.[67]

Like most of the Rappahannock Huguenots, Lewis Latané was a native of one of the Atlantic provinces of western France. Nothing is known of Lewis's childhood in France or the precise date of his immigration to England. Unlike John Bertrand, Latané did not go to England after being educated and ordained in France. Assuming he arrived in England soon after Protestantism was outlawed in France, he would have been thirteen or fourteen years old. Latané grew to adulthood in a French exile community, received a B.A. at Queen's College, Oxford, and then spent three years as a theology student in Bristol. The French Church in Bristol and the ministers of the Savoy Church in London recommended him to the Bishop of London for ordination.[68] Lewis did not have to go through the ecclesiastical re-tooling process that was so much a part of the experience of the Huguenot-Anglican ministers who arrived in the colony in the 1680s.

There is evidence Latané was committed to supporting the Huguenot refugees who were continuing to arrive in Virginia after him. In 1702, he traveled to the York River to meet the *Nassau* on its return voyage to the colony. Latané was there to welcome a small group of French refugees as they arrived in Virginia.[69] With both Latané and the wealthy court justice Paul Micou living in Essex County, it increasingly became a center of Huguenot exile activity in the early decades of the eighteenth century.

Like many Chesapeake-area immigrants, Lewis Latané saw his family disrupted by the high mortality rates of the region. Records suggest he was married three times. His first wife, whose name is unknown, and an infant traveled with him to Virginia on the *Nassau*. Lewis's daughter Charlotte (husband, Abram Montague) was the only surviving child of this marriage. The date of Lewis's marriage to his second wife, Phoebe, is not known, but she died in January 1711. Lewis and Phoebe had five children: Phebe, Susanna, Henry, William, and Henrietta. Of these children, only Susanna and Henrietta (husband, William Jones) lived into adulthood. The boys, Henry and William, died tragically of small pox while attending school in Liverpool in 1724. Lewis married Mary Deane in 1716, and she gave birth to four children: Catherine in 1717, Lewis in 1720, John in 1722 (wife, Mary Allen), and Maryanne in 1725 (husband, John Clements). Of these, Catherine and Lewis died in infancy.[70]

Both of Lewis's Virginia marriages were to women from prominent colonial families. His wife Phoebe had been married to William Peachey until his death in the late 1690s. She had a son from this marriage named Samuel. She was the daughter of Phoebe Smith, though it is not known by which of her mother's two husbands, William Hodgkins or William Slaughter. She was the granddaughter of Toby Smith and Phoebe Fauntleroy, who settled along the Rappahannock River in 1652. Phoebe's grandparents were part of the influential Underwood/Williamson/Fauntleroy clan that dominated the governance of Rappahannock County and its parishes during the 1650s and 1660s.[71] Mary Deane, Lewis's next wife, was born in England about 1685. While the identity of her parents is not known, Mary was apparently a relative of Robert Beverley (c. 1673–1722), who wrote the 1705 history of the colony. Beverley gave his blessing to Mary's marriage to Lewis through a dowery gift of 663 acres. Mary maintained a long-term friendship with Robert's son William Beverley.[72]

Unfortunately the surviving records tell us very little about Latané's thirty-two-year ministry at South Farnham Parish. The inventory listing of the approximately 150 books in his library may, however, offer some insight into the nature of his ministry. His Huguenot identity is affirmed by his French Bible and works of John Calvin, Pierre du Moulin, and Philippe Duplessis-Mornay. Lewis's bilingual ministry is confirmed by his French-to-English and Latin-to-French dictionaries. Lewis's library included about twenty-eight publications on theological subjects representing a wide variety of theological positions from the Scholastic Calvinism of Pierre Du Moulin to the Armenian writings of Archbishop William Laud. Lewis's eight collections of published sermons, five volumes dealing with catechisms, seven books on church polity, and three "how to" works on communicating with Quakers, Catholics, and atheists demonstrate the practical emphasis of his ministry. Eleven biblical studies and the same number of books on church history resourced his preaching and teaching ministry. Not surprisingly, he had a first edition of the 1705 classic work by his parishioner Robert Beverley, *The History and Present State of Virginia* with its engraved illustrations by Bertrand relative Simon Gribelin. Because Latané received the greatest part of his education in England, it is not surprising that most titles were in English rather than French. His bilingual facility is demonstrated by extant correspondence with his brother Henry in London, some of which was in French and some in English.[73]

Another interesting window into Latané's ministry is his response to the "Paper of Enquiries" sent by the new Bishop of London, Edmund Gibson (1669–1748), soon after taking office in 1723. Gibson sent this survey to all the Anglican parishes in British North America.[74] Latané's responses to the survey raise a number of significant issues. The expansive geographical setting of the parish, forty miles long and eight miles wide, created many challenges for the 200 families who traveled to church by foot or by horse. The leaders of the parish addressed this issue by constructing two churches in different parts of the parish, the upper Piscataway church and the lower Piscataway church.[75] Nonetheless, Latané concluded the parish was not able to properly nurture its youth in the faith.

The role of African Virginians in the parish was another important issue raised by Bishop Gibson. In this case, the wording of the survey and Latané's response are significant. Question: "Are there any Infidels, bond or free, within your Parish; and what means are used for their conversion?" Response: "The infidels in the Parish are slaves; the means for their conversion is divine service, performed at the Church every Sunday which few of them attend to." Latané's apparently dismissive response raises questions that cannot be answered. Were enslaved persons not attending services because they chose not to do so, or did their masters discourage or forbid them from going? Did Latané believe the minister or the parish should reach out in any way to offer Christian instruction and support to enslaved persons as Huguenot-Anglicans Elie Neau and Francis Le Jau were doing in New York and South Carolina? Bishop Gibson might well have included this question in response to a moving letter he received in 1723 from enslaved persons in Virginia begging for release from bondage and to be educated in the faith.[76] The bishop's interest in more aggressive action by both enslavers and ministers to instruct the enslaved in the Christian faith is demonstrated by pastoral letters he published in 1727. While Latané's Huguenot ministerial colleagues Peter Fontaine, Francis Fontaine, and James Marye showed interest in educating the enslaved, his response suggests he had not yet embraced the new emphasis of the Bishop of London.[77]

Latané's response to the survey also reveals the South Farnham vestry had not presented him to the governor for induction into his position as minister of the parish. Induction gave ministers a form of tenure that made it difficult for their parishes to dismiss them. Virginia vestries were notorious for refusing to recommend their ministers for induction because they wanted to retain the option of firing them without cause. As described in Chapters 3 and 6 of this study, the records suggest John Bertrand was not inducted into either of the parishes he served and that in both cases vestries dismissed him.

During the first two decades of the eighteenth century, the tide was beginning to turn against local officials who sought to maintain full control over their parishes and resisted Bishop Compton's reforms. In 1710, Andrew Jackson, Lancaster's well-respected Scots-Irish Presbyterian pastor, died. Colonial authorities were by then fully prepared to aggressively intervene to enforce the English imperialist ecclesiastical policy at the local level. In Lancaster, Andrew Jackson's next two successors, John Bell[78] and David Currie,[79] led the county into the low-church Anglicanism of eighteenth-century Virginia that could incorporate a surplice and a Geneva pulpit gown in the same service. The residents of the county who were unwilling to make that journey with Bell and Currie were able to attend the services of Presbyterian preachers who were registering as dissenters in the Rappahannock region during the 1720s.[80] County and vestry officials were becoming less able to fire ministers without cause or to maintain the long-established autonomous ecclesiastical identities of their parishes.[81]

The contentious relationship between Lewis Latané and his South Farnham vestry became a test case for Anglican reform in 1716. The extant records do not reveal the source of the conflict, but it escalated to the level of a vestry decision not to renew the minister's annual contract. Lewis's contemporary Hugh Jones, formerly minister at Jamestown, described this incident in 1724 and noted with ridicule the vestry's unconvincing rationale for the firing, their inability to understand their pastor's sermons because he spoke with "a small tang of the French." Jones understood the vestry would not have waited fifteen years to move against Lewis if he were truly unable to preach effectively in English.[82] Whatever the issue of dispute might have been, the vestry believed it possessed full authority to dismiss Latané because he had never been inducted. It is reasonable to assume officials in Williamsburg were informed in advance about the troubles brewing at South Farnham, perhaps by Paul Micou. When the church wardens at South Farnham enforced the vestry's termination decision by locking Latané out of the church, the lieutenant governor Alexander Spotswood sent a scathing letter to the vestry:

> As no vestry in England ever pretended to set themselves up as judges over their ministers, so I know no law of this country that has given such authority to the vestry here. If a clergyman transgresses against the canons of the church, he is to be tried before a proper judicature. . . . In case of the misbehavior of your minister, you may be his accusers, but in no case his judges. . . . But your

churchwardens, ordering the Church to be shut up, and thereby taking upon them to lay the parish under an interdict, is such an exorbitant act of power, that even the Pope of Rome never pretended to a greater; and if your churchwardens persist in it, they will find themselves involved in greater troubles than they are aware of.[83]

Spotswood made good on his threat. He placed the issue before the Council in Williamsburg, and that governing body took the following action to force the vestry to rescind its dismissal of its minister: "It is the unanimous opinion of this Board that the said Vestry have no power to turn out their Minister in the manner they have done. And therefore, it is ordered that the Church Wardens cause the door of the Church to be opened, and that the said Mr. Latané be permitted to exercise his Ministerial Function therein."[84] The Council went on to issue the additional warning that the vestry would face serious repercussions if it failed to pay their minister's salary.

The action of the Council in this case suggested the induction of a minister no longer mattered. Its language assigned to Latané the rights previously associated with induction. This was a very different response from the one John Bertrand received in 1693, when the Council refused to reverse his firing by the vestry of North Farnham Parish. Latané kept his position and continued to serve in his dual-track ministry to the parish and the Rappahannock Refuge for sixteen more years until his death. This incident suggests the unchecked power of the vestries to run the Virginia parishes as they saw fit had finally been broken, though not yet eliminated. In 1719, a convention of Virginia ministers complained about the power of their vestries to dismiss them.[85] Henry Compton's bilingual Huguenot-Anglican ministers of the 1680s and 1690s had effectively prepared the ground for the Anglican reform the bishop had long envisioned. Bertrand's bilingual successor in the Rappahannock Refuge became an early beneficiary of this reform, which would later be codified by the Virginia Assembly in 1749.[86]

During the first four decades of the eighteenth century, French exiles continued to immigrate to the Rappahannock region. In June 1716, a Huguenot named John Fontaine was passing through Essex County and recorded in his diary his experience of worshipping at South Farnham Church and hearing a very good sermon by Mr. de Latané. John was the son of Jaques Fontaine, a Huguenot minister who grew up in Saintonge and wrote about the persecution of Protestants in Cozes in the 1680s, as noted in Chapter 1 of this study. Jaques fled to England in 1686 and went on to Ireland, where he eventually settled in Dublin. There he raised and educated five sons and two daughters. The siblings formed a family partnership, following Saintonge tradition, and decided to invest their pooled resources in British America. They chose John to tour the colonies to evaluate opportunities for trade, and to purchase a plantation in the place he thought most promising for the family. Arriving in Virginia in the spring of 1715, John called on Huguenots and government officials in Williamsburg and in New York City. He also made a quick trip through Pennsylvania and Delaware, exploring intercolonial and transatlantic trading opportunities. He acquired a plantation for the family partnership in King William County, along the southwest edge of the Rappahannock Refuge. As four of his siblings were making their way to the King William County plantation, John Fontaine went back to Ireland, probably intending to coordinate transatlantic trade, which never materialized. He later moved to London and then to Wales, never returning to Virginia.[87]

John's brother Peter Fontaine (1691–1759) and his wife, Elizabeth Fourreau, arrived in Virginia in October 1716. A graduate of Trinity College in Dublin, Peter was ordained to the Anglican ministry by Bishop of London John Robinson in February 1716.[88] By 1720, he was serving Westover Parish, where he remained until his death. James Fontaine (1686–1746) and his wife, Lucretia Desjarrie, were the next to arrive, in October 1717. James, who was not a minister, settled in the Rappahannock Refuge at the King William plantation John had purchased. The next Fontaine sibling to immigrate to the new world was Mary Ann (1690–1755) and her husband, a French refugee named Matthew Maury. They arrived in the colony before 1720 and established their own plantation on a section of John Fontaine's King William patent. Francis Fontaine (1697–1749) was the last of the siblings to settle in the colony. Like his brother Peter, Francis was a graduate of Trinity College Dublin and was ordained by Bishop Robinson before sailing to the new world in 1721 with his wife, Marie Glannison.[89] Francis briefly served Rappahannock Huguenots at Saint Margaret's Parish in King William, but soon moved on to Yorkhampton Parish in York County while teaching Hebrew at the College of William and Mary from 1729–1731. Peter and Francis Fontaine's long-tenured ministries in Virginia would prove to be an important resource for Huguenot-Anglicans in the colony. Like John Bertrand and Lewis Latané, Peter and Francis continued to serve their parishes in Virginia to the end of their lives.[90]

Francis arrived in Virginia about the same time as another Trinity graduate who might have been from a Huguenot or Walloon family that fled to Ireland. Lawrence De Butts was ordained by Bishop Robinson in June 1721 and licensed to serve in Virginia the following month. De Butts subsequently found a position in the Rappahannock region, where he served as minister of Washington Parish in Westmoreland County from 1721 to 1728. Because nothing is known of De Butts's family in Ireland, his ethnic identity is a matter of speculation. While he later served in Truro Parish in Fairfax County, by 1734 he had moved to Maryland.[91]

John Moncure (c. 1709–1764) was a Huguenot descendant who clearly fits the pattern of the Fontaines. After growing up in Scotland, Moncure migrated to the Rappahannock region in 1735 to serve as a tutor. A few years later, he traveled to England, where he was ordained and licensed for ministry in Virginia by Bishop of London Edmund Gibson in December 1737. The following year, he became the minister of the Overwharton Parish in Stafford County, where he served until his death in 1764.[92]

John Fontaine never returned to Virginia, but he maintained a channel of communication with Lewis Latané about Huguenots who were moving to the colony. Lewis's papers include a 1720 letter from John Fontaine, written from Dublin. John asked the minister to find a position for a Mr. Dalliriens, the son of a Huguenot friend who had just arrived in Virginia and wanted to become a merchant. Fontaine hoped the young man could be apprenticed to Robert Beverley.[93]

The presence of Peter and Francis Fontaine in the colony would eventually prove important for the Manakin Town settlement. The French refugees in the Piedmont faced many challenges, including limited economic opportunities and conflict within the community. They also had a difficult relationship with colonial authorities, who found the refugees to be troublesome and requested no more be sent.[94] The conflict at Manakin Town usually embroiled the pastors and some of the leading members of the community.[95] The first minister, Benjamin de Joux, died in 1703. Claude Philippe de Richebourg, another original Manakin settler, quickly replaced de Joux. In 1711, de Richebourg chose to leave Manakin Town to join a group of Manakin settlers who had earlier moved on to a new settlement in present-day North Carolina. In 1714, the next full-time minister, John Cairon, arrived in Virginia but died the following year. There would be no more Huguenot-Anglican ministers in full-time service to the struggling parish at Manakin Town. The vestry paid its *lecteur* to read services while ministers from nearby parishes made occasional visits to address the worship and pastoral needs of the community. Two of the pastors who made regular trips to Manakin Town in the early 1720s were Peter and Francis Fontaine.[96] By 1728, leaders of the King William Parish were scrambling to keep their small, impoverished French parish from being folded into a larger, English-speaking one.[97]

In the spring of 1730, the pastoral leadership of the Manakin Town parish was stabilized for a time when it obtained the part-time services of a dual-track French minister named James Marye (d. 1767). Marye was a Catholic priest in France who went to England, converted to the Anglican faith, and sought recognition as a minister. In England, he married Letitia Maria Ann Staige, the daughter of an Anglican clergyman.[98] Catholic priests who converted took instruction but did not have to be re-ordained in the Church of England as French Protestant ministers did. In 1729, Marye was licensed to serve in Virginia, perhaps in response to Lieutenant Governor William Gooch's 1728 request to the Bishop of London for a minister who could preach in French as well as English. When Marye arrived in Virginia in 1730, Gooch noted with satisfaction that Marye could serve two neighboring parishes: St. James Northam in Goochland County, where he would preach in English, and King William Parish at Manakin Town, where he could preach in French.[99] A King William Vestry Book entry in August 1732 confirms this dual-track relationship was supported by the SPG as Gooch had proposed in 1728.[100] Unfortunately for the Manakin Town Huguenots, Marye's bilingual ministry with them ended in 1735, when he moved to a more distant Virginia parish.[101]

The Manakin Huguenots were slower to gain proficiency in English than their Rappahannock Huguenot counterparts. Living in a homogeneous French community afforded the Manakin settlers less interaction with English speakers and fewer opportunities to develop fluency in English. However, their inability to secure the regular services of French-speaking ministers after 1715, except for their five-year relationship with James Marye, moved their King William Parish toward a fairly rapid transition to worshipping in English. In the 1740s, the parish agreed to a contract with an English minister requiring him to preach only four of his seventeen annual sermons in French.[102]

Had the Manakin Huguenots been able to continue employing French ministers, they likely would have followed a pattern similar to the Huguenot settlement in New Rochelle, New York, after it conformed to Anglicanism in 1709. The New Rochelle Church benefited from the long-term pastorate of Pierre Stouppe from 1724 to 1760. In 1744, Stouppe reported preaching twice each Sunday at New Rochelle, using French in the morning and English in the afternoon. Members of the New Rochelle community who preferred worshipping in French were not abruptly forced out of their comfort zone as the Manakin Huguenots were.[103]

While English surnames were increasingly listed in the parish records at Manakin Town by the middle of the eighteenth century, the community remained mostly French because of the ownership of so much of the surrounding land by Huguenot families. However, the French presence in the area did not expand, as the population of the parish remained in the 250–300 range for many decades.[104] By contrast, the appearance of additional Huguenot surnames in the counties of the Rappahannock region between 1710 and 1740 suggests this larger and more widely dispersed Refuge continued to attract Huguenot-connected emigrants such as the Fontaines, Maurys, John Moncure, and Mr. Dalliriens during the first four decades of the eighteenth century.

There was, perhaps, an even more significant contrast between the Rappahannock and Manakin Huguenots by the end of the 1730s. Rappahannock Huguenot leaders were using the Refuge as a springboard into the Virginia aristocracy in a way that was unimaginable for Manakin Huguenots. Both Paul Micou and Lewis Latané entered exogamous marriages with women from Virginia gentry families. Over the next three generations, descendants of Micou, Latané, and John Bertrand formed marriages with members of elite Virginia families such as the Balls, Berkeleys, Burwells, Carters, Cockes, Fauntleroys, Lees, Lightfoots, and Wormeleys.[105]

The Rappahannock Huguenots suffered a major setback in 1733, when the thirty-two-year ministry of Lewis Latané at South Farnham Parish came to an end. In April of that year, Mary Deane Latané filed the will of her husband.[106] The exact date of Lewis's death is unknown. It is believed he was buried at *Langley*, the plantation where he lived and that passed into the ownership of his son John. With the death of Latané, there apparently was no resident bilingual Huguenot-Anglican minister serving a Rappahannock River parish for the first time in forty-six years. By the middle of the 1730s, the Huguenot-Anglican Refuge in Virginia was moving into a new era.

NOTES

1. Edward Porter Alexander, ed., *The Journal of John Fontaine: An Irish Huguenot Son in Spain and Virginia, 1710–1719* (Williamsburg, VA, 1972), 86.

2. LC WB, *8,* 1690–1709, 105.

3. Katherine Carté, *Religion and the American Revolution: An Imperial History* (Chapel Hill, NC, 2021), 44–48.

4. William A. Bultmann, "The SPG and the French Huguenots in Colonial America," *Historical Magazine of the Protestant Episcopal Church* 20 (1951), 156–72.

5. Van Ruymbeke, *From New Babylon to Eden*, 131; Carlo, *Huguenot Refugees in Colonial New York*, 78–82.

6. Stanwood, *The Empire Reformed*, 20.

7. Lambert, *The Protestant International and the Huguenot Migration to Virginia*, 136, 154, 155, 160, and 162.

8. Ibid., 136 and 154. For the passenger list of the *Mary and Ann,* see Brock, 253–55. For the *Peter and Anthony*, see Brock, 14–16.

9. Lambert, *The Protestant International and the Huguenot Migration to Virginia*, 145–54.

10. James L Bugg Jr, "The French Huguenot Frontier Settlement of Manakin Town," VMHB 61, no. 4 (October 1953), 359–94.

11. Brock, 19; Durand, 29, 131, and 133; WMQ 9, 123–24.

12. Brock, 14–15; Headley, *Wills of Richmond County, Virginia,* 22; Dorman, EC Records, 1706–1711, 1717–1719, 69 and 72.

13. Lambert, *The Protestant International and the Huguenot Migration to Virginia*, 161.

14. Brock, 29–32; Appendix B-III (Braban, Chaperon, Cheneau, des Maizeaux, Merchand, Laborie, Latané, and Roy).

15. SP, EC RB, 1699–1702, 33, 83, 87, and 117; SP, RC OB, 1697–1699, 86 and 110; Meade, *Old Churches, Old Ministers, and Old Families of Virginia*, vol. 1, 384; Manross, ed., *The Fulham Papers*, 159 and 162.

16. Gwynn, *Huguenots in Britain I*, 335.

17. RBP, Ms 1, folio 88 (Latané), HL.

18. Latané, *Parson Latané*, 21.

19. Baird, vol. 2, 144–45; Lucy Temple Latané, *Parson Latané, 1672–1732* (Charlottesville, VA, 1936); #98729, CCEd.

20. Davis, *William Fitzhugh and His Chesapeake World*, 45.

21. Brock, 44.

22. Davis, *William Fitzhugh and His Chesapeake World*, 54.

23. Records show that at least one of the servants (Joan Denin) gained her freedom, increasing the households documented between 1701 and 1710 to seventy-seven.

24. SP, SC DWB, 1699–1709, 46. For eight Huguenots living side by side on the lower bank of Cedar Run near Brent Town in the part of Stafford County that would become Prince William, see Harrison, *Landmarks of Old Prince William*, 189–90.

25. Barbara Beigun, *Land and Heritage in the Virginia Tidewater: A History of King and Queen County* (Richmond, 1993), 35, 36, and 39–41.

26. Appendices A and B document a total of 252 French-surnamed households and fifty-three indentured servants in the counties of the Rappahannock region between 1677 and 1710. Records show that eleven of the indentured servants gained their freedom and helped to form nine additional households, to bring the household total to 261.

27. Butler, *The Huguenots in America*, 46–49.

28. Van Ruymbeke, *From New Babylon to Eden*, 106, and 113–16.

29. French ministers were long-tenured in Old Rappahannock, Richmond, Lancaster, and Essex Counties, where 53.5 percent of the documented Rappahannock Huguenots lived. French ministers held short-term positions in New Kent and Westmoreland Counties, where 15.4 precent of the Rappahannock Huguenots were located.

30. Van Ruymbeke, *From New Babylon to Eden*, 114–15.

31. Bugg, "The French Huguenot Frontier Settlement of Manakin Town," 391–92.

32. Butler, *The Huguenots in America*, 46–49.

33. Francis Louis Michel, "Report of the Journey of Francis Louis Michel from Berne, Switzerland, to Virginia, October 2, 1701–December 1, 1702," ed. and trans. William J. Hinke, VMHB 24 (1916), 113–41; Beverley, *The History and Present State of Virginia*, 225.

34. See Appendix A for the identification of Huguenot households that acquired land in Virginia.

35. Durand, 111–12.

36. McIlwaine, *Executive Journals*, vol. 3, 99, 139, and 261. For a detailed study of Manakin Town land grants and their recipients, see Priscilla Hariss Cabell, *Turff & Twigg: Volume I, The French Lands* (Richmond, VA, 1988).

37. Nugent, *Cavaliers and Pioneers*, vol. 3, 139, 140, 169, and 184.

38. SP, EC DWB, 1695–1699, 69–70.

39. SP, EC WB, 1735–1743, 11–12; SP, RC DB, 1701–1704, 33–34; SP, EC DB, 1721–1724, 41 and 48; LOP No. 13, 1725–1730, 281; Dorman, EC DWB No. 13, 1707–1711, 21; Ryland, "Paul Micou, Chyrurgeon," 245; Fleet, vol. 2, 13, 31, and 44; Micou, "Paul Micou, Huguenot Physician and His Descendants," 363–64; Nicklin, "An Annotated Copy of the Rent Roll of 1704," 402; John Bailey Calvert Nicklin, "Quit Rent Roll for the Year 1715—Essex County, Virginia," WMQ 18, no. 2 (April 1938), 205.

40. Dorman, EC RB, 1706–1707, 1717–1719, 41 and 70; LOP No. 11, 1719–1724, 147.

41. Freeman, *Young Washington*, vol. 1, 489–95.

42. Carl F. Canon, *Robert "King" Carter of Corrotoman* (Duke University Phd. Thesis, Durham, NC, 1956), 268–78; Walsh, *Motives of Honor, Pleasure, and Profit*, 256–60.

43. Freeman, *Young Washington*, vol. 1, 489.

44. LC OB 4, 1696–1702, 156.

45. Isaac, *The Transformation of Virginia*, 57; SP, LC OB 4, 1699–1701, 103; LC OB, 1696–1702, 156.

46. LC OB 5, 1702–1713, 18; SP, LC OB, 1695–1699, 43–47.

47. LC OB 5, 1702–1713, 43, 44, 51, 57, 59, 61, and 67.

48. LC OB 5, 1702–1713, 102 and 113.

49. LC DB 9, 1701–1706, 25 (Thomas Cooper), 45 (Thomas Hinde); SP, LC DB, 1701–1706, 45–46 (Thomas Mackey), 66 (William Lawson); LC OB, 5, 1702–1713, 18 (William Fletcher).

50. LC WB 10, 1709–1727, 392–97; LC OB 7, 1721–1729, 65; Lee, *A Brief History of Belle Isle Plantation*, 41–76; Fairfax Papers, BR 295 (2b), BR Box 233, Richmond County Farnham Parish Rental Roll for 1744, Huntington Library, San Marino, California.

51. Fleet, vol. 2, 242.

52. Ryland, "Paul Micou. Chyrugeon," 241–46.

53. McIlwaine, *Executive Journals*, vol. 3, xix and 244.

54. Dorman, Caroline County, Virginia OB, 1732–1740, 1.

55. SP, King George County, Virginia DB, 1721–1735, 34–35; Mary Marshall Brewer, *King George County, Virginia Orders, 1736–1740* (Lewes, DE), 32.

56. Fleet, vol. 1, 295, 306, 310–11, vols. 2, 9, 11, 13, 31, 44, and 80; Dorman, *Caroline County, Virginia OB, Part 1*, 1; Meade, *Old Churches, Ministers, and Families of Virginia*, vol. 1, 405; Brock, xvii.

57. Joshua Fry married Mary Hill Micou about the time of Paul Micou's death in 1736. Micou, "Paul Micou, Huguenot Physician, and his Descendants," 367–69; James B. Slaughter, *Settlers, Southerners, Americans: The History of Essex County, Virginia, 1608–1984* (Tappahannock, VA, 1985), 57.

58. Fleet, vol. 1, 314.

59. LC OB 5, 1702–1713, 255, 278–79, and 296; Lee, *A Brief History of Belle Isle Plantation*, 59.

60. LC WB, 10, 376–78 (Charles Ewell); LC WB, No. 16, 148–49 (William Bertrand); and LC WB, 20, folio 142–44, 1–4 (Thomas Bertrand Griffin).

South Farnham Parish, 1733 155

61. LC DWB 12, 1726–1736, 144, 157–59; EC WB 5, 1730–1735, 128.
62. SP, EC WB, 1735–1743, 11–12.
63. Jones, *The Present State of Virginia*, 70.
64. Whelan, "The Extraordinary Voyage of Elie Neau," 499–527.
65. Denzil T. Clifton, "Anglicanism and Negro Slavery in Colonial America," *Historical Magazine of the Protestant Episcopal Church* 39, no. 1 (March 1970), 60–62.
66. Ibid., 63–64.
67. For slave labor as a key building block of the British empire, see Greene, "From John Smith to Adam Smith," 295–96.
68. Gwynn, *Huguenots in Britain I*, 335.
69. Michel, "Report of the Journey of Francis Louis Michel," 137–38.
70. Latané, *Pastor Latané*, 38–45; Brock, 29.
71. Latané, *Parson Latané*, 37–40; SP, LC DW 1652–1657, 81–82; Stanard, "Abstracts of Land Patents," VMHB 3, 60–66.
72. Latané, *Parson Latané*, 37–41, 59–62; Dorman, EC RB, 1706–1707, 1717–1719, 70.
73. Latané, *Parson Latané*, 51–55, 73–76.
74. Perry, ed., *Historical Collections*, 285–86; Latané, *Parson Latané*, 31–32.
75. Mason, "The Colonial Churches of Essex and Richmond Counties," 9–15.
76. Thomas N. Ingersoll, ed., "'Release us out of this Cruell Bondegg': An Appeal from Virginia in 1723," WMQ 51, no. 4 (October 1994), 781–82.
77. Perry, ed., *Historical Collections*, 270–72, 281–83, and 285–86; Joan Louise Rezner, *The Anglican Church in Virginia, 1723–1743* (Williamsburg, VA, M.A. Thesis, William and Mary College, 1968), 68–75.
78. John Bell served as minister of Lancaster's Anglican congregations from 1712 until his death in 1743. #15065, #15071, and #73826, CCEd.
79. Anglican-ordained David Currie followed John Bell, serving from 1743 until his death in 1791. Otto Lohrenz, "An Analysis of the the Life and Career of the Reverend David Currie, Lancaster County, Virginia, 1743–1791," *Anglican and Episcopal History* 61, no. 2 (1992), 142–66; Museum of Historic Christ Church, Irvington, Virginia.
80. Jett, *Lancaster County, Virginia*, 100.
81. Bell, *Empire, Religion, and Revolution*, 90, 109–21.
82. Jones, *The Present State of Virginia*, 104–05.
83. Latané, *Parson Latané*, 25–26; Mead, *Old Churches, Ministers, and Families of Virginia*, vol. 1, 395.
84. McIlwaine, *Executive Journals*, vol. 3, 438.
85. Convention of the Clergy of the Colony of Virginia to the Bishop of London, April 10, 1719, in Perry, ed., *Historical Collections,* 212–15.
86. Isaac, *The Transformation of Virginia*, 145.
87. Fontaine, *Memoirs of the Reverend Jaques Fontaine*, 190–96; Alexander, ed., *The Journal of John Fontaine*, 110–26; Ann Maury, *Memoirs of a Huguenot Family* (New York, 1852), 245–310.
88. CCEd #72214 and #72228.
89. #72704 and #72705, CCEd.

90. Craig M. Kilby, "John Fontaine and the First Germanna Colony, Part III," Germanna Foundation (May 2009), germanna.org.

91. Nelson, *A Blessed Company,* 97.

92. Meade, *Old Churches, Ministers, and Families of Virginia,* vol. 2, 198–202; #73855, #73864, and #74611, CCEd.

93. Latané, *Parson Latané,* 78–79.

94. McIlwaine, *Executive Journals,* vol. 2, 126–28 and 261.

95. McIlwaine, *Executive Journals,* vol. 3, 143.

96. R. H. Fife, ed., "The Vestry Book of King William Parish, Virginia, VA, 1707–1750," VMHB 12, no. 1 (July 1904), 24–26, and 29; Lambert, *The Protestant International and the Huguenot Migration to Virginia,* 171–74; Stanwood, *The Global Refuge,* 150–54.

97. Inhabitants of King William Parish in Manacan Town, Virginia, to Mr. Nearne (Extract), July 4, 1728, in Perry, ed., *Historical Collections,* 353.

98. Brock, 183.

99. #108102, CCEd; George McLaren Bryden, "The Virginia Clergy: Governor Gooch's Letters to the Bishop of London, 1727–1749," VMHB 32, no. 3 (July 1924), 225–26 and 234–35.

100. Ibid., 225–26; Fife, ed., "The Vestry Book of King William Parish, VA, 1707–1750," VMHB 13, no 1 (July 1905), 69.

101. St. George's Parish (Spotsylvania County, Virginia) Vestry Book, 1726–1745, March 4, 1735, Midwest Genealogy Center, Lee's Summit, Missouri; SP, Spotsylvania County, Virginia OB, 1734–1735, 90.

102. Fife, ed., "The Vestry Book of King William Parish, VA, 1707–1750," VMHB 12, no. 1, 30, and 12, no. 4 (April 1905), 380, and 13, no. 2 (October 1905), 183.

103. Carlo, *Huguenot Refugees in Colonial New York,* 62–64.

104. Bugg, "The French Huguenot Frontier Settlement of Manakin Town," 391–93.

105. Fischer, *Albions's Seed,* 216; Latané, *Parson Latané,* 93–97; Micou, "Paul Micou, Huguenot Physician, and his Descendants," VMHB 46, 367–70, VMHB 47, 66–78; Lee, *A Brief History of Belle Isle Plantation,* 85–87, and 120–21.

106. SP, ECWB, 1735–1743, 12–13.

Conclusion

The Huguenot-Anglican Project in America, 1761

> Being sorry and penitent for my sins past, I humbly implore my Saviour Jesus Christ that he would receive my soul into his hands and take me into the heavenly mansion prepared for all the Elect.
>
> —John Bertrand, preamble to his will, December 1700

By 1740, the distinctively Huguenot-Anglican Refuge in the Rappahannock region of Virginia, advertised in Europe by Durand de Dauphiné, influenced by London's French Church of the Savoy, and faithful to Bishop Compton's vision of a Protestant empire, had proved resilient. The 1701 pastoral leadership transition from John Bertrand to Lewis Latané had been successful, and by the end of the 1730s, yet another French exile minister was well established in an Anglican parish along the Rappahannock.[1]

In 1735, James Marye, the French convert from Catholicism, left his dual-tract ministry serving the Manakin Town parish to move to St. George's Parish in Spotsylvania County.[2] Spotsylvania was created in 1720, as Virginians were beginning to move away from the rivers toward the mountains. The new county was carved out of the frontier areas of Essex, King and Queen, and King William Counties, extending from the head of the Rappahannock River to the head of the Mattapony River. The two main churches of this parish, originally called Rappahannock and Mattapony, served Huguenots living along these two rivers. The Rappahannock Church was located in the new settlement of Fredericksburg. While St. George's Parish was a considerable distance upriver from the North and South Farnham parishes, where the Rappahannock Refuge began, it was well located for the Huguenots who had moved during the early 1700s to the Stafford and Mattapony River areas in search of land. Marye's hiring suggests that as Rappahannock Huguenots were moving upriver, the center of the Refuge was shifting geographically as well. The relocation of this French exile minister to St. George's Parish further suggests Huguenot-Anglicans in the upper Rappahannock River area were not yet ready to give up their ethnic and religious identity.

Approving James Marye's move to Spotsylvania might have given pause to Lieutenant Governor William Gooch, who had lobbied to have a French minister sent to Virginia with SPG funding to serve the Manakin Huguenots. However, the long-established presence of Rappahannock Huguenots within the bounds of St. George's Parish might have smoothed the way for Gooch's concurrence. Marye made his home near Fredericksburg and was naturalized in 1743. Records show he was baptizing African Virginian children by 1751, when the vestry instructed him to no longer baptize black children with the white children of the parish. Marye served the parish until his death in 1767, when his son, James Marye Jr. (1731–1780), succeeded him as minister and remained in that role until his death.[3] Marye's long ministry to the Rappahannock and Mattapony churches helped strengthen the Huguenot-Anglican identity of 1687 emigrant descendants.

While the Rappahannock Huguenots lived in rural settings, they faced very different challenges from those faced by Huguenots in the homogeneous rural communities in Virginia, New York, and South Carolina. In some ways, Rappahannock Huguenots had more in common with Huguenots in the cities of Boston, Charlestown, and New York City. Like these city dwellers, the Huguenots along the Rappahannock were an ethnic minority group frequently interacting with English colonials, building relationships with them, and often choosing to enter exogamous marriages with them. During the first four decades of the eighteenth century, the growing practice of exogamous marriage in Boston, Charlestown, and New York City coincided with Huguenots moving into the culturally dominant English congregations, usually Anglican. Sometimes Huguenots in these cities maintained joint memberships in both French and English congregations. In either case, the process helped to put the independent French congregations, where worship was conducted exclusively in French, into precipitous decline. One historian has described what happened in these three cities as the "thorough disintegration of the Huguenots as a cohesive refugee group."[4]

This historical assessment cannot be easily applied to the Rappahannock Huguenots, where the purpose of their migration was never to create a cohesive refugee group or to stave off the process of "disintegration." The purpose of the Huguenot-Anglican migration to Virginia was always the quick "integration" of French Protestant emigrants into the parishes and social structures of English colonial society. In this respect, the Rappahannock Refuge was fundamentally different from other Huguenot communities in

Conclusion 159

America, rural and urban. Beginning with John Bertrand, the Rappahannock Refuge was about learning to live in two spheres, the public and the private. Bertrand spoke English in public settings and French with his family, as William Fitzhugh confirmed in 1690, after his sons had been living with the Bertrands.[5] For the Rappahannock Huguenot-Anglican ministers, an important purpose of their "half-way house" French-language services was to prepare the refugees for worship in the public arena of their Anglican parishes, where only English was spoken. Bilingualism soon became an economic necessity for many Huguenots in urban centers, but it would take decades to emerge in the homogeneous rural Huguenot communities.[6]

While John Bertrand and Lewis Latané helped create this distinct Refuge by teaching the refugees to use English in the public arena, it is likely James Marye had a different mission. His role was almost certainly to encourage refugee descendants to keep French at the center of their family and close friendship interactions so that a form of bilingualism might continue to exist for those who were willing to practice it. The combined ministries of Marye and his son from 1735 to 1780 helped keep bilingualism alive for Rappahannock Huguenot descendants to the end of the colonial era.

The resilience and geographical reach of the Rappahannock Refuge is demonstrated by the 1730 marriage of Charlotte Ewell to Darby Gallahough. Charlotte was a child of the exogamous marriage between Mary Ann Bertrand and Charles Ewell. She was a granddaughter of John and Charlotte Bertrand who grew up on their Lancaster County plantation. As a young child, she would have known the emigrant grandmother for whom she was named. Darby, a ship carpenter, was the son of Jacques Gallahough and Marie Roussel, Huguenot emigrants who arrived in Virginia about 1690. Records suggest Marie was an indentured servant. It is likely Darby grew up on his father's lease in the Huguenot community near Brent Town in the part of Stafford County that would become Prince William in 1730. After their marriage, they lived in Prince William where Charlotte, who survived her husband, was last documented in 1783.[7] Following the example of her parents, Charlotte joined with five of her siblings in forming a Saintonge-style family partnership. The partners moved to the Port of Dumfries, one of the largest ports in British America, on the Potomac River in Prince William County, to operate a store, trade in tobacco, and launch a corporation to produce iron for export to Great Britain. Two of Charlotte's brothers, one of whom chose a French name for his plantation, soon became court justices in their new county.[8]

The shared history and relationships that helped sustain the descendants of the Rappahannock Huguenot emigrants were often tied to the Anglican congregations that had employed French ministers. By 1739, William Bertrand was on the vestry of St. Mary's Whitechapel, where his father had served as minister four decades earlier. William was still a member of the vestry in 1752, when the parish merged with Christ Church, the other Anglican parish in Lancaster.[9] This merger of the two Lancaster County parishes was likely an indicator of the decline of the Anglican Church in the county after the emergence of the Great Awakening, a spiritual renewal movement sweeping through the colonies at this time.[10] In 1758, a Presbyterian Meeting House was constructed in Lancaster County, and it attracted some of Lancaster's leading citizens, including William Bertrand's nephew Solomon Ewell, who by the early 1760s was also a member of his Anglican vestry. The meeting house was drawing large crowds in Lancaster with guest preachers such as Samuel Davies, future president of the College of New Jersey, which later became Princeton University. Davies drew 800 to 900 worshippers to the meeting house in 1759. He was a New Side Presbyterian whose preaching was grounded in the enthusiasm of the Great Awakening. Davies had oratorical skills the local Anglican clergy could not match. Records also show these New Side Presbyterians, following the lead of Samuel Davies, were making a concerted effort to include African Virginians in their community of faith. On September 11, 1763, the sacrament of the Lord's Supper was served to 115 white and eighty-five black congregants of Lancaster's Presbyterian Meeting House.[11]

The interest in New Side Presbyterianism in Lancaster made the county a receptive venue for the preaching of George Whitfield, an English Anglican minister of Calvinist persuasion and pioneer of the first Great Awakening. Whitfield arrived in the county the last week of August 1763. He stayed in Lancaster about a week, preaching to large crowds and leading worship at the Presbyterian Meeting House. He was a spell-binding orator who usually preached outdoors because the crowds were too large for the existing buildings. In another demonstration of Great Awakening activity in Lancaster, Baptist preachers were registering as dissenters and touring the county by 1760.[12] While William Bertrand and other Huguenot descendants remained faithful to their Anglican parishes, they might well have recognized that Virginia's established church was entering a time of profound crisis.

Support for the break with Great Britain was very strong in the counties along the Rappahannock River. When the Lancaster Court justices swore allegiance to the new commonwealth on July 16, 1776, William Bertrand's grandson and heir, Thomas Bertrand Griffin, participated as the clerk of the court. At the time, Griffin was also serving as lieutenant colonel of the Lancaster militia.[13] His fellow Bertrand descendants were heavily invested in the struggle for American independence as well. Records confirm at least twelve other great-grandsons of John Bertrand served in revolutionary military forces.[14] Thomas Bertrand Griffin's brother Cyrus served in the wartime Continental Congress and was its last president during 1787–1788.[15] A grandson of James Foushee,[16] three descendants of Paul Micou, and two of Lewis Latané are also known to have served the revolutionary cause.[17]

The identification of the Anglican Church with the government and policies of the king against whom most Virginians were rebelling led many to leave the church during and after the Revolution. The loss of public funding for clergy salaries and buildings in 1777 and the ensuing disestablishment of the Anglican Church in Virginia in 1786 destroyed the long-standing institutional underpinning of the Anglican parishes along the Rappahannock.[18] In 1800, Charles Ewell, great-grandson of John and Charlotte Bertrand, donated the land for the first Methodist church built in Prince William County.[19] Some of John and Charlotte's great-grandchildren, however, remained loyal to the Anglican Church. Jesse Ewell was a delegate to the 1785 General Convention in Philadelphia as it adopted canons for the government of an American Episcopal Church.[20] Cyrus Griffin, fresh from voting to approve the *Virginia Statute for Religious Freedom,* which disestablished the Anglican Church, served as a Lancaster delegate to the 1786 Virginia Anglican Convention that tried to chart a new way forward for a restructured church.[21]

This proved to be a torturous journey for the Anglican congregations along the Rappahannock. By 1790, the Whitechapel Church was abandoned. During the four decades it was closed, the building suffered significant damage. The chancel and lower nave at the east end of the church collapsed. The high pulpit from which John Bertrand had preached disappeared. Seats, doors, and furnishings were pilfered. Some of the tombstones in the cemetery disappeared. A major reconstruction of the Whitechapel Church was necessary for it to reopen as an Episcopal congregation in 1832.[22] A similar process played out for most of the Anglican churches in the Rappahannock region. By 1802, the North Farnham Church was no longer a place of worship. Over the next thirty-two years, it was used as a granary, a stable, and a distillery, with significant damage to the building. Yet, like Whitechapel, North Farnham was repaired and brought back to life as an Episcopal congregation in 1834. Vauter's Church in Essex County followed the same pattern, closing its doors during the decade after the Revolution and reopening in 1822. Its building apparently suffered relatively little damage thanks to a neighboring landowner who claimed ownership of the church and threatened to sue anyone who damaged it.[23] Sadly, most of the seventeenth- and eighteenth-century records of these Anglican parishes were never recovered, leaving the pastoral activities of Henry Compton's Huguenot-Anglican ministers shrouded in mystery.

In 1736, three years after the death of Lewis Latané, Paul Micou died. One of the last remaining French emigrants of the late 1680s, Micou personified both the identity of the Rappahannock Refuge and the aspirations of his fellow exiles through his rapid integration into Virginia's colonial elite. His will named his wife, Margaret, seven children, and two grandchildren through his deceased daughter, Elizabeth. By the terms of the will, Paul Micou Jr. received the *Port Micou* plantation, where his father was buried.[24] These plantation burials were contrary to the policy of Bishop Compton, who wanted Virginians to bury their dead at their churches rather than their plantations, a practice he labeled a "profane custom."[25] A large stone marker identifying Micou's place of burial remained on the grounds of *Port Micou* as late as 1938, when the property was no longer owned by his descendants.[26] The marker was moved sometime after that to Vauter's Episcopal Church, where it resides today behind a church in which Paul Micou worshipped. While it took more than 200 years to undo Micou's embrace of the "profane custom," in this case Bishop Compton's policy finally prevailed.

Gravestone of Paul Micou (1659–1736)
Photo by the author. Courtesy Vauter's Episcopal Church, Loretto, Virginia

While some of the early Huguenot communities in other colonies apparently tried to insulate themselves from English cultural and religious influences, the Huguenot-Anglicans in Virginia sought to straddle their French and English identities. The wills of John Bertrand and Paul Micou offer some clues about how this process unfolded. John Bertrand's will followed English tradition by leaving his plantation to his son William and by entailing it to prevent his heirs from selling, mortgaging, or bequeathing the plantation outside the family.[27] However, making his wife the sole administrator of his estate, naming their daughter Mary Ann as next in line to inherit the plantation ahead of John's nephew in London, and giving this daughter a full share in the personal property of the estate was a striking departure from English practice in favor of Saintonge inheritance customs.[28] While most of Paul Micou's will was consistent with English practice and tradition, it stipulated that Anglican burial practice not be observed at his death. For Virginians of Paul Micou's stature, the preaching of a sermon was the central event of their funerals, for which the minister received a fee. Paul's will directed there be no funeral sermon following his death.[29] This provision suggests Micou wanted his body to be committed to the earth according to the traditional Huguenot practice of immediate burial without sermon or prayers.[30]

Paul Micou's will also shows the influence of the ambivalent policy on slavery adopted by the National Synod of the French Reformed Church in the previous century. The policy, apparently crafted to guide La Rochelle merchants who were participating in the Atlantic slave trade, did not condemn the practice of slavery but mandated humane treatment of the enslaved. Micou's will suggests he took this mandate seriously. The will named all the African Virginians to be transferred and carefully described their family relationships. In this way, the language of Micou's will emphasized the humanity of these enslaved workers in a colonial context in which their humanity was typically denied. For Micou, these African Virginians were much more than a source of labor. They were husbands and wives, fathers and mothers, sons and daughters.[31]

The rapid integration of Rappahannock Huguenots into their Anglican parishes helps explain why this migration remained so long hidden from historians and why there is so little local memory of it. Where Virginia Huguenot memory exists, it is tied to the activities of the Richmond-based Huguenot Society for the Founders of Manakin. Its founding myth, centered on the refugee ships sponsored by William III that arrived in Virginia in 1700 and 1701, makes no provision for a seventeenth-century Refuge in the Rappahannock region. Up to the present time, there has apparently been no origin narrative for the Rappahannock Refuge. Certainly, none was passed on to the descendants of John Bertrand, Paul Micou, or Lewis Latané. Later generations of these families remembered these men were Huguenot emigrants and speculated about where they grew up in France. Their descendants passed on legends about them that were sometimes, but not always, factually accurate. Family researchers gathered information about where they lived and some of their activities in Virginia, but until recently remained unaware they were part of a major Huguenot migration. Bertrand and Micou descendants also remained unaware that these men knew each other in France. Descendants researching other Rappahannock-region Huguenots have followed a similar path. Some have traced their ancestors to England and France, but have labored without the tools to connect them to a larger Huguenot refugee community in Virginia.[32]

While the origin of the Huguenot-Anglican Refuge in Virginia cannot be fully documented, linking Durand de Dauphiné's 1687 chronology with John Bertrand's arrival in Rappahannock County later the same year forms an intriguing narrative. Durand reported having a December 19, 1686, conversation with Virginia's governor, Francis Howard, Baron of Effingham. They met at *Rosegill,* the plantation of Ralph Wormeley, on the banks of the Rappahannock River in Middlesex County. The governor invited Durand to lead a Huguenot migration to Virginia and proposed the creative deployment of a few Huguenot ministers to preach in French to Huguenot refugees *and* to serve Anglican parishes that were struggling to find competent pastors. According to Durand's narrative, the governor followed their conversation with a letter to the Bishop of London, who was responsible for recruiting and commissioning ministers for the colony. A few days later, Durand traveled with Ralph Wormeley, following the Rappahannock River west into Rappahannock County. The Frenchman vividly described the beauty of the rolling landscape and its potential for Huguenot settlers seeking to secure land on which to produce wine and other crops. According to Durand, Wormeley offered all his extensive land holdings in Rappahannock County to Huguenots at very favorable terms. Durand continued to follow the river, arriving in Stafford County on Christmas Eve. There he stayed with William Fitzhugh and learned of another opportunity for Huguenots to acquire land for a reasonable price near the planned Brent Town settlement in Stafford. Durand decided to return to England to promote these two Virginia counties, which he believed to be superior to any other location for Huguenot settlement in English America. On March 15, 1687, Durand boarded a ship bound for England. He arrived in London on May 7, hoping to have a conversation with the Bishop of London.[33] On July 7, 1687, Durand published his French-language tract at The Hague to advertise the Rappahannock region to Huguenot refugees in Europe.[34]

At this point, the origin narrative shifts from Durand's chronology to seventeenth-century Virginia records, cross-referenced with records from England and western France. By the end of 1687, John Bertrand had arrived in Rappahannock County, where Paul Micou and other Huguenot exiles from Bertrand's hometown of Cozes, France, were subsequently documented. Bertrand then became the first Huguenot minister to perform the creative dual-track ministry Governor Howard had envisioned the previous year, offering French Protestant worship to newly arriving Huguenot refugees *and* serving the North Farnham Anglican parish. Some of these Huguenot emigrants subsequently succeeded in securing land. With both French preaching and land being extended to Huguenot emigrants in the Rappahannock region, a robust Refuge gradually formed.

As origin narratives are tested, the contours of memory may be partially reconstructed through present-day institutions of the Rappahannock region. The Belle Isle State Park in Lancaster County, Virginia, has preserved the 924-acre plantation of John Bertrand. Artifacts from the turn-of-the-eighteenth-century Bertrand home, excavated by the William and Mary Center for Archeological Research, may one day be exhibited in the park visitor center. While early parish records have not survived for the Episcopal congregations that received seventeenth-century Huguenot exiles, the memory of the Refuge lives in their architectural structures. The original center section of St. Mary's Whitechapel Episcopal Church in Lancaster was the building where John Bertrand preached during the 1690s. Whitechapel's 1702 Decalogue, a common feature of Protestant Churches in France, was added the year after Bertrand's death as Huguenots were continuing to arrive in the region, and some were moving into this parish. Paul Micou worshipped in the present building of Vauter's Episcopal Church in Loretto, which was constructed about 1719, enlarged four years prior to his death, and where his burial stone now resides.[35]

In 1761, William Bertrand died at the Lancaster County plantation his parents purchased in 1692. William's death came seventy-four years after his parents had arrived in Virginia and just over a century after the death of his grandfather in Cozes. In 1761, the cultural, geographic, and religious structures that supported the Rappahannock Refuge were coming apart as Virginia was entering an era of dramatic change. Third- and fourth-generation descendants were well-established colonial citizens, and many were participating in the accelerating population movement of Virginians westward. At the same time, some descendants had shifted their religious loyalties in response to the Great Awakening.[36] While it is not possible to chart the end of the Rappahannock Refuge, the evidence suggests it held together longer than Huguenot networks in British American urban centers, but it faded more quickly than those in homogenous rural communities.

Nonetheless, recognizable vestiges of Rappahannock Huguenot identity remained for at least three decades after William Bertrand's death in 1761. James Marye's Rappahannock Anglican ministry still had a handful of years to run as his son prepared to follow him in St. George's Parish. William Bertrand's grandson and heir, Thomas Bertrand Griffin, built an elegant Georgian house at the Bertrand plantation in 1767 with the help of his wife, who was a great-granddaughter of Robert Carter. Griffin then gave the plantation the French name that continues to brand it: *Belle Isle*.[37] The ethnic identity and bilingual character of these Bertrand descendants in the late eighteenth century was likely one of the motivating factors behind the effort of William's grandson Cyrus Griffin to lobby President Washington (unsuccessfully) to appoint him Thomas Jefferson's successor as American ambassador to France in 1789.[38]

Long before 1761, the success of the large Huguenot-Anglican Refuge in Virginia had convincingly demonstrated the decisive influence of London's French Church of the Savoy on the Huguenot diaspora in British America. The Savoy Church emphasis on blending into the dominant culture rather than remaining autonomous from it encouraged the widespread practices of exogamous marriage and slaveholding by Huguenots in America.[39] Its "half-way house" style of Anglicanism, emphasizing French-language worship, Presbyterian-Anglican liturgical practices, and Amyraldean Calvinist theology gave French Protestant refugees a way to be both Huguenot and Anglican in the new world. Though John Bertrand was a dedicated advocate for Bishop Compton's Anglican reform in Virginia, he could also use Calvinist language in the preamble of his will to anticipate the "heavenly mansion prepared for all the Elect."[40] It was this version of Anglican faith that proved persuasive to a large segment of Huguenot exiles in British America and helped the Savoy Church contest the Threadneedle Street Church's position as the center of the English Huguenot world.[41]

At the same time, the search for an autonomous Huguenot identity through the independent French churches in America had failed. The gradual disintegration of the French congregations that embraced the Threadneedle Street model in Boston, Charleston, and New York City in turn weakened the rural congregations that depended on them. The problems experienced by these churches were exacerbated by the Anglican sympathies of some of their members and pastors.[42] The failure of autonomous Huguenot identity in America was confirmed by the adoption of the "half-way house" Anglicanism of the Savoy Church by independent Huguenot congregations in South Carolina and New York with the encouragement of the SPG.[43] The growing Huguenot-Anglican preference of French Protestant refugees in eighteenth-century America[44] offers a stark contrast with the dominant pattern among Huguenot exiles in England, where 75 percent had attached themselves to non-conformist French Reformed congregations by the early 1700s.[45]

One of the most prominent Huguenot refugees who migrated to the Anglican Church in America was the New England merchant Gabriel Bernon, who arrived in Boston in 1688 after being smuggled out of a La Rochelle prison in a wine cask the previous year. His papers reveal his extensive correspondence with Huguenots throughout the American colonies and in Europe. After moving from Boston and its independent Huguenot congregation to Rhode Island by the end of the 1690s, Bernon helped organize three Anglican congregations there.[46] In 1725, at the age of eighty-one, he blamed Puritan dissenters for the English Civil War in language that was reminiscent of the Huguenot theologian Moïse Amyraut: "The arbitrary power of the Presbyterians under Oliver Cromwell set England ablaze, the Father against the Mother, the brother against the sister, the mother-in-law against the daughter-in-law, and Independents against the Crown and the Church . . . which seems to me the most deplorable thing in the world."[47] This was the critique of English Puritan ecclesiology Amyraldean Huguenots internalized before they left France, making them natural allies of Anglican leaders like Henry Compton. John Bertrand's brother Paul, who was trained in Amyraut's theology at Saumur, made a similar argument in a 1684 letter archived in Compton's papers.[48] This critique almost certainly animated the Huguenot-Anglican leaders of the Rappahannock Refuge as they worked to overcome Puritan influence in Virginia's parishes and advocated for Anglican conformity among Huguenots in America.

The dual-track ministries and imperialist Protestant project of Bishop Compton's French exile ministers proved surprisingly effective as they helped shape a Huguenot migration to America that was larger and more Anglican than scholars have generally understood. Their work also fueled an underlying Huguenot-Anglican project in America: the remarkably effective integration of French Protestant refugee families into English colonial society. The distinctively Huguenot-Anglican Refuge in Virginia, true to the aspirations of Durand de Dauphiné and John Bertrand, led the way toward rapid religious and social conformity by Huguenots in British America.

NOTES

1. For John Bertrand's will, see LC WB 8, 1690–1709, 105.
2. SP, Spotsylvania County, Virginia OB, 1734–1735, 90; Philip Slaughter, *History of St. George's Parish in the county of Spotsylvania, and the diocese of Virginia* (Richmond, VA, 1890), 17.
3. Carrol H. Quenzel, *The History and Background of St. George's Episcopal Church, Fredericksburg, Virginia* (Richmond, 1951), 11–14 and 16–17.
4. Butler, *The Huguenots in America*, 81–91, 131–38, and 186–97.
5. Davis, *William Fitzhugh and His Chesapeake World*, 271.
6. Carlo, *Huguenot Refugees in Colonial New York*, 169–72.
7. George Harrison Sanford King, Mss 1k5823a, Virginia Historical Society Library, Richmond.
8. Lee, *A Brief History of Belle Isle Plantation*, 72–74.
9. St. Mary's Whitechapel Parish Vestry Book, 1739–1752, Mary Ball Washington Library, Lancaster, Virginia.
10. Jett, *Lancaster County, Virginia*, 100.

11. "Journal of Colonel James Gordon, Lancaster County, Virginia," WMQ 11, no. 2 (October 1902), 102 and vol. 12, no. 1 (July 1903), 9; Isaac, *The Transformation of Virginia*, 154.

12. Jett, *Lancaster County, Virginia*, 102–04, and 106–07.

13. Benjamin J. Hillman, ed., *Executive Journals of the Council of Virginia*, vol. 6 (June 20, 1754—May 3, 1775) (Richmond, VA, 1966), 405; Jett, *Lancaster County, Virginia*, 113.

14. Bertrand descendants serving in the revolutionary military forces included Thomas Bertrand Griffin, Corbin Griffin, Leroy Griffin, Samuel Griffin, William Griffin, James Ewell (1), Jesse Ewell, Thomas Ewell, Charles Ewell, James Ewell (2), Charles Gallahue, Jeremiah Gallahue, and Thomas Montague. Lee, *A Brief History of Belle Isle Plantation*, 95–103; Robert Wuthnow, "Captain Charles Ewell" (unpublished essay, 2022); Robert Wuthnow, "Militia Story" (unpublished essay, 2022).

15. United States Congress, *Biographical Dictionary of the United States Congress, 1774–present*, Griffin, Cyrus (1748–1810), (Washington DC, 1998).

16. "To Thomas Jefferson from William Foushee, 13 September 1801," in *The Papers of Thomas Jefferson*, vol. 35, 1 August–30 November 1801, ed. Barbara B. Oberg (Princeton, NJ, 2008), 278–79.

17. "Revolutionary War Listing," Essex County, Virginia, for William Latané, Paul Micou, and Richard Montague; The American Revolution Institute of the Society of the Cincinnati for Henry Micou; Micou, "Paul Micou, Huguenot Physician and His Descendants," VMHB 47, 77, for two Henry Micous.

18. Thomas E. Buckley, "Establishing New Bases for Religious Authority," in *From Jamestown to Jefferson: The Evolution of Religious Freedom in Virginia*, eds., Paul Rasor and Richard E. Bond (Charlottesville, VA, 2011), 146; Bell, *Empire, Religion, and Revolution*, 10–11, 170–74; Isaac, *The Transformation of Virginia*, 312–17.

19. Susan R. Morton, "Survey Report, Old Methodist Church Site," October 6, 1937, LVA.

20. Historic Dumfries, Inc., *Records of Dettingen Parish, Prince William County, Virginia, 1745–1802* (Berwyn Heights, MD, 2007), 67–68.

21. Tupper, ed., *Christ Church Parish, Lancaster County, Virginia Vestry Book, 1739–1786*, 93.

22. Elizabeth C. Pierce, "A Brief History of St. Mary's Whitechapel Episcopal Church," 2, Mary Ball Washington Library, Lancaster, Virginia; Page Henley, St. Mary's Whitechapel historian, in an email with the author December 8, 2014.

23. Mason, "The Colonial Churches of Essex and Richmond Counties," 13–15, and 18.

24. SP WB 6, 1735–1743, 11–12.

25. Carpenter, *The Protestant Bishop*, 256.

26. Micou, "Paul Micou, Huguenot Physician and His Descendants," 362–70.

27. LC WB 8, 1690–1709, 105–05a.

28. Carlo, *Huguenot Refugees in Colonial New York*, 147–48.

29. SP, EC WB, 1735–1743, 89–90.

30. Bernard Roussel, "'Ensevelir honnestement les corps": funeral corteges and Huguenot culture," in *Society and Culture in the Huguenot World, 1559–1685*, eds.

Raymond A. Mentzer and Andrew Spicer (Cambridge, UK, 2002), 193–208; Yves Krumenacker, "Huguenot Death in the Seventeenth Century: Discourse and Reality," trans. T. Evans, in *The Huguenots: France, Exile, and Diaspora*, eds. Jane McKee and Randolph Vigne (Brighton, UK, 2013), 17–27.

31. SP, EC WB, 1735–1743, 11–12.

32. William C. Bryant, "Pierre (Peter) Riviere: Huguenot Planter of Lancaster County and Progenitor of the Revere Family of Virginia," *Northern Neck of Virginia Historical Magazine* (December 2009), 7138–52; Steven G. Fancy and Sue Reneau Damewood, "Genealogy of the Reno/Reneau Family in America, 1600–1930," Bull Run Regional Library, Manassas, Virginia.

33. Durand, 143–78.

34. Ibid., 12.

35. Mason, "The Colonial Churches of Essex and Richmond Counties," 13–15.

36. For the cultural and religious revolution that was underway in Virginia by the 1760s, see Isaac, *The Transformation of Virginia*, 137–38.

37. Lee, *A Brief History of Belle Isle Plantation*, 79–82; Camille Wells, "Belle Isle" (unpublished essay, 2014).

38. "Letter to Thomas Jefferson from Cyrus Griffin, 11 December 1789," in *The Papers of Thomas Jefferson,* vol. 16, 30 November–4 July, ed., Julian P. Boyd (Princeton, NJ, 1961), 14–15.

39. For the common social and religious patterns that emerged among Huguenots across the English American colonies, see Jon Butler, "The Huguenots and the American Immigrant Experience," in *Memory and Identity: The Huguenots in France and the Atlantic Diaspora*, eds. Van Ruymbeke and Sparks, 194–203.

40. LC WB 8, 1690–1709, 105.

41. Stanwood, *The Global Refuge*, 141–42.

42. Butler, *The Huguenots in America*, 111–12.

43. Van Ruymbeke, *From New Babylon to Eden*, 131; Carlo, *Huguenot Refugees in Colonial New York*, 78–82.

44. For the argument that Huguenots in the American colonies almost unanimously embraced Anglicanism, see Robert M. Kingdon, "Why Did the Huguenot Refugees in the American Colonies Become Episcopalian?" *Historical Magazine of the Protestant Episcopal Church* 49, no. 4 (December 1980), 317–35. For a more nuanced discussion of this issue, see Paula Wheeler Carlo, "Huguenot Congregations in Colonial New York and Massachusetts: Reassessing the Paradigm of Anglican Conformity," in *A Companion to the Huguenots,* eds. Mentzer and Van Ruymbeke, 371–93.

45. Gwynn, *Huguenot Heritage*, 131–32.

46. Catharine Randall, *From a Far Country: Camisards and Huguenots in the Atlantic World* (Athens, GA, 2009), 70–78.

47. Van Ruymbeke, *From New Babylon to Eden*, 155.

48. Paul Bertrand, April 13, 1684, Rawlinson Papers, Ms C 984, Bodleian Library, Oxford University.

Abbreviations

ADCMLR	Archives Departmentales de la Charente-Maritime LaRochelle
Agnew	David C. A. Agnew, *Protestant Exiles from France*
Baird	Charles W. Baird, *History of the Huguenot Emigration to America*
Brock	R. A. Brock, ed., *Huguenot Emigration to Virgina*
CCEd	Clergy of the Church of England Database
CZ	*Papiers des Baptêmes de l'Église Réformée de Cozes* (Cozes Protestant Baptism Register)
DB	County Deed Book
Dorman	John Frederick Dorman, Series of Published Virginia County Records
Durand	Durand de Dauphiné, *A Huguenot Exile in Virginia*
DWB	County Deed and Will Book
EC	Essex County, Virginia
FCL	Robin Gwynn, ed., *The Minutes of the Consistory of the French Church of London, Threadneedle Street*
Fleet	Beverley Fleet, *Virginia Colonial Abstracts*
HL	Huguenot Library, University College, London
KGC	King George County, Virginia
KQC	King and Queen County, Virginia
KWC	King William County, Virginia
LMA	London Metropolitan Archives
LC	Lancaster County, Virginia
LCA	Lancaster County Archives, Lancaster, Virginia
LVA	Library of Virginia, Richmond, Virginia
LOP	Land Office Patents, Library of Virginia, Richmond, Virginia
MC	Middlesex County, Virginia

Minet	William and Susan Minet, ed., *Le Livre . . . a la Savoye, Le Livre . . . de Threadneedle Street,* and *Registers of . . . Savoy, Spring Garden, and Les Grecs*
NC	Northumberland County, Virginia
NNG	Northern Neck Grants, Library of Virginia, Richmond
OB	County Order Book
ORC	[Old] Rappahannock County, Virginia
PWC	Prince William County, Virginia
RB	County Record Book
RBP	Royal Bounty Papers, Huguenot Library, University College, London
RC	Richmond County, Virginia
RCA	Richmond County Archives, Warsaw, Virginia
SC	Stafford County, Virginia
Shaw	William A. Shaw, *Letters of Denization and Acts of Naturalization*
SHPF	Bibliothèque de la Society de l'Histoire Du Protestantisme Français Paris
SP	Ruth and Sam Sparacio, Series of Published Virginia County Records
VMHB	*The Virginia Magazine of History and Biography*
WB	County Will Book
WC	Westmoreland County, Virginia
WMCAR-2006	William and Mary Center for Archeological Research, Archeological Evaluation of Sites 44LA147 and 44LA175, Belle Isle State Park, Lancaster County, Virginia.
WMCAR-2020	William and Mary Center for Archeological Research, Interim Management Summary: Archeological Evaluation of Site 44LA147, Belle Isle State Park, Lancaster County, Virginia.
WMQ	*William and Mary Quarterly*

Appendix A
Rappahannock Huguenot Refugees, 1677–1710

Interpreting the Refugee Chart:
Names are listed as rendered in Virginia records with French variant surname spellings in italics. Names of spouses are given in parentheses followed by the county and the earliest year the name is documented there. The placement of an asterisk after the county indicates the acquisition of land in that county. Occupations of refugees and names of masters of Huguenot servants are provided within brackets. Sources for corroborating Huguenot identity (see the source abbreviation list) are provided last with upper case spelling designating full name document matches and lower case indicating surname only matches. The "VA Record" notation designates persons who are identified as Huguenots in Virginia records. Because of gaps in the extant records, it is possible some of these refugees arrived in Virginia earlier than the year listed for them.

Part I: Households Initially Documented 1677–1685:

1. James Andres/*André*, Rappahannock,* 1679 (cz)
2. William Barbee (Elizabeth), Middlesex,* 1685 (rbp)
3. Nicholas Bernard/Burnard (Elisabeth Revett), Stafford,* 1682 (FCL, cz)
4. Stephen Besson, Stafford,* 1684 (rbp, agnew)
5. William Brassie/Breese/*Brossier*, Lancaster, 1679 [surgeon] (cz)
6. Aime/Adam Brittaine, Middlesex, 1677 [overseer] (VA record)
7. James Certaine/*Certainy*, Westmoreland, 1681, Stafford, 1692 (rbp, minet)
8. Henry Chappell/*Chappelle*, Rappahannock, 1685, Richmond, 1693 (fcl)
9. Thomas Charles, Westmoreland, 1681 (agnew, minet)

10. John Colleyvow, Rappahannock,* 1683, Essex* 1698 [pharmacist] (AGNEW)
11. James Dabney/*Dabin* (Ann Sherwood) Northumberland, 1679, Rappahannock,* 1690/King and Queen,* 1701, King William, 1703 (cz)
12. Robert Daubinet/*Daubigne/Daubonne*, Westmoreland, 1683 (rbp)
13. Nicholas Deluis/Delues, Rappahannock, 1684 (cz)
14. Nicholas Demall/*Deméon*, Westmoreland, 1680 (baird)
15. Peter Deschazant/de Shazer/Deshasero, New Kent (later King and Queen/King William), 1681 (FM)
16. Luke Demerritt/*Demet* (Mary), Northumberland, 1679, Richmond,* 1699, Westmoreland, 1702 (rbp)
17. Thomas Demery/Dimery/*Demarais*, Middlesex, 1678, Lancaster, 1678 (agnew)
18. Owen Dermott/*Demet*, Northumberland, 1682 [teacher] (rbp)
19. John Deverdell/*Deville*, Middlesex, 1682 (rbp)
20. Charles Duet/*Douet*, Westmoreland, 1683 (rbp)
21. Peter Foxen/*Faucon,* Rappahannock,* 1684 [constable] (fcl)
22. Henry Gauler/*Gallet/Gaulier*, Rappahannock,* 1684 (rbp, minet)
23. William Guyat, Middlesex, 1681 (agnew)
24. George Herriott/*Heruat*, New Kent (later King and Queen/King William), 1678 (cz)
25. George Lascaille/*Lajaille*, Rappahannock, 1681 (CZ)
26. James Levitt/*Lavotte*, Rappahannock, 1681 (fcl)
27. Gedeon Macon/*Marcon* (Martha Woodward), New Kent (later King and Queen/King William),* 1680 (minet, cz)
28. John Maison/*Maisonneuve/Maisant*, Middlesex, 1684 (rbp, minet)
29. George Mallet, Lancaster, 1685 (cz, rbp, agnew)
30. David Mazey, Lancaster, 1678 (agnew)
31. Joseph Moucher/*Moucheron*, Lancaster, 1683 (rbp)
32. Josué Norment/*Normant/Normand* (Anne), New Kent (later King and Queen/King William),* 1682 (rbp, minet)
33. Leonard Osier/Ossier/*Ozias*, Westmoreland, 1681 (rbp)
34. Robert Pardoe/*Parcot/Perdu*, Rappahannock, 1683 (baird)
35. Richard Person, Rappahannock, 1679 (shaw)
36. Peter Pheradine/*Peridié*, Lancaster, 1678 (rbp)
37. Richard Philiter/*Pelletant/Pellitier*, Rappahannock, 1679, Stafford, 1693 (cz, shaw)
38. Christopher Pridum/*Preudhomme,* Rappahannock, 1678 (shaw)
39. Francis Quarles/*Queila*, Rappahannock, 1685 (rbp)
40. James Quarles/*Queila*, New Kent (later King and Queen/King William),* 1683 (rbp)
41. John Quarles/*Queila*, Rappahannock, 1685, King William,* 1702 (rbp)

42. John Simone/*Simeon*, Lancaster, 1681 (SHAW, cz, rbp)
43. John Tillett, Stafford,* 1691 [arrived in Gloucester Co. about 1678] (AGNEW)
44. Charles Valland/*Vaillant/Vallan*, Northumberland, 1679 (rbp, shaw)
45. Claude Vallet/*Veillet* (alias Champagne) (Ann), Middlesex, 1684 (CZ)

Refugees Arriving as Indentured Servants:

1. Thomas Bowyer/*Bouyer*, Northumberland, 1683 {John Nichols} (cz)
2. Lewis DeBurbon/*Dubourdieu*, Middlesex, 1682 {Robert Price} (rbp)
3. Henry de Boys/*Dubois*, Northumberland, 1683 {William Bashaw} [orphan] (cz)
4. Samuel Gerrard/*Geraud*, Rappahannock, 1685 {William Travis} (rbp, agnew)
5. Jane Leucas/*Lucas*, Middlesex, 1684 {Captain Whitaker} (cz, rbp)
6. John LeMarr, Middlesex, 1685 {Christopher Robinson} (fm, minet)
7. Edward Poore/*Poirer*, Middlesex, 1681 {Robert Smith} (cz)
8. James Taffe/*Tiffeay*, Northumberland, 1678, {Samuel Mackneil} (rbp)
9. Refugees Arriving as Indentured Servants and Gaining Freedom:
10. Cyprian Prou (Margaret) Rappahannock, 1684?, Richmond,* 1696 [tailor, indenture contract in London in 1684, gained freedom before 1696, constable] (FCL, MINET, agnew)
11. Margaret Prou (Cyprien), Rappahannock, 1684?, Richmond, 1704, [indenture contract in London in 1684, gained freedom before 1696] (agnew, minet, fcl)
12. Elias Hughes Sale/*Sallé*, Rappahannock, 1685 {Thomas Glasscock} [gained freedom in 1685] (fm)

Part II: Households Initially Documented 1686–1700:

1. Absolom Abbey/*Abbé*, Stafford, 1689, Westmoreland, 1703 (fcl, rbp)
2. John Amee/Amis/*Amés/Aimé* (Rebecca), Stafford, 1689 (RBP)
3. Peter Aveline, Richmond, 1698 (FCL, agnew)
4. John Bache, Stafford, 1691 (AGNEW)
5. Peter Bache (Dorothy), Stafford, * 1686 (agnew)
6. Peter Baile/*Bayle/Bale* Stafford, * 1694 (FCL, RBP)
7. John Barnard/Bernard (Margaret), Richmond, 1698, Westmoreland, * 1710 (CZ, RBP, SHAW)
8. John Bertrand (Charlotte Jolly), Rappahannock, 1688/Richmond, 1692, Lancaster,* 1692 [minister/merchant/teacher] (John: CZ, RBP, AGNEW) (Charlotte: CZ, RBP)

9. James Boiseau, New Kent (later King William/King and Queen), 1690 [minister] (RBP, AGNEW)
10. John Bonnevill, Richmond, 1695 (agnew)
11. Jean Boucher/*Bouchier*, Rappahannock, 1691 (CZ, RBP)
12. John Brages/*Brase*, Rappahannock,* 1687, [carpenter] (minet)
13. John Brassier/Brazier/*Brossier* (Elizabeth Holt), Rappahannock, 1688, Essex,* 1692, [carpenter] (CZ)
14. William Breton Richmond, 1697/Stafford, 1706, Westmoreland, 1707 [ship captain] (cz)
15. James Burnard/Bernard, Stafford, 1690 (MINET, cz, rbp)
16. Moses Burnard/Bernard, Stafford, 1692 (MINET, cz, rbp)
17. Marquis Calmes/*Calmels/Calmetz*, Lancaster, 1694/Stafford,* 1706 (RBP, AGNEW, FM)
18. John Champ/*Deschamps* (Elizabeth Reyly), Stafford, 1687, Richmond,* 1695, Westmoreland, 1703 (cz, baird, agnew)
19. William Champ/*Deschamps*, New Kent (later King and Queen),* 1687, Stafford,* 1702 (cz, baird, agnew)
20. Alexander Chappell/*Chappelle*, Stafford, 1692/Richmond, 1693, Essex, 1693 [physician] (fcl)
21. Moses Chappell/*Chappelle* (Dorothy), Essex, 1695 (fcl)
22. John Charteris/Chartris/Chartres/*Chartier,* Richmond, 1699, [merchant, in Liverpool by 1704] (SHAW, MINET, fcl)
23. Stephen Chaukerett/*Chaudoré/Chaboner* (Hannah/Elizabeth), Northumberland,* 1688 [constable in Fairfield Parish] (baird, minet)
24. John de la Chaumette, Stafford, 1688 (RBP)
25. Morrice Clerke/*Clercq*, Stafford,* 1690, Richmond,* 1711 (baird)
26. Richard Collett/*Colet* (Sarah) Essex, 1695 (minet, agnew),
27. Michall Connele (Katherine), Richmond, 1694 [weaver of tapestries] (CZ)
28. James Conill, Stafford, 1700 (cz)
29. William Constantine/*Constantin*, Rappahannock, 1686 (agnew, fcl, rbp)
30. Charles Coshee/*Couchier/Couscher,* Richmond, 1692 (cz, rbp)
31. Thomas Cotance/*Coutant/Cotin*, Lancaster, 1695 (cz, fm, fcl, rbp)
32. Henry Curry/*Cury, Currie,* Essex, 1692 (brock, minet)
33. Edward Danellin/*Denillanialle* (Jane Smith), Essex, 1695 [tavern keeper] (CZ)
34. James Debore/Deboree/*Delaborie*, Richmond, 1694 (CZ)
35. Samuel Deboree/*Delaborie*, Richmond, 1695 (cz)
36. Lewis Debria (Elizabeth), Westmoreland, 1698 (fm)
37. Bryan Dehorter/*Duhorte,* Rappahannock, 1688 (minet, brock)
38. Abraham Delander/*Delalande/des Landes* (Mary), Stafford, c. 1690 (CZ, RBP)

Appendix A 177

39. Samuel Demonvill/*de Monbeville* (Hannah Cox Lampkin), Westmoreland,* 1691, Richmond, 1693, Stafford* 1714 (CZ, FM)
40. Alexander Denain/Denin/Denaux, Essex,* 1692 (cz, baird)
41. Abraham Depree (Rebecca/Elizabeth Smith), Middlesex, 1687, Rappahannock, 1688, Essex, 1693, Stafford, 1703 [builder of tobacco houses] (RBP)
42. David Depue, Northumberland, 1689 (cz)
43. Charles Dermott/*Demet*, Northumberland, 1699 (rbp)
44. John Devall/*Duvall*, Rappahannock, 1690 (fm)
45. Jacob Devalliard, Essex,* 1698 [physician] (rbp)
46. Thomas Deviant/*Devion*, Westmoreland, 1695 (rbp)
47. Isaac Duchemin Stafford, c. 1690, Westmoreland,* 1697 (RBP)
48. Samuel Duchemin Stafford, c. 1690, Westmoreland,* 1697, Richmond,* 1708, Essex* 1714 (RBP)
49. Frances DuCondry/*De Cow/Decoux*, Stafford, 1699 (baird)
50. Lewis Fardo/*Fard*, Rappahannock,* 1688 (fcl)
51. Abraham Farrow/*Fallow/Fallour/Fouron* (Margaret Mason) Stafford,* 1690 [millwright] (cz)
52. John Faver/Favour/*Fabure/Faviere* (Mary), Rappahannock, 1690, Westmoreland, 1698, Richmond, 1699, [naturalized 1711] (CZ, FCL, SHAW)
53. Henry Faucon, Stafford, 1689 (rbp, agnew, minet)
54. James Foushee/*Foucher/Fouchier* (Marie, Ruth Mitchell), Richmond,* 1694/Lancaster, 1724 (CZ, VA Record)
55. John Foushee/*Foucher/Fouchier*, Rappahannock, 1691 (CZ, RBP)
56. James Gallahough/*Galliott* (Mary Roussal), Stafford, 1690 (cz)
57. Ann Galard/*Gaillard*, Richmond, 1695 (CZ, RBP, FCL)
58. John Galley/*Galais* (Elizabeth), Richmond, 1693 (FCL, SHAW, cz)
59. Henry Gallop/*Gallopin/Galope,* Richmond,* 1697 (rbp, minet)
60. Robert Gallop/*Gallopin/Galope,* Richmond, 1698 (rbp, minet)
61. Mark Gendron (Mary), Lancaster,* 1698, Essex, 1698 [merchant] (agnew, shaw)
62. William Gueffe/*Gouffe*, Stafford, 1691 (agnew)
63. John Guyatt/*Gayot*, Stafford, 1690 (AGNEW, MINET)
64. William Herson/*Hersan/Hersent,* Stafford, 1691 (rbp, fm)
65. Peter Huett, Richmond, 1699 (FCL, RBP, MINET)
66. Samuel Jaques, Essex, 1693, (cz, fcl)
67. John Lahore/Lehore/*Lehueur*, Lancaster, 1687 (agnew)
68. Jean Lainy/Launy/*Lainé/Launay*, Rappahannock, 1686 (MINET, rbp, fcl)
69. Joan Lamy, Essex, 1696, (cz, fcl, rbp)
70. Thomas Lande/*Delalande,* Stafford, 1691, (cz, agnew)

Appendix A

71. Nathaniel Landers/*Delalande*, Rappahannock, 1690 (cz, agnew)
72. John Lastree/*Lastre,* Rappahannock,* 1689 (rbp)
73. Nicholas Laurans, Westmoreland, 1694 (CZ, RBP)
74. John Lavag/*Lavau,* Rappahannock,* 1691 (fcl)
75. _____ LeClair/*Clair* (Ann Platt), Stafford,* 1698 (rbp)
76. John Mallie/*Malle*, Lancaster, 1692 (cz, minet)
77. Nicholas Maniere/*Moynier*, Stafford, 1690 (cz, agnew)
78. Thomas Marchant, Richmond, 1698 (agnew, rbp, fcl)
79. Arnold Marr/*Marchais* (Mary), King and Queen (later King William),* 1696 (cz)
80. John Marr/*Marchais/Marre* Stafford, 1700, King William, 1703, Richmond,* 1712 (VA Record, CZ, FM)
81. Richard Marr/*Marchais*, King and Queen (later King William),* 1700 (cz)
82. John Masson, Westmoreland, 1691 [ministerial candidate, teacher] (CZ, RBP)
83. Robert Maupin/*Mopin*, Northumberland, 1699 (fm, shaw)
84. Edward Maurin/*Morin*, Essex, 1693 (cz, agnew)
85. Martin Mazey/*Mauzy/Mosey,* Rappahannock, 1691, Essex, 1693 (rbp, fcl)
86. John Mauzy/Mosey, Stafford, 1700 (agnew)
87. Michel Mauzy/Mosey Stafford, 1689 (RBP, AGNEW)
88. Paul Micou (Margaret Thatcher/Cammock) Rappahannock, 1690, Richmond,* 1693, Essex* 1693, Westmoreland, 1701, Stafford 1706 [physician/merchant/court justice] (CZ)
89. Giles Monparson/*Monpincon,* Rappahannock, 1689 (fcl)
90. Nicholas Morcan/*Marcon*, Essex, 1700 (cz)
91. Nicholas Moreau, New Kent (later King and Queen), 1696, Essex, 1698, Richmond, 1699, Westmoreland, 1700, [minister/physician] (RBP, cz)
92. Elias Morrice/*Morisse/Maurice* (Bridgett), Westmoreland,* 1693 (CZ)
93. John Morrice/*Morisse/Maurice* (Elisabeth), Westmoreland, 1698 (CZ)
94. Robert Mussen/*Musson*, Westmoreland, 1691 (baird)
95. Robert Napier/*Nareit/Nauguier* (Mary Perrin), King and Queen (later King William),* 1690 (fcl, agnew)
96. Joshua Nason/*Naissan/Nezereau* Essex,* 1692, King and Queen, 1702 (rbp, minet)
97. Thomas Nason/*Naissan/Nezereau,* Stafford, 1691 (rbp, minet)
98. Peter Ollane/*Ollineau*, Richmond, 1694 (cz)
99. William Palisson/*Pelisson*, Westmoreland, 1698 (cz, rbp, agnew)
100. Charles Pampillion/*Papillon*, Lancaster, 1700 (rbp, baird)
101. Simon Pascoe/Passo/Pascaud/*Passeau,* Essex, 1699 (cz)
102. Vincent Pass/*Pas,* Rappahannock, 1688 (minet)

103. John Person, Rappahannock, 1690 (SHAW, minet)
104. James Pesson/*Pessé/Person,* Richmond, 1696 (minet, shaw)
105. Samuel Ponye/*Ponge,* Rappahannock,* 1686 (rbp)
106. Elizabeth Poore/*Poirie,* Richmond, 1698 (fcl, rbp)
107. Thomas Quetance/*Quantine* Lancaster, 1693 (cz)
108. Benjamin Renoe/*Renaud* (Mary), Stafford, 1688 (RBP, cz)
109. Bernard Renoe/*Renaud,* Essex, 1695 (cz, rbp)
110. Lewis Renoe/*Renaud* (Anna), Stafford,* 1688 (RBP, cz)
111. James Roy/*Leroy,* Rappahannock, 1691, Richmond, 1692 (CZ, RBP, FCL, AGNEW)
112. Thomas Roy/*Leroy,* Essex, 1697 (cz, rbp, fcl)
113. Richard Sables/*Seble,* Rappahannock, 1691, Richmond, 1695 (rbp)
114. Peter St. Leger (Elisabeth), Rappahannock, 1688 (rbp, fcl)
115. Peter Salinger/Sullenger/*Selingue* (Elizabeth Dixon), Rappahannock, 1692, Essex* 1696 (RBP)
116. John Salmon/*Salemon,* Essex, 1695 (cz, shaw)
117. Stephen Sebastian/Sabastian/*Sabatier/Sabaties* (Elizabeth), Stafford, 1689, Richmond, 1705, [cooper] (fcl, rbp, shaw)
118. John Shaproone/*Shaperon,* Richmond, 1695 (RBP, FCL)
119. Charles Tebo/*Thibaud* (Frances), Rappahannock, 1689 (cz)
120. Francis Terrett/*Terets,* Richmond,* 1700 (minet)
121. Thomas Terrett/*Terets,* Westmoreland,* 1692 (minet)
122. Simon Tomasin/*Thomassin* (Patience) Stafford, 1686, Richmond,* 1696 [carpenter] (shaw)
123. John Travallion, Essex, 1695 (RBP)
124. Peter Trebble/Tribell/*Trible,* Essex,* 1695, [cooper], (agnew)
125. Charles Vallieur (Jane Welsh), Richmond, 1693 (rbp)
126. Bartholomew Vawter/Vauter/*Vautier* (Anna), Rappahannock,* 1687, Essex,* 1693 (rbp, fcl, shaw)
127. John Vihice/*Vias,* Rappahannock, 1690 (cz, rbp)
128. Edward Vergin/*Vergne,* Richmond, 1694 (rbp, fcl)
129. George Violett/*Viala,* Northumberland, 1699 [later became indentured servant of Thomas Brewer after becoming indigent] (RBP, minet)
130. Job Virgett/*Virger/Verger* (Elizabeth Shipley), Essex,* 1695 (rbp, agnew, shaw, minet)
131. John Virgett/*Virger/Verger* (Elizabeth Gray), Essex, 1692 (RBP, AGNEW, SH, MINET)

Refugees Arriving as Indentured Servants:

1. Peter Barnard, Rappahannock, 1686 {James Taylor} (MINET, cz, agnew)
2. Morris Brassell/*Brasseau,* Northumberland, 1699 {Richard Key} (rbp)

3. Jeffery Brassier/*Brossier*, Lancaster, 1700 {John Bertrand} (cz)
4. John Britton, Richmond, 1696 {John Champ} (cz, VA Record)
5. Margaret Conniel, Lancaster, 1695 {William Edmonds} (cz)
6. Anne Corbet/*Courbet*, Lancaster, 1688 {Mrs. Wallis} (brock)
7. James Deboe, Rappahannock, 1690) {William Loyd} (CZ)
8. Ellinore Deinne/*Dejenne*, Lancaster, 1699 {John Bertrand} (fcl)
9. Elizabeth Desborough/*Debrosses/Desbrousses*, Stafford, 1690 {George Luke} (cz)
10. Jacob Devall/*Duvall/Davall*, Richmond, 1698 {William Brokenbough} (fm, shaw)
11. Robert Furney/*Fournier*, Lancaster, 1699 {John Bertrand} (cz, rbp)
12. Peter Geniox/*Gehneau/Generaud*, Lancaster, 1700 {Mark Gendron} (cz)
13. Michaell Gwin/*Guerin/Gouin,* Lancaster, 1692 {Martha Norris} (fcl, rbp)
14. Henry Hases/*de la Haise,* Rappahannock, 1690 {Thomas Tensley} (fcl)
15. George Herron/*Heron,* Richmond, 1699 {John Baker} (rbp, fcl)
16. Sarah Lafeavour/*LeFevre* Rappahannock, 1689, Richmond, 1693 {William Ball} (fm)
17. Peter Lander/*Lalande*, Essex, 1694 {Henry Pickett} (CZ, AGNEW, MINET)
18. Hugh Moyniere/*Moynier,* Richmond, 1699 {William Strother} (cz, agnew)
19. Dorothy Paget/*Page*, Stafford, 1692 {Richard Fossaker} (cz, minet)
20. Mary Pew/*Dupeu*, Richmond, 1700 {Roland Lawson} (baird)
21. John Poore/*Poirier*, Northumberland, 1698 {Samuel Griffin, William Keene} (cz, rbp)
22. John Pourgin/*Pourpin*, Lancaster, 1686 {unknown} (rbp)
23. Edward Salmon/*Salemon*, Essex, 1700 {Thomas Covington} (cz)
24. John Violett/*Viala*, Stafford, 1692 {Giles Vandecastaill} (minet, rbp)

Refugees Arriving as Indentured Servants and Gaining Freedom:

1. Andrew Barbee/*Barbé,* Lancaster, 1689, Stafford,* 1691 {John Chin} [servant in Lancaster, gained freedom 1689] (rbp)
2. Richard Levicount/*Leconte,* Richmond, 1696 {George Hopkins} [gained freedom by 1708] (fcl)
3. James Mussen/*Musson*, Stafford, 1691 {William Williams} [gained freedom 1691, collector of quit rents, 1692] (baird)
4. Thomas Pin/*du Pin*, Lancaster, 1686 {John Pinchard} [gained freedom by 1695] (agnew, shaw)

5. Marie Russell/*Roussal* (James Gallahough), Stafford, 1690, Westmoreland, 1702 {Edmond Helder, William Downing} [gained freedom in 1690] (RBP)
6. Richard Savour/*Sauver* Richmond, 1699 {John Rankin} [gained freedom 1707] (brock, fcl)
7. Henry Tuff/Tuffe/*Tiffeay*, Lancaster, 1688 {Elizabeth Wilkes/Spencer} [gained freedom in 1691, shoemaker] (rbp)

Part III: Households Initially Documented 1701–1710:

1. John Angoon, Lancaster, 1705 (VA Record)
2. Catherine Aveline, Richmond, 1704 (agnew)
3. Pierre Batu, Stafford, 1702 (VA Record)
4. Peter Boname/*Bonhomme*, Lancaster, 1701 (CZ, RBP)
5. Joseph Boucher/*Bouchier*, Stafford, 1703 (cz)
6. Daniel Braban, King William, 1702 [immigrated on the Nassau, 1701] (VA Record, BROCK)
7. James Breton, King William, 1706 (cz)
8. Joseph Brossier, Richmond, 1704 (cz)
9. Thomas Cabinett/*Cabinne,* Richmond, 1708 (minet)
10. Jean Calvert, Stafford, 1702 [moved to Manakin by 1705] (VA Record, BROCK)
11. John Chaproone/*Chapron*/*Chaperon,* Richmond,* 1704 [immigrated on the *Nassau* 1701] (BROCK, RBP, FCL)
12. Estienne/Stephen Chenault/Cheneau (Mary Elizabeth Howlett), Essex, 1714 [immigrated on the *Nassau* 1701] (BROCK, cz, rbp)
13. Clement Chevalle, Stafford,* c. 1704 (VA Record, cz)
14. Jean Cochelle, Stafford, 1702 (VA Record)
15. Daniel Collett/*Colet,* Lancaster, 1706, Richmond, 1708 (AGNEW)
16. John Collier/*Colier,* Stafford, 1704, King and Queen,* 1711 (SHAW, agnew)
17. Simon Coniel (Elizabeth), Stafford,* 1701 (cz)
18. Peter Coronett, Lancaster, 1705 (VA Record, minet)
19. George Dabney/*Dabin*, King and Queen,* 1701, King William, 1703 (cz)
20. Sarah Dabney/*Dabin*, King and Queen,* 1701 [sister of James and George] (cz)
21. Dennis Danvergne/*Danerville* (Anne) Northumberland, 1702 [merchant] (rbp)
22. William Deball/*Debaud*, Westmoreland, 1707 (rbp)
23. Joseph Delaney/*Delaunay,* Westmoreland, 1706, Essex, 1720 (fcl)
24. Michall Dermott/*Demet*, Westmoreland, 1707, Stafford,* 1712 (rbp)

Appendix A

25. Louis Dienbaum, Stafford, 1702 (VA Record)
26. John de Jarnat/Dejarnet/*de Jernac*, King William, c. 1710 (VA Record, FM, cz)
27. Rynhart de la Fayolle, Stafford,* c. 1704 (VA Record)
28. Andrew Delaps/*Delprat* (Ann) Stafford, 1709 (rbp)
29. Peters de Perrue, Lancaster, 1705 (VA Record)
30. William des Meaux, King William, c. 1710 (VA Record)
31. Benjamin Deverell/*Deville* (Rachel), Richmond, 1702 [merchant, wife in Bristol, England] (rb)
32. Theodore Durosou/de Rousseau, Richmond,* 1714 [immigrated on the *Peter and Anthony* 1700] (BROCK, FM, cz)
33. Daniel Duval, King William, c. 1710 (baird, fm)
34. Henry Hardin/*Hardouin*, Stafford,* c. 1710 (FM, brock)
35. John Hardin/*Hardouin*, Westmoreland, 1706 (SHAW, fm, brock)
36. Peter Huzaro/*Heuzé*, Richmond, 1709 (RBP, minet)
37. Maurice Jolly, Westmoreland, 1703 (CZ, RBP)
38. James Joyeux, Essex, 1710 [ministerial candidate] (RBP, SHAW, brock)
39. Antoine Laborie, Stafford, 1702 [immigrated on the *Nassau* 1701] (VA Record, BROCK)
40. Isaac Lafite, Stafford, 1702 [moved to Manakin by 1705] (VA Record, BROCK, MINET)
41. Francis Lafon/*Delafon*, Essex, 1710 (CZ, RBP, SHAW)
42. Nicholas Lafon/*Delafon*, Essex, c. 1710 (CZ, FM)
43. Lewis Latané (Phebe Smith, Mary Deane), Essex,* 1701/Spotsylvania,* 1722 [minister, immigrated on the *Nassau* 1701] (BROCK, VA Record, RBP)
44. Peter Lavere/*Lavigne*, Lancaster, 1701 (CZ)
45. Peter Lehew, Stafford,* c. 1704 (VA Record, FM)
46. Jean Malscet, Lancaster, 1705 (VA Record)
47. John Manear/Muneer/*Moynier/Mounier* (Anne), Richmond,* 1706 (RBP, cz)
48. William Marchant, Essex,* 1708 (agnew, rbp, fcl)
49. Abraham Marchant, Essex,* 1710 (agnew, rbp, fcl)
50. John Marrone/*Marione*, Stafford, 1702, [ministerial candidate] (RBP, fcl)
51. Abraham Micheau, Stafford, 1702 [moved to Manakin by 1705] (VA Record, CZ, BROCK)
52. John Orion/Oria/Orial/Oriot (Mary), Stafford, 1702, Richmond,* 1708 (AGNEW, SHAW)
53. Stephen Palliseres/*Pelissier*, Stafford, 1705 (rbp)
54. Charles Peraut/Perault, Stafford, 1702 [moved to Manakin by 1705] (VA Record, BROCK, cz)
55. Guillaume Polant, Stafford, 1702 (VA Record)

Appendix A 183

56. Robert Poore/*Poirier*, Westmoreland, 1706 (cz, rbp)
57. Edward Poulin/*Poulain*, Essex, 1702 (rbp, fcl)
58. Edward Prue/*Prou,* Richmond, 1708 (agnew, minet)
59. Benjamin Quellen/*Quillet*, Westmoreland, 1701 (rbp)
60. Henry Ravenall/*Ravenal,* Richmond, 1710 (minet, rbp, fm)
61. Eliene Reinbou, Stafford, 1702 (VA Record)
62. Marie Rienmande, Stafford, 1702 (VA Record)
63. Peter Riviere, Lancaster,* 1702 (VA Record, BROCK, cz)
64. Maurice Robert (Rosamann), King William,* 1702 (CZ)
65. Jean Rocheblau, Stafford, 1702 (VA Record)
66. Hece/Helie/Hillaire Rouseau, Stafford, 1702 (VA Record, cz)
67. John Roy/*Leroy* (Dorothy Taliaferro Buckner Smith), Essex,* 1716, [tobacco receiver, immigrated on the *Nassau,* 1701] (CZ, BROCK, FM)
68. William Roy/*Leroy* (Hannah Spires), Essex,* 1704 (cz)
69. Nicholas Savin (Catherine?), Stafford, 1701 (brock, agnew, fcl)
70. Matthew Seay, King William, *1703 (brock, agnew)
71. Lewis Tacquet, Stafford,* c. 1704 (VA Record)
72. Daniel Tebbs/*Thibaut*, Westmoreland,* 1706, Stafford,* 1716 [factor for English merchant, under-sheriff, listed as carpenter in RBP] (CZ, RBP)
73. Isaac Trocq (Mary Cammock), Essex,* 1717, Richmond, 1718 [immigrated on the *Peter and Anthony* 1700] (BROCK)
74. Stephen Veneard/*Vignaud,* Westmoreland, 1707 (cz)
75. Thomas Verloe/*Varlé/Veillou,* Richmond, 1710 (minet)
76. Jean Vigne/*Vigneau,* King William, c. 1710 (SHAW, cz)

Refugees Arriving as Indentured Servants:

1. Mary Carnee/*Carniere,* Richmond, 1710 {Thomas Pace} (minet)
2. Pierre des Maizeaux, King William, 1702 {Daniel Braban} [immigrated on the Nassau 1701] (BROCK, VA Record)
3. Margaret Gerrard, Lancaster, 1701 {Thomas Martin} (cz)
4. George Guy, Richmond, 1705 {Peter Kippax} (agnew, fcl, minet)
5. Elizabeth Maurice, Richmond, 1706 {Charles Barber} (cz, agnew)
6. James Merchand, Essex, 1704, {Lewis Latané}, [immigrated on the Nassau 1701] (VA Record, BROCK)
7. Margaret Morrice, Stafford, 1701 {John Mountjoy} (cz, agnew)
8. William Pew/*Dupeu,* Westmoreland, 1708 {Dorothy Veale} (baird)
9. Maurice Phin/*du Pin,* Lancaster, 1702 {John Mott} (agnew)
10. Frances Poore/*Poirier,* Lancaster, 1706 {Charlotte Bertrand} (cz, fcl, rbp)

Refugees Arriving as Indentured Servants and Gaining Freedom:

1. Joan Denin, Richmond, 1705 {Thomas Deacus} [gained freedom in 1705] (AGNEW)

Appendix B

Documenting Rappahannock Huguenot Refugees, 1677–1710

Interpreting the Chart:

The refugees are listed by the county in which they were first documented with their names following the source and page number on which they were initially listed. For source abbreviations, see the list included in this study. This chart also includes a rough tally of the number of refugees in each county.

Rappahannock County—Forty-Nine Refugees, 1677–1692:

SP, ORC DWB, 1678/9–1682, 12 (Richard Person), 13 (Christopher Pridum), 29 (Richard Philitar), 97 (George Lascaille, James Levitt).

SP, ORC DB, 1682–1686, 75 (James Andres), 12 (John Colleyvow), 93 (Nicholas Deluis), 18 (Robert Pardoe), 96 (Henry Chappell).

SP, ORC WB, 1682–1687, 52 (Peter Foxon), 66 (Francis Quarles, John Quarles).

SP, ORC OB, 1683–1685, 81 (Henry Gauler), 97 (Samuel Gerrard), 64 (Elias Hughes Sale).

SP, ORC OB, 1685–1687, 59 (Peter Barnard, William Constantine).

SP, ORC DB, 1686–1688, 30 (Samuel Ponye), 46 (Jean Lainy/Launy), 79 (Lewis Fardo).

ORC OB, 2, 1686–1692, 71–72 (John Bertrand), 254 (John Foushee).

SP, ORC OB, 1687–1689, 12 (Bryan Dehorter), 29 (John Brazier), 33 (Vincent Pass), 46 (Bartholomew Vauter), 80 (John Brages), 93 (Giles Monparson), 94 (Sarah Lafeavor), 101 (Charles Tebo).

SP, ORC DB, 1688–1692, 48 (John Lastree), 78 (John Vihice), 105 (Nathaniel Landers), 107 (John Lavag).

SP, ORC OB, 1689–1692, 2 (John Person), 4 (James Deboe) 8 (John Devall), 9 (Henry Hases), 42 (Paul Micou), 48 (Jean Boucher), 7 (Peter St. Leger), 84 (Martin Mazey), 101 (Pierre Salinger).

Fleet, vol. 1, 241 (James Roy), 262 (Richard Sables).

King, *The Registers of North Farnham Parish, 1663–1814,* 62 (John Faver).

Plantation Indentures, Greater London Record Office, SR02006a, LVA (Cyprian Prou, Margaret Prou).

Richmond County (formerly Rappahannock)—Forty-Five Refugees, 1692–1710:

SP, RC OB, 1692–1694, 90 (James Foushee), 68 (Charles Vallieur), 8 (Charles Coshee), 89 (Peter Ollane), 63 (John Galley).

SP, RC DB, 1692–1695, 82 (Edward Vergin).

SP, RC OB, 1694–1697, 126 (William Breton), 13 (James Deboree), 25 (Samuel Deboree), 40 (Ann Galard), 56 (John Shaperoone), 59 (Michall Connele), 103 (John Britton), 115 (Richard Levicount).

SP, RC DB, 1695–1701, 7 (John Bonnevill), 36 (James Pesson), 65 (Robert Gallop), 69 (Elizabeth Poore), 100 (Francis Terrett).

SP, RC OB, 1697–1699, 12 (Henry Gallop), 82 (Peter Huett), 33 (Peter Aveline), 27 (John Barnard), 49 (Thomas Marchant), 59 (Jacob Devall), 71 (George Herron), 85 (Hugh Moyniere), 86 (Richard Savour).

SP, RC OB, 1699–1701, 6 (John Chartris), 38 (Mary Pew).

SP, RC DB, 1701–1704, 59 (Joseph Brossier).

SP, RC OB, 1702–1704, 27 (Benjamin Deverell), 115 (Catherine Aveline), 122 (John Chaproone).

SP, RC OB, 1704–1705, 56 (George Guy), 76 (Joan Denin).

SP, RC OB, 1705–1706, 18 (Elizabeth Maurice).

SP, RC OB, 1707–1708, 73 (Edward Prue).

SP, RC OB, 1708–1709, 11 (Thomas Cabinett), 46 (Peter Huzaro).

SP, RC OB, 1709–1710, 69 (Mary Carnee).

SP, RC OB, 1710–1711, 20 (Thomas Verloe), 40 (Henry Ravenall).

Headley, *Wills of Richmond County, Virginia,* 22 (Theodore Durosou), 37 (John Manear).

Essex County (formerly Rappahannock)—Thirty-Four Refugees, 1692–1710:

Wright, *Essex County, Virginia Marriage References*, 120 (Nicholas Lafon), 174 (William Roy), 55 (Edward Danellin), 122 (John Salmon), 209 (Job Virgett, John Virgett).

SP, EC DWB, 1692–1693, 9 (Joshua Nason), 11 (Henry Curry), 62 (Alexander Denain).
SP, EC DWB, 1694–1695, 10 (Peter Lander), 30 (Peter Trebble), 42 (Moses Chappell), 46 (John Travallion), 50 (Bernard Renoe), 86 (Edward Maurin).
SP, EC DWB, 1695–1697, 44 (Joan Lamy).
SP, EC OB, 1695–1699, 40 (Thomas Roy), 62 (Richard Collett), 91 (Jacob Devalliard).
SP, RC OB, 1697–1699, 86 (Nicholas Moreau).
SP, EC DWB, 1699–1701, 84 (Edward Salmon).
SP, EC OB, 1699–1702, 30 (Nicholas Morcan), 97 (Simon Pascoe).
SP, EC DWB, 1701–1703, 27 (Lewis Latané), 87 (Edward Poulin).
Dorman, EC RB, 1706–1707, 1717–1719, 72 (Isaac Trocq).
Dorman, EC DWB No. 13, 1707–1711, 4 (James Joyeux), 20 (William Marchant), 100 (Francis Lafon), 109 (Abraham Marchant).
Fleet, vol. 1, 253 (Samuel Jaques), vol. 2, 33 (Estienne/Stephen Chenault), 79 (John Roy).
McIlwaine, *Executive Journals*, vol. 2, 382 (James Merchand).

Stafford County—Sixty-Eight Refugees, 1677–1710:

SP, SC DWB, 1686–1689, 44 (Nicholas Bernard), 55 (Stephen Besson), 7 (Peter Bache), 79 (Lewis Renoe, Benjamin Renoe), 110 (John Champ), 112 (Absolon Abbey), 114 (Stephen Sebastian), 115 (John Amee).
SP, SC OB, 1664–1668/1689–1690, 136 (Abraham Farrow), 75 (John Guyatt), 123 (James Gallahough, Marie Roussal), 126 (Nicholas Maniere), 64–65 (Elizabeth Desborough).
SP, SC DWB, 1689–1693, 24 (James Burnard), 30 (Simon Tomasin), 52 (Henry Faucon), 43 and 70 (Michel Mauzy/Mosey), 68 (William Gueffe), 72 (John Bache), 81 (Thomas Lande), 90 (John Violett), 108 (Moses Burnard), 134 (Morrice Clerke).
SP, SC OB, 1691–1692, 6 (James Mussen), 35 (William Herson), 42 (John Tillett), 52 (Thomas Nason), 112 (Dorothy Paget).
SP, SC OB, 1692–1693, 45 (Alexander Chappell).
SP, SC DWB, 1699–1709, 3 (Frances DuCondry), 8 (John Mauzy), 17 (John Marr), 59 (_____ LeClair), 55 (Abraham Delander), 37 (Nicholas Savin), 46 (Pierre Batu, Jean Calvert, Jean Cochelle, Simon Coniel, Louis Dienbaum, Antoine Laborie, Isaac Lafite, Abraham Michau, Charles Peraut/Perault, Guillaume Polant, Eliene Rienbou, Marie Rienmande, Jean Rocheblau, Hece/Helie/Hillaire Rousau), 51 (Margaret Morrice), 52 (John Marrone, John Orian), 59 (Joseph Boucher), 90 (John

Collier), 164 (Andrew Delaps), 165 (Rynhart de la Fayolle/Flagal), 104 (Stephen Palliseres).

Harrison, *Landmarks of Prince William*, 189–190 (Clement Chevalle, Peter Lehew, Lewis Tacquet, Isaac Ducheminia, Samuel Ducheminia).

NNG No. 2, 1694–1700, 103 (Peter Baile).

Colonial Muster Roll: Stafford 1701, RELIC, Bull Run Regional Library, 2300 (James Conill).

Tobacco Tenders, Stafford, 1724, RELIC, Bull Run Regional Library, 8410 (John de la Chaumette).

NNG No. 5, 1713–1719, 60, (Henry Hardin).

Lancaster County—Thirty-Five Refugees, 1677–1710:

SP, LC DWB, 1661–1702, 124 (Mark Gendron).

SP, LC OB, 1674–1678, 63 (George Mallet).

SP, LC WB, 1675–1689, 33 (Peter Pheradine).

SP, LC OB, 1678–1681, 50 (William Breese), 89 (John Simone).

SP, LC OB, 1682–1687, 29 (Joseph Moucher), 84 (Thomas Pin), 92 (John Pourgin).

SP, LC OB, 1687–1691, 17 (John Lahore) 24 (Henry Tuffe), 37 (Anne Corbet), 50 (Andrew Barbee).

SP, LC OB, 1691–1695, 19 (Michaell Gwin), 39 (John Mallie), 68 (Thomas Quetance), 87 (Marquis Calmes), 90 (Margaret Conniel).

SP, LC OB, 1695–1699, 3 (Thomas Cotance, David Mazy).

SP, NC OB, 1699–1700, 2 (Robert Furney).

SP, LC OB, 1699–1701, 12 (Ellinor Deinne), 74 (Charles Pampillion), 77 (Jeffrey Brassier, Peter Geniox), 84 (Peter Lavere), 87 (Margaret Gerard), 90 (Peter Boname).

SP, LC OB, 1701–1703, 99 (Maurice Phin)

SP, LC DWB, 1701–1706, 54 (John Angoon, Peter Corronett, Peters de Perrue, Jean Malscet), 73 (Daniel Collett).

SP, LC DB, 1706–1710, 13 (Frances Poore).

William C. Bryant, Jr., "Pierre (Peter) Riviere: Huguenot Planter of Lancaster County and Progenitor of the Riviere Family of Virginia," *Northern Neck of Virginia Magazine* 59, no. 1 (December, 2009), 7138–7152 (Pierre Riviere).

Westmoreland County—Twenty-Six Refugees, 1677–1710:

Dorman, WC DB, 1665–1677 (Part Four, Appended DWB #4, 1707–1709), 64 (Daniel Tebbs), 78 (Joseph Delaney).

Dorman, WC OB, 1675/6–1688/9 (Part One, 1675/6–1679), 24 (Nicholas Demall).

Dorman, WC OB, 1675/6–1688/9 (Part Two, 1679–1682), 63 (Thomas Charles).

Dorman, WC OB, 1675/6–1688/9 (Part Three, 1682–1684), 17 (James Certaine), 14 (Charles Duet, Robert Daubinet).

WC OB 1690–1698, 5a (John Masson).

Dorman, WC OB, 1690–1698 (Part One, 1690/91–1692), 6 (Samuel Demonvill, Robert Musson), 41 (Leonard Ossier).

Dorman, WC OB, 1690–1698, Part Two, 1692–1694, 38 (Elias Morrice), 70 (Nicholas Laurans).

Dorman, WC DWB No. 2, 1691–1699, 9 (Thomas Deviant), 67 (William Palisson).

Dorman, WC OB, 1698–1705, Part One, 1698–1699, 9, 10, and 51 (John Morrice).

Fothergill, *Wills of Westmoreland County, Virginia, 1654–1800*, 24 (Lewis Debria).

Dorman, WC DWB, No. 3, 1701–1707, 1 (Benjamin Quellen), 50 (Maurice Jolly).

Dorman, WC OB, 1705–1721 (1705–1707), 35 (Robert Poore), 38 (John Hardin), 53 (Michall Dermott), 57 (William Deball), 76 (Stephen Veneard).

Dorman, WC OB, 1705–1721 (1707–1709), 39 (William Pew).

NNG No. 1, 1690–1692, 172 (Thomas Terrett).

New Kent (1677), King and Queen (1691), and King William (1702) Counties—Twenty-One Refugees, 1677–1710:

Nugent, vol. 2, 185 (George Herriott), 218 (Peter Deschazant), 260 (James Quarles).

Nugent, vol. 3, 46 (Gedeon Macon, Sarah Dabney).

SP, KWC OB, 1702–1705, 42 (Josue Norment), 68 (Matthew Seay).

Weis, *Colonial Clergy of Virginia*, 6 (James Boisseau).

Beverly Conolly, ed., KWC RB, 1702–1806 (Athens, GA, 2006), 3 (Maurice Robert), 4 (George Dabney), 5 (Richard Marr), 14 (Arnold Marr), 16 (Robert Napier), 19 (James Breton).

Fleet, vol. 2, 239 (William Champ).

Cameron Allen, "Huguenot Migrations," in Kenn Stryker-Rodda, ed., *Genealogical Research, Volume 2 by the American Society of Genealogists* (Washington DC, 1971), 282 (Jean de Jarnat, William des Meaux, Daniel Duvall, Jean Vigne).

McIlwaine, *Executive Journals,* vol. 2, 246 (Pierre des Maizeaux/Peter May, Daniel Braban/Daniell Brabant).

Northumberland County—Fifteen Refugees, 1677–1710:

SP, NC OB, 1677–1679, 40 (James Taffe), 79 (James Dabney), 80 (Charles Valland).

SP, NC OB, 1683–1686, 2 (Thomas Bowyer), 42 (Owen Dermott).

SP, NC OB, 1699–1700, 1 (Morris Brassell), 23 (George Violett), 37 (Robert Maupin).

SP, NC OB, 1702–1704, 3 (Dennis Danvergne).

Charles and Virginia Hamrick, NC OB, 1678–1699, Part One, 1678–1687 (Athens, GA), 28 (Luke Demerritt), 154 (Henry de Boys).

Hamrick, NC OB, 1678–1699, Part Two, 1687–1699, 430 (Stephen Chaukerett), 458 (David Depue) 823 (John Poore).

Fleet, vol. 1, 521 (Charles Dermott).

Middlesex County—Twelve Refugees, 1677–1710:

Kilby, *Christ Church Parish Register, Middlesex, County, Virginia, 1651–1821,* 9 (William Barbee), 73 (Abraham Depree, John Deverdell), 226 (Claude Vallet).

SP, MC OB, 1673–1678, 75 (Aime Brittaine).

SP, MC OB, 1677–1680, 19 (Thomas Dimery).

SP, MC OB, 1680–1686, 19 (Edward Poore), 26 (Lewis DeBurbon), 32 (William Guyat), 69 (John Maison), 78 (Jane Lucas), 85 (John LeMarr).

Bibliography

A true copy of the oaths that are appointed by act of Parliament, made in the first year of their present Majesties reign; to be taken instead of the oaths of supremacy and allegiance and the declaration appointed to be repeated and subscribe. Boston, 1692. Library of Congress.

Accomack County Order Book, 1697–1705. Accomack County Archives, Accomac, Virginia.

"Account of the Proceedings of the Clergy of Virginia at the Church at Williamsburg, 1705." In *Historical Collections Relating to the American Colonial Church,* edited by William Stevens Perry, vol. 1, 144–53. Hartford, CT: Church Press Company, 1870.

Agnew, David C. A. *Protestant Exiles from France in the Reign of Louis XIV: or, The Huguenot Refugees and Their Descendants In Great Britain and Ireland.* London: Reeves and Turner, 1874.

Alexander, Edward Porter, ed. *The Journal of John Fontaine: An Irish Huguenot Son in Spain and Virginia, 1710–1719.* Williamsburg, VA: The Colonial Williamsburg Foundation, 1972.

Allen, Cameron. "Huguenot Migrations." In *Genealogical Research, Volume 2, by The American Society of Genealogists,* edited by Kenn Stryker-Rodda, 256–90. Washington DC: The American Society of Genealogists, 1971.

Amyraut, Moyse. *Brief Traitte de la Predestination et de ses Principales Dependances.* Saumur: Jean Lesnier, 1634.

———. Introduction, *Commentary on the Psalms of David,* 1662. In Geiter, Mary K. and Speck, W. A. "Moise Amyraut and Charles II." *The Huguenot Society Journal* 30, no. 2, (2014): appendix, 166–80. Translated by Janet Davies.

Anselme, Pere. *Histoire Genealogique et Chronologique de la Maison Royale de France,* vol. 4. Paris: Guillaume Cevelier, 1712.

Appleby, David J. "From Ejectment to Toleration in England, 1662–1689." In *The Great Ejectment of 1662,* edited by Alan P. Sell. Eugene, OR: Pickwick Publications, 2012.

Archive Nationale, TT. 246. SHPF.

Armstrong, Brian C. *Calvinism and the Amyraut Heresy: Protestant Scholasticism and Humanism in Seventeenth-Century France.* Madison, WI: University of Wisconsin Press, 1969.

Armytage, G. J., ed. *Allegations for Marriage Licenses Issued by the Vicar-General of the Archbishop of Canterbury, July 1679 to June 1687.* London: Harleian Society, 1886.

Auziere, Saintonge Eglises, NS 585. SHPF.

Bailyn, Bernard. "Politics and Social Structure in Virginia." In *Seventeenth-Century America: Essays in Colonial History,* edited by James Morton Smith, 90–115. Chapel Hill: University of North Carolina Press, 1959.

Bain, Robert A. "The Composition and Publication of *The Present State of Virginia and the College.*" *Early American Literature* 6, no. 1, Special Southern Issue (Spring 1971): 31–54.

Baird, Charles W. *History of the Huguenot Emigration to America,* vols. 1 and 2. New York: Dodd, Mead, 1885.

Bell, James B. *Empire, Religion and Revolution in Early Virginia, 1607–1786.* Basingstoke, UK: Palgrave Macmillan, 2013.

Bertrand, John and Charlotte Jolly Marriage Record. Register of the Parish Church of St. Paul's Covent Garden, September 24, 1686. Guildhall Library, London.

Bertrand, John Ordination Record #9535/3. Guildhall Library, London.

Bertrand, Monsieur (Paul), to the Bishop of London, September 12, 1689. In *Archives of Maryland,* edited by W. H. Brown, vol. 1, 114–18. Baltimore: Maryland Historical Society, 1883.

Bertrand, Paul. Letter in the papers of Henry Compton, Bishop of London, 13 Avril 1684. Rawlinson Papers, Ms. C984. Bodleian Library, Oxford.

Bertrand, Paul and Marie Gribelin Marriage Record. October 29, 1685. FM 1/10. Lambeth Palace Library, London.

Beverley, Robert. *The History and Present State of Virginia by Robert Beverley: A New Edition with an Introduction by Susan Scott Parish.* Chapel Hill: The University of North Carolina Press, 2013.

Billings, Warren M. ed. *Papers of Francis Howard, Baron Howard of Effingham, 1643–1695.* Richmond: Library of Virginia, 1989.

———. "The Law of Servants and Slaves in Seventeenth-Century Virginia." VMHB 99, no. 1 (January 1991): 45–62.

———. *Virginia's Viceroy: Their Majesties' Governor General: Francis Howard, Baron of Effingham.* Fairfax, VA: George Mason University Press, 1991.

Blair, James and John Locke. "Some of the Chief Grievances of the Present Constitution of Virginia, with an Essay Towards the Remedies Thereof." Edited by Michael G. Kammen. In Michael G. Kammen, "Virginia at the Close of the Seventeenth Century: An Appraisal by James Blair and John Locke." VMHB 74, no. 2 (April 1966): 153–69.

Boddie, John Bennett. *Seventeenth Century Isle of Wight County, Virginia.* Baltimore: Genealogical Publishing Company, 1973.

Bond, Edward L. *Damned Souls in a Tobacco Colony: Religion in Seventeenth-Century Virginia.* Macon, GA: Mercer University Press, 2000.

Bonnin, Jean-Claude and Nicholas Faucherre. *The Towers of La Rochelle.* Paris: Centre des Monuments Nationaux, 2004.

Bosher, J. F. "Huguenot Merchants and the Protestant International in the Seventeenth Century." WMQ 52 (Jan. 1995): 77–102.

Boucher, Philip P. "Revisioning the French Atlantic." In *The Atlantic World and Virginia, 1550–1624*, edited by Peter C. Mancall, 274–306. Chapel Hill: University of North Carolina Press, 2007.

Bradley, Michael Raymond. *The Puritans of Virginia: Their Influence on the Religious Life of the Old Dominion, 1607–1659.* Nashville: Vanderbilt University Phd. Dissertation, 1971.

Brett, Vanessa. *Bertrand's Toyshop in Bath: Luxury Retailing, 1685–1765.* Wetherby, UK: Oblong Creative Ltd, 2014.

Brewer, Mary Marshall. *King George County, Virginia Orders, 1736–1740.* Lewes, DE: Colonial Roots, 2007.

Brock, R. A., ed. *Documents, chiefly unpublished, relating to the Huguenot emigration to Virginia and the settlement of Manakin-Town* . . . Baltimore: Genealogical Publishing Company, 1962.

Brown, Katharine A. *Robert "King" Carter: Builder of Christ Church.* Irvington, VA: Historic Christ Church Foundation, 2010.

Brown, Stuart E. Jr. *Annals of Clarke County, Virginia.* Berryville, VA: Virginia Book, 1983.

Bryant, William C., Jr. "Pierre (Peter) Riviere: Huguenot Planter of Lancaster County and Progenitor of the Riviere Family of Virginia." *Northern Neck of Virginia Magazine* 59, no. 1 (December 2009): 7138–52.

Brydon, George MacLaren. *Religious Life of Virginia in the Seventeenth Century: Faith of Our Fathers.* Williamsburg, VA: Virginia 350th Anniversary Celebration Corporation, 1957.

———. "The Huguenots of Manakin Town and Their Times: An Address Delivered before the Annual Meeting of the Huguenot Society of Manakin Town on April 14, 1934." VMHB 42, no. 4 (October 1934): 325–35.

———. "The Virginia Clergy: Governor Gooch's Letters to the Bishop of London, 1727–1749." VMHB 32, no. 3 (July 1924): 209–36.

———. *Virginia's Mother Church and the Political Conditions Under Which It Grew.* Richmond: Virginia Historical Society, 1947.

Buckley, Thomas E. "Establishing New Bases for Religious Authority." In *From Jamestown to Jefferson: The Evolution of Religious Freedom in Virginia*, edited by Paul Rasor and Richard E. Bond, 138–65. Charlottesville: University of Virginia Press, 2011.

Bugg, James L., Jr. "The French Huguenot Frontier Settlement of Manakin Town." VMHB 61, no. 4 (October 1953): 359–94.

Bulletin de la Société des Archives historiques de la Saintonge et de l'Aunis 7 1880.

Bultmann, William A. "The SPG and the French Huguenots in Colonial America." *Historical Magazine of the Protestant Episcopal Church* 20 (1951): 156–72.

Butler, Jon. *Awash in a Sea of Faith: Christianizing the American People.* Cambridge, MA: Harvard University Press, 1992.

———. "The Huguenots and the American Immigrant Experience." In *Memory and Identity: The Huguenots in France and the Atlantic Diaspora*, edited by Bertrand Van Ruymbeke and Randy J. Sparks, 194–203. Columbia: University of South Carolina Press, 2008.

———. *The Huguenots in America: A Refugee People in a New World Society*. Cambridge, MA: Harvard University Press, 1983.

Butterfield, Kevin. "Puritans and Religious Strife in Colonial Virginia." VMHB 109, no. 1 (2001): 5–37.

Cabell, Priscilla Hariss. *Turff & Twigg: Volume One, The French Lands*. Richmond: Printed by the Author, 1988.

Canon, Carl F. *Robert "King" Carter of Corrotoman*. Durham: Duke University Phd. Dissertation, 1956.

Carlo, Paula Wheeler. "Huguenot Congregations in Colonial New York and Massachusetts: Reassessing the Paradigm of Anglican Conformity." In *A Companion to the Huguenots*, edited by Raymond A. Mentzer and Bertrand Van Ruymbeke, 371–93. Leiden: Brill, 2016.

———. "Huguenot Identity and Protestant Unity in Colonial Massachusetts: the Reverend Andre Le Mercier and the 'Sociable Spirit.'" *Historical Journal of Massachusetts* 40, nos. 1 and 2 (Summer 2012): 122–47.

———. *Huguenot Refugees in Colonial New York: Becoming American in the Hudson Valley*. Brighton, UK: Sussex Academic Press, 2005.

Caroline County, Virginia Court Order Book, 1740–1742. Caroline County Archives, Bowling Green, Virginia.

Carpenter, Edward. *The Protestant Bishop: Being the Life of Henry Compton, 1632–1713, Bishop of London*. London: Longmans Green, 1956.

Carté, Katherine. *Religion and the American Revolution: An Imperial History*. Chapel Hill: University of North Carolina Press, 2021.

Chamberlayne, C. G. *The Vestry Book of Christ Church Parish, Middlesex County, Virginia, 1663–1767*. Richmond: Old Dominion Press, 1927.

———. *The Vestry Book and Register of of St. Peters Parish, New Kent, and James City Counties, Virginia, 1684–1786*. Richmond: Division of Purchase and Printing, 1937.

Chamier, Anthony. "A Refugee Minister Comes to London: Daniel Chamier, 1661–1698." *The Huguenot Society Journal* 30, no. 1 (2013): 52–72.

Chappell, Carolyn Lougee. "Family Bonds Across the Refuge." In *Memory and Identity*: *The Huguenots in France and the Atlantic Diaspora*, edited by Bertrand Van Ruymbeke and Randy J. Sparks, 172–93. Columbia: University of South Carolina Press, 2008.

Chasseboeuf, Frédéric. *Châteaux, Manoirs, et Logis: La Charente-Maritime*, vol. 2. Prahecq, France: Patrimoines Médias, 2008.

Church of England. Clergy of the Church of England Database. #218493 (John Amerand/Armourier). #15065, #15071, #73826 (John Bell). #97040 (John Bertrand). # 97436 (Paul Bertrand). #97686, #85066 (James Boisseau). #178298 (John/Alexander Burnett). #91098, #127063 (Amory Butler, Sr.). #99371, #99372 (John Cairon). #772778, #74466 (Lawrence De Butts). #98702, #98703 (Benjamin de Joux). #98676, #98677 (Claude Philippe de Richebourg). #101399, #135799, #135800, #23842 (Benjamin Doggett). #86798 (Francis Doughty). #72704, #72705 (Francis Fontaine). #72214, #72228 (Peter Fontaine). #82288 (John Gordon). #6554 (Samuel Gray). #26310 (Charles Grimes). #82132 (Abraham Kenyon). #98729 (Louis Latané). #108102 (James Marye). #16848 (John Masson). #92506, #82019 (Deuel Pead). #102340 (John Scrimgeour). #90466 (William White). #78001 (Paul Williams). #97244 (John Wood).

Church of England. *Book of Common Prayer from the Original Manuscript attached to The Act of Uniformity of 1662.* Cambridge, UK: John Baskerville, 1760.

Clarke, W. M., ed. *Colonial Churches: A Series of Sketches of Churches in the Original Colony of Virginia.* Richmond: Southern Churchman, 1907.

Clement, John. "Clergymen Licensed Overseas by the Bishop of London, 1696–1710 and 1715–1716." *Historical Magazine of the Protestant Episcopal Church* 16 (December 1947): 318–49.

Clifton, Denzil T. "Anglicanism and Negro Slavery in Colonial America." *Historical Magazine of the Protestant Episcopal Church* 39, no. 1 (March 1970), 29–70.

Colonial Muster Roll: Stafford 1701. Bull Run Regional Library, Manassas, Virginia.

Colonial Tithables, Research Notes no. 17, 2. LVA.

Colonial Williamsburg Digital Library. *Virginia Gazette*, Dixon, May 7, 1778, 8, column 1.

Colyer-Ferguson, T. C., ed. *The Registers of the French Church, Threadneedle Street, London*, vol. 3. Aberdeen, UK: Aberdeen University Press, 1906.

Connolly, Beverly, ed. *King William County, Virginia Records, 1702–1806.* Athens, GA: New Papyrus Publishing, 2006.

Controle des Actes de Cozes. Cozes Hotel de Ville, Cozes, France.

Convention of the Clergy of the Colony of Virginia to the Bishop of London, April 10, 1719. *Historical Collections Relating to the American Colonial Church*, edited by William Stevens Perry, vol. 1. Hartford, CT: 1870: 212–15.

Coombs, John C. "A New Chronology for the Rise of Slavery in Early Virginia." *WMQ* 68, no. 3 (July 2011): 332–60.

———. "Others Not Christians in the Service of the English." *VMHB* 127, no. 3 (2019): 212–38.

Cotton, Jane Baldwin, and R. B. Henry, eds. *Maryland Calendar of Wills,* vol. 4. *Baltimore*: Kohn and Pollock, 1928.

Cottret, Bernard. "Frenchmen by Birth, Huguenots by the Grace of God." In *Memory and Identity: The Huguenots in France and the Atlantac Diaspora,* edited by Bertrand Van Ruymbeke and Randy Sparks, 310–24. Columbia: University of South Carolina Press, 2003.

———. *The Huguenots in England: Immigration and Settlement, c. 1550–1700.* Translated by Peregrine and Adriana Stevenson. Cambridge: Cambridge University Press, 1992.

Crozier, William Armstrong, ed. *Virginia County Records, vol. 2, Virginia County Militia, 1651–1776.* Baltimore: Genealogical Publishing Company, 1905.

Dangibeaud, Charles. *Minutes de Notaires: Notes de Lecture.* BR 5842 and PF 7320. *ADCMLR*.

Daulnis Famille, G 34/D2. SHPF.

Davis, Richard Beale, ed. "A Sermon Preached at James City in Virginia the 23rd of April 1686 Before the Loyal Society of Citizens Born in and about London and Inhabiting Virginia by Deuel Pead." WMQ 17 (1960), 371–94.

———. *Intellectual life in the Colonial South, 1585–1763.* Knoxville: University of Tennessee Press, 1978.

———, ed. *William Fitzhugh and His Chesapeake World 1676–1701: The Fitzhugh Letters and Other Documents,* Chapel Hill: North Carolina University Press, 1963.

Davison, Bertha Lawrence Newton. "First Fifty Years in the Life of Cople Parish." *Northern Neck of Virginia Historical Magazine* 40, no. 1 (December 1990): 4578–615.

De Schickler, Le Baron F. *Les Eglises Du Refuge En Angleterre,* tome deuxième. Paris:Librairie Fischbacher, 1892.

Dorman, John Frederick. Caroline County, Virginia OB, 1732–1740. Washington, DC: Printed by the Author, 1965.

———. Essex County (hereafter EC) DWB, No. 13, 1707–1711. Washington, DC: Printed by the Author, 1963.

———. EC RB, 1706–1707, 1717–1719. Washington, DC: Printed by the Author, 1963.

———. EC RB, 1717–1722. Washington, DC: Printed by the Author, 1959.

———. Prince William County WB C 1733–1744. Washington, DC: Printed by the Author, 1956.

———. Westmoreland County (hereafter WC) DWB, 1665–1677, Part Three. Washington, DC: Printed by the Author, 1974.

———. WC DWB, 1665–1677, Part Four, Appended WC DWB, No. 4, 1707–1709. Washington, DC: Printed by the Author, 1975.

———. WC OB, 1675/6–1688/9, Part Two. Washington, DC: Printed by the Author, 1983.

———. WC OB, 1690–1698, Part Two, 1692–1694. Washington, DC: Printed by the Author, 1963.

———. WC OB, 1698–1705, Part One, 1698–1699. Washington DC: Printed by the Author, 1978.

———. WC OB, 1698–1705, Part Two, 1700–1701.

———. WC DWB, No, 2, 1691–1699. Washington DC: Printed by the Author, 1965.

———. WC DWB, No. 3, 1701–1707. Washington DC: Printed by the Author, 1967.

———. WC OB, 1705–1721. Washington DC: Printed by the Author, 1990.

Dowdey, Clifford. *The Virginia Dynasties: The Emergence of "King" Carter and the Golden Age.* Boston: Little, Brown, 1969.

Durand de Dauphiné. *A Huguenot Exile in Virginia, or Voyages of a Frenchman exiled for his Religion with a description of Virginia and Maryland.* Edited by Gilbert Chinard. New York: The Press of the Pioneers, Inc., 1934.

Durel, John. *A View of the Government and Public Worship of God in the Reformed Churches Beyond the Seas: Wherein is Shewed Their Conformity and Agreement with the Church of England, as it is Established by the Act of Uniformity.* London: J. G. for R. Royston, 1662.

———. *La Liturgie, Ou Formulaire Des Prieres Publiques, Selon l'ausage de L'Eglise Anglicane.* London: Chez Paul Vaillant dans le Strand, 1748.

Elliott, J. H. "The Iberian Atlantic and Virginia." In *The Atlantic World and Virginia, 1550–1624*, edited by Peter C. Mancall, 541–57. Chapel Hill: University of North Carolina Press.

Essex County Will Book 5, 1730–1735, 128. Essex County Archives, Tappahannock, Virginia.

Fairfax Papers. BR Box 227 (2), folio 16. Huntington Library, San Marino, California.

———. BR Box 227 (3), folio 119. Huntington Library, San Marino, California.

———. BR Box 227 (8), Grants from Proprietary, 1713–1714. Huntington Library, San Marino, California.

———. BR Box 233, Box VII. White Chapel Parish Rental Roll for 1750. Huntington Library, San Marino, California.

———. BR Box 295 (2b), Richmond County Farnham Parish Rental Roll for 1744. Huntington Library, San Marino, California.

Fausz, J. Frederick. "Richard Bennett." In *The Dictionary of Virginia Biography, Encyclopedia Virginia.* Virginia Foundation for the Humanities, 5 July 2014.

Fife, R. H., ed. and trans. "The Vestry Book of King William Parish, Virginia, 1707–1750." VMHB 11, no. 3 (January 1904): 289–304, VMHB 11, no. 4 (April 1904): 425–40, VMHB 12, no. 1 (July 1904): 17–32.

Firth, C. H. and R. S. Raitt, eds. *Acts and Ordinances of the Interregnum, 1642–1660.* London: H. M. Stationary Office, 1911.

Fischer, David Hackett. *Albion's Seed: Four British Folkways in America.* New York: Oxford University Press, 1989.

Fleet, Beverley. *Virginia Colonial Abstracts*, vol. 1 and 2. Baltimore: Genealogical Publishing Company, 1961.

Flower, Sibylla Jane. *A Walk Round Fulham Palace and Its Garden.* London: Friends of Fulham Palace, 2002.

Fontaine, Jaques. *Memoirs of the Reverend Jaques Fontaine, 1658–1728.* Edited by Dianne W. Ressinger. London: The Huguenot Society of Great Britain and Ireland, 1992.

Forlacroix, Elisabeth and Olga de Saint-Afrique. *Les Pasteurs d'Aunis, Saintonge, et Angoumois devant la Revocation: Dictionnaire.* Paris: Rivages des Cantons, 2010.

Foster, Joseph, ed. *Alumni Oxonienses, the members of the University of Oxford, 1500–1714 . . .* Oxford: Parker and Company, 1891.

Fothergill, Augusta B. "Underwood Family of Virginia (Continued)." VMHB 39, no. 3 (July 1931): 272–76.

———. *Wills of Westmoreland County, Virginia, 1654–1800.* Richmond: Appeals Press, 1925.

Foushee, William. "To Thomas Jefferson from William Foushee, 13 September 1801." In *The Papers of Thomas Jefferson,* vol. 35, 1 August8—30 November 1801, edited by Barbara B. Oberg, 278–79. Princeton: Princeton University Press, 2008.

Freeman, Douglas Southall. *Young Washington*, vol. I, Appendix I-1, 447–513. New York: Charles Scribner's Sons, 1948.

French Church of the Savoy Census. Louis Casimir de la Rochefoucauld Household, November 29, 1681. MR/R/R/032/08. LMA.

Gannon, Peter Steven, ed. *Huguenot Refugees in the Settling of Colonial America.* New York: Huguenot Society of America, 1985.

Geiter, Mary K. and W. A. Speck. "Moise Amyraut and Charles II." *The Huguenot Society Journal* 30, no. 2 (2014): 157–80.

Glozier, Matthew. *The Huguenot Soldiers of William of Orange and the "Glorious Revolution of 1688: The Lions of Judah.* Brighton, UK: Sussex Academic Press, 2002.

Green, Michael. "A Huguenot Education for the Early Modern Nobility." *Huguenot Society Journal* 30, no. 1 (2013): 73–91.

Green, Raleigh Travers. *Genealogical and Historical Notes on Culpeper County, Virginia.* Culpeper, Virginia: Printed by the author, 1900.

Greene, Jack P. "From John Smith to Adam Smith: Virginia and the Founding Conventions of English Long-Distance Settler Colonization." In *Virginia 1619: Slavery and Freedom in the Making of English America,* edited by Paul Musselwhite, Peter C. Mancall, and James Horn, 282–307. Chapel Hill: University of North Carolina Press, 2019.

Griffin, Cyrus. "Letter to Thomas Jefferson from Cyrus Griffin, 11 December 1789." In *The Papers of Thomas Jefferson,* vol. 16, 30 November–4 July, edited by Julian P. Boyd, 14–15. Princeton: Princeton University Press, 1961.

Gwynn, Robin. *Huguenot Heritage: The History and Contribution of the Huguenots in Britain.* Brighton, UK: Sussex Academic Press, 2011.

———. *Minutes of the Consistory of the French Church of London, Threadneedle Street: Calendared with an historical introduction and commentary by Robin Gwynn.* London: Huguenot Society of Great Britain and Ireland, 1994.

———. "Strains of Worship: The Huguenots and Non-Conformity." In *The Huguenots: History and Memory in Transnational Context,* edited by David J. B. Trim, 121–51. Leiden: Brill, 2011.

———. *The Huguenots in Later Stuart Britain, Volume I—Crisis, Renewal, and the Minister's Dilemma.* Brighton, UK: Sussex Academic Press, 2015.

———. *The Huguenots in Later Stuart Britain, Volume II—Settlement, Churches, and the Role of London.* Brighton, UK: Sussex Academic Press, 2018.

———. *The Huguenots of London.* Brighton, UK: The Alpha Press, 1998.

Haag, Eugene and Emile Haag, eds. *La France Protestante, Deuxieme Edition,* Tome Deuxieme. Paris: Librairie Sandoz et Fishbacher, 1877.

Haffenden, Philip S. "The Anglican Church in Restoration Colonial Policy." In *Seventeenth-Century America: Essays in Colonial History,* edited by James Morton Smith, 166–91. Chapel Hill: University of North Carolina Press, 1959.

Harrison, Fairfax. *Landmarks of Old Prince William: A Study of Origins in Northern Virginia.* Richmond: Printed by the Author, 1924.

Hartwell, Henry, James Blair, and Edward Chilton. *The Present State of Virginia, and the College.* Edited by Hunter Dickinson Farish. Williamsburg, VA: Colonial Williamsburg, 1940.

Hatfield, April Lee. *Atlantic Virginia: Intercolonial Relationships in the Seventeenth Century.* Philadelphia: University of Pennsylvania Press, 2004.

———. "Dutch and New Netherland Merchants in the Seventeenth-Century English Chesapeake." In *The Atlantic Economy During the Seventeenth and Eighteenth Centuries: Organization, Operation, Practice, and Personnel,* edited by Peter A. Coclanis, 205–28. Columbia: University of South Carolina Press, 2005.

Hay, George to James Monroe, November 22, 1824. Mss 2H3218al. Virginia Historical Society Library, Richmond.

Headley, Robert K. *Married Well and Often: Marriages of the Northern Neck of Virginia, 1649–1800.* Baltimore: Genealogical Publishing Company, 2003.

———. *Wills of Richmond County, Virginia, 1699–1800.* Baltimore: Genealogical Publishing Company, 1983.

Hening, William Waller, ed. *Statutes at Large: Being a Collection of All the Laws of Virginia,* vol. 6 and 9. New York: R. and W. and G. Bartow, 1821.

Hening, William Waller and Samuel Shepherd, eds. *The Statutes at Large of Virginia from October 1792 to December 1806,* vol. 1. Richmond: 1835–36.

Hillman, Benjamin J., ed. *Executive Journals of the Council of Virginia,* vol. 6. Richmond: Virginia State Library, 1966.

Historic Dumfries, Inc. *Records of Dettingen Parish, Prince William County, Virginia, 1745–1802.* Berwyn Heights, MD: Heritage Books, 2007.

Hnatkovich, Philip J. *The Atlantic Gate: The Anglo-Huguenot Channel Community, 1553–1665.* State College: Penn State University Phd. Dissertation, 2014.

Holifield, E. B. "Worship." In *Encyclopedia of the Reformed Faith,* edited by Donald McKim, 410–12. Louisville, KY: Westminster/John Knox Press, 1992.

Hopkins, William Lindsay. *Isle of Wight County, Virginia Deeds, 1647–1710, Court Orders, 1693–1695, and Guardian Accounts, 1740–1767.* Athens, GA: New Papyrus Publishing, 1994.

Horn, James. *Adapting to a New World: English Society in the Seventeenth-Century Chesapeake.* Chapel Hill: University of North Carolina Press, 1994.

Howell, Roger, Jr. "The Vocation of the Lord: Aspects of the Huguenot Contribution to the English Speaking World." *Anglican and Episcopal History* 61, no. 2 (1987): 133–51.

Huguenot Ancestors Authenticated List. The Huguenot Society of the Founders of Manakin in the Colony of Virginia Library, Midlothian.

Ingersoll, Thomas N., ed. "'Release us out of this Cruell Bondegg': An Appeal from Virginia in 1723." *WMQ* 51, no. 4 (October 1994): 781–82.

Inhabitants of King William Parish in Manacan Town, Virginia, to Mr. Nearne (Extract), July 4, 1728. In William Stevens Perry, ed. *Historical Collections Relating to the American Colonial Church,* vol. 1, 353. Hartford, CT: Church Press Company, 1870.

Isaac, Rhys. *The Transformation of Virginia, 1740–1790.* Chapel Hill: University of North Carolina Press, 1999.

James River Institute for Archeology, Inc. *Phase I Archeological Survey of Belle Isle, Lancaster County, Virginia.* Jamestown, VA, 1992.

Jett, Carolyn H. *Lancaster County, Virginia: Where the River Meets the Bay.* Lancaster, VA: The Lancaster County History Book Committee, 2003.

———. "The Strange Case of Col. Robert 'King' Carter Versus Capt. Richard Haynie." *The Bulletin of the Northumberland County Historical Society* 39 (2002): 15–20.

Jolly, Henry. 1655 Baptism Record. NS, 284. SHPF.

Jones, Hugh. *The Present State of Virginia.* London: J. Clarke, 1724.

Jones, John Gwynfor. "The Growth of Puritanism, c. 1559–1662." In *The Great Ejectment of 1662: Its Antecedents, Aftermath, and Ecumenical Significance*, edited by Alan P. Sell, 3–66. Eugene, OR: Pickwick Publications, 2012.

"Journal of Colonel James Gordon, Lancaster County, Virginia." WMQ 11, no. 2 (October 1902): 98–112.

———. WMQ 12, no. 1 (July 1903), 1–12.

Kamil, Neal. *Fortress of the Soul: Violence, Metaphysics, and Material Life in the Huguenots New World, 1517–1751.* Baltimore: John Hopkins University Press, 2005.

Kammen, Michael G. "Virginia at the Close of the Seventeenth Century: An Appraisal by James Blair and John Locke." VMHB 74, no. 2 (April 1966): 141–69.

Kaplan, Barbara Beigun. *Land and Heritage in the Virginia Tidewater: A History of King and Queen County.* Richmond: Cadmus Fine Books, 1993.

Keesecker, William F., ed. *A Calvin Reader: Reflections on Living.* Philadelphia: The Westminster Press, 1985.

Kidd, Thomas S. *The Protestant Interest: New England After Puritanism.* New Haven: Yale University Press, 2013.

Kilby, Craig M. *Christ Church Parish Register, Middlesex County Virginia, 1651–1821: An Interpretive Reconstruction.* Athens, GA: New Papyrus Publishing, 2014.

———. "John Fontaine and the First Germanna Colony, Part III." Germanna Foundation (May 2009).

———. *Lancaster County, Virginia Will Book 10, 1709–1727.* Athens, GA: New Papyrus Publishing, 2014.

King, George Harrison Sanford. Msslk5823a. Virginia Historical Society Library, Richmond.

———, ed. *The Register of Overwharton Parish, Stafford County, Virginia, 1723–1758, and Sundry Historical and Genealogical Notes.* Fredericksburg, VA: Printed by the Author, 1961.

———, ed. *The Registers of North Farnham Parish, 1663–1814 and Lunenburg Parish, 1783–1800, Richmond County, Virginia.* Fredericksburg, VA: Printed by the Author, 1966.

Kingdon, Robert M. "Why Did the Huguenot Refugees in the American Colonies Become Episcopalian?" *Historical Magazine of the Protestant Episcopal Church* 49, no. 4 (December 1980): 317–35.

Krumenacker, Yves. "Huguenot Death in the Seventeenth Century: Discourse and Reality." Translated by T. Evans. In *The Huguenots: France, Exile, and Diaspora*, edited by Jane McKee and Randolph Vigne, 17–27. Brighton, UK: Sussex Academic Press, 2013.

Labrousse, Elisabeth. *Bayle*. Oxford: Oxford University Press, 1983.
———. "Great Britain as Envisaged by the Huguenots of the Seventeenth Century." In *Huguenots in Britain and their French Background, 1550–1800*, edited by Irene Scouloudi. Basingstoke, UK: Palgrave Macmillan, 1987.
Lachenicht, Susanne. "Diasporic Networks and Immigration Policies." In *A Companion to the Huguenots*, edited by Raymond A. Mentzer and Bertrand Van Ruymbeke, 249–72. Leiden: Brill, 2016.
———. "Huguenot Immigrants and the Formation of National Identities, 1546–1787." *Historical Journal* 50, no. 2 (June 2007): 309–31.
———, ed. *Religious Refugees in Europe, Asia, and North America, 6th–21st century*. Hamburg: LIT Verlag, 2007.
Lambert, David. *The Protestant International and the Huguenot Migration to Virginia*. New York: Peter Lang, 2010.
Lancaster County Individual Tithables, 1653–1720. Mary Ball Washington Library, Lancaster, Virginia.
Lancaster County, Virginia Deed Book, 1652–1657 (hereafter LC DB). Lancaster County Archives, Lancaster, Virginia (hereafter LCA)
LC DB 9, 1701–1706. LCA.
LC DB 11, 1714–1728. LCA.
LC DB 19, 1770–1782. LCA.
Lancaster County, Virginia Deed and Will Book 2 (hereafter LC DWB). LCA.
LC DWB 7, 1687–1700. LCA.
LC DWB 12, 1726–1736, 144, 157–59. LCA.
LC DWB 13, 1736–1743, 21–22. LCA.
LC DWB 14, 1743–1750. LCA.
Lancaster County, Virginia Order Book 1 (hereafter LC OB). LCA.
LC OB, 1656–1666. LCA.
LC OB, 1686–1696. LCA.
LC OB, 1696–1701, vol. 4. LCA.
LC OB 5, 1702–1713. LCA.
LC OB 7, 1721–1729. LCA.
LC OB 12, 1734–1735. LCA.
LC OB 12, 1764–1767. LCA.
Lancaster County, Virginia Register of Marriages, 16 December, 1724. LCA.
Lancaster County, Virginia Will Book, vol. 5 (hereafter LC WB). LCA.
LC WB, vol. 5, 1674–1689. LCA.
LC WB 8 1690–1709, 105–05a. LCA.
LC WB 10, 1709–1727, 376–78. LCA.
LC WB 16, 1758–1763, 105–06,148–49. LCA
LC WB 20, folio 120. LCA.
Land Office Patents no. 2, 1643–1651, 288 (hereafter LOP). LVA.
LOP no. 4, 1655–1664, 137, 223. LVA
LOP no. 5, 1661–1666, vol. 1 and 2, Part 1–369, 537. LVA.
LOP no. 6, 1666–1679, Part 1 and 2, 138. LVA.
LOP no. 8, 1689–1695, 115, 207, 274. LVA.

LOP no. 9, 1697–1706, 348, 352, 445, 667. LVA.
LOP no. 10, 1710–1719, 10. LVA.
LOP no. 11, 1719–1724, 147. LVA.
LOP no. 13, 1725–1730, 281. LVA.
LOP no 17, 1735–1738, 434. LVA.
Lart, Charles Edmund. *Huguenot Pedigrees.* Baltimore: Genealogical Publishing Company, 1967.
Latané, Lucy Temple. *Parson Latané, 1672–1732.* Charlottesville, VA: Michie Printers, 1936.
Lee, Grace Lawless. *The Huguenot Settlements of Ireland.* Berwyn Heights, MD: Heritage Books, 2008.
Lee, Lonnie H. *A Brief History of Belle Isle Plantation, Lancaster County, Virginia, 1650–1782.* Berwyn Heights, MD: Heritage Books, 2020.
———. "The Transatlantic Legacy of the Protestant Church of Cozes." *Huguenot Society Journal* 32 (2019): 36–54.
Le Fanu, T. P. and W. H. Manchee, eds. *Dublin and Portarlington Veterans, King William III's Army.* London: Huguenot Society of London, 1946.
Le Fanu, Thomas Philip, ed. *Registers of the French Church at Portarlington, Ireland.* London: Spottswoode and Company, 1908.
Leith, John H. *Introduction to the Reformed Tradition: A Way of Being the Christian Community.* Atlanta: John Knox Press, 1977.
Liste Generalle De Tous Les Francois Protestants Establys Dans La Paroisse Du Roy Guillaume, Compte De Henrico En Virginia, Y Compris Les Femmes, Enfants, Veuses, Et Orphelins [1714]. The Huguenot Society of the Founders of Manakin in the Colony of Virginia Library, Midlothian.
Loose Wills (Will of Thomas Powell). LVA.
Lorenz, Otto. "An Analysis of the Life and Career of the Reverend David Currie, Lancaster County, Virginia, 1743–1791." *Anglican and Episcopal History* 61, no. 2 (1992): 142–66.
Lougee, Carolyn Chappell. *Facing the Revocation: Huguenot Families, Faith, and the King's Will.* New York: Oxford University Press, 2017.
Lounsbury, Carl R. *The Courthouses of Early Virginia: An Architectural History.* Charlottesville: University Press of Virginia, 2005.
Maag, Karin. "Pulpit and Pen: Pastors and Professors as Shapers of the Huguenot Tradition." In *A Companion to the Huguenots,* edited by Raymond A. Mentzer and Bertrand Van Ruymbeke, 154. Leiden: Brill, 2016.
MacCulloch, Diarmaid. *The Reformation: A History.* New York: Penguin Books, 2003.
MacNeil, Karen. *The Wine Bible.* New York: Workman Publishing, 2001.
Makemie, Francis to Increase Mather, July 22, 1684. In I. Marshall Page. *The Life Story of Rev. Francis Makemie.* Grand Rapids, MI: William B. Eerdmans Publishing Company, 1938: 63–64.
——— to Increase Mather, July 28, 1685. In I. Marshall Page. *The Life Story of Rev. Francis Makemie.* Grand Rapids, MI: William B. Eerdmans Publishing Company, 1938: 65.

Manross, William Wilson, ed. *The Fulham Papers in the Lambeth Palace Library, American Colonial Section, Calendar and Indexes*. Oxford: Clarendon Press, 1965.

Mason, George Carrington. "The Colonial Churches of Essex and Richmond Counties." VMHB 53, no. 1 (January 1945): 3–20.

———. "The Colonial Churches of King and Queen and King William Counties, Virginia." WMQ 23, no. 4 (October 1943): 440–64.

———. "The Colonial Churches of Northumberland and Lancaster Counties, Virginia." VMHB 54, no. 2 (April 1946): 137–51.

———. "The Colonial Churches of Northumberland and Lancaster Counties (concluded)." VMHB 54, no. 3 (July 1946): 233–43.

———. "The Colonial Churches of Spotsylvania and Caroline Counties, Virginia." VMHB 58, no. 4 (October 1950): 442–72.

———. "The Colonial Churches of Westmoreland and King George Counties, Virginia, Part I." VMHB 56, no. 2 (April 1948): 154–72.

———. "The Colonial Churches of Westmoreland and King George Counties, Virginia, Part II." VMHB 56, no. 3 (July 1948): 280–93.

Maury, Ann. *Memoirs of a Huguenot Family*. New York: 1852.

McCartney, Martha W. *Virginia Immigrants and Adventurers, 1607–1635: A Biographical Dictionary*. Baltimore: Genealogical Publishing Company, 2007.

McIlwaine, H. L., ed. *Executive Journals of the Council of Colonial Virginia*, vol. 1–3. Richmond: D. Bottom, 1925, 1927, 1928.

McKee, Jane and Randolph Vigne, eds. *The Huguenots: France, Exile, and Diaspora*. Brighton, UK: Sussex Academic Press, 2013.

McNeill, John T. *The History and Character of Calvinism*. Oxford: Oxford University Press, 1954.

Meade, William. *Old Churches, Ministers, and Families of Virginia*. Philadelphia: J. B. Lippincott, 1861.

Mentzer, Raymond A. *Blood and Belief: Family Survival and Confessional Identity Among the Provincial Huguenot Nobility*. West Lafayette: Purdue University Press, 1993.

Mentzer, Raymond A. and Bertrand Van Ruymbeke, eds. *A Companion to the Huguenots*. Leiden: Brill, 2016.

Mentzer, Raymond A. and Andrew Spicer, eds. *Society and Culture in the Huguenot World, 1559–1685*. Cambridge: Cambridge University Press, 2002.

Meyer, Judith Pugh. *Reformation in La Rochelle: Tradition and Change in Early Modern Europe, 1500–1568*. Geneva: Librairie Droz S. A., 1996.

Michel, Francis Louis. "Report of the Journey of Francis Louis Michel from Berne, Switzerland, to Virginia, October 2, 1701–December 1, 1702." Edited and translated by William J. Hinke. VMHB 24 (1916), 113–41.

Micou, Mary D. "The Colonial Churches of York County, Virginia." In *Colonial Churches: A series of Sketches of Churches in the Original Colony of Virginia*, edited by W. M. Clarke, 240–44. Richmond: Southern Churchman, 1907.

Micou, Paul. "Paul Micou, Huguenot Physician and His Descendants." VMHB 46, no. 4 (October 1938): 362–70. VMHB 47, no. 1 (January 1939), 66–78.

Minet, William and Susan Minet, eds. *Le Livre Des Conversions et de Reconnaissances Faites; a la Savoye, 1684–1702*. London: Huguenot Society of Great Britain and Ireland Publications, 1914.

———. *Le Livre Des Tesmoignages de L'Eglise de Threadneedle Street, 1669–1789*. London: Huguenot Society of Great Britain and Ireland Publications, 1909.

———. *Registers of the Churches of the Savoy, Spring Gardens, and Les Grecs*. Lymington, UK: Huguenot Society of Great Britain and Ireland Publications, 1922.

Moens, William J. C., ed. *The Registers of the French Church, Threadneedle Street, London, 1637–1685*. Lymington, UK: Huguenot Society of Great Britain and Ireland Publications, 1899.

Moré, Les. "Descendances et familles allées (XVIe–XIXe siècles)." *Généalogies Protestantes (Angoumois, Aunis, Guyenne, Saintonge)* (2021): 10–365.

Moreau, Nicholas to William Lloyd, Bishop of Lichfield and Coventry, April 12, 1697. In William Stevens Perry, ed. *Historical Collections Relating to the American Colonial Church*, vol. 1, 29–32. Hartford, CT: Church Press Company, 1870.

Morris, Sandra. "Legacy of a Bishop: The Trees and Shrubs of Fulham Palace Gardens Introduced 1675–1713." *Garden History* 19, no. 1 (Spring 1991): 47–59.

Morton, Susan R. "Survey Report, Old Methodist Church Site." October 6, 1937, LVA.

Nash, R. C. "Huguenot Merchants and the Development of South Carolina's Slave-Plantation and Atlantic Trading Economy, 1680–1775." In *Memory and Identity: The Huguenots in France and the Atlantic Diaspora*, edited by Bertrand Van Ruymbeke and Randy J. Sparks, 194–203. Columbia: University of South Carolina Press, 2003.

National Society of Colonial Dames of America (Virginia), ed. *Christ Church Middlesex County Parish Register*. Richmond: 1897.

Nelson, John K. *A Blessed Company: Parishes, Parsons, and Parishioners in Anglican Virginia, 1690–1776*. Chapel Hill: North Carolina University Press, 2001.

Nicklin, John Bailey Calvert. "An Annotated Copy of the Rent Roll of 1704." WMQ 21, no. 4 (October 1941): 397–405.

———. "Quit Rent Roll for the Year 1715—Essex County, Virginia." WMQ 18, no. 2 (April 1938): 203–06.

Northern Neck Grants no. 1, 1690–1692, 16–18, 96, 172 (hereafter NNG). LVA.

NNG no. 2, 1694–1700, 76–77, 103, 112–13, 120–21, 293–95. LVA.

NNG no. 3, 1703–1710, 23, 147. LVA.

NNG no. 4, 1710–1712, 43, 53, 94, 103. LVA.

NNG no. 5, 1713–1719, 60, 65, 103, 189. LVA.

NNG A, 1722–1726, 128. LVA.

NNG B, 1726–1729, 107, 134, 184. LVA.

NNG F, 1742–1754, 274. LVA.

Northey, Edward. "Sir Edward Northey's Opinion concerning Induction of Ministers in Virginia," July 29, 1703. In William Stevens Perry, ed., *Historical Collections*, vol. 1, 127–28. Hartford, CT: Church Press Company, 1870.

Notaire Bargignac. 3E, 128/49, folio 23, January 4, 1692. ADCMLR.

Notaire Bargignac. 3E, 128/52, folio 143–44, 1695. ADCMLR.

Notaire Tourneur. 3E, 26/1086, folio 121–22, and 298, May 1, 1690. ADCMLR.

Notaire Tourneur. 3E, 26/1086, folio 244–45, May 1, 1693. ADCMLR.
Notaire Tourneur. 3E, 26/1086, folio 298, May 1, 1693. ADCMLR.
"Notes from the Council and General Court Records, 1641–1672." General Court Will Book Number 2, 37. VMHB 8, no. 3 (January 1901), 244.
Nugent, Nell, M. *Cavaliers and Pioneers, A Calendar of Virginia Land Grants, 1623–1800*, vols. 1, 2, and 3. Richmond: Press of the Dietz Printing Company, 1934.
Old Rappahannock County Order Book 2, 1686–1692 (hereafter ORC OB). Richmond County Archives, Warsaw, Virginia (hereafter RCA).
ORC DB, 1668–1672. RCA
ORC DWB 1, 1665–1677. RCA
ORC DWB 1, 1677–1682. RCA.
ORC DWB 8. RCA.
Page, I. Marshall. *The Life Story of Rev. Francis Makemie*. Grand Rapids, MI: William B. Eerdmans Publishing Company, 1938.
Painter, Andrew A. *Virginia Wine: Four Centuries of Change*. Fairfax, VA: George Mason University Press, 2018.
Palmer, William P., ed. *Calendar of Virginia State Papers and Other Manuscripts, 1652–1781*, vol. 7. Richmond: R. F. Walker, 1875.
Papiers des Baptêmes de l'Eglise Réformée de Cozes . . . Fevrier 1656–Juillet 1668. I–43. ADCMLR.
Parish, Susan Scott. "Introduction." In Robert Beverley, *The History and Present State of Virginia: A New Edition with an Introduction by Susan Scott Parish*, xi–xxxviii. Chapel Hill: The University of North Carolina Press, 2013.
Perry, William Stevens, ed. *Historical Collections Relating to the American Colonial Church*, vol. 1. Hartford, CT: Church Press Company, 1870.
Pierce, Elizabeth C. "A Brief History of St. Mary's Whitechapel Episcopal Church." Mary Ball Washington Library, Lancaster, Virginia.
Prince William County Deed Book D. Prince William County Archives, Manassas, Virginia.
Prince William County Land Causes, 1789–1793. Prince William County Archives, Manassas, Virginia.
Purkiss, Diane. *The English Civil War: Papists, Gentlewomen, Soldiers, and Witchfinders in the Birth of Modern Britain*. New York: Basic Books, 2006.
Quenzel, Carrol H. *The History and Background of St. George's Episcopal Church, Fredericksburg, Virginia*. Richmond: Clyde W. Saunders and Sons, 1951.
Raimo, John W. *Biographical Directory of American Colonial and Revolutionary Governors, 1607–1789*. Westport, CT: Meckler Books, 1980.
Raithby, John, ed. *Statutes of the Realm*. London: 1810–1828.
Randall, Catherine. *From a Far Country: Camisards and Huguenots in the Atlantic World*. Athens, GA: University of Georgia Press, 2009.
Rasor, Paul and Richard E, Bond, eds. *From Jamestown to Jefferson: The Evolution of Religious Freedom in Virginia*. Charlottesville: University of Virginia Press, 2011.
Rezner, Joan Louise. *The Anglican Church in Virginia, 1723–1743*. Williamsburg, VA: M.A. Thesis, William and Mary College, 1968.

"Revue de Saintonge & d'Aunis," *Bulletin de la Société des Archives historiques de la Saintonge et de l'Aunis* 15.
Richmond County Order Book, 1699–1701 (hereafter RC OB). RCA.
RC OB, 1702–1704. RCA.
RC OB 2, 1692–1694. RCA.
Rightmyer, Nelson W. "List of Anglican Clergy Receiving a Bounty for Overseas Service, 1680–1688." *Historical Magazine of the Protestant Episcopal Church* 17 (June 1948): 174–82.
Robbins, Kevin C. *City on the Ocean Sea, La Rochelle, 1530–1650: Urban Society, Religion, and Politics on the French Atlantic Frontier.* Leiden: Brill, 1997.
Root, Winfred T. "Lords of Trade and Plantations, 1675–1696," *American Historical Review* 23, no. 1 (October 1917): 29–41.
Roper, Louis H. and Bertrand Van Ruymbeke, eds. *Constructing Early Modern Empires: Proprietary Ventures in the Atlantic World, 1500–1750*, 1–18. Leiden: Brill, 2007.
Rouse, Parke. *James Blair of Virginia.* Chapel Hill: University of North Carolina Press, 1971.
Roussel, Bernard. "'Ensevelir honnestement les corps": funeral corteges and Huguenot culture." In *Society and Culture in the Huguenot World, 1559–1685*, edited by Raymond A. Mentzer and Andrew Spicer, 193–208. Cambridge: Cambridge University Press, 2002.
"Royal Bounty Papers." Ms 1 (hereafter RBP). Library of the Huguenot Society of Great Britain and Ireland, University College, London (hereafter HL).
RBP. Ms 2/3, Ms 2/4, Ms 2/5, Ms 2/6, Ms 2/7. HL.
RBP. Ms 4/1, Ms 4/2. HL.
RBP. Ms 8. HL.
RBP. Ms 9/2, Ms 9/3, Ms 9/4, Ms 9/6, Ms 9/7, Ms 9/8. HL.
RBP. Ms 11. HL.
RBP. Ms 15. HL.
RBP. Ms 17/1, Ms 17/2, Ms 17/3, Ms 17/4, and Ms 17/5. HL.
Ryland, Elizabeth Hawes. "Paul Micou, Chyrurgeon." WMQ 16, no. 2 (April 1936): 241–46.
Sainsbury, W. Noel, ed. *Calendar of State Papers, Colonial Series, vol. 1, America and West Indies, 1574–1660.* London, 1860: 98–121.
Saint Denis Chateaux. Inventaire du Patrimoine Cultural, 2008–2013. Region Poitou Charentes.
St. George's Parish (Spotsylvania County, Virginia) Vestry Book, 1726–1745. Midwest Genealogy Center, Lee's Summit, Missouri.
St. Mary's Whitechapel Parish Vestry Book, 1739–1752. Mary Ball Washington Library, Lancaster, Virginia.
Saintonge Pasteurs, A-D, Bertrand (Paul), 67. SHPF.
Salmon, Emily Jones and John Salmon. "Tobacco in Colonial Virginia." *Encyclopedia Virginia*, Virginia Foundation for the Humanities.

Scott, Kenneth and Kenn Stryker-Rodda, eds. *Denizations, Naturalizations, and Oaths of Allegiance in Colonial New York.* Baltimore: Genealogical Publishing Company, 1975.

Scott, P. G. "James Blair and the Scottish Church: A New Source." WMQ 33, no. 2 (April, 1976): 300–08.

Scott, Robert Forsyth. *St. John's College, Cambridge.* London: J. M. Dent, 1907.

Scouloudi, Irene, ed. *Huguenots in Britain and their French Background, 1550–1800.* Basingstoke, UK: Palgrave Macmillan, 1987.

Seacord, Morgan H. *Biographical Sketches and Indexes of the Huguenot Settlers of New Rochelle, 1687–1776.* New Rochelle: Huguenot and Historical Association of New Rochelle, NY, 1941.

Seiler, William H. "Land Processioning in Colonial Virginia." WMQ 6, 3rd series (1949): 426–30.

———. "The Anglican Parish Vestry in Colonial Virginia." *The Journal of Southern History* 22, no. 3 (August 1956): 310–37.

Sell, Alan P. F., ed. *The Great Ejectment of 1662: Its Antecedents, Aftermath, and Ecumenical Significance.* Eugene, OR: Pickwick Publications, 2012.

Shaw, William A. *A History of the English Church During the Civil Wars and Under the Commonwealth.* London: Longmans Green, 1900.

———. *Letters of Denization and Acts of Naturalization for Aliens in England and Ireland, 1603–1700.* Lymington, UK: Huguenot Society of Great Britain and Ireland Publications, 1911.

Slaughter, James B. *Settlers, Southerners, Americans: The History of Essex County, Virginia, 1608–1984.* Tappahannock, VA: Essex County Board of Supervisors, 1985.

Slaughter, Philip. *History of St. George's Parish in the county of Spotsylvania, and the diocese of Virginia.* Edited by R. A. Brock. Richmond: Randolph and English, 1890.

———. *Memoir of Col. Joshua Fry, Sometime Professor in William and Mary College.* Richmond: Randolph and English, 1880.

Smylie, James H. *A Brief History of the Presbyterians.* Louisville, KY: Geneva Press, 1996.

Societe de l'Histoire Du Protestantisme Francais Paris. *Bulletin Historique et Litteraire*, Tome XXXIV, Troisieme Series, Quatrieme Anee.

Sparacio, Ruth and Sam Sparacio. Essex County (hereafter EC) DWB, 1692–1693. McLean, VA: Antient Press, 1991.

———. EC DWB, 1693–1694. McLean, VA: Antient Press, 1991.

———. EC DWB, 1694–1695. McLean, VA: Antient Press, 1991.

———. EC DWB, 1695–1697. Berwyn Heights, MD: Heritage Press, 2020.

———. EC OB, 1695–1699. McLean, VA: Antient Press, 1991.

———. EC DWB, 1697–1699. McLean, VA: Antient Press, 1991.

———. EC DWB, 1699–1701. McLean, VA: Antient Press, 1991.

———. EC OB, 1699–1702. McLean, VA: Antient Press, 1991.

———. EC DWB, 1701–1703. Berwyn Heights, MD: Heritage Press, 2020.

———. EC DB, 1711–1721. McLean, VA: Antient Press, 1992.

———. EC DB, 1721–1724. McLean, VA: Antient Press, 1988.

Bibliography

———. EC WB, 1735–1743. McLean, VA: Antient Press, 1989.
———. King William County (hereafter KWC) RB, 1702–1705. McLean, VA: Antient Press, 1996.
———. KWC RB, 1705–1721. McLean, VA: Antient Press, 1996.
———. Lancaster County (hereafter LC) DWB, 1654–1661. McLean, VA: Antient Press, 1991.
———. LC DWB, 1652–1657. McLean, VA: Antient Press, 1991.
———. LC OB, 1656–1661. McLean, VA: Antient Press, 1993.
———. LC OB, 1662–1666. McLean, VA: Antient Press, 1993.
———. LC OB, 1666–1669. McLean, VA: Antient Press, 1993.
———. LC DWB, 1661–1702. McLean, VA: Antient Press, 1991.
———. LC OB, 1666–1669. McLean, VA: Antient Press, 1993.
———. LC OB, 1670–1674. McLean, VA: Antient Press, 1993.
———. LC OB, 1674–1678. McLean, VA: Antient Press, 1993.
———. LC WB, 1675–1689. McLean, VA: Antient Press, 1992.
———. LC OB, 1678–1681. McLean, VA: Antient Press, 1993.
———. LC OB, 1682–1687. McLean, VA: Antient Press, 1995.
———. LC OB, 1687–1691. McLean, VA: Antient Press, 1995.
———. LC WB, 1690–1709. McLean, VA: Antient Press, 1992.
———. LC OB, 1691–1695. McLean, VA: Antient Press, 1995.
———. LC OB, 1695–1699. McLean, VA: Antient Press, 1998.
———. LC OB, 1699–1701. McLean, VA: Antient Press, 1998.
———. LC DB, 1701–1706. McLean, VA: Antient Press, 1995.
———. LC OB, 1703–1706. McLean, VA: Antient Press, 1999.
———. LC DB, 1706–1710. McLean, VA: Antient Press, 1995.
———. Middlesex County (hereafter MC) OB, 1673–1678. McLean, VA: Antient Press, 1989.
———. MC OB, 1677–1680. McLean, VA: Antient Press, 1989.
———. MC OB, 1680–1686. McLean, VA: Antient Press, 1994.
———. MC OB, 1690–1694. McLean, VA: Antient Press, 1994.
———. Northumberland County (hereafter NC) OB, 1669–1673. McLean, VA: Antient Press, 1995.
———. NC OB, 1677–1679. McLean, VA: Antient Press, 1998.
———. NC OB, 1683–1686. Berwyn Heights, MD: Heritage Books, 2019.
———. NC OB, 1699–1700. McLean, VA: Antient Press, 1998.
———. NC OB, 1702–1704. McLean, VA: Antient Press, 1998.
———. Old Rappahannock County (hereafter ORC) DWB, No. 1, 1656–1664. McLean, VA: Antient Press, 1989.
———. ORC DWB, 1665–1677. McLean, VA: Antient Press, 1989.
———. ORC DWB, 1670–1672. McLean, VA: Antient Press, 1989.
———. ORC DWB, 1672–1673/4. McLean, VA: Antient Press, 1989.
———. ORC DB, 1673/4–1676. McLean, VA: Antient Press, 1989.
———. ORC DWB, 1678/9–1682. McLean, VA: Antient Press, 1990.
———. ORC DB, 1682–1686. McLean, VA: Antient Press, 1990.
———. ORC WB, 1682–1687. Berwyn Heights, MD: Heritage Books, 2018.

———. ORC OB, 1683–1685. McLean, VA: Antient Press, 1990.
———. ORC OB, 1685–1687. McLean, VA: Antient Press, 1990.
———. ORC DB, 1686–1688. McLean, VA: Antient Press, 1990.
———. ORC OB, 1687–1689. McLean, VA: Antient Press, 1990.
———. ORC DB, 1688–1692. McLean, VA: Antient Press, 1990.
———. ORC OB, 1689–1692. Berwyn Heights, MD: Heritage Books, 2018.
———. Prince William County OB, 1754–1755. McLean, VA: Antient Press, 1988.
———. Richmond County (hereafter RC) OB, 1692–1694. McLean, VA: Antient Press, 1991.
———. RC DB, 1692–1695. McLean, VA: Antient Press, 1991.
———. RC OB, 1694–1697. McLean, VA: Antient Press, 1991.
———. RC DB, 1695–1701. McLean, VA: Antient Press, 1991.
———. RC OB, 1697–1699. McLean, VA: Antient Press, 1991.
———. RC OB, 1699–1701. McLean, VA: Antient Press, 1991.
———. RC DB, 1701–1704. McLean, VA: Antient Press, 1991.
———. RC OB, 1702–1704. McLean, VA: Antient Press, 1991.
———. RC OB, 1704–1705. McLean, VA: Antient Press, 1996.
———. RC OB, 1705–1706. McLean, VA: Antient Press, 1996.
———. RC DB, 1705–1708. McLean, VA: Antient Press, 1991.
———. RC OB, 1707–1708. McLean, VA: Antient Press, 1997.
———. RC OB, 1708–1709. McLean, VA: Antient Press, 1997.
———. RC OB, 1709–1710. McLean, VA: Antient Press, 1997.
———. Spotsylvania County OB, 1734–1735. McLean, VA: Antient Press, 1991.
———. Stafford County (hereafter SC) OB, 1664–1668 and 1689–1690. McLean, VA: Antient Press, 1987.
———. SC DWB, 1686–1689. McLean, VA: Antient Press, 1989.
———. SC DWB, 1689–1693. McLean, VA: Antient Press, 1989.
———. SC OB, 1691–1692. McLean, VA: Antient Press, 1987.
———. SC OB, 1692–1693. McLean, VA: Antient Press, 1988.
———. SC DWB, 1699–1709. McLean, VA: Antient Press, 1989.
Stanard, W. G., ed. "Abstracts of Virginia Land Patents." VMHB 3, no. 1 (July 1895): 60–66.
———. "Abstracts of Rappahannock County Wills." VMHB 5, no. 3 (Jan 1898): 283.
———. "Christ Church, Lancaster County, Virginia." In *Colonial Churches: A Series of Sketches of Churches in the Original Colony of Virginia*, edited by W. M. Clarke, 93–106. Richmond: Southern Churchman, 1907.
Stanwood, Owen. "Between Eden and Empire: Huguenot Refugees and the Promise of New Worlds." *American Historical Review* (December 2013): 1319–44.
———. *The Empire Reformed: English America in the Age of the Glorious Revolution.* Philadelphia: University of Pennsylvania Press, 2011.
———. *The Global Refuge: Huguenots in an Age of Empire.* New York: Oxford University Press, 2020.
———. "The Huguenot Refuge and European Imperialism." In *A Companion to the Huguenots,* edited by Raymond A. Mentzer and Bertrand Van Ruymbeke, 394–421. Leiden: Brill, 2016.

Syndics of Cambridge University Library. UA Subscriptions 2.
Tarter, Brent. "Bacon's Rebellion, the Grievances of the People, and the Political Culture of Seventeenth-Century Virginia," VMHB 119, no. 1 (2011): 2–41.
———. "Evidence of Religion in Seventeenth Century Virginia." In *From Jamestown to Jefferson: The Evolution of Religious Freedom in Virginia*, edited by Paul Rasor and Richard E. Bond. Charlottesville: University of Virginia Press, 2011.
———. "Reflections on the Church of England in Colonial Virginia." VMHB 112, no. 4 (2004): 338–71.
Teagle, Robert. "Mean Tobacco and a Well-Beloved Minister: Andrew Jackson of Christ Church Parish, 1686–1710." *Northern Neck of Virginia Historical Magazine* 52 (December 2002): 6227–44.
The Huguenot Society of Great Britain and Ireland. *Proceedings of the Huguenot Society of London*, vol. 7 (1901–1904): 148–49.
The Virginia Gazette. Dixon and Hunter. May 8, 1778, 7. Colonial Williamsburg Digital Library.
"The Vestry Book of King William Parish, Virginia, 1707–1750 (Continued)." VMHB 12, no. 1 (July 1904), 17–32.
The Virginia Magazine of History and Biography 1, no. 3 (Jan. 1894): 254–56.
———5, no. 3 (Jan 1898): 290.
———8, no. 3 (Jan. 1901): 244, 308.
———19, no. 4 (Oct. 1911): 417.
TLC Genealogy. *Richmond County Virginia Miscellaneous Records, 1699–1724.*
Tobacco Tenders: Stafford, 1724. Bull Run Regional Library, Manassas, Virginia.
Treasure, Geoffrey. *The Huguenots*. New Haven: Yale University Press, 2013.
Trim, David J. B. "The Huguenots and the European Wars of Religion." In *The Huguenots: History and Memory in Transnational Context*, edited by David J. B. Trim, 153–92. Leiden: Brill, 2011.
———. "The Huguenots and the Experience of Exile (Sixteenth to Twentieth Centuries): History, Memory, and Transnationalism." In *The Huguenots: History and Memory in Transnational Context*, edited by David J. B. Trim, 1–42. Leiden: Brill, 2011.
Tupper, Margaret H., ed. *Christ Church Parish, Lancaster County, Virginia Vestry Book, 1739–1786.* Irvington, VA: Foundation for Historic Christ Church, 1990.
Uhrbrock, Richard S. "Francis Makemie (c. 1658–1708)." *Colonial Genealogist* 8, no. 3 (1976): 115–25, no. 4 (1977): 189–95.
Un Album Bernois de 1672, 514–15. SHPF.
United States Congress. *Biographical Dictionary of the United States Congress, 1774–present, Cyrus Griffin (1748–1810)*. Washington, DC: United States Congress, 1998.
Upton, Dale. *Holy Things and Profane: Anglican Parish Churches in Colonial Virginia.* New Haven: Yale University Press, 1997.
Van der Linden, David. "The Economy of Exile: Huguenot Migration from Dieppe to Rotterdam, 1685–1700." In *The Huguenots: France, Exile, and Diaspora*, edited by Jane McKee and Randolph Vigne, 99–112. Brighton, UK: Sussex Academic Press, 2013.

Van Ruymbeke, Bertrand. *From New Babylon to Eden: The Huguenots and Their Migration to Colonial South Carolina.* Columbia: University of South Carolina Press, 2006.

―――. "*Le Refuge*: History and Memory from the 1770s to the Present." In *A Companion to the Huguenots,* edited by Raymond A. Mentzer and Bertrand Van Ruymbeke, 427. Leiden: Brill, 2016.

―――. "Minority Survival: The Huguenot Paradigm in France and the Diaspora." In *Memory and Identity: The Huguenots in France and the Atlantic Diaspora,* edited by Bertrand Van Ruymbeke and Randy Sparks, 1–16. Columbia: University of South Carolina Press, 2008.

―――. "Refuge or Diaspora: Historiographical Reflections on the Huguenot Dispersion in the Atlantic World." In *Religious Refugees in Europe, Asia, and North America, 6th–21st century,* edited by Susanne Lachenicht. Hamburg: LIT Verlag, 2007.

Van Ruymbeke, Bertrand and Randy Sparks, eds. *Memory and Identity: The Huguenots in France and the Atlantic Diaspora.* Columbia: University of South Carolina Press, 2003.

Van Stam, F. P. *The Controversy Over the Theology of Saumur, 1635–1650: Disrupting Debates Among the Huguenots in Complicated Circumstances.* Amsterdam: Holland University Press, 1988.

Various Authors. *Colonial Records of Virginia.* Baltimore: Genealogical Publishing Company, 1964.

Venn, J. A. and John Venn, eds. *Alumni Cantabrigienses: a biographical list of all known students, graduates, and holders of office at the University of Cambridge.* Cambridge: Cambridge University Press, 1922–1954.

"Virginia Huguenot Naturalization, 1705." Library of the Huguenot Society of the Founders of Manakin, Richmond.

"Virginia Naturalizations, 1657–1776." Research Notes Number 9. LVA.

Voorhis, Manning C. "Crown Versus Council in the Virginia Land Policy." WMQ 3, no. 4, 3rd series (Oct. 1946): 499–514.

Wagner, Henry. Family File on Jolit. HL.

Walsh, Lorena S. *Motives of Honor, Pleasure, and Profit: Plantation Management in the Colonial Chesapeake, 1607–1763.* Chapel Hill: The University of North Carolina Press, 2010.

Warner, Thomas Hoskins. *History of Old Rappahannock County, Virginia, 1656–1692.* Tappahannock, VA: P. P. Warner, 1965.

Warren, Barbara. "Gossip and Slander in Northumberland County in the Last Half of the Seventeenth Century." *Bulletin of the Northumberland Historical Society* 60 (2003): 41–52.

Watson, Marcia. *Hugo,* e-letter of the Huguenot Society of Australia Inc., no. 15, (February 2017).

Wawrzyczek, Irmina. "The Women of Accomack County versus Henry Smith: Gender, Legal Recourse, and the Social Order in Seventeenth-Century Virginia." VMHB 105, no. 1 (Winter, 1997): 5–26.

Weis, Frederick Louis. *Colonial Clergy of Virginia, North Carolina, and South Carolina.* Boston: Society of the Descendants of the Colonial Clergy, 1955.

Weiss, Charles. *History of the French Protestant refugees, from the revocation of the edict of Nantes to the present time.* Translated by Frederick Hardman. Edinburgh: W. Blackwood, 1854.

Wellenreuther, Hermann. "The Meaning of Early Modern North Atlantic History: Jacob Leisler, Commerce, Piety, Kinship, and Politics." In *Jacob Leisler's Atlantic World in the Later Seventeenth Century: Essays on Religion, Militia, Trade, and Networks*, edited by Hermann Wellenreuther, 149–72. Munster: LIT Verlag, 2009.

Wells, Camille. "Belle Isle." Unpublished essay, 2014.

Westmoreland County Order Book, 1690–1698 (hereafter WC OB). Westmoreland County Archives, Montross, Virginia.

WC DWB, 1698. Westmoreland County Archives, Montross, Virginia.

Wheeler, Robert A. *Lancaster County, Virginia, 1650–1750: The Evolution of a Southern Tidewater Community.* Providence, RI: Brown University Phd. Dissertation, 1972.

Whelan, Ruth. "The Extraordinary Voyage of Elie Neau (1662–1722): Naturalized Englishman and French Protestant Galley Slave." *Proceedings of the Huguenot Society of Great Britain and Ireland*, 29, no. 4, (2011), 499–527.

William and Mary Center for Archeological Research. William H. Moore, David W. Lewes, and Joe B. Jones. *Archeological Evaluation of Sites 44LA147 and 44LA175, Belle Isle State Park, Lancaster County, Virginia.* Williamsburg, VA, 2006.

William and Mary Center for Archeological Research. Thomas F. Higgins III and Joe B. Jones. *Interim Management Summary: Archeological Evaluation of Site 44LA147, Associated with the Proposed Belle Isle State Park Shoreline Stabilization Project, Lancaster County, Virginia.* Williamsburg, Virginia, 2020.

William and Mary Quarterly Magazine, 1st Series, 2, no. 3 (January 1894), 179–80. Report from the Justices of Princess Anne County to the Council of Virginia, October 4, 1699.

———. 17, no. 2 (October 1908): 75–76.

Winfrie, Waverly K., ed. "The Laws of Virginia Being a Supplement to Hening's *The Statutes at Large*, 1700–1750." Richmond: LVA, 1971: 39–41.

Winner, Lauren. *A Cheerful and Comfortable Faith: Anglican Religious Practice in the Elite Households of Eighteenth-Century Virginia.* New Haven: Yale University Press, 2010.

Withington, Lothrop. "Virginia Gleanings in England (Continued)." VMHB 13, no. 2 (October 1905).

Wittmeyer, Alfred V., ed. *Register of the Births, Marriages, and Deaths of the "Eglise Francaise a la Nouvelle York," from 1688 to 1804.* New York: 1886.

Wood, Betty. "Servant Women and Sex in the Seventeenth-Century Chesapeake." In *Women in Early America*, edited by Thomas A. Foster, 95–117. New York: New York University Press, 2015.

Wright, F. Edward. *Essex County, Virginia Marriage References and Family Relationships, 1620–1800.* Lewes, DE: Colonial Roots, 2013.

Wuthnow, Robert. "Captain Charles Ewell." Unpublished essay, 2022.
———. "Militia Story." Unpublished essay, 2022.
Yannis, Suire. Region Poitou-Charentes, Inventaire du patrimoine culturel.

Index

Act of Toleration (1689), 61, 120
Act of Uniformity (1662), 23, 116
American Revolution, 160–161
Amyraut, Moïse, xi–xii, 24–26, 31;
   and Charles II, 25–26;
   and French Calvinist controversy, xii, 24–25;
   as professor at Saumur Academy, xii, 24;
   and Puritans in England, 25–26, 167;
   and the Saumur theology, 24–25, 28–29, 39n36, 167
André, Jean, 1, 11, 16, 19n39, 81n13
André, Judith, 7, 16, 30, 68, 81n13
André, Marie, 1, 6, 10, 15, 30
André family, 14–15
Andros, Edmund (governor of Virginia), 97, 100, 122, 129n73
Anglican Church in Virginia, 111, 133–134, 160–161, 167;
   and the *Book of Common Prayer*, xii–xiii, xv, 25–26, 51, 54–55, 114–116, 119, 121;
   and the commissary of the bishop of London, xviii, 50, 57, 97, 111–113, 119, 122–123;
   as the established church of Virginia, xvi, 4, 33, 50;
   and governance by vestries, xiv, 50–60, 111–119, 122–124, 142, 147–148;
   and the governor, 50–52, 112–114, 118–119, 122–123, 129n56, 147–148, 151, 158, 164–165;
   and Henry Compton's reforms, xiv, 31–32, 37, 50–51, 56–57, 60, 62, 105, 112–113, 117–124, 129n57, 133, 147–148;
   and Huguenot emigrants, xvi, 4, 48–49, 59–60, 125, 158–159, 163, 167;
   and induction of ministers, 50, 53, 147–148;
   Puritan influence of, 54, 113–116, 121;
   and salaries of ministers, 51, 53–54, 161;
   and slavery, xviii, 50, 70–71, 144, 146;
   and the surplice or Genevan pulpit gown, 121, 123;
   See also Blair, James; Church of England; Compton, Henry
Anne of Austria (queen of France and Navarre), 5

Index

Baird, Charles W., 9
Ball, James, 141–142
Ball, Mary Ann Bertrand Ewell
  Ballandine, 47, 128n44, 141–143, 159, 163
Ball family, 118, 152
Ballandine, William, 141
baptism, 2, 30–31, 44, 56, 113;
    and congregational size, 5, 17n4;
    for the enslaved, 143–144, 146, 158;
    as practiced in Cozes, 5–7;
    sponsors of, 6, 14, 16, 36, 38n8, 42n83
Bell, John, 147, 155n78
Belle Isle Plantation. *See* Bertrand Plantation
Benoist, Jean, 14
Benoist, Marie, 14
Berkeley, William (governor of Virginia), 88, 105n8
Berkeley family, 152
Bernon, Gabriel, 14, 68–69, 81n11, 166–167
Bertrand, Charlotte Jolly, 83n51, 137, 143, 159;
    background of, xi, 7, 16, 30, 36, 44, 81n13;
    and the Bertrand plantation, 140–141;
    emigration of, 15, 32, 46;
    marriage and children of, xii, 30–31, 40n50, 47, 137, 141;
    as merchant, 15, 68–69, 104–105, 140–141
Bertrand, John (Jean), 38n8, 81n13, 83n51, 152, 159, 167;
    Anglican ordination of, xi, 10, 21–24, 37n1;
    background of, xi, 1–2, 17n2, 30, 44, 81n13;
    and Calvinism, 24–28, 55–56, 123–124, 166;
    and conflict with Robert Carter, 100–102, 124;
    death of, 133, 136, 140, 157, 163;
    emigration of, xiv–xvi, 10, 15, 23, 26–27, 31–37, 43–50, 164;
    and enslaved workers, xviii, 70, 81n22, 143–144;
    and indentured servants, 57–58, 70, 143;
    marriage and children of, xi–xii, 30–31, 40n50, 47, 137, 141;
    as merchant, 15, 67–69, 104–105;
    as minister in Virginia, xi–xii, xiv–xvi, 15, 50–62, 63n32, 66n74, 74–75, 112–113, 120–125, 128n52, 130n85, 131n90, 147–149, 165;
    and the Northern Neck Proprietary, xvii–xviii, 77–78, 85, 91, 95–100, 105, 139;
    and plantation boundary controversy, xvii–xviii, 78–80, 85, 91–101;
    and relationship with William Fitzhugh, 75–77, 100–103, 137, 159;
    as tutor, 28–29, 39n39, 75–76
Bertrand, Marie Gribelin, 31, 40n53, 46
Bertrand, Mary Ann (daughter of John Bertrand). *See* Ball, Mary Ann Bertrand Ewell Ballandine
Bertrand, Mary Ann (daughter of William Bertrand). *See* Griffin, Mary Ann Bertrand
Bertrand, Paul (father), xvi, 1, 6, 10–11, 30
Bertrand, Paul (son), 36, 39n39;
    background of, 1, 11, 17n2;
    and correspondence with Henry Compton, 28, 39n35, 47, 169n48;
    death of, 47;
    emigration of, 10, 15, 26;
    marriage and children of, 31, 47;
    and ministry at Rye, 27–29;
    and ministry in Maryland, 46–47;
    ordination of, 24, 27;

Index 217

and the Saumur
   theology, 24–28, 31
Bertrand Plantation, xvii, 61–62, 67–80,
   82n48, 83n51, 104, 107n61, 108n93,
   140–141, 163, 165;
   and boundary dispute, xvii–xviii,
      78–80, 85, 91–101
Bertrand, Susannah Foushee,
   109n96, 141
Bertrand, William:
   and the Bertrand plantation,
      82n48, 108n93, 141–143,
      163, 165–166;
   birth of, 47;
   death of, 165–166;
   and enslaved workers, 143;
   marriage and children of,
      109n96, 141;
   and the Whitechapel vestry, 160
Bertrand family, 47, 152, 160–161
Beverley, Robert, 98, 112, 145–146, 150
bilingualism, xi, xv, 33, 51, 59, 111,
   145–146, 148, 151–152, 159, 166
Blair, James, 128n42, 129n69;
   as commissary, xviii, 50, 57,
      111–113, 119, 129n71;
   and conflict with Governor
      Andros, 122–123, 129n73;
   reporting to the Board of Trade,
      85, 97, 104;
   See also Anglican Church
      in Virginia
Board of Trade, London, xviii,
   85, 96–98, 101, 103–104,
   106n46, 124, 139
Bordeaux, France, 1, 4, 11, 38n17, 70
Boisseau, James, xiv, xvi, 32, 59
Bourdon, Judith, 14
Boyne, Battle of, 37
Braban, Daniell, 135, 152n14
Brent, George, 41n76, 46, 77, 83n69, 95
Brent Town, xxin18, 33, 41n76, 41n77,
   45–46, 49, 77, 103–104, 108n83,
   153n24, 159, 164
Browne, Ann. *See* Tomlyn, Ann Browne

Browne, Nathaniel, 73, 79–80, 84n74–
   77, 91–94, 99
Burwell family, 152
Butler, Jon, 137

Cairon, John (Jean), 32, 150
Calmes, Marquis, 35, 41n77, 49
Calvin, John, 1–3, 24, 55, 123,
   130n79, 145
Calvinism, 24–28, 55–56, 123–
   124, 145, 166
Cammock, Margaret, 48
Cammock, Margaret Thatcher. *See*
   Micou, Margaret Thatcher Cammock
Caribbean:
   Huguenots in, 9, 69;
   slave system in, 70
Carlo, Paula Wheeler, 65n72, 169n44
Carter, Robert, 78, 84n72, 113, 165;
   as agent of the Northern Neck
      Proprietary, 130n80, 139–140;
   and conflict with John Bertrand,
      xviii, 100–102, 124;
   in opposition to the Northern
      Neck Proprietary, xvii–xviii,
      90, 95–96, 98
Carter family, 117, 152
Catesby, Jane. *See* Kyrby, Jane
   Catesby Powell
Catholic Church:
   and the advance of militant
      Catholicism, 28, 32, 56;
   in the Chesapeake region,
      46–47, 146, 150;
   and converts to the Church of
      England, xvii, 151–152, 157;
   in France, xvii, 3–5, 8, 16,
      25, 38n13;
   and Huguenot converts in France,
      10, 12, 16, 81n15;
   promoted in England by James II,
      xi–xii, 35–37;
   and the Puritan critique of the
      Church of England, 54, 113;
   See also Louis XIV

Index

Chaperon, Jean, 135
Charles I (king of England),
    22, 25–26, 27
Charles II (king of England), 22, 115;
    and *Act of Uniformity*, 23, 25–26;
    and the Northern Neck
        Proprietary, xvii, 86,
        87–88, 100;
    and trade policies, 67
Charlestown (Charleston), South
    Carolina, xii, 13, 137, 158, 166
Cheneau, Estienne, 135
Chevalle, Clement, 41n77, 103
Christ Church Parish, Lancaster County,
    Virginia, 75, 119–121, 123–124,
    128n49, 155n79, 160
Christ Church Parish, Middlesex
    County, Virginia, 64n42, 115, 117,
    126n28, 130n86
Church of England, 34, 50, 55,
    117, 133, 151;
    and the *Book of Common
        Prayer*, xii–xiii, xv, 21,
        25–26, 51, 54–56, 75, 114–
        116, 119, 121, 124;
    and ordination of Huguenot
        refugee ministers, xi, xiv,
        10,15, 21–24, 27, 59–60, 136;
    and Puritans, 25, 54–56,
        113–116, 167;
    and the recruitment of ministers
        for the colonies, xiv,
        28, 31–32, 46, 51, 112,
        117–119, 124, 127n41,
        133–134, 144;
    and the settlement of Charles II,
        25, 115–116, 118;
    and slavery, xviii,
        70–71, 144, 146;
    See also Anglican Church in
        Virginia; Compton, Henry
citizenship. *See* naturalization
Clayton, John, 121, 128n42
Cocke family, 152

Compton, Henry (bishop of London),
    22, 127n41, 157, 162, 167;
    and Anglican reform in Virginia,
        xiv, 31–32, 50–51, 54,
        56–57, 60, 62, 111–113, 117–
        124, 129n57, 133, 147–148;
    and conflict with James II,
        xii, 35–36;
    and Huguenots in England,
        xi–xiv, 21, 26–28, 35–36,
        59, 136, 144;
    and William III and Mary II, xii,
        23, 36, 46;
    See also Anglican Church in
        Virginia; Church of England
Connele family, 34
Cople Parish, Virginia, 60,
    127n40, 130n82
Cozes, France:
    and the Dragonnades, 10–12;
    and the Huguenot diaspora, 9–10,
        12, 16, 23–24, 27–28;
    and Huguenots in English
        America, xvi, xviii,
        14–16, 34–35, 44, 60,
        68–69, 104, 165;
    and the local nobility, 7,
        16, 28–30;
    Protestant baptism record of,
        5–7, 14, 47;
    Protestant identity of, 1–2, 4–6, 8;
    and its Protestant ministers, 1–2,
        5–6, 8–11, 15–17, 30, 47, 60
Crew, Nathaniel (bishop of Durham),
    36, 129n56
Culpepper, Catherine, 88
Culpepper, Margaret (Margaretta von
    Hesse), 88
Culpepper, Thomas (second baron
    Culpepper of Thoresway and
    governor of Virginia), 88–89, 105n8
Currie, David, 147, 155n79

Dacres, Ann Powell, 74, 77, 80,
    82n47, 106n31

Index

Dacres, Charles, 55, 74, 127n40
Dade, Francis, 90, 100
Dalliriens, Monsieur, 150–151
Danellin, Edward, 34, 42n82, 63n25
Daulnis Family, 36, 42n94
Davies, Samuel, 160
Davis, John, 61, 125, 127n40, 128n42, 130n85, 130n89
Deane, Mary. *See* Latané, Mary Deane
De Butts, Lawrence, 149–150
Deep Creek Plantation. *See* Bertrand Plantation
Demonvill, Samuel, 49
des Maizeaux, Pierre, 135
d'Etaples, Jacques Lefevre, 2
de Joux, Benjamin, 32, 59, 134, 150
Depree, Abraham, 35
de Richebourg, Claude Philippe, 32, 59, 150
de Rosseaux, Theodore, 102, 135
Doggett, Benjamin, 115–117, 123, 127n31, 127n40
Doughty, Francis, 55, 115, 126n27
Dozier, Leonard, 102, 108n76
du Moulin, Pierre, 24, 145
Duchemin, Isaac, 41n77, 104, 108n83
Duchemin, Samuel, 41n77, 104, 108n83
Durand de Dauphiné, xiv–xvi, 34, 41n73, 43, 49–50, 76, 133, 135, 157, 167;
    and French ministers for Virginia, xv–xvi, 33, 44, 51, 59, 164;
    and Huguenot land acquisition, xv–xvi, 32–33, 44, 103, 137–138, 164
Durel, John, xii–xiii, 26–27, 127n31
Dragonnades, xix, 10–12

economic opportunities:
    for Huguenots in Saintonge, 1–2, 6;
    for Manakin Huguenots, 134–135, 150;
    for New Rochelle Huguenots, 14;
    for Rappahannock Huguenots, 48–49, 134–135
Edict of Fontainebleau (1685), 12
Edict of Nantes (1598), 3, 9–10, 12, 44
English Civil War, 22, 26, 167
enslaved persons, 50;
    baptism of, 143–144, 146, 158;
    catechism classes for, 144, 146;
    and the Church of England, xviii, 70–71, 144, 146;
    and the French Reformed Church, xviii, 13, 70–71, 163;
    and Huguenots in Virginia, 13, 70, 81n22, 141, 143, 146, 163;
    and the labor system of Virginia, xv, xviii, 71;
    as a liquid asset, 142–143;
    and registration of enslaved children, 70;
    theological implications of, 13, 68, 71;
    and transatlantic trade in, 13, 70, 163
Ewell, Charles (father), 82n48, 128n44, 141, 143, 159
Ewell, Charles (son), 141–142
Ewell, Charlotte. *See* Gallahue, Charlotte Ewell
Ewell family, 141, 159–161, 168n14

Fairfax, Thomas (fifth Lord Fairfax of Cameron), 88, 95–96, 139
Fauntleroy, Margaret Micou, 141, 143
Fauntleroy, Moore, 141
Fauntleroy family, 83n55, 145, 152
Fitzhugh, Henry, 76
Fitzhugh, William (father), 33, 46, 136–137, 164;
    as agent of the Northern Neck Proprietary, xvii–xviii, 79, 90–92, 95–98, 100–104, 139–140;
    and relationship with John Bertrand, 63n32, 67, 75–77, 159

Fitzhugh, William (son), 75
Fleete, Henry, 114, 126n15
Fleetwood, William (bishop of St. Asaph), 70–71
Fontaine, Francis, 146, 149–150
Fontaine, James, 149
Fontaine, Jaques, 11–12, 19n39, 108n95, 148
Fontaine, John, 133, 148–150
Fontaine, Mary Ann. *See* Maury, Mary Ann Fontaine
Fontaine, Peter, 146, 149–150
Fontaine family, 149–151
Forrestier, Pierre, 10–11
Fouace, Stephen, 32, 59, 111, 128n52
Foushee, James, 34, 42n83, 49, 102, 104, 109n96, 135, 141, 143, 161
Foushee, Marie, 34, 104, 135, 141
Foushee, Ruth Mitchell, 177
Foushee, Susannah. *See* Bertrand, Susannah Foushee
Foushee family, 34, 42n83, 104, 109n97, 135
French Church in Bristol, England, 144
French Church in New Rochelle, New York, 60, 66n72, 134, 151
French Church of London on Threadneedle Street, xix, 26–31, 34–35, 40n44, 166;
 and Huguenots in the new world, xii–xiv, 34–35;
 and support of the refugee church at Rye, 27–29
French Church of the Savoy, Westminster, xix, 26, 28–31, 35–37, 127n31, 144;
 and Huguenots in the new world, xii, xiv, 44, 157, 166;
 and worship style, xii, 26–27, 34, 39n28, 55, 59–60, 134
French Reformed Church, xii, xvi, 2;
 and its Amyraldean wing, 24–27, 31, 35, 37, 166;
 and slavery, xviii, 13, 70–71, 163
Fry, Joshua, 141–142, 154n57

Fry–Jefferson Map, 142
Fry, Mary Micou Hill, 141–142, 154n57

Gallahough, James (Jacques), 41n77, 103–104, 159
Gallahough, Marie Roussel, 159
Gallahough/Gallahue, Darby, 103, 108n88, 159
Gallahue, Charlotte Ewell, 108n88, 159
Gibson, Edmund (bishop of London), 146, 150
Glorious Revolution (1689), 36–37, 46, 56, 61, 71, 119–120, 129n61
Gooch, William (lieutenant governor of Virginia), 150–151, 158
Great Awakening, 160, 165
Gribelin, Marie. *See* Bertrand, Marie Gribelin
Gribelin, Simon, 31, 36, 146
Griffin, Cyrus, 161, 166
Griffin, Mary Ann Bertrand, 141
Griffin, Thomas Bertrand, 81n25, 107n61, 143, 160–161, 165–166, 168n14
Griffin family, 141, 168n14
Guyenne Province, France, 136

The Hague, Netherlands, xiv, 32, 34, 164
Hayward, Nicholas, 33, 41n76, 49, 67, 75–76, 83n60, 108n83
Henry IV (king of France and Navarre), 3;
 See also Edict of Nantes
Hill, Leonard, 141
Howard, Francis (baron of Effingham and governor of Virginia), 41n74, 50–51, 88, 95, 100, 118–119, 129n56;
 and invitation to French ministers, xv, xviii, xxin18, 33, 51, 59, 136, 164–165

indentured servants, xvi, xix, xxin21,
    xxiin33, 49–50, 62n2, 70, 100–101,
    135, 143, 159;
  and acquiring land, 102–103;
  sexual abuse of, xviii, 57–58

Jackson, Andrew, 75, 113, 118–124,
    128n48, 128n54, 130n80,
    130n87, 147
Jefferson, Peter, 142
Jefferson, Thomas, 142, 166
Jewin Street French Church, London, 35
Jolly, Charles (Seigneur de Chadignac),
    7, 15–16, 19n39, 30
Jolly, Charlotte. *See* Bertrand,
    Charlotte Jolly
Jolly de Chadignac family, xi, 7, 11,
    15–16, 19n39, 30, 36, 44, 68, 69
Jones, Hugh, 147

Kamil, Neil, 3
Kingdon, Robert M., 169n44
King William Parish, Virginia, 135,
    150–151, 157
Kyrby, Jane Catesby Powell, 73–74, 78
Kyrby, John, 73–75, 77–80, 83n54, 94

Laborie, Antoine, 135
La Chaumette, John de, 35, 41n77
La Fayolle, Rynhart de, 41n77, 103
Lancaster County, Virginia Court,
    51–52, 85, 92–102, 105, 139–141
land acquisition, xvi, xix, 75, 77–80, 90,
    102–105, 137–141, 153n34, 153n36;
  through Brent Town leases,
    46, 104, 159;
  according to Durand, xv, 33,
    44, 164–165;
  through the Northern Neck
    Proprietary, xvii–xviii, 49,
    85–86, 98–99, 140
La Rochefoucauld, Francois de
    (Seigneur Du Parc d'Archaic),
    7, 16, 28–29

La Rochefoucauld, Louis Casimir de
    (Sieur de Fontrouet), 28, 40n40
La Rochefoucauld family, 7,
    16, 28–29, 69
La Rochelle, France, 1–6, 14, 38n13,
    69–70, 163, 166
Lascaille, George, 34, 42n84
Latané, Lewis, xviii, 150, 161, 163;
  background of, 136, 144;
  death of, 152, 162;
  emigration of, 59, 135;
  and enslaved workers, 143;
  and land acquisition, 139;
  marriage and children of,
    49, 145, 152;
  and ministry in Virginia, xiv,
    xvi, 32, 49, 59, 136, 144–
    149, 157, 159
Latané, Mary Deane, 139, 145, 152
Latané, Phoebe Peachey, 145
Latané family, 145, 161
Lee, Richard, 97–98
Lee family, 152
Lehew, Peter, 41n77, 103
Leisler, Jacob, 68
Le Jau, Francis, 32, 144, 146
Lightfoot family, 152
Lloyd, William (bishop of
    Lichfield), 125n1
Locke, John, xviii, 76, 85,
    96–97, 103–104
Lomax, Judith Micou, 141
Lomax, Lundsford, 141
London:
  Huguenot exile community in, xi–
    xii, xix, 10, 15, 21–24, 26–32,
    34–35, 37, 44–45, 69;
  as seat of imperial planning,
    xvii–xviii, 43, 85, 89, 95–98,
    104, 112–113, 119, 124,
    129n73, 139, 157;
  See also Board of Trade, London;
    Compton, Henry
Lords of Trade, London, 88–89, 95–96,
    106n46, 112, 129n57

Louis XIII (king of France), 3, 5, 31
Louis XIV (king of France), xi–xii,
    xvi, 5, 8–13, 16, 24, 26, 36–37, 43,
    48, 56, 144
Loyd, John, 61, 74–75, 77–78,
    84n72, 91, 140
Loyd, Thomas, 94
Loyd, William, 74–75, 78, 83n55
Lynnhaven Parish, 118

Mackie, Josias, 118–120,
    128n42, 128n54
Makemie, Francis, 118, 128n42, 128n48
Manakin Town Huguenot Settlement,
    xvii, 102, 152, 163;
        founding of, 13, 134–135, 138;
        and land grants to settlers, 138–
            139, 153n36;
        ministers of, 59, 150–
            151, 157–158;
        worship practices of, 60, 150–151
Marr, John, 41n77, 103
marriage patterns, 49, 141, 152,
    158–159, 166
Martiau, Nicholas, 4
Mary II (queen of England), 23,
    37, 46, 119
Mary and Ann (refugee ship),
    134–135, 152n8
Marye, James (father), xvii, 146, 150–
    151, 157–159, 165
Marye, James (son), 158, 165
Marye, Letitia Maria Ann
    Staige, 150–151
Masson, Jean (father), 2, 5–6,
    9–11, 15–17, 60
Masson, John (son), 15, 60
Mattapony Church of St. George's
    Parish, Virginia, 157–158
Maury, Mary Ann Fontaine, 149, 151
Maury, Matthew, 149, 151
Mazarin, Cardinal, 25
Meade, William, 120
Merchand, James, 135
Michel, Francis Louis, 138

Micou, Elizabeth. *See* Scott,
    Elizabeth Micou.
Micou, Henry, 141
Micou, James, 48, 141
Micou, John, 141–142
Micou, Judith. *See* Lomax, Judith Micou
Micou, Margaret Thatcher Cammock,
    49, 70, 135, 141, 162
Micou, Margaret Fauntleroy. *See*
    Fauntleroy, Margaret Micou
Micou, Mary. *See* Fry, Mary Micou Hill
Micou, Paul (father), xviii–xix, 103,
    137, 147, 164–165;
        background of, 6, 15–16,
            42n82, 44;
        as court justice in Essex County,
            49, 125, 142, 144;
        death of, 154n57, 161–162;
        emigration of, xvi, 15–16,
            33–34, 47–48;
        and enslaved workers,
            69–70, 143, 163;
        and land acquisition, 33, 67–69,
            138–139, 141, 163;
        marriage and children of, 48, 135,
            141–143, 152, 162;
        as merchant, xvi, 15,
            67–69, 104, 141;
        as physician, xvi, 15,
            47–48, 111, 141
Micou, Paul (son), 141–142, 162
Micou family, 6, 15–16, 34, 42n82, 48,
    69, 142, 152, 161, 168n17
Moncure, John, 149–151
Monroe, James (fifth president of the
    United States), 104, 109n97
Montauban Academy, France, 2, 38n17
Moreau, Nicholas, xiv, xvi, 32, 49, 59,
    111, 122, 124–125, 135–136
Morin, Michel, 47, 63n13
Morrice family, 34

Nassau (refugee ship), 135–
    137, 144–145

Native Americans, 46, 72, 82n27, 134, 142
naturalization, 36, 102–103, 135, 138
Navigation Acts, 67
Neau, Elie, 143–144
New Rochelle, New York, 13–15, 60, 66n72, 134, 137, 151
New York City, xii, 10, 13–14, 68–69, 137, 144, 149, 158, 166
New York (colony), xvi, 12–14, 34, 60, 68, 133, 137–138, 151, 158, 166
Nicholson, Francis (lieutenant governor of Virginia), 89, 97, 100, 119–122, 135–136
Nine Years War, 56, 104, 108n95
Norser, Thomas, 84n74, 91–93, 106n24
Northern Neck Proprietary, xvii, 77, 79, 83n69, 85–105, 139–140
North Farnham Parish, Virginia, 48, 58–60, 124–125, 161;
    ministers of, xi, 50, 52, 54–56, 61–62, 66n74, 74–75, 78, 115, 126n27, 127n40, 130n85, 130n89, 131n90, 148, 165

Overwharton Parish, Virginia, 150

Papin family, 5, 9, 10, 68–69
Paris, 3, 11, 25, 35
Pead, Deuel, 64n42, 117, 121, 128n42, 130n86
Pelletreau, Jean (uncle), 9, 14
Pelletreau, Jean (nephew), 14
Pelletreau, Paul, 9, 14
Pelletreau family, 9, 14, 68–69
Peter and Anthony (refugee ship), 134–135
Piscataway Churches (Lower and Upper), South Farnham Parish, Virginia, 146
Poitou Province, France, xix, 2, 10
Port Micou Plantation, 139, 141–142, 162
Powell, Ann. *See* Dacres, Ann Powell

Powell, Rawleigh, 73–75, 78–80, 82n48, 93, 106n31
Powell, Thomas, 73–75, 78–79, 82n34–35, 82n38, 91, 93–94, 98, 104
Powell family, 73, 82n35
Powell's Quarter. *See* Bertrand Plantation
Presbyterians, 57, 118, 129n69;
    and the *Directory for the Public Worship of God*, 114–116, 123–124;
    and the Genevan pulpit gown, 121, 123;
    and the meeting house in Lancaster, 160;
    and ministers in Anglican parishes, xiv, 55, 113–116, 118–121, 123–124, 128n54, 129n62, 130n85, 147;
    and new side Presbyterian activity in Virginia, 147, 160;
    and the Presbyterian Puritan wing of the Church of England, 25, 114–117, 167;
    and the Westminster Confession of Faith, 115, 123;
    and worship practices in Anglican parishes, xiv, 54, 113–116;
    and worship practices of the French Church of the Savoy, xii, 26, 34–35, 166
processioning of plantation boundary lines, 80, 94
Prou, Cyprien, xix, 103
Prou, Margaret, xix, 103
psalm singing, 26, 29;
    Louis XIV's prohibition of, 8–9
Puritans, xiv;
    and the Church of England, 25, 54, 56, 113–116;
    and ministers in Anglican parishes, 61, 115;
    and worship practices in Anglican parishes, 55, 113–114
Puylaurens, France, 38n17

Rappahannock Church of St. George's Parish, Virginia, 157–158
Redouet, Antoine (baron de Sance), 3–4
Renoe, Anne, 35
Renoe, Benjamin, 35, 41n77, 102
Renoe, Lewis, 35, 41n77, 102–103
Renoe, Mary, 35
Richelieu, Cardinal, 3, 25
Robinson, John (bishop of London), 149
Roussel, Marie. *See* Gallahough, Marie Roussel
Roy Family, 34, 42n82, 48, 63n25, 135
Royal Bounty:
    for Huguenot relief in England, 32, 35, 41n58, 44, 60, 81n11, 136;
    for transporting ministers to English America, 31, 41n58, 136

Rye, England, 27–29, 56,

Saint Denis Parish, South Carolina, 133
Saintes, France, 2, 7, 11, 16, 68
Saint James Goosecreek Parish, South Carolina, 134, 144
Saint James Santee Parish, South Carolina, 134
Saint John's Berkeley Parish, South Carolina, 134
Saint Margaret's Parish, Virginia, 149
Saintonge Province, France:
    and the Huguenot diaspora, 11 16, 24, 30, 36, 44, 135;
    and its Protestant identity, xi, 1–3, 7, 15;
    and trade, 4, 14, 43, 68, 70, 140;
    and wine production, 43, 69, 81n13, 104
Saint Paul's Covent Garden Church, Westminster, England, 30–31, 40n50
Saumur Academy, France, xii, 24–25, 28–29, 35, 167
Saumur theology. *See* Amyraut, Moïse
Scott, Elizabeth Micou, 141

Scott, James, 141
Servant, Bertrand, 135
Sittenbourne Parish, Virginia, 48, 55, 61, 115–116, 124, 126n27, 130n84
slavery. *See* enslaved persons
Smith, John (Captain), 72
Society for the Propagation of the Gospel (SPG), 133, 144, 151, 158
South Carolina, 86, 133;
    and Huguenot migration to, xii, xiv–xvi, 4, 12–15, 32, 34, 43, 60, 133, 137–138, 158, 166;
    and ministers in, 32, 62n5, 144, 146;
    and promotional literature about, 43, 60, 41n73
South Farnham Parish, Virginia, 52, 139, 142, 147–148, 152, 157;
    ministers of, 59, 121, 125, 136, 145, 152
Spotswood, Alexander (lieutenant governor of Virginia), 147–148
St. George's Parish, Virginia, 157–158, 165
St. James Northam Parish, Virginia, 151
St. John's Parish, Virginia, 59
St. Mary's Whitechapel Parish, Virginia, 52, 80, 84n79, 159–161, 165;
    ministers of, 74–75, 115, 118, 120–125, 130n85, 130n87
St. Peter's Parish, Virginia, 59
Stanwood, Owen, 134
Stouppe, Pierre, 151
Synod of Dordt, 24
Sysderf, Thomas (bishop of Orkney) 115, 127n31

Tacquet, Lewis, 41n77, 103–104
Tavernor/George/Nicolas/Clerke partnership, 4, 66n77, 125
Tavernor, John, 61, 66n77, 78, 84n72, 125
testamentary practices, 140, 162–163
Tomlyn, Ann Browne, 92–94, 99, 106n31

Tomlyn, Stephen, 92–94, 99
Tourtellot, Abraham, 14–15, 68
Trocq, Isaac, 135
Truro Parish, Virginia, 149
Tuckney, Anthony, 115, 127n29

Underwood, William, 114, 126n15,
Underwood family, 145

Vallet, Claude, 34
Van den Bosch, Laurentius, 32
Van Ruymbeke, Bertrand,
  38n12, 62n5, 137
Vauter's Church, Loretto, Virginia,
  161–162, 165
Vezey, George, 79, 84n75–77,
  92, 106n38
Virginia Council of State, 33, 88, 104,
  135, 129n60, 135, 141–142;
    and anti-Puritan pronouncements,
      54, 119–120;
    and the curtailment of its powers
      by the Board of Trade,
      97–98, 104, 124;
    as the general court of the colony,
      52, 61, 89, 93–94, 96, 98,
      100, 102, 148;
    and granting unassigned land,
      xvii, 85–86, 95;
    and opposition to the Northern
      Neck Proprietary, xvii–
      xviii, 89–90
Virginia House of Burgesses, xvii, 70,
  95, 100, 114, 139
Virginia Statute for Religious Freedom
  (1786), 161

Waldensian Protestants, 13

Walloons, 4, 13, 48, 149
Washington, George (first president of
  the United States), 4, 141, 166
Washington, Mary Ball, 141
Washington Parish, Virginia, 117, 124,
  130n83, 149
Wells, Camille, 107n61
Westover Parish, Virginia, 149
Whitfield, George, 160
Wicomico Parish, Virginia, 115,
  126n26, 127n40
William III (prince of Orange and king
  of England), 23, 88, 119;
    and invasion of England, xi–xii,
      36–37, 46;
    and military opposition to Louis
      XIV, 16, 37, 56;
    as sponsor of 1700–1701
      Huguenot migration, xvii,
      xix, 13, 43–44, 59, 134,
      136, 138, 163
William and Elizabeth (refugee
  ship), 136
wine production:
    as an English imperialist
      objective, xv, 33;
    in Saintonge, xvi, 4, 43,
      69, 81n13;
    in Virginia, 104, 109n97, 138, 164
women:
    as indentured servants, 57–58;
    as merchants, 68–69, 81n13,
      104, 140–141
Wormeley, Ralph, 33, 164
Wormeley family, 152

Yorkhampton Parish, Virginia, 149

About the Author

The **Reverend Dr. Lonnie H. Lee** is a native of Wichita, Kansas, and a graduate of the University of Kansas, Princeton Theological Seminary, and Austin Presbyterian Theological Seminary. He is married to Barbara Gail Dove, and they have two sons and two granddaughters. Dr. Lee served as pastor of four Presbyterian congregations in Oklahoma, Texas, and Illinois. From 1995 to 2012, he was senior pastor of the 1,200-member Westminster Presbyterian Church of Springfield, Illinois. He presently lives in Olathe, Kansas, where he has served in leadership roles with Heartland Presbytery and taught church history courses at the 4,000-member Village Presbyterian Church of Prairie Village, Kansas. His long-standing interest in church history has inspired his in-depth study of the Huguenot diaspora through extensive research in Virginia, Great Britain, and France. His article, "The Transatlantic Legacy of the Protestant Church of Cozes," was published in Great Britain in 2019 by the *Huguenot Society Journal*. His first book, *A Brief History of Belle Isle Plantation, Lancaster County, Virginia, 1650–1782*, was published by Heritage Books in 2020. Another article, "Huguenot-Anglicans in Seventeenth-Century Virginia," was published in *Anglican and Episcopal History* in 2022. This book is the result of his latest research on the Huguenot migration to Virginia.